INTRODUCTION TO MANAGEMENT

Nicole Yeaman
March 2008.
from
Judyn
Matthewman.

Also by Richard Pettinger

Introduction to Corporate Strategy
Introduction to Organisational Behaviour
A Practical Introduction to Human Resource Management
Preparing and Handling Industrial Tribunal Cases
The Management of Discipline and Grievances
Managing the Flexible Workforce
Measuring Business and Managerial Performance (with Rebecca Frith)

INTRODUCTION TO MANAGEMENT

Second Edition

Richard Pettinger

First edition 1994
Reprinted twice
Second edition 1997

Published 1997 by
THE MACMILLAN PRESS LTD
Houndmills, Basingstoke, Hampshire RG21 6XS
and London
Companies and representatives
throughout the world

ISBN 0–333–68745–0

A catalogue record for this book is available
from the British Library.

This book is printed on paper suitable for recycling and made from fully managed and sustained forest sources.

10   9   8   7   6   5   4   3   2
06   05   04   03   02   01   00   99   98   97

Copy-edited and typeset by Povey–Edmondson
Okehampton and Rochdale, England

Printed in Great Britain by
Antony Rowe Ltd
Chippenham, Wiltshire

Contents

List of figures and summary boxes

■ Figures

■ Summary boxes

Preface

Everywhere in the world there is a revolution going on, a transformation of business and of the services needed and wanted by people. At the heart of this revolution is management. This is underlined by a realisation that, whatever the merits of how this was conducted in the past, new ways and new methods are essential for the future; above all, this means a better understanding of what management actually is.

The background against which this revolution takes place is one of economic, social and political turbulence and upheaval. The global environment is both unstable and volatile. The sophisticated post-industrial new economies of the West are undergoing radical transformation, driven by a combination of recession, technological advance and competition from emerging nations. This is exacerbated by the need for levels of investment and other resource commitments over periods of time that run contrary to prevailing political and economic pressures. The economies of the Far East have generated a business and commercial power bloc in the period since the Second World War that dominates the global electrical and consumer goods markets and makes them major operators in the car, white goods and finance sectors. This has been achieved from a combination of investment, technology and organisation founded in the reconstruction and regeneration of the world devastated by the Second World War.

Ever-greater strains and demands are placed on the finite and diminishing resources of the world by an ever-increasing global population. These have therefore to be arranged, planned, ordered and organised to ensure that they are used to greatest possible advantage. In the particular context of pressure on the one hand and finity on the other, this constitutes a drive for constant improvement in efficiency, effectiveness, maximisation and optimisation.

This is the framework of the 'business sphere' – that is, the environment of business, and background against which business is conducted. It forms the backcloth to the 'management sphere' – the actual and conceptual environment (global, organisational and departmental) in which the practice of management is conducted. The work is carried out in and by 'organisations' – that is, combinations of human and other resources drawn together for a distinctive business or social purpose.

The standpoint adopted in response to this is straightforward: management is a statement of excellence and quality and of expertise. There is a body of knowledge and skills that must be acquired by anyone who wishes to be a part of the managing – the direction and ordering – of the situation. There are capabilities and capacities required in people in the pursuit of this. High standards of behaviour, ethics and performance are required. There is a personal commitment necessary in terms of energy, commitment, enthusiasm and ambition. There is increasingly a standard of education and training necessary, both as a prerequisite to entry to the field and in the maintenance of effective and current performance in it. Finally, in common with all true experts there must be personal pride and joy in the work itself, in the organisation in which it is carried out, and in the particular department in which the manager is working.

The nature of this expertise is complex and diverse. The practice of management requires both the recognition of this complexity, and the capacity to reconcile the conflicting elements present in the pursuit of it. For the purposes of introducing the scale and scope of this expertise and in order to provide a framework for the recognition and understanding of it, the book is organised as follows.

Chapter 1 is an introduction and overview of what management is and what it should be, and this is followed by an historical summary and review in Chapter 2, to establish the development of the expertise to date.

Chapter 3 is an introduction to organisation behaviour and an illustration and analysis of its key features. Chapter 4 then relates the processes of managing organisations, the importance of their structures, systems and cultures and the means by which these are envisioned and energised.

This is followed by an illustration and consideration of the nature and context of distinctive management functions that are carried out by organisations in the pursuit of their stated purposes. Starting with a consideration of strategy and policy formulation in Chapter 5, the book then addresses the particular concerns of marketing, human resources, industrial relations and employment law (Chapters 6–7). Chapter 8 addresses the nature and complexity of operations management. Chapters 9–10 consider the qualitative and financial aspects of management, from a managerial (rather than technical) standpoint.

The purpose of the last part of the book (Chapters 11–12) is to address the major current issues related to managing in the changing and volatile environment already referred to; and the particular current concerns of excellence and quality. There is also a short section on Japanese management.

This last bears another word here. Both academics and practitioners have looked at Japanese business and management practices in detail and depth in their attempts to explain the great economic successes that have been achieved in that country and by its companies since 1945. There is a relationship to be drawn between this and the practices adopted, and they thus merit particular consideration.

To bring the threads of these opening remarks together – the elements feed off each other. Good management engenders good business, good business creates good organisations, good organisations attract, retain and develop good managers who in turn improve both the quality of organisations and of the business that they conduct. Organisations thus cannot afford bad managers or their bad practices.

The main conclusion drawn is in relation to the constant expansion of the subject, both as a field of study and as an area of practice; and of the consequent necessity of those who work in it to keep up to date with developments, to read, to acknowledge and to accept their responsibilities for their own continuous professional expansion and to act upon all of this. The commitment needed for this matches that of any classical profession – such as medicine or the law.

This is an illustration and summary of the scope and coverage of the book. The overall purpose is to introduce concepts and features of the management sphere to the student coming to the subject for the first time; to those commencing professional studies and professional examinations who require an introduction to management or a general management reader; to those studying management as part of a technological, technical, engineering or computer course; and as a contribution to the level and content of the debate in the field.

RICHARD PETTINGER

Acknowledgements

The genesis of this book lay in the undergraduate Management Principles course of the Bartlett School of Architecture, Building, Environmental Design and Planning, University College London. In the pursuit and completion of this project, therefore, special thanks and acknowledgement are due to Graham Winch, John Andrews, Victor Torrance and Barbara Young of the Bartlett School.

Many other people also contributed. Peter Lawrence, Professor of Comparative Management at the Loughborough University Business School, reviewed the manuscript and made many positive and helpful comments and suggestions. Stephen Rutt and Jane Powell at the publishers were a constant and positive source of help and guidance throughout. Many people made helpful comments and suggestions for the preparation of the second edition. Peter Lawrence provided a full and comprehensive review of the first edition. I am indebted to Kelvin Cheatle, Director of Human Resources at Broadmoor Hospital; Jim and Margaret Malpas and Sandra Madigan and Ian Robinson of Malpas Flexible Learning Ltd, a top-quality professional education and training company and consultancy; David Scott of the Artisan Group; Jo Thomas, who provided much additional material; Andrew Jordan of BT; Ram Ahronov of UCL; and to Rebecca Frith, who typed and edited the manuscript. I am also grateful to Keith Sanders, Ken Batchelor, Michael Hutton, James Pollock, and Janet and John Doyle for their constant support and encouragement, and Keith Povey for overseeing the copy-editing.

RICHARD PETTINGER

The author and publishers wish to thank the following for permission to reproduce copyright material: Sanyo Industries UK Ltd (for their staff handbook); Irwin Publishers for material from C.R. Christensen *et al.*, *Business Policy: Text and Cases*, 1987.

Every effort has been made to trace all the copyright-holders, but if any have been inadvertently overlooked the publishers will be pleased to make the necessary arrangement at the first opportunity.

CHAPTER 1

Introduction

The purpose of this chapter is to identify the range of general and universal concepts and elements that ought to be present in any worthwhile study of the subject of management. These are highlighted in themselves and then drawn together in so far as this is possible. However, many of these elements are disparate or divergent and it is essential to recognise them as such.

Many definitions of what management is exist. Henri Fayol, in the early twentieth century, defined it as the process of 'forecasting, planning, organising, commanding, coordinating and controlling'. E. F. L. Brech called it 'the social process of planning, coordination, control and motivation'. Writing in the 1980s Tom Peters defined it as 'organisational direction based on sound common sense, pride in the organisation and enthusiasm for its works'. It is clear that management is partly the process of getting things done through people; and partly the creative and energetic combination of scarce resources into effective and profitable activities and the combination of the skill and talents of the individuals concerned with doing this.

Management is conducted in organisations. A context must be established. Organisations are variously described as: 'systems of inter-dependent human beings' (D. S. Pugh); a 'joint function of human characteristics, the task to be accomplished and its environment' (H. Simon). Organisations may be seen as combinations of resources brought together for a purpose; they have a life and a permanent identity of their own; and are energised by people.

■ Background to management

Management is variously defined as science, profession and art. The truth of its status lies somewhere between the three; and that it has strong elements of each is incontrovertible.

There are precise elements, scientific and exact aspects that have to be learned and assimilated. Any manager must have a good grasp of certain quantitative methods and financial and statistical data, as well as certain, less scientific but well tried and tested elements such as human motivations, and the effect of different payment systems on the performance of different occupations.

It is a profession in so far as there is a general recognition that there are certain knowledge, skills and aptitudes that must be assimilated and understood by anyone who aspires to be a truly effective manager. Management is not a true or traditional profession in the sense that it is not a fully self-regulating occupation, and nor is there yet a named qualification that must be achieved before one is allowed to practise. However, pressure to be both educated and qualified is growing universally. There is a recognition also of the correlation between this and expert and effective practice.

Management is an art in the sense that within these confines and strictures there is great scope for the use of creativity, imagination, initiative and invention within the overall sphere of the occupation. The scientific methods and body of knowledge referred to must be applied in their own way to each and any given situation, issue or problem. This is the creative aspect of the manager's role and function; and anyone in a managerial position who seeks for prescriptive solutions to organisational problems is likely to fail.

The subject of management is thus concerned with both the precise and the vague; the ordered and the creative. Within these broad concepts it is possible to pin down certain elements that are present in all effective management and successful managers.

The most critical of these elements are communication and decision-making. Anyone who aspires to management must understand the processes involved and be able to carry them out effectively in their own situation. They are dealt with extensively elsewhere in this book and form a common and continuous thread throughout. They are fundamental to the success of any managerial activity.

The overall managerial task is concerned with getting things done through people; the combination and ordering of a variety of resources for given productive purposes; the actions and processes involved in the combination of those resources; and the balancing of resource utilisation with the commercial, environmental and operational variables of quantity, quality and time; and coping with change and uncertainty. This task is, in turn, broad and strategic at the top of organisations where the manager is concerned with broad direction and the future; and narrower, concerned with short term and operational matters at the lower levels of organisations. In all cases, it is the ability to communicate effectively, and to take effective decisions, that are fundamental to any successful managerial activity.

■ The professionalisation of management

The best managers are, therefore, highly professional, committed and dedicated operators; highly trained and educated; with excellent analytical and critical faculties. Beyond this, there is a body of skills and aptitudes, knowledge, attitudes and behaviour which the effective manager must have and be able to draw upon.

What is required of the effective manager reads, if one is not careful, like a checklist for life. The basis of this forms the rationale for the scope of this book.

In summary, managers must have the strategic planning and organisational skills necessary to determine and carry out the directive functions required in the particular situation. They must understand the basic aspects of human behaviour and motivation if they are to stand any chance at all of getting effective work out of the staff. They must have a basic grasp of quantitative and analytical methods enabling them to recognise those activities which are truly profitable and effective and those that are not. They must be familiar with information systems and the information itself. They must be able to draw accurate conclusions from it. They must be able both to ask for information, and to present information in ways that the organisation as a whole and its individual operations require. They must be able to manage, maintain, develop and improve the human resource. They must have a good knowledge of the law as it impinges on their particular managerial activities and be able to work within it. They must understand and be able to apply strategic processes, priorities, schedules, timetables and techniques. They must be able to work to deadlines and within resource constraints. They must have basic skills and aptitudes in marketing and presentation. They must set standards of performance for themselves, their peers, their subordinates and the organisation as a whole and take early active steps to remedy that performance when it falls.

Related to this, the personal qualities required include ambition, energy, great commitment, self-motivation, job, product and service knowledge, drive and enthusiasm, creativity and imagination, a thirst for knowledge, a commitment to improvement, a commitment to continuous development, personal and professional, the ability to grow and broaden the outlook and vision of the organisation concerned, a positive and dynamic attitude, self-discipline, empathy with the staff, a love of the organisation and pride and enthusiasm in the job, its people, its products, its services, its customers and clients (see Summary Box 1.1). These personal qualities provide the springboard for the successful and professional operator.

There is a certain background that is required. This relates to the knowledge, understanding and grasp of basic economic concepts, the relationship between organisations and their environment, current issues and affairs, constraints on the ability to conduct business, assimilation of the knowledge that is comprised in the subject areas of: strategy and policy; marketing; behavioural sciences; personnel and industrial relations; production, operations, systems, service, projects and facilities management; and the management of initiative and innovation. Currently, much of this is formalised and achieved through the study of business at school, college and university. This is by no means a universal requirement, however – there have been countless successful managers who never had this benefit. However, their success was undoubtedly based on their own ability, however gained, in these areas.

There is the recognition that management is a global activity, that lessons can be both learned and offered, from and to the rest of the world. The business sphere consists of Western Europe, North America, Japan, Korea, the Philippines, Malaysia, Indonesia, the Middle East, Australia, New Zealand and South

---

SUMMARY BOX 1.1   Professions

- The 'classical' professions are medicine, law, the priesthood and the army. The following properties were held to distinguish these from the rest of society.
- Distinctive expertise: not available elsewhere in society or in its individual members
- Distinctive body of knowledge: required by all those who aspire to practice in the profession
- Entry barriers: in the form of examinations, time serving, learning from experts
- Formal qualifications: given as the result of acquiring the body of knowledge and clearing the entry barriers
- High status: professions are at the top of the occupational tree
- Distinctive morality: for medicine, the commitment to keep people alive as long as possible; for law, a commitment to represent the client's best interests; for the church, a commitment to godliness and to serve the congregation's best interest; for the army, to fight within stated rules of law
- High value: professions make a distinctive and positive contribution to both the organisations and individual members of the society
- Self-regulating: professions set their own rules, codes of conduct, standards of performance and qualifications
- Self-disciplining: professions establish their own bodies for dealing with problems, complaints, allegations of malpractice
- Unlimited reward levels: according to preferred levels of charges and the demands of society
- Life membership: dismissal at the behest of the profession; ceasing to work for one employer does not constitute loss of profession
- Personal commitment: to high standards of practice and morality; commitment to deliver the best possible in all circumstances
- Self-discipline: commitment to personal standards of behaviour in the pursuit of professional excellence
- Continuous development: of knowledge and skills; a commitment to keep abreast of all developments and initiatives in the field
- Governance: by institutions established by the profession itself.

Notes:
1. In absolute terms 'management' falls short in most areas. Formal qualifications are not a great prerequisite to practice (though they are highly desirable and evermore sought after). Discipline and regulation of managers is still over-whelmingly a matter for organisations and not management institutions. There is some influence over reward levels and training and development. Measures of status and value are uneven. Management institutions act as focal points for debate; and they also have a lobbying function. They do not act as regulators
2. There is a clear drive towards the professionalisation of management. This is based on attention to expertise, knowledge and qualifications, and the relationship between these and the value added to organisations by expert managers
3. In 1995, Handy proposed that all business school graduates should be required to take the equivalent of the hippocratic oath, thus committing themselves to best practice and high standards and quality of performance.

Africa, where managerial practices are well documented. These will impinge on and be modified by the business emergence of the former communist bloc and USSR, South and Central America, India and Pakistan, and China. All of these are industrialising and commercialising and having their own influence on business practices. In the future, this will undoubtedly include the rest of Africa, and the more remote parts of Asia. It must be recognised, finally, that management is currently being conducted in a changing and turbulent environment. This has itself changed over the period since 1945 and the reconstruction of the world damaged by the Second World War. Then, everything was arranged to try and bring order, stability and performance steadiness to business, service and the markets and spheres in which they operated. Today, all that has gone, and the processes of technological advance, management education, automation, social change, political development together with the globalisation of business and commerce ensure that all concepts of management are in turn subject to continuous change and revision. Truly expert and committed managers will always ensure that they keep themselves up-to-date with everything that impinges on both their job and their chosen profession. Many managerial institutions now insist that their members keep records of all continuous professional development activities that they undertake and, indeed, insist on this as a condition of continuing membership.

If management is viewed in this way, it is a highly professional activity and one that demands a set body of expertise and a large measure of commitment on the part of its practitioners. In traditional terms, management falls short of the full status of profession in that the elements outlined here do not constitute yet a formal entry barrier (in medicine, the law, the clergy and the military, it is essential to have the stated qualifications before being allowed to practise). However, there is currently a combination of pressures – from the EC, North America and local considerations of contract compliance and tendering, especially in public services, the proliferation of business and management, schools and education, the decline of traditional, industrial and commercial sectors, and the growth in awareness of this as a critical operational area – that are coming together to ensure the recognition of management as an expertise in its own right and, in turn, ensuring its increased professionalism and status.

■ Management as a field of study

The importance of management as a field of study has therefore never been greater; and it is growing all the time. Organisations that are well managed, that have excellent and competent managers, gain competitive and operational advantages, quite apart from anything to do with the quality or value of their products and services. There is a competitive advantage in having high quality staff in any field and this extends to those who manage them.

■ Management research and literature

There is a great proliferation of this at present – textbooks, how-to books, personal and organisational histories, professional and commercial journals and periodicals, computer-based packages, databases, leaflets, checklists; and also university and commercial research programmes, monographs and learned papers.

The result is that in the total management sphere there is a great body of knowledge and experience on which to draw and from which to learn. Written at all levels and to cover all shades of interest the range now extends from tiny anecdotes or proverbial words of wisdom to extensive, analytical and top quality theses on business strategy, quantitative methods, marketing and other resource management.

Both aspiring and practising managers have obligations to their profession, to their organisation and to themselves, to equip themselves with a leavening of this material. It represents both interest and concern with the occupation, and the standards of knowledge, experience and enlightenment required. It mirrors the march of progress in the field, and the importance increasingly placed by organisations on having expert, trained, educated and capable managers.

The range and scope of literature becomes apparent through the course of any study of the field. Certain strands may, however, be usefully identified.

Some of it is intellectually extremely challenging. The ability, both to understand and to be an effective practitioner also in certain aspects of the managerial sphere, requires a high degree of intellectual capacity, higher education and a basic grasp of some mathematical and economic theories as well as behavioural and operational matters.

Some of it addresses precise or defined issues that have a direct bearing on the business sphere. This is especially true of the areas of leadership, motivation, perception, the formation of attitudes, standards and values which have both their own body of knowledge in their own right, and which then require translation into particular managerial situations in different ways.

Some of it dwells heavily on empirical research, case histories and anecdotal examples. This enables studies of the relationships between variables in given situations to be undertaken and assimilated, and 'what if' and other hypothetical discussions to take place in relation to real events of the past, but in overtly 'safe' situations at present. The body of the general knowledge and experience of the manager is thus developed and extended, as are his critical faculty and awareness and overall view of the sphere.

Some of it illustrates particular successes and failures; this is especially true of the swelling array of books produced by successful business people. The lessons to be drawn here are often in the mind of the reader. Such books tend to reinforce certain aspects only of the whole managerial sphere. They provide a very useful library of what has worked in practice for comparison against a theoretical or academic base. They contribute to the overall fund of empirical and anecdotal experience from which the manager may draw.

Some of it aims to popularise, de-mystify and familiarise that which other parts of it would appear to shroud in mystery. Prominent among these works are the writings of Tom Peters, Rosabeth Moss Kanter, Walter Goldsmith, David Clutterbuck, John Harvey-Jones and Ronnie Lessem. In these cases the material is tackled in reverse. Basics and fundamentals of management are illustrated with famous and high profile success stories so that lessons are learned that way. The works of Tom Peters, especially, are peppered with anecdotes that the student or reader should remember; these gather a life of their own in his exciting, vivid and stirring language. The stories are also much better learned because they are positive rather than negative in their telling.

Some of it, finally, represents a more general illustration of the sphere at large. This purposes to provide the first step towards enlightenment and understanding and also to set out the range and complexity of the profession of management. This material is for use both at the point of entry to the profession and also for general reading once within it.

Whatever the 'category', and these have been defined for illustrative purposes only, all the material should inspire, energise, enthuse and enlighten those who read it. It should be credible and accurate. There is also a clear requirements of the motivation of the manager or aspiring manager to read into and around the chosen subject and profession as part of the commitment to it. Inevitably some parts will inspire and enthuse more than others; while other parts of it will have less meaning and relevance. Only by getting involved, however, is it possible to create and develop and analytical and critical faculty and draw general lessons from those areas where there is no direct interest or experience (see Summary Box 1.2).

Finally, all the literature, books and works must be seen in their own context. Not all management literature retains its currency. Some may be highly useful and valuable for a limited period of time only; or an essential though transient stepping stone along the path of progress. It should be seen for what it is – the configuration of the current state of learning at a given point. It is constantly being updated and added to in terms of volume, quality and enlightenment.

■ Conclusion

Management impinges on all aspects of life. The main concern here is with the effects on, and effectiveness in, the direction of business, industry, commercial and public services, and the non-profit-making sector.

However, many of the principles and practices to be applied have relevance across the whole of life – the organisation of family outings, weekend sporting and leisure activities, religious and social functions.

SUMMARY BOX 1.2   Fashions and Fads

'Fashions and fads' is a useful way of describing directive and prescriptive approaches to management issues and problems. Some current issues are as follows.

- **Job evaluation**: the analysis of job and work activities according to present criteria in order to rank them in importance, status, values and place on the pay scale. In practice, job evaluation tends to be rigid, inconsistent and divisive.
- **Business process re-engineering (BPR)**: attention to administration, supervision and procedures for the purposes of simplicity, clarification and speed of operation. The premise is that these improvements are always possible. In practice, business process re-engineering tends to be applied prescriptively to all functions without reference to organisational effectiveness or wider aspects of operations.
- **Total quality management (TQM)**: attention to every aspect of organisational practice in pursuit of continuous improvement, the highest possible standards of practice, products, services and customer service. In practice, TQM tends to be prescriptive in approach and dominated by paperwork and administration systems rather than attention to products and customers.
- **Right first time, every time**: this rolls easily off the tongue/pen; it is a direct contradiction of the view that everything can be improved.
- **Benchmarking**: benchmarks set standards of activity against which other activities can be compared and rated; benchmarking also applies to placing people on salary scales, activity scales, job importance scales and other matters to do with status. In practice, it is usually rigid, inconsistent and divisive.
- **Virtual organisation**: organisation structures based on technology rather than physical presence. A useful concept that tends to get drowned, either by cost-cutting or technological processes, or conventional, adversarial supervision.

The major contribution of each (and all fashions and fads) is to broaden the debate on management issues, and to get people thinking about progress and improvement. Their weakness is apparent when they are grasped as perfection, the absolute truth, instant solutions to all-round management problems.

Finally, anyone who is truly dedicated and professional in whatever sphere should be determined to keep themselves abreast of progress and development in their chosen field. In this respect, the manager is no different from any other true and dedicated professional. It represents personal commitment to their chosen field, a consequence of going into it in the first place. More generally, customers and clients of any professional expect to be dealt with on a current rather than historic basis. This must apply, above all, to the truly professional manager.

CHAPTER 2

Historical perspective

■ Early studies

The subject of management has been studied over the centuries with the view of establishing what constitutes a successful manager or, in the closely related field, what constitutes a successful leader. The subject of leadership is dealt with fully later in the book. At this stage, suffice it to say that while the two concepts are closely related, they are not synonymous – a good leader is not necessarily a good manager; nor is a good manager always a brilliant leader (though they should always be at least capable).

The purpose here is to illustrate the extent to which management has been studied over the centuries, and the concepts developed; to briefly introduce and discuss the work of the major contributors to the subject over the period since the industrialisation of the western world; and to look finally at those works, writers and practices that are of importance in the study and analysis of the subjects in the late twentieth century.

The subject of management has been developed from the earliest points of civilisation. Religious writings identify the fundamental elements of strength of character and purpose, positive morality and love of truth that anyone who aspires to a position of authority should have. Both archaeologists and those interested in the organisational aspects have long concerned themselves with how the resources necessary to build the pyramids and temples of Egypt and South America were coordinated. They have speculated on the means by which these might have been achieved, without coming to definite conclusions overall.

Common threads running through the lives of the twelve Caesars, as told by Suetonius writing in the first century AD, related their moral and ethical purposes, their ambition, their policies for Rome and the Roman Empire and the standpoints for these, to their overall success. Also identified were elements that were necessary to survive in the situation and the extent to which they were successful in the pursuit of this. Julius Caesar, himself a writer of note, dealt extensively with the vision, strategic and tactical awareness that he required to be successful in his twin careers of general and emperor. Later, histories of the Frankish Kingdom in the Middle Ages ascribe strong leadership, a clarity of purpose and the ability to persuade a range of disparate elements to a single point of view, as characteristics of Charles Martel and Charlemagne in the establishment of the nation of France.

The nature and importance of power and influence were clearly established. Niccolo Machiavelli, the Florentine, writing in the fifteen century, developed this much further. His book, *The Prince*, recognised as an early authority on leadership, pushes back the ethical and moral boundaries and advocated the subordination of means to ends. He marks political awareness and astuteness and the ability to translate innate abilities into particular situations as further key characteristics; if one did not understand the environment and could not operate within it, one could not be truly effective.

The main common element of these historic studies was the separation of the role of the leader and the characteristics required of the leader from the remainder of business, political and military activities (see Summary Box 2.1). A good soldier did not necessarily make a good leader; on the other hand to be a good leader of soldiers, it was necessary to have a good knowledge of what the components of soldiering were, and to be able to combine this with the other characteristics necessary, of ordering and directing and planning.

SUMMARY BOX 2.1   The Divine Right of Kings

This is a concept established by various dynasties, in various parts of the world, throughout the centuries. The notion that the king was appointed and anointed by divine intervention, had the additional effect of making any attempt on his life or well-being not only a crime of high treason, but also a crime against God. Anyone who raised questions about performance of the king or, in extreme situations, their hand against him, therefore faced retribution both here and in the after-life.

It is an early example of a cultural barrier.

Prior to the western industrial revolution, therefore, there was a large, if uncoordinated and undervalued, body of knowledge and experience available from which conclusions about the prevailing and ideal nature of leadership and management could be drawn.

The industrial revolution in Great Britain and Europe over the eighteenth and nineteenth centuries brought great social and political ferment and upheaval, as well as economic restructuring. In particular, the shift to a money, wage-earning economy in the cities transformed the lives of the masses of people. It ran alongside explosions of population and technological advance, creating an urban workforce available to meet the demands of the new factories, mills, transport and infrastructure industries that were springing up at the time.

Out of this ferment and transformation came particular initiatives, writings and scholarship both in relation to work and also on the implications of the relationship between the ways of working and the society at large. Some of these are now considered. The coverage is illustrative, rather than comprehensive, with the purpose of demonstrating the great range of ways in which the subject has been tackled. It also constitutes an introduction to both concepts and authorities which have been and remain important, notorious and controversial in the field.

■ Marxism

The ferment of ideas that ran concurrently with the industrial and social upheaval brought with it the concept of communism. Written and developed by Karl Marx and Friedrich Engels, the *Communist Manifesto* propounded that industrial society as it stood was to be a place of permanent upheaval and revolution; that the workers, the wage slaves, would not tolerate the current state of industrial society, but would rather overthrow it and seize control of it for themselves. Egalitarian in concept, it rejected the then emerging concepts of capitalism, bourgeoisie (the middle and professional classes), and the fledgeling wage–work bargain. Largely discredited as a philosophy (above all by the collapse of the communist bloc which *called itself* Marxist), Marxism never succeeded in translation into an effective code for the organisation of work. However, it does illustrate the extreme or radical perspective on working situations; the extent to which the workforce may become alienated either from the organisation for which they work or from its managers. It also voices genuine concerns for the standards, dignity and rights of those who work for others in the pursuit of supporting their own lives. It became the cornerstone of the trade union movement in the UK and elsewhere. The attraction lay in the egalitarianism preached and the utopian vision of shared ownership of the means of production and economic activity.

■ Bureaucracy and the permanence of organisations

The work of Max Weber (1864–1920) developed the concept of the permanence and continuity of organisations. This was the basis of the theory of **bureaucracy**. Weber saw bureaucracy as an organisational form based on an hierarchy of offices and systems of rules and with the purpose of ensuring the permanence of the organisation, even though job holders within it might come and go. The knowledge, practice and experience of the organisation would be preserved in files, thus ensuring permanence and continuity. Authority in such circumstances is described as legal–rational, where the position of the office holder is enshrined in an organisation structure and fully understood and accepted by all job holders. The organisation itself is continuous and permanent. Work is specialised and defined by job title and job description. The organisation is hierarchical, where one level is subject to control by that or those above it. Everything that is done in the name of the organisation and its officials is recorded. Job holders are appointed on the basis of technical competence; the jobs exist in their own right; job holders have no other rights to the job. Ownership and control of the organisation are separated; effectively the owners of an organisation appoint others to run it on their behalf. The work and the control of it is enshrined in rule books and procedures which must be obeyed and followed. Order and efficiency are thus brought to this state of permanence.

Thus, the overall purpose of bureaucratic structure was, and remains, to attain the maximum degree of efficiency possible and to ensure the permanence of the organisation. As organisations grow in size and complexity, the bureaucracy itself has to be managed. Failure to do this leads to red tape, excessive procedures, obscure and conflicting rules and regulations. In the worst cases, the rules and procedures become themselves all-important to the detriment of the product or service that is being offered.

■ The origins of welfarism

The Cadbury family who pioneered and built up the chocolate and cocoa industries in Great Britain in the nineteenth century came from a strong religious tradition (they were Quakers). Determined to be both profitable and ethical, they sought to ensure certain standards of living and quality of life for those who worked for them. They built both their factories and the housing for their staff as a model industrial village at Bourneville on the (then) edge of Birmingham. The village included basic housing and sanitation, green spaces, schools for the children and company shops which sold food of a good quality. The purpose was to ensure that the staff were kept fit, healthy and motivated to work in the chocolate factories, producing good quality products. Other Quaker foundations operated along similar lines, for example the Fry and Terry companies (which also produced chocolate).

This was by no means the rule, and many employers continued to treat their people very harshly, keeping them in bad conditions, under-paying them and using fear as the driving force. Graphical and apocryphal descriptions may be found in the poetry of William Blake and *The Water Babies* by Charles Kingsley. However, the work of the Cadburys is important as one of the most enduring early industrial examples of the relationship between concern for the staff and commercial permanence, profitability and success.

■ Henri Fayol

The work of Henri Fayol (1841–1925) is important because he was the first to attempt a fully comprehensive definition of industrial management. It was published in 1916 under the title *General and Industrial Administration*. It identified the components of any industrial undertaking under the headings of technical; commercial; financial; security; accounting; and managerial. This last group of components comprised forecasting, planning, organisation, command, coordination and control of the others; the overall function is to unify and direct the organisation and its resources in productive activities. He also listed 14 'principles of management' on which he claimed to have based his own managerial practice and style and which he cited as the foundation of his own success:

1. **Division of work,** the ordering and specialisation of tasks and jobs necessary for greater efficiency and ease of control
2. **Authority and responsibility,** the right to give commands and the acceptance of the consequences of giving those commands
3. **Unity of command,** each employee has an identified and recognised superior or commander
4. **Unity of direction,** one commander for each activity or objective
5. The **subordination** of **individual** interests to the **organisational** interest
6. **Remuneration** and **reward** in a **fair and equitable manner** to all
7. **Centralisation** and **centrality** of control
8. A discernible **top-to-bottom line of authority**
9. **Order** as a principle of organisation, the arrangement and coordination of activities
10. **Equity,** the principle of dealing fairly with everybody who works for the organisation
11. **Employee discipline,** ensuring that everybody receives the same standard of treatment at the organisation
12. **Stability of job tenure,** by which all employees should be given continuity of employment in the interests of building up expertise
13. Encouragement of **initiative** on the part of everyone who works in the organisation
14. **Esprit de corps,** the generation of organisation, team and group identity, willingness and motivation to work

Fayol's work stands as the first attempt to produce a theory of management and set of management principles. Fayol also recognised that these principles did not constitute an end in themselves; that their emphasis would vary between situations; and that they would require interpretation and application on the part of those managing the situation.

■ Scientific management

The concept of scientific management, that is the taking of a precise approach to the problems of work and work organisation, was pioneered by Frederick Winslow Taylor (1856–1917). His hypothesis was based on the premise that the proper organisation of the workforce and work methods would improve efficiency. It was based on the experience of his career in the US steel industry. He propounded a mental and attitudinal revolution on the part of both managers and workers. Work should be a cooperative effort between managers and workers. Work organisation should be such that it removed all responsibility from the workers, leaving them only with their particular task. By specialising and training in this task, the individual worker would become 'perfect' in his job performance; work could thus be organised into production lines and items produced efficiently and to a constant standard as a result. Precise performance standards would be predetermined by job observation and analysis and a best method arrived at; this would become the normal way of working. Everyone would benefit – the organisation because it cut out all wasteful and inefficient use of resources; managers because they had a known standard of work to set and observe; and workers because they would always do the job the same way. Everyone would benefit financially also from the increase in output, sales and profits and the reflection of this in high wage and salary levels. In a famous innovation at the Bethlehem Steel Works, USA, where he also worked, Taylor optimised productive labour at the ore and coal stock piles by providing various sizes of shovels from which the men could choose to ensure that they used that which was best suited to them. He reduced handling costs per tonne by a half over a three-year period. He also reduced the size of the workforce required to do this from 400 to 140.

The great advances that Taylor and those that also followed the scientific school made were in the standardisation of work, the ability to put concepts of productivity and efficiency into practice. The work foreshadowed the production line and other standardised and automated efforts and techniques that have been used for mass produced goods and commodities ever since. In the pursuit of this, scientific management also helped create the boredom, disaffection and alienation of the workforces producing these goods that still remain as issues to be addressed and resolved in the 1990s and beyond.

■ The human relations school

The most famous and pioneering work carried out in this field of management was the Hawthorne Studies at The Western Electric Company in Chicago. These studies were carried out over the period 1924–1936. Originally designed to draw conclusions between the working environment and work output they finished as major studies of work groups, social factors and employee attitudes and values, and the effect of these at the place of work.

The Hawthorne Works employed over 30,000 people at the time, making telephone equipment. Elton Mayo, Professor of Industrial Research at Harvard University, was called in to advise the company because there was both poor productivity and a high level of employee dissatisfaction.

The first of the experiments was based on the hypothesis that productivity would improve if working conditions were improved. The first stage was the improvement of the lighting for a group of female workers; to give a measure of validity to the results, a control group was established whose lighting was to remain consistent. However, the output of both groups improved and continued to improve whether the lighting was increased or decreased. The second stage extended the experiments to include rest pauses, variations in starting and finishing times, and variations in the timing and length of the lunch break. At each stage the output of both groups rose until the point at which the women in the experimental group complained that they had too many breaks and that their work rhythm was being disrupted. The third stage was a major attitude survey of over 20,000 of the company's employees. This was conducted over the period 1928–1930. The fourth and final stage consisted of observation in depth of both the informal and formal working groups in 1932. The final stage (1936) drew all threads together and resulted in the commencement of personnel counselling schemes and other staff related activities based on the overall conclusions drawn by Mayo and his team from Harvard and also the company's own researchers.

These may be summarised as follows:

1. **Individuals** need to be given importance in their own right, and must also be seen as group or team members
2. **The need to belong** at the workplace is of fundamental importance, as critical in its own way as both pay and rewards and working conditions
3. There is both a **formal and informal** organisation, with formal and informal groups and structures; the informal exerts a strong influence over the formal
4. People respond positively to active involvement in work.

What started out as a survey of the working environment thus finished as the first major piece of research on the attitudes and values prevalent among those drawn together into working situations. The Hawthorne Studies gave rise to concepts of social man and human relations at the workplace. They were the first to place importance on them and to set concepts of groups, behaviour, personal value and identity importance in industrial and commercial situations.

■ Winning friends and influencing people

The work of Dale Carnegie deserves a mention here. He was a pioneer of some of the concepts that have now become part of the mainstream of good business and management practices.

Carnegie identified the barriers and blockages to profitable and effective activity. He summarised this as 'overcoming fears'. The starting point for nearly all transactions was having to deal with humans on a face to face basis as the prerequisite for commercial success.

To do this successfully he identified certain fundamental techniques for handling people. The main factor is **empathy**: the ability to put yourself in the other person's position, seeing things from their point of view, understanding their wants, needs, hopes and fears; and understanding what they want from the transaction (not your wonderful product *per se*, but rather the benefits that are expected to accrue). The customer is at the centre of the transaction and therefore, is entitled to feel important and to have their wants and needs attended to and satisfied.

Carnegie identified other characteristics in support of this that would reinforce the effective capabilities of anyone who deals with customers. These are: learning to take a genuine interest in people; the development of a positive persona; listening attentively and responding to the needs of the customers, encouraging them to talk; speaking in terms of their interests; and being sincere. Language used should always be positive and couched in terms that encourage progress and positive responses. Staff should never argue with customers.

More generally, Carnegie preached the value of positive rather than negative criticism – above all, when it is necessary to tell someone that they are wrong, sticking to the wrong deed rather than criticising their personality. The person in question should also be allowed to save face. Criticism should always be followed by constructive help and followed by an item of praise. In general all people should be praised and valued and given a high reputation – the organisation is going to need these qualities, and not those engendered by any lasting resentment.

Carnegie also preached the more general virtues of honesty, openness, self-respect, commitment and clarity of purpose as being central to business and commercial success.

The lessons taught by Carnegie run throughout the whole of the philosophy of human relations and are to be found in the practices of many successful companies and those regarded as 'excellent'. The importance of, and central position of, 'the customer' is a feature current in the offerings of business schools in the last decade of the twentieth century, as well as being a critical factor in the successes of Japanese industry and commerce.

■ The 'Affluent Worker' studies

The affluent worker studies were carried out at Luton, UK, in the early 1960s. There were three companies studied, Vauxhall Cars, La Porte Chemicals, and Skefco Engineering. The stated purpose was to give an account of the attitudes and behaviour of a sample of affluent workers, male high wage earners at mass or flow companies; and to attempt to explain them. Both the firms and the area were considered highly profitable and prosperous.

The main findings were as follows. The job was overwhelmingly a means to an end on the part of the workforce, that of earning enough to support life away from the company. The affluent workers had little or no identity with the place of work or with their colleagues; this was especially true of those doing unskilled jobs.

Some skilled workers would discuss work issues and problems with colleagues. The unskilled would not. In general, the workforces felt no involvement with either the company, their colleagues or the work. Generally, positive attitudes towards the company prevailed, but again these were related to the instrumental approaches to employment adopted; the companies were expected both to increase in prosperity and to provide increased wages and standards of living. The companies were perceived to be 'good employers' for similar reasons.

The matters to which the affluent workers were found to be actively hostile were those concerning supervision. The preferred style of supervision was described as 'hands off'; any more active supervision was perceived to be intrusive. Work study and efficiency drives were also opposed.

There was a very high degree of trade union membership (87% overall), though few of the affluent workers became actively involved in either national or branch union activities. Union membership was perceived as an insurance policy. The main point of contact between workers and union was the shop steward, who was expected to take an active interest, where necessary, in their concerns.

No association was found between job satisfaction and current employment. It was purely a 'wage–work bargain', a means to an end. The most important relationship in the life of the worker was that with his family. The workers did not generally socialise with each other, either at work or in the community; thus membership of workplace social clubs was also low.

The view of the future adopted was also instrumental. There was no general aspiration to supervisory positions especially for their intrinsic benefits. The affluent workers would rather have their own high wages than the status and responsibility of being the foreman. More generally, the future was regarded in terms of increased profitability and prosperity, an expectation that wages would grow and that standards of living and of life would, in consequence, grow with them.

The studies illustrated the sources and background of the attitudes and behaviour inherent in this instrumental view of employment. More generally, the studies concluded that levels of workplace satisfaction were conditional upon continued stability and prosperity; and that there were universal expectations of continuing growth in the situation.

■ The intrapreneur

Intrapreneur is the name given to 'the enterprising individual in the successful business'. Identifiable within this concept are two main strands, the characteristics of the individuals who can be developed as intrapreneurs, and the nature of organisations that can develop them.

The characteristics identified as being essential within individuals are:

- **Commercial insight** and market and environmental awareness and understanding
- **Personal strength of character** and persistence in the approach to business matters and issues, professional stamina and staying power
- **Innovative and creative approaches** to problems and the development of the creative faculties

- The ability to manage and direct **change**
- The capacity for **analysis, organisation** and **control** of activities
- The ability to **get on with people** at all levels, to animate them and to enable others to perform their jobs effectively and successfully.

Organisations must have the following attributes:

- The ability to **recognise the talents and potential** of individuals and to harness those in mutually beneficial and profitable activities
- The ability to **learn and develop** more quickly than the rate of organisational change
- The capacity to provide both **intrinsic** and **extrinsic rewards** commensurate with both organisational profit and individual capabilities.

The overall purpose is the creation of an environment where both business activities and talented individuals can come together for the generation of successful, dynamic and profitable business activities. 'Intrapreneuring' is the ability to both nurture and harmonise these talents in this way.

■ The Peter Principle

Lawrence J. Peter worked as teacher, psychologist, counsellor and consultant in different parts of the American education sphere during the post-war era. This included education in prisons and dealing with emotionally disadvantaged and disturbed children.

The Peter Principle was published in 1969. It is based on the assumption and invariable actuality that people gain promotion to their level of incompetence – as long as they are successful in one job they will be considered a suitable candidate for the next by the organisation in question; and only when they are not successful in that job will they not be considered for the next promotion (see Summary Box 2.2). The book is written in an essentially racy and light-hearted way; the lessons to be learned are nevertheless important.

Promotions are clearly being made on a false premise, that of competence in the current job rather than the competence required for the new one. It follows from this that assessments for promotion are fundamentally flawed, based on

---

SUMMARY BOX 2.2   The Peter Principle

'The head's friends saw that the head was no use as a head, so they made her an inspector, to interfere with other heads. And when they found she wasn't much good even at that, they got her into Parliament, where she lived happily ever after.'

Source: C.S. Lewis, *The Silver Chair* (1953).

the wrongful appraisal of the wrong set of characteristics. More generally, what is 'sound performance' in one job may simply be identifiable on the basis that the individual is not actually doing any harm.

In the management sphere the application of the 'Peter Principle' is only too universal. Time and again promotion to supervisory and management grades from within the ranks is based upon the operative's performance in those ranks rather than on any aptitude for supervision, management or direction. Organisations thus not only gain an incompetent or inadequate supervisor, they also lose a highly competent technician. This remains true for all walks of life – the best nurses do not *per se* make the best hospital directors; the best teachers do not make the best school heads; the best drivers do not make the best transport fleet managers.

The lessons to be drawn from this may be summarised as the ability to identify genuine levels and requirements of performance and attributes required to carry them out, and to set criteria against which they can be measured accurately. People may then be placed in jobs that they can do and for which they are best suited. Aptitude for promotion, or any other preferred job for that matter, can then be assessed on the basis of matching personal qualities with desired performance and organisational appointments made accordingly. Finally, the principle also has implications for growing and nurturing your own experts and managers and for succession and continuity planning.

■ Studying organisations

Pioneering and seminal work in this field has been carried out by Charles B. Handy of the London Business School. Over the period since 1950, he has consulted and written extensively on the concepts, complexities, functions and interrelationships within organisations.

Handy's work emphasises the importance of this field of study itself, to both the aspiring and the practising manager. It is concerned with illustrating and discussing and analysing the basic concepts, and also with translating these into a useful and comprehensible body of managerial knowledge and experience.

Handy's work focuses on the following distinctive areas. There are fundamental universal concepts and principles – motivation, leadership, power and influence, groups, the individual, roles and interactions – found in all situations. These are then applied to particular situations, and the ways in which they combine together and become effective are studied. These are concerned with the staffing structure, style and systems of organisations and their managers. The other concern is the fluid nature of the organisations themselves, their propensities to expand, contract, change their style and way of working, their requirements for efficiency and effectiveness, both as business-like, commercial undertakings and also in the harmonisation and reconciliation of human interactions in this pursuit.

Handy was the first to articulate and elucidate, on a wide scale, the general concepts of the **core and peripheral workforce**, an organisation style and structure that identified a core group of staff – the establishment that would serve the organisation permanently and be on its payroll, provide its life and its style, its permanence and continuity; and the peripheral – who would be on a much looser contract, brought in when necessary either to carry out tasks that their specialism allowed or to cope with periods of pressure or overload on the organisation.

Handy developed this concept a stage further into that of the 'Shamrock' organisation, identifying more precisely the nature of the peripheral workforce as having distinct elements (the petals of the shamrock). These consisted of sub-contractors, specialists and the unskilled. The concept is based on the thesis that organisations cannot and will not carry these staff on their payrolls if their services are only required at particular points of the business calendar.

Handy is the major authority on the understanding of, and complexities of, organisations; he is also both pioneer of, and a mirror of, the leadership and directional aspects essential for organisation success.

■ Business policy and strategy

The importance of this as part of the field of the study of management was first fully developed by H.I. Ansoff, who postulated theories concerning both the totality of, and complexities of, organisational and operational strategy. This work was carried out in the 1950s and 1960s.

Ansoff's stance was based in the concern found among business managers of identifying rational and accurate ways in which organisations could both adjust to and also exploit changes in their environment. Such ways he described as:

- **Traditional**, micro-economic theories of the firm which, while taking full account of 'the organisation in its environment', took no account of either its operational or behavioural procedures and practices
- The need to reconcile a **range of decision classes** – strategic, administrative and operational – in both the allocation of, and competition for, the organisation's resources, priority, time and attention
- **Transition** from one state to another due to changes in technology, markets, working practices, size or scale of the firm and its operations
- The application of **science and technology** to the process of management which was ever-increasing at the time. This generated both interest and acceptance of more analytical approaches.

The work of Ansoff was pioneering in what was then recognised as a complex field of study, and one that offered great scope for research from both an academic point of view and also in the interest of the pursuit of profitable business.

Ansoff was the first academic to adopt this area as a field of genuine enquiry, and to focus on the widest concept of what strategy is and what it should cover in the business sphere. The work carried out drew conclusions based not only on the strategy, but also the organisational processes that were established to achieve it. The work looked forward. It recognised the inevitability of change and the turmoil and turbulence that this would cause to organisations and their environment. Ansoff was among the very first (academic, research or business theorist) to propound the concept of strategies for change and the active processes required in its management.

The major authority on business policy and strategy is, currently, Michael E. Porter, of the Harvard Business School. As expert, consultant and academic, he has conducted in-depth analyses of strategy processes, competitive positioning and competitive advantage, developing and refining the key concepts outlined above and also delving much deeper into the complexities that constitute effective corporate strategies.

This has included substantial analyses of the interrelationships between organisations and their environment; and between each other in particular industrial and commercial sectors. In turn, he has related this to both the diversification and complexity of the organisations themselves that operate in particular spheres. He has isolated the concepts of defensive and offensive strategies and when each should be used. His work has produced a comprehensive set of tools, techniques and methods for the analysis of companies, industries, sectors and markets.

Porter's concept of the analysis of the 'value chain' (see Figure 2.1) identifies the elements that are critical in the devising and assessment of profitable or effective strategy, where the particular links in the chain lie, and the effect of each upon the whole of the strategy adopted. These links include: costs and their behaviour; the separation and combination of activities; the technology that is available and the ability of the organisation to use it; the identification of good and bad aspects of operations in the organisation and the market; the identification of good and bad industrial and commercial sectors and competitors within them. These are then related both to the segments in which the organisation is to operate and the structures and sub-structures that it adopts in order to do this effectively.

Business and public policy and strategy is currently a major field of enquiry. This derives from the change, turmoil and turbulence that is present and endemic throughout the business sphere at present. As organisations get better at it, and understand the importance of conducting it and formulating it effectively, and in line with their own capabilities and capacities, they gain great advantages in their ability to compete in their chosen field.

■ Organisations, management and technology

The relationships between the technology required to conduct certain industrial and production activities and the nature and style of organisation required to

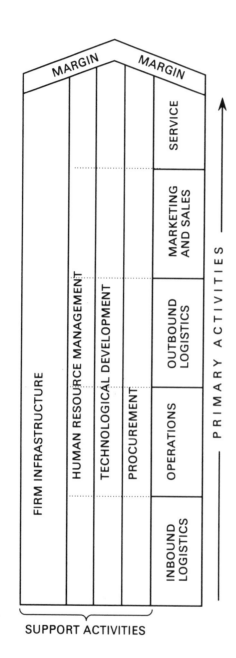

Notes: The value chain breaks an organisation down into its component parts in order to understand the source of, and behaviour of, costs; and actual and potential sources of differentiation. It isolates and identifies the 'building blocks' by which an organisation creates an offering of value to its customers and clients:

- It is a tool for the general examination of an organisation's competitive position, and means of cost determination.
- It identifies the range and mix characteristics necessary to design, produce, deliver and support its offerings.
- The value chain should be identified at 'business unit' level, for greatest possible clarity and accuracy.

Figure 2.1   The Value Chain

Source: Michael E. Porter. Used with permission from the Free Press Inc., a division of Macmillan.

1.

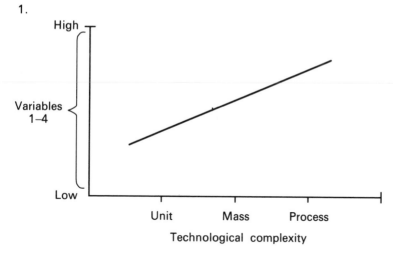

Technological complexity

Variables: 1. Number of levels in management hierarchy
2. Ratio of managers and supervisors to total staff
3. Ratio of direct to indirect labour
4. Proportion of graduates among supervisory staff engaged in production.

2.

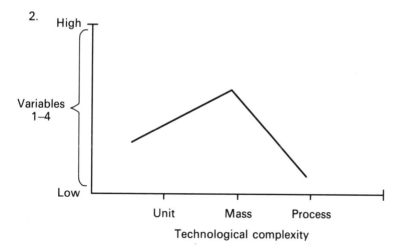

Technological complexity

Variables: 1. Span of total of first time supervisors
2. Organisation flexibility/inflexibility
3. Amount of written communication
4. Specialistion between functions of management, technical expertise; the time–staff structure.

Figure 2.2 Organisations and technology

Source: P. A. Lawrence (1985). Used with permission.

energise this was studied by Joan Woodward, who conducted research among the manufacturing firms of South East Essex in the post-war conditions of the 1950s. The research looked at the organisational aspects of the levels and complexities of authority and hierarchy and spans of control in these organisations (see Figure 2.2). It also considered the nature and division of work – the clarity of the definition of jobs and duties, and the ways in which specialist and functional divisions were drawn. Finally, the nature of communications activities and systems in the organisations was analysed.

The conclusions drawn related the differences in these organisational aspects to the different technologies used in them. The technology was found to impinge on all factors – organisational objectives, lines of authority, roles and responsibilities and the structure of management committees. The nature, complexity and personality of systems for control were also found to be related to the technological processes in place.

The work also defined the levels of production process and complexity in technological terms that are now universally understood and used: those of unit production, batch production, mass production and flow production. It further developed the relationship between these and the nature and complexity of organisation required in each case, and above all in regard to the highly capital intensive mass and flow activities.

Mechanistic and organic/organismic management systems

These model systems of management were proposed by T. Burns and G. M. Stalker in 'The Management of Innovation' (1966). The mechanistic system of organisation was found to be appropriate to conditions of relative stability. They are highly structured, and those working in them have rigorous formal job descriptions, clearly defined roles and precise positions in the hierarchies (see Figure 2.3). Direction of the organisation is handed down via the hierarchy from the top; and communication is similarly 'vertical'. The organisation insists on loyalty and obedience from its members, both to superior officers, and also to itself. Finally, it is the ability of the functionary to operate within the constraints of the organisation that is required.

The organic/organismic model is suitable to unstable, turbulent and changing conditions. The organisation is constantly breaking new ground, addressing new problems, and meeting the unforeseen, and a highly specialised structure cannot accommodate this. What is required is fluidity, continual adjustment, task redefinition, and flexibility (see Figure 2.4). Groups and departments and teams are constantly formed and reformed. Communication is at every level, and between every level. The means of control is regarded as a network rather than a

1.

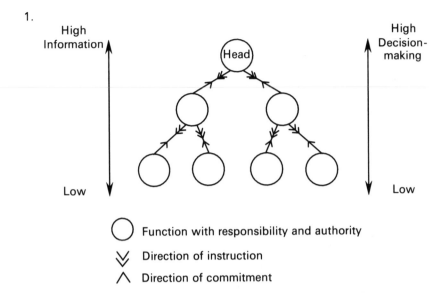

High
Information

High
Decision-
making

Low

Low

○   Function with responsibility and authority

⋁   Direction of instruction

⋀   Direction of commitment

Figure 2.3   Organisation structures: mechanistic

Source: P.A. Lawrence (1985) (after Burns and Stalker).

2.

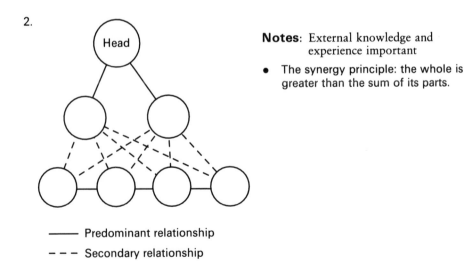

Notes: External knowledge and
experience important

● The synergy principle: the whole is
greater than the sum of its parts.

——— Predominant relationship

– – – Secondary relationship

Figure 2.4   Organisation structures: organic/organismic

Source: P.A. Lawrence (1985) (after Burns and Stalker).

a personal commitment to it, that goes beyond the purely operational or functional.

Burns and Stalker develop their theme a stage further, to ascertain whether it was possible to move from the mechanistic to the organismic. The conclusion was that they doubted that it could. When mechanistic organisations seek change, committee and working party systems are created and liaison officer posts are established. Additional stresses are placed on the existing structure and channels of communication of the organisation, compounding the difficulties, and clouding the issues that are to be faced. The consequences are that progress tends to be stifled rather than facilitated.

■ Socio-technical systems

The concept of the 'socio-technical' workplace system was proposed as the result of studies carried out at the instigation of the Tavistock Institute of Human Relations during the 1940s, 1950s and 1960s. The work was conducted in a variety of situations, including coal mines, cotton mills, and prisons.

The 'socio-technical' definition was arrived at because the researchers (E. Trist, G. Bamforth) found that it was not enough to regard work methods as purely functional or operational. The organisation and autonomy of the work group itself had to be considered as part of the design of the activities to be carried out; and if this was disturbed there was an increase in disputes, grievances, absenteeism, and arguments over pay. Consequently, both the social and technical (or operational) aspects had to be addressed if truly effective work methods were to be devised.

Other findings and conclusions of the socio-technical approach should be illustrated. The autonomy of the work group, and its self-identity, is of critical importance, and if it is disturbed, either by intrusive supervision, technological or operational change, this again leads to increases in disputes and absenteeism. There was found to be a clear relationship between the social effectiveness of the group and its work output. As far as work performance was concerned, groups and individuals took a high degree of pride and satisfaction in task achievement, and in having the ability to be involved in the whole operation (rather than just a part of it). They established an 'ideal' size of work group, as consisting of eight persons. There was also found to be a high level of willingness to cooperate on the part of operatives, provided that the environment and approach to the work was also right.

The main contribution is to identify, and support, the need for all work, work patterns and methods, to meet social and psychological needs, as well as those related simply to the task in hand. The work also reinforces ideas of motivation that relate to job enrichment and enlargement; to the provision of a quality working environment; and to the importance of means of supervision.

■ Excellence

The genesis of the work that subsequently grew into the management concept of 'excellence', was a review carried out in the latter part of the 1970s by McKinsey, the international management consulting firm, of its thinking and approach to business strategy and organisation effectiveness. This review was itself founded in a dissatisfaction with conventional approaches to these matters.

The approach adopted was to study both businesses and managers of high repute and/or high performance, and to try and isolate those qualities and characteristics that made them so. A model (the 7–S model; see Figure 2.5) for the design and description of organisations was also proposed. Those working on the study also identified those attributes that they felt ought to be present in such organisations and persons, and to test them against those studied.

In all, 62 organisations were studied. They were drawn from all sectors of US industry and commerce, and included many global firms (e.g., Boeing, McDonald's, Hewlett Packard, 3M).

'High performing' took on a variety of meanings – profitability; a global organisation such as IBM; a strong positive image such as Marks & Spencer; a strong domestic organisation (Sainsbury's in the UK or 3M in the USA); a strong player in a slumped or declining market; and also related other aspects such as a strong general image; customer confidence; and staff and customer loyalty.

These characteristics may be summarised as follows:

1. The leadership and management of business organisations requires **vision**, energy, dynamism and positivism; the placing of the customer and his needs and wants at the centre of the business; and the ability to change and improve as a permanent organisational feature
2. The closeness of the relationship between the **organisation** and its **customers** and **clients** must be maintained; if this is lost the customers will go elsewhere
3. The commitment, motivation, ability, training and development of all **staff** at all levels of the organisation are critical to the continuation of its success; closely related to this is a shared vision or shared values to which all members of the organisation must ascribe; staff must be held in high respect and well rewarded
4. **Supervision** levels, hierarchies, regional and head office establishments must be kept to a minimum; the purpose of these establishments is to service those who generate business of the organisation and not to impose a superstructure on them; such establishments should also be flexible and responsive and not hierarchical and inert
5. Organisations must stick to their **core business**; that which they are good at; and that which is profitable and effective
6. Organisations must constantly **innovate and improve**, update working practices, staff abilities, technology, customer response times and methods. They should constantly seek new applications and new markets for their existing products and services
7. Organisations must be **receptive** to ideas and influences from outside, and be able to evaluate them for use and value to them in their own circumstances
8. The bias of the organisation must be towards **action** not procedure.

SUMMARY BOX 2.3   Eight Characteristics of Excellent Management Practice

---

1. **Bias for action** – do it, fix it, try it.
2. **Closeness to the customer** – listen intently and regularly to the customer and provide quality, service and reliability in response to customer needs.
3. **Autonomy and entrepreneurship** – innovation and risk taking as an expected way of doing things, rather than conformity and conservatism.
4. **Productivity through people** – employees are seen as the source of quality and productivity.
5. **Hands-on, value driven** – the basic philosophy of the organisation is well-defined and articulated.
6. **Stick to knitting** – stay close to what you can do well.
7. **Simple form lean staff** – structural arrangements and systems are simple, with small headquarters staff.
8. **Simultaneous loose-tight properties** – centralised control of values, but operational decentralisation and autonomy.

Source: Peters and Waterman (1982).

The 7–S
Framework

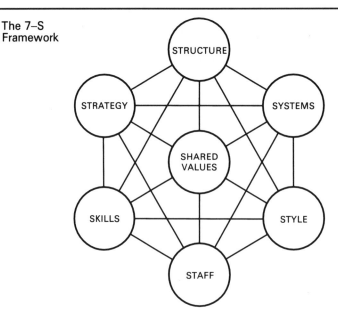

Purpose: a configuration of organisation, pattern and design that reflects the essential attributes that must be addressed in the establishment and development of an excellent organisation.

Figure 2.5   The concept of excellence applied to organisations

Source: Peters and Waterman (1982).

Various models are proposed as to how this can best be achieved, what the components of excellent organisations are, and how to develop organisations in such ways as they become excellent (see Summary Box 2.3 and Figure 2.5). Related aspects are also considered, the style of supervision adopted, strategic and policy aspects, innovation, staff performance, salaries and wages, conflicts and disputes at the workplace, the nature of the work carried out and the attitudes of organisations to both their staff and customers.

The key findings were as follows:

1. **The essential nature of organisation culture.** In the organisations studied this was: a belief in being the best; a belief in the importance of the staff and individuals as well as in their contribution to the organisation; a belief in, and obsession with, quality and service; a belief that organisation members should innovate and have their creative capacities harnessed; a belief in the importance of excellent communication among all staff; a belief in the concept of simultaneous loose–tight properties – measures of control that allow for operational flexibility; a belief in the continuous cycle of development; and a recognition that there is always room for improvement. Attention to detail – the necessity to ensure that whatever the excellence of the strategic vision, it must always be carefully and accurately carried out. The belief in the importance of economic growth and profit motive.
2. **The importance of macro-organisational analysis.** This was the approach used to establish the concepts and elements that were present in the organisations described as 'excellent'.

   Essentially, this is dependent upon the strength and style of leadership – the drive, determination, core values and strategic vision necessary to energise and make profitable the organisation's activities. In time, this becomes 'the way things are done here'. Managers underpin this through their day-to-day activities – those issues they concern themselves with, those matters on which they spend resources, those people with whom they spend time. It is therefore a combination both of what they do and also of how they do it and messages are given off by this to the rest of the organisation. Above all, the leader of the organisation expresses the true organisational value through the means by which s/he conducts her/himself in all activities.

These values become an integral part of the structures and systems of the organisation that affect all its activities. If the management style is energetic and positive, this is reflected in the ways in which senior managers wish to have things done.

The next part of the Peters and Waterman study was to look at the particular performance indicators of the organisation. These came from all areas of activity. They included asset growth and returns on capital invested; the organisations studied and from which the lessons were drawn had rates of return on these factors of between 10 and 60 times the sectoral average. Absenteeism was another factor studied. In a US Steel Works studied by Peters he found an uncertificated sickness rate of two-fifths of 1% – against a national average of 6% and a sectoral average of 9%. Organisation reputation was another factor assessed; this was conducted across all its activities – marketing, human resource policies, customer care and customer relations, equality of opportunity – and also across its wider general reputation in the environment and community – in which it invariably perceived itself to have a direct stake, interest and wider responsibility.

The other contribution of the excellence studies was to identify these characteristics as being essential to both organisation and managerial success (see Summary Box 2.4). The role of the senior manager is therefore the management of the organisation's culture, style and values; designer and director of strategy; and assessor of progress against precisely stated performance indicators – that is, the manager of the 'simultaneous loose–tight properties'.

The person most responsible for energising and popularising this work is Tom Peters. Working extensively in organisations and drawing his conclusions from this work, he has published a range of management books that have the purpose of illustrating these findings and ensuring their promulgation to the widest audience possible. Alongside this is a more general approach of the excellence studies to reach parts of the business and management sphere not so far touched by other works. What has happened as a result therefore is both promotion of a wide-ranging debate and the popularisation of the subject-matter. This may well turn out to be the major enduring contribution of the excellence studies.

SUMMARY BOX 2.4   Criteria for Excellence

- High growth of assets, value, turnover and profits
- Consistent reputation in sector as leader and pioneer
- Solid and positive reputation with customers, community and general public.

Source: W. Goldsmith and D. Clutterbuck (1990).

- Professional organisations are lean and empowered
- Professional staff require flat structures and autonomy for effective performance
- Processes and procedures are speedy, simple and effective.

Source: C.B. Handy (1984).

- Excellence is performance thousands and thousands of percentage points over sectoral norms.

Source: T. Peters (1982).

- Innovation and development leading to maximisation and optimisation of the human resource
- Innovation in quality of working life
- Promotion of full and genuine equality of opportunity
- Models of good practice, offer their example to the world, and are pleased and proud to be studied.

Source: R.M. Kanter (1985).

■ Change

The subject of change forms a continuous thread throughout this book. It merits introduction here as a key area of concern in current management studies. We have already made reference to the current turbulent nature of the business sphere. The changes that have impinged in general on society over the period since the end of the Second World War and more particularly since the 1960s in turn impinge on the management of organisations. These changes may be summarised as:

(1) **Technological,** affecting all social, economic and business activities; rendering many organisations and occupations obsolete and creating new ones; and opening up new spheres of activity bringing travel transport, distribution, telecommunication, industry, goods and services on to a global scale.

(2) **Social,** the changing of the lives of people from the fundamentals of life expectancy and lifestyle choice to the ability to buy and possess items; to travel; to be educated; to receive ever-increasing standards of health care, personal insurance and information; to be fed; higher standards of social security and stability; increased leisure time and choice of leisure pursuits; and all commensurate with increases in disposable income and purchasing power and choices of purchase.

(3) **Eco-political,** resulting in changes in all government forms; the state of flux of the EC and the adoption of supernational laws and directives and the single European market; the collapse of the communist bloc and the USSR; the fragmentation of the former Yugoslavia; the emergence of Taiwan, South Africa, Korea, Malaysia and Vietnam as spheres of political and economic influence taking their places in the business sphere.

(4) **Expectational,** in which the changes may be expressed as from stability to the state of change itself, a permanent state of flux; the change from the expectation of working for one company or organisation to working for many, and the realisation that the former is increasingly unlikely; change in occupation, training and profession is an increased expectation; changes in political governments and the instrument of state is an expectation. Organisations change their business (e.g., Virgin, from music into air travel) and expect their staff to change with them. Hospitals in the UK in the 1990s are being reconstituted as business units and offering medical services at a price or charge, and they expect their staff and patients to go along with this. The business sphere is indeed 'thriving on chaos' and 'learning to love change', and this is ever-more expected on the part of those who manage it.

Understanding, controlling and managing this process is fundamental to its success. Rather than either passive acceptance or allowing it to happen, managers must assume responsibility for the direction of the change process and the activities required to make it effective and successful.

■ Conclusions

The overall purpose here has been to illustrate the complexity, range and scale of the subject-matter that is to be considered, the widely differing standpoints from which it has been tackled, and the progression of it as a field of study. The balance of the material quoted reflects the particular concern with it over the period since 1945 and its emergence as an area critical to both business and economic success, and also the wider prosperity of society at large.

It is not at all an exhaustive coverage. However, it does attempt to itemise major staging posts and fields of enquiry, and to illustrate the variety of studies that have been undertaken. Each study indicated addresses different parts of the business and management sphere. Each makes its own particular contribution to the whole field; none provides a comprehensive coverage of it. What is clear, however, is that it is an ever-broadening sphere. The works illustrated here demonstrate just how far this has developed and the variety of approaches that have been taken in the pursuit of this.

There is no doubt that there has been a shift in approach to regard management as an occupation in its own right. What has been less certain is what the actual composition of this occupation and profession is. This chapter has attempted to illustrate the basis of this and to introduce some of the major concepts, studies and ideas that have contributed to the state of its development.

Some more specific conclusions can also be drawn from this material. Management direction and leadership are separate from the functions, operations and activities of the organisation. Ability to generate confidence, loyalty, trust and faith of all those in the organisation is essential. It is necessary to establish the identity of a common purpose to which everybody in the organisation can aspire and to which all the resources of the organisation are concentrated. People must be rewarded in response to the efforts that they put into the achievement of the organisation's purposes. Both the organisation and its managers must have knowledge of and ability to operate in the chosen environment and to influence this as far as they possibly can. Within particular constraints, organisations establish their own ways of working, cultural norms, procedures and practices, as part of the process of making effective their daily operations. There is the recognition that business and managerial practice takes place in what is both a global and turbulent environment. The ability to operate within this is critical to continuity and success.

This, then, represents the backcloth against which the rest of the book is written. It enables a broad understanding of where the current state of the management art/science/profession is drawn and where the current matters of importance and concern within it lie. It also indicates the range and complexity of the qualities and capacities required of the manager.

CHAPTER 3

Organisational and behavioural aspects

■ Introduction

The purpose of this chapter is to identify and discuss the range and complexity of the behavioural, qualitative and psychological concepts that are a necessary background and prerequisite to managerial effectiveness.

It is necessary to have a general level of understanding in these areas as part of the knowledge background which is in turn essential for the adoption of, and implementation of, adequate and suitable staff and organisational management styles. More specifically, identity with the organisation and its work can only be achieved if an understanding of the people who work in it, their wants and needs, hopes, fears, desires and aspirations, is first acquired. Commonality of purpose – team spirit or Fayol's esprit de corps – can similarly be contemplated only when the widely conflicting and divergent reasons and objectives that people have in work situations are themselves fully understood; and means of harmonising and energising these can only be successful if seen from this standpoint.

The aspects discussed are arranged under five generic headings:

- **Leadership**, qualities and capabilities; power and influence; and the role and function of the chief executive or organisation leader.
- **Conflict**, sources, existence, management and containment.
- **Motivation**, the ability and capacity of both organisations and the individuals who work within them to energise themselves, their talents and attributes in productive, effective, relevant and harmonious activities.
- **Groups**, their formation, composition, energising and empowerment and including elements related to both the work in hand and the maintenance and development of the group as an entity with its own life and standing.
- **Individuals**, their roles and responsibilities in the organisation and how these are to be harmonised and reconciled in the pursuit of productive endeavour and activity.

■ Leadership

Leadership is concerned with getting results through people, and all that entails and implies – the organisation of the staff into productive teams, groups, departments; the creation of human structures; their motivation and direction;

the resolution of conflicts at the workplace (both inherent and operational); creating vision and direction for the whole undertaking; and providing resources in support of this.

The problems of leadership have been recognised for thousands of years, as we have seen (Chapter 1), and approaches to them have taken many different forms. The main issues concerned are:

- Getting **optimum performance** from the workforce, in whatever terms that is defined.
- Ensuring **continuity**, development and improvement in the workforce itself.
- Relating the **skills and capacities** of the workforce to the job, task and functional requirements; and meeting the intrinsic expectations of the job.
- Taking active responsibility for results.

Approaches to these problems in the business sphere have covered a wide spectrum. At the one extreme, organisations have sought to recruit their managers from the aristocracy or officer classes, where 'leadership' was deemed to have been an in-bred or else a 'natural quality'. At the other, lists of qualities, skills and attributes have been isolated, and individuals put through training

---

SUMMARY BOX 3.1   Leadership Styles

Autocratic (Benevolent or Tyrannical*)	Participative	
	Consultative	Democratic
1. Leader makes all final decisions for the group	1. Leader makes decisions after consultation with group	1. Decisions made by the group – by consultation, or vote if necessary
2. Close supervision, variety of styles	2. Total communication between leader and members	Voting based on the principle of one man – one vote majority rules
3. Individual members' interests subordinate to the organisation	3. Leader is supportive and developmental	2. All members bound by the group decision and support it
4. Subordinates treated without regard for their views	4. Leader is accessible and discursive	3. All members may contribute to discussion
5. Great demands placed on staff	5. Questioning approach encouraged	4. Development of coalitions and cliques
6. Questioning discouraged	6. Modus operandi largely unspecified	5. Leadership role is assumed by Chairman

*Difference is in attitude and approach, not content.

programmes devised around these. In between the two, academic and organisational research has identified and codified a variety of different approaches.

In outline, these are as follows:

■ Trait theories

The basis of these theories is that there is a body of traits or characteristics which are present in successful and effective leaders. The great limitation on this approach is the great diversity of characteristics identified across a range of situations; and the identification of very few traits common to all, in all situations. The concept of 'success' is widely open to interpretation, as is the presence of, and ability to identify integrity.

The traits that are identified most often are: intelligence; initiative; self-assurance; the ability to take an overview; good health; enthusiasm; determination and decisiveness; ambition, commitment, energy and drive; and integrity and honesty.

■ Style theories

These identify leadership as being somewhere on an 'authoritarian – participative' continuum. There is an emotive leaning towards the notion that the more participative or supportive the style of the leader, the better the organisation is for all those who have to work in it (see Summary Box 3.1). While this may to some extent be borne out by levels of grievance and dissension, there is no direct or simple correlation demonstrated between this and profitability, or other measures of business success.

■ Contingency theories

These relate both traits and style to the situation, the environment, the technology and the work to be done, and recognise that this is fluid rather than static. This concerns the position of the leader within the group, and whether they are physically or psychologically distant or close to it.

■ Action centred leadership

This concentrates on the interrelationship of three specific components of the work sphere – the maintenance of the work group; the tasks and their performance; and the position of the individual (see Summary Box 3.2). Again the situation is regarded as fluid, and flexibility is required in any leader who is to be effective.

SUMMARY BOX 3.2   The Leadership Functions Model

The leader must address the key issues of achieving the task, building the team and developing individuals. The leader who concentrates only on the task by for example going all out for production schedules while neglecting the training, encouragement and motivation of the group will always have problems of dissonance and dysfunction.

The leader who concentrates only on creating team spirit while neglecting the job or individuals will not get maximum involvement and commitment, which only comes from an environment that is both harmonious and genuinely productive. Staff members would therefore lack any true achievement or feeling of success.

ACHIEVING THE TASK

BUILDING AND DEVELOPING THE TEAM

CONCERN FOR THE INDIVIDUAL

The key leadership functions required are

DIRECTION	PLANNING
COMMUNICATION	APPRAISAL
COORDINATION	CONTROL
ASSESSMENT	DEVELOPMENT

Source: John Adair (1975).

■ Theories of 'best fit'

The approach in this case derives from each of the others. It recognises that no one approach provides the complete picture or answer. It balances the universal elements of the leader, the subordinates, the task, the technology and the environment; and recognises that there are common elements and attributes on which to draw.

Leadership is not the same as management but a part of it, and leadership qualities, activities and aspects are essential in anyone who aspires to a truly managerial position.

■ Charisma

This is the element of the power, authority and influence of the leaders or managers that arises from their person and personality. It is generally enhanced by the success of the person in the position; and by other related aspects such as their own expertise, or ways of working; it is enhanced also by the self-belief and self confidence of the leader or manager. Charismatic influence depends heavily on the identification with this person by subordinates or followers. Defeat and failure affect the confidence elements of this, and the charismatic leader will suffer loss of personal (as well as professional) reputation as a result. Both leaders and managers may attribute their successes to the force of their personality, only to find that when failure occurs, the organisation falls back on its operational rather than personal elements to rescue the situation; in such a case, the leader loses both position and reputation, but the organisation and its work continue.

■ Situational knowledge and expertise

It follows from this that the best functionary does not necessarily make the best leader of functionaries – none of the characteristics thus far identified is to do with technical excellence. However, it is necessary to reconcile the tenet of 'authority flows from one who knows', and the expectations of the workforce that their manager is an expert in the field, with the qualities necessary to lead and direct them, and to organise the work.

It often happens that the functional expert is promoted into a managerial position, with the consequent loss to the organisation of their technical brilliance, but without a gain in expertise in what is a management rather than a technical position.

So a balance must be struck. The leader cannot lead without a sound knowledge of the work, the technology, the environment, and the professional and technical expertise of those actually carrying out the work.

There is a responsibility incumbent on organisations either to train the technically-oriented functionaries for management before giving them a managerial or executive position; or to induct and ground those already trained as managers in the technical environment.

There have been a great many studies of leaders, directors and managers, from all walks of life (see Summary Box 3.3). They are all inconclusive, in that none of them identifies all the attributes necessary to lead, direct or manage, in all situations. However, the following characteristics are found to be applicable to most situations:

- **Communication**: with both staff and customers, regularly, continuously, and in ways in which they both understand and respond to
- **Decision-making**: the ability to take the right decisions in given situations, to take responsibility and be accountable for them, and to understand the consequences of particular courses of action
- **Commitment**: to both particular matters in hand, and also the wider aspects of the business as a whole; this includes an inherent willingness to draw on one's personal as well as professional energies
- **Staff**: respecting them, trusting them, committing oneself to them, developing them, understanding them and their aspirations and reconciling these with the matters in hand, having confidence in them
- **Quality**: a commitment to a quality of product or service that, whatever the matter in hand, the customer receives high value and high satisfaction and will seek to return for more if required
- **A given set of values** with which others will identify and commit themselves, *or* which they will reject: there are few examples of leaders, directors or managers, who succeed by being all things to all people in all situations
- **Personal characteristics**: of vision, enthusiasm, strength of character, commitment, energy, and interest are common in successful leaders, directors and managers
- **Positive attitudes**: common in successful leaders, directors and managers, and these are transmitted to their staff and customers
- **Mutuality and dependency** of the leader, director or manager and their staff: successful (truly successful) leaders, directors and managers know their own weaknesses, the importance and value of the people with them; above all, they know what they cannot do, and when and where to go for help and support in these areas
- Personal and professional responsibility, authority and accountability.

SUMMARY BOX 3.3   Case Approaches to Leadership and Management

By studying a range of leaders and managers from a variety of situations and backgrounds – sport, politics, history, the military, exploration, religion, and also business – it is possible to infer and draw conclusions in regard to their success or otherwise, and the reasons for this. Their contribution can be assessed and analysed, as can other elements and factors present.

The main constraint on the approach relates to the ability only to see these contributions, elements and factors, in the given situation, and without being able to translate the situational aspects in the case to all examples. Any conclusions thus arrived at have first to be related to current situations if lessons thus learned are to be put into practice.

There is inherent in all of this a body of skills, knowledge, attitudes and behaviour that must be learned, assimilated, adopted or developed in those who aspire to positions that are truly managerial.

From this, it is possible to outline some archetypes of organisation managers and managerial styles, relating both leadership and operational elements.

An outline of archetype organisation managers

W. Reddin developed the 3–D theory, modelled in Figure 3.1 to show these archetypes:

■ Relaxed bureaucrats

People who (in the lowest reading) display insufficient interest in task and relationship interface. Where their enthusiasm for the job is too low, a tendency towards secrecy and lack of commitment may be hindering resource performance and that of the subordinates.

■ Missionaries

People who put harmony and relationships above other considerations. They are ineffective because their desire to see themselves, and be seen, as a 'good person' prevents them from risking a disruption of relationships in order to get production.

■ Autocrats

People who put the immediate task before all other considerations. They are ineffective in that they make it obvious that they have no concern for relationships and have little confidence in others. While many may fear them they also dislike them and are thus motivated to work only when they apply direct pressure.

■ Compromisers

People who recognise the advantages of being oriented to both task and relationships but who are incapable or unwilling to make sound decisions. Ambivalence and compromise are their stock in trade. The strongest influence in their decision-making is the most recent or heaviest pressure.

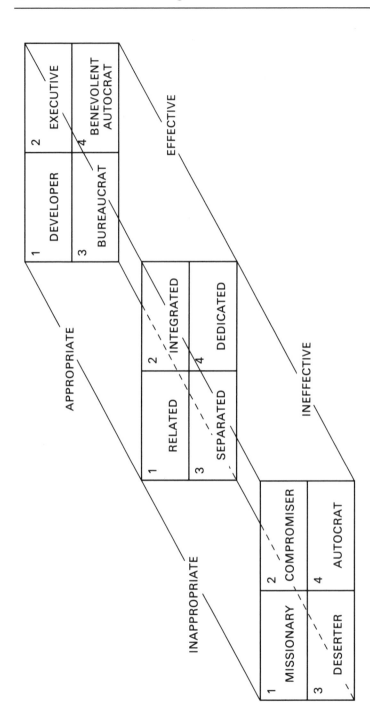

Figure 3.1   The 3-D theory

Purpose: The middle set of boxes identifies the four archetype leaders of Reddin's theory. These archetypes may then be translated into APPROPRIATE EFFECTIVE or INAPPROPRIATE INEFFECTIVE personal types.

Source: Reddin (1970).

■ Effective bureaucrats

People who simply follow the rules without due concern for the finer aspects of the task or the relationships associated with it. They are skilled at maintaining morale and being effective, in spite of a lack of any real interest in either task or relationships.

■ Developers

People who place implicit trust in people, seeing the job as primarily concerned with developing the talents of others and of providing a work atmosphere conducive to maximising individual satisfaction and motivation; effective in that the work environment created is conducive to subordinates developing commitment to both themselves and the job. While successful in obtaining high production, the high relationships orientation on occasions leads them to put the personal development of others before short or long run production, even though this personal development may be unrelated to the job and the development of successors to their position.

■ Benevolent autocrats

Benevolent Autocrats place implicit trust in themselves and are concerned with both the immediate and long run task. They are effective in that they have a skill in inducing others to do what they want them to do without creating such resentment that production and output fall.

■ Executives

Executives see their job as effectively maximising the effort of others in relation to the short and long run task. They set high standards for production and performance and recognise that because of individual differences and expectations they will have to treat everyone differently. They are effective in that their commitment to both task and relationships is evident to all. This acts as a powerful motivator. Their effectiveness is in obtaining results within these dimensions.

A similar approach is taken by Blake and Mouton (see Summary Box 3.4 and Figure 3.2).

■ Power in organisations

It is first useful to distinguish between **authority** and **power**:

SUMMARY BOX 3.4   The Managerial Grid

The managerial grid is a configuration of management styles based on the matching of two dimensions of managerial concern – those of 'concern for people' and 'concern for production/output'. Each of these dimensions is plotted on a nine point graph scale (see Figure 3.2) and an assessment made of the managerial style according to where they come out on each. Thus a low score (1–1) on each axis reflects poverty in managerial style; a high score (9–9) on each reflects a high degree of balance, concern and commitment in each area, and the implication from this is that an adequate, effective and successful managerial style is in place.

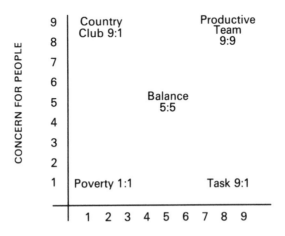

Figure 3.2   The managerial grid

Other styles that Blake and Mouton identified were:

- **9–1: The country club** – production is incidental; concern for the staff and people is everything.
- **1–9: Task orientation** – production is everything; concern for the staff is subordinated to production, effectiveness. Staff management mainly takes the form of planning and control activities; organisational activity is concerned only with output.
- **5–5: Balance** – a medium degree of expertise, commitment and concern in both areas; likely to produce adequate or satisfactory performance.

- The 9–9 score is indicated as 'the best' by Blake and Mouton. This illustrates the target to be striven for, and the organisation's current position, in relation to each axis. The information on which the position on the grid is based is drawn from structured questionnaires, issued to all managers and supervisors in the organisation, section, unit or department to be assessed.

Source: Blake and Mouton (1986).

■ Authority

Authority is the recognition of the right to restrict freedom to act (recognition is the key factor, i.e., the existence of authority is dependent upon shared values between those involved).

Authority refers to the establishment of accepted rules and norms of behaviour which limit conflict (Note: a rule is a contract between those involved).

■ Power

- The ability to influence the attitudes and behaviour of others or, more strongly, an ability to get B to do something which B would not otherwise do!

Authority is thus a relationship; power is a resource.

■ Types of power and authority

In order to be able to understand the behaviour of people in organisations more fully it is useful to examine the different types of power and authority which exist. Weber defined three categories of authority:

1. **Charismatic**: refers to a special aspect of a leader's personality. This is the ability to dominate and lead others to an unusual degree. Extreme examples are Napoleon and John F. Kennedy. Many examples exist at more modest levels, however, in most organisations.
2. **Traditional**: refers to kinship as a basis for allocating power. Typically son follows father. In its purest form it is increasingly rare in organisations.
3. **Legal–rational**: rules and norms, legitimised by law and custom, provide the justification for the possession of power by certain persons. The rules may apply to electoral processes in, for example, government and committees, or they may apply to the selection processes used to make appointments within a hierarchy. A further aspect of the rules will be the definition of the responsibilities of roles and the relations which exist between jobs.
   All formalised hierarchical organisations are of this type.

French and Raven (in D. Cartwright, *Studies in Social Power* (1959) have distinguished five categories of power:

1. **Reward power**: persons with authority over others have the ability to give (or withhold) rewards. These may vary from pay increases to words of praise. This power clearly may be used to influence the behaviour of the subordinate in places of work.
2. **Physical power**: this is the use and threatened use of physical force. Although this is the least acceptable form of power and is never formally used in normal organisations it is a factor in the behaviour of some physically powerful managers and employees. It may be clearly present in such activities as lock-outs and picketing.
3. **Expert power**: knowledge is power. Greater knowledge gives greater power. The expert accountant has power precisely because he is an expert accountant. This power is significant only if the less knowledgeable acknowledge that fact. This is probably the most acceptable and least offensive form of power. In consequence strenuous but spurious efforts may be made by some to claim its possession.
4. **Referent power**: this is power based on the personal friendships of superiors and subordinates. In most relationships where it exists it is likely to be less significant than one or more of the other types.
5. **Legitimate power**: if a subordinate believes that he is a subordinate then he legitimises the power of his superiors. Legitimate power exists in other contexts, e.g. legal power, and parental power.
   In organisations it is typified by hierarchy, chain of command, spans of control, delegation and job specifications. Legitimate power exists in a role, not a person, although it may be supported by, say, expert power in a particular case.

Amitai Etzioni in *Power in Organisations* (1964) defined three power resources:

- **Coercive**: the ability to order or force someone to do something that they would not otherwise do.
- **Remunerative**: the ability to influence someone's standard and style of living.
- **Normative**: the ability to set standards and types of behaviour that enable the ways in which people will act to be predicted with a good degree of certainty.

■ Summary

Power is a fundamental human need. People must be able to control, order and influence their environment at all times, so that it is not a threat, and so that it is of positive use.

In an organisation power is the fuel which feeds the 'motor' (usually 'motors', sometimes not working in unison) on which the work, output and change all depend.

In organisations power always exists. It is a question of locating it.

It is also a motivating factor for all (although in differing degrees for different persons and roles), with different expectations and aspirations reflected in its usage.

It has effects within the organisation in terms of performance: work is done, goals are pursued.

The exercise of power has effects upon those using it and also upon those on whom it is used.

■ Summary of leadership qualities

Whichever model of leadership is taken, or whichever is appropriate to particular situations, certain common aspects clearly present themselves:

1. **The situation and environment**: an understanding of it, and ability to recognise what can and cannot be controlled or influenced, the relationship between the organisation and its environment. The ability to be flexible and responsive to the situation environment 'mix'
2. **Culture, values and ethics**: and standards, in that these are manifest in the leader and set by him/her for his/her fellow followers
3. **Qualities**: honesty, integrity, loyalty, enthusiasm, ambition, drive, commitment, standard setting, communication and decision-making
4. **The matter in hand**: and its relationship with the ways in which problems are to be resolved or implemented, with timescales and projected outcomes
5. **Measures of success and failure**: who judges, how they are judged, criteria set, financial indicators, ethical indicators, other performance criteria, opportunities and consequences
6. **Concern for people**: staff, clients and wider public
7. **Flexibility**: the ability and willingness to change methods, practices, behaviour (and ultimately attitudes, values and beliefs); and to accommodate situational, environmental and operational factors as they change
8. **Distance**: both physical and psychological distance normally constitute barriers to the leaders' relationships with their people.

■ The chief executive

This is the term to be used for the 'business leader'; and requires the adaptation of the qualities and aptitudes given above into the particular sphere of business management.

The business leader or Chief Executive (CE), may be seen as follows: the Organisation Leader; the Personal Leader; and the Chief Architect of Organisation Purpose. The task of the CE in any business is one of great complexity and variety. It requires successful action in both the variety of tasks and variety of roles that the CE may be called upon to carry out (Christensen). The task is wide-ranging and complex, requiring great energy as well as skill and knowledge.

Corporate CEs are responsible for everything that goes on in their organisations, presiding over (very often) highly complex, and technologically sophisticated organisations, about which they must have knowledge, but very often this will be at the level of a general understanding only. They must also know and be able to work in the organisation's markets, and the environment and political sphere of the business being conducted. They carry the ultimate burden of success or failure of the organisation, and are answerable to shareholders or boards of directors or governors for the results obtained. They must be able to handle crises and emergencies in such a way that confidence and credibility are maintained.

CEs must be able to harness general qualities into resourcefulness on the part of the organisation, in whichever sphere or situation they find themselves representing it. They must be able to gain commitment to purpose of a divergent and disparate group of specialist and technological functionaries, and to provide the coordination and harmonisation rationale for this. They must be able to engage in the process of 'creative maintenance and development' of the organisation and its capabilities. They must be able to resolve dilemmas and conflicts relating to organisational, departmental and individual aims and objectives; technology; production and marketing considerations; economic, social, political and ethical factors; and the wider relationship between the organisation and its environment, customers and staff. They will finally have a vision of the organisation's direction and future, and of the path required to take it there.

They set the standards of behaviour expected and implied within the organisation. This happens anyway, either because standards are positively set, or because they have been allowed to emerge without proper direction. In any case, the staff of an organisation set standards of behaviour that they believe to mirror the ways in which their top managers would act in the same circumstances.

An example of this is graphically given in the findings of the enquiry into the *Herald of Free Enterprise* disaster of 1987. The *Herald of Free Enterprise* was a car and passenger ferry operated by Townsend Thoresen Ltd, between Dover, France and Belgium. On 3 March 1987, it turned over on a sandbank outside the harbour at Zeebrugge, Belgium, and 190 (out of the 500 on board) people lost their lives. The prime reason for this was that the bow doors were left open, and the sea rushed in, causing the instability in the ship which in turn caused it to roll over. Nobody had thought that it was important enough to ensure that the doors were shut *before* the ship set sail; the enquiry went on, moreover, to state that the staff had behaved exactly as they felt that they were expected to behave by the company's top management, and indeed, how they felt that the top managers would have behaved in that situation.

In general terms, the CE presents a combination of energy, style, vigour, drive, image, aura, enthusiasm and ambition, as the 'shining light' of the organisation, and that with which more junior staff will (or will not) identify. This is true whether the CE is very high profile; or in negative terms, anonymous (where the staff will follow the same qualities in anonymous and indifferent ways); again, either positive or negative, life is given to the style of the organisation and its staff.

The CE is responsible for both the generation of strategic and business objectives and the range of choices available to the organisation; and also for the choice of direction from this range of alternatives. From this, a CE is responsible for ensuring that the choice finally taken is successful. CEs must be able to evaluate, in strategic and global terms, these proposals; and in operational terms, the abilities and capacities of the organisation to translate them into successful and profitable business or service activities.

The CE is responsible also for the continuous processes involved in monitoring and evaluating the strategy adopted, and the policies and procedures used for its implementation. CEs are responsible for foreseeing the next phase of corporate, business and service development and initiative. They are responsible for foreseeing and averting failure in given initiatives; where it becomes clear that a disaster is looming, it is the duty of the CE to devise and implement proposals for averting it.

Closely related to this is the ethical and moral stance that the CE sets for the organisation; again this can be inferred from the example above – nobody thought that it was *wrong* to leave the ferry's bow doors open (let alone dangerous or stupid). This in turn has implications for wider issues of confidence and public support for the organisation, as much for the way that things are done, as for what is actually done.

The CE must maintain both credibility and confidence in all aspects indicated; and once this is lost, the CE has no future at the organisation (lesser functionaries or employees may have, or be given, time to repair such a situation – the CE, invariably, does not). Staff, managers, shareholders and stakeholders, customers, clients, the general public may all have a legitimate view on this and a contribution to it depending upon the nature of the organisation. A vote of no confidence passed by directors, shareholders, boards of governors, and (sometimes) the organisation's staff, lead inevitably to the removal or resignation of the CE.

Once the CE has lost the support or confidence of any of these groups, they will normally leave, in the interests of limiting any damage or loss of reputation to the organisation (see Summary Box 3.5). CEs do not have long notice periods for the same reason; both resignation and dismissal are normally instant at least at the point of publication or promulgation, as is the next CE's appointment. The wider interests must be preserved and this is the consequent nature of any enforced or voluntary changeover.

The CE, in general, is responsible and answerable to all relevant interest groups. Increasingly for large sophisticated companies and organisations this means maintaining the confidence of institutional shareholders. For public and municipal services and authorities this means maintaining this confidence with elected members and boards of governors.

Ideally therefore the succession will be managed in a preconceived and orderly manner. This takes the form of either grooming a 'crown prince' from within the organisation, who also enjoys the confidence of these interest groups; or, of seeking out someone well in advance of the intended succession time through the

---

SUMMARY BOX 3.5   Instant Departures

- **Margaret Thatcher**, UK Prime Minister from 1979 until 1990, won a vote of confidence from her party in November 1990, but not by a large enough majority. She lost her job four days later.

- **John Akers** resigned from his position of CE at IBM in January 1993. This was after the company had declared the then highest ever corporate loss of 5 billion dollars and followed this with a staff resizing policy for the first time.

- **Lord King** left British Airways in February 1993, following an encroachment and dirty tricks scandal involving the company's relationship with the Virgin Atlantic Group.

- **Robert Stempel** left his position as CE of General Motors following disastrous results world-wide in November 1992.

- **James Robinson** stood down from the position of CE at American Express in January 1993 following the declaration of greatly reduced operating profits for 1992.

- **David Young** left Cable & Wireless in November 1995 following a Boardroom upheaval. It was felt that he would be unable to continue with the full backing of every member of the Board in the future.

In all cases the person named left their job before they had intended to do so, and as the consequence of the circumstances noted. This does not mean that the results declared were their fault; however in each case the sacrifice of them for the greater good of the organisation in question was felt to be the most appropriate course of action.

---

combination of head hunting, the directoral circuit, reputation and achievement in other organisations.

The performance of the CE, finally, may also be acceptable in one role but not in others. For example, a CE who is also the founding entrepreneur of the company may indeed be a great visionary or designer or marketeer in his own right. In most cases, however, he also needs the additional support of a team of general and expert managers of wide experience and acumen at this level, if an organisation that is to be effectively directed is to be achieved.

■ CE examples

We can now look briefly at two case studies of CE behaviour.

- **John Brown**
John Brown founded his own engineering business in the 1960s. It became very

successful, supplying a range of components to the automotive industries. It gained an excellent and thoroughly deserved reputation for supplying high quality products to deadlines.

Brown floated the company on the stock exchange. The Board of Directors was elected by the new shareholders. He became chief executive, and later, company president.

At this time the first serious complaints came about. They were not enough to damage the firm's overall reputation but did give cause for concern. The problems were analysed and they all had the following elements.

They were all from firms with whom Brown's had been dealing since the early days, customers that John Brown himself had gained, and who had supported him and put faith in him. John Brown was continuing to contact his old friends at these companies, persons like himself, who also were now figureheads. He was then interfering in the ordering, processing and dispatching activities and chasing them up personally.

It took several weeks, including the rigorous keeping of a diary and an activity sampling exercise to illustrate this to Brown and to indicate to him that what he was doing now was both unproductive and actively harmful to the reputation and future of the company.

- **Steve Shirley**

Stephanie (Steve) Shirley founded F International in 1964.

It represented the incorporation of her life's work, vision and concept that she had previously established and which was simply called Freelance Programmers.

F International is a computer software, programming and project company that draws on the talents and skills of a large body of women, who work from and at home, on a freelance basis, devising and implementing software solutions and products for the computer industry. Steve Shirley's vision was to provide an organisation that would both generate work for this niche of the population and, also, raise awareness of it among industrial and commercial sectors.

The work of the organisation is essentially project-orientated and highly creative. As commissions come in, teams and groups are created from among the pool of freelancers to work on the matters required. Shirley, having created the company, has stood back from it. A Board of Directors and senior management team are employed. Shirley's brief is on the creative, visionary and animating side, looking for new projects and directions in which to go.

■ Organisational conflict

There are various sources of conflict in organisations:

1. The **job** and its professional or technical context, training required, the structure of work and of organisation, its formal objectives
2. The **person** and his or her personality, personal objectives, ethics, expectations, aspirations, beliefs, values
3. The **organisation** itself, and its ways of working and organising its activities
4. The **traditions** of the sector, company or organisation in question, especially those to do with management style, staff and industrial relations.

For the individual organisational conflict arises fundamentally from ideology, objectives and territory:

- **Ideology:** a set of beliefs about human behaviour, values and standards
- **Objectives:** those things, economic and psychological, which we want from an employing organisation
- **Territory:** an important aspect of objectives; while it is sometimes visible in terms literally of possession of 'living space' it is more usually expressed in organisations in terms of rewards, job security and career prospects; this is important especially in a comparative context, i.e. how people see their situation in comparison with others.

Organisational conflict thus arises from the incompatibility of objectives, practices or attitudes between individuals and groups within an organisation.

Note that conflict may **feed on itself**. Conflict initially emerging from the nature of the job may create and magnify conflict at a personal level.

■ Conflict theory

Conflict theory is concerned with providing a basic conceptual framework and a language which will enable persons in organisations to develop a fuller understanding of the nature of conflict. Also, and most importantly for managers, it concludes with proposals for using conflict positively and beneficially from the organisation's standpoint.

There are four aspects:

1. **The parties** to the conflict
    - The simplest form of conflict involves only two parties. Much organisational conflict concerns more, and often many more, than two parties. One of the problems facing a manager is being able to define clearly the parties to a conflict. Differences of perception and communication problems at different levels of an organisation can cause difficulties in this connection.
2. **The issues**
    - The topics in dispute
    - The perceptions of the parties to the dispute in this respect
    - The interests of those concerned and involved; and
    - whether there is a hierarchy of contentious issues and matters to be resolved.
3. **The dynamics of the conflict**
    - The causes of the initial conflict; its nature and style
    - The extent to which it is formal and how far informal
    - The extent to which it is structural or professional or departmental or institutional or personalised
    - The length of time that it has been going on for, the attitudes of the different players in the conflict; the conflicting interests of those concerned
    - The extent to which it is possible to predict certain developments or outcomes unless certain action is taken
    - The range of possible outcomes, both positive and negative
    - These aspects are concerned with defining and analysing the nature of conflict. They present essential input to the managerial decision-making process which is the fourth aspect.
4. **The management of conflict**
    - Management's first priority must be to try to control or at least influence the conflict

- Uncontrolled conflict is a symptom of an uncontrolled organisation and an unmanaged organisation; the organisation becomes a ship without a rudder; it is the negation of management.

Hence managerial objectives in dealing with conflict must be:

1. The development of the conflict into **constructive competition** or useful argument
2. If this is not possible, then to **contain** and **control** the conflict and to minimise its dysfunctional effects.
3. Removal of the causes of conflict.

■ Strategies for the management of conflict

These therefore include the following:

1. **Developing rules**, procedures and precedents to minimise the emergence of conflict and then, to the extent that it still occurs, to minimise its undesirable effects and maximise its desirable ones
2. Ensuring that **communications** are effective in minimising conflict; bad communications may cause conflict or magnify minor conflicts to dangerous proportions
3. Separation of **sources of potential conflict**; this may be done geographically or structurally
4. **Arbitration machinery** may be permanently available as a strategy of last resort
5. **Confrontation** may be used to try to bring all participants to the conflict together in an attempt to use the dysfunctional aspects of the conflict as a warning to them; **accurate prediction** of the outcome of such a tactic is usually difficult
6. **Benign neglect**: the application of the dictum that 'a problem deferred is a problem half-solved'. Usually benign neglect can be used only as a temporary measure while more information is being gathered or a more structured approach is being formulated.

■ Symptoms of conflict

These are as follows; and every manager must be aware of them, and respond to them when they start to occur.

1. **Declining organisational performance**: this is the most important functional and practical symptom; declining performance trends in a section or department often accompany the growth of conflict.
2. **Declining morale**: indicated by rising rates of labour turnover, sickness and absence; conflict aggravates these problems.

Managerial energy devoted to dealing with organisational conflict represents energy *not* spent producing the output of the organisation. There is an opportunity cost aspect here. It represents a diversion of managerial time and effort away from achieving the prime purposes of the organisation.

■ Motivation

The ability to gain the commitment and motivation of staff in organisations has been recognised as important in certain sectors of the business sphere. It is now more universally accepted as a critical business and organisational activity, and one that has highly profitable returns and implications for the extent of the returns on investment that is made in the human resource.

There is a correlation between organisations that go to a lot of trouble to motivate their staff, and profitable business performance. There is also a correlation at national level – Japanese organisations recognise this question much more widely than elsewhere. However, such organisations transcend such compartmentalisation in reality, and may be found in all sectors, in all nations, of the business sphere.

The ability to motivate staff in the workplace stems from the understanding, on the part of the organisation concerned, of the following:

1. A general appreciation of how human beings **behave** in particular situations, and in response to their needs to satisfy and fulfil basic drives, instincts, needs and wants. Some of these are instinctive, others are the product of the civilisation in which they live, and the socialisation processes contained therein. Others still are the product of the occupation held by the individual and the education, training, ethics, standards and aspirations thus instilled. Finally, the organisation itself impinges on the behaviour of the human being, in terms of the structure, style, shared values and work practices adopted.
2. An understanding of the nature of the **work** that must be carried out, and the effects that this will have, or is likely to have, on those who are to do it. This has to do with the extent of intrinsic satisfaction and fulfilment that is present in the work; the interface between the human resource and technology; and, again the style of management and supervision that is to be adopted.
3. The wider standards and expectations of the **relationships** between humans at the workplace. The background and aura for this is created by management, and infuses everyone (positively or negatively) at the workplace. At its best, it contains a variety of elements including: enthusiasm and commitment on the part of everyone to the organisation and its products, services and customers; a corporate belief in the organisation and all its works; a measure of involvement in the implementation of policy and achievement of objectives by all concerned; a clearly established and understood set of principles and operational standards by which the organisation functions; the taking of pride by all members of staff in the organisation and all its works; adequate, effective and relevant communication processes and methods; and preventative approaches to problems and commitment to resolve them quickly when they arise.

   Conversely, there must be a recognition, on the part of organisations and their managers, that where these elements are not present, or where they are diluted, not believed in, or not valued, there will be a tendency towards de-motivation and alienation on the part of the staff.
4. Organisations **cannot be all things to all people**. They can only accommodate a range of divergent interests and aspirations among the staff in so far as these can be made to accord with their overall purposes and values. Dysfunctions arising from their divergences and conflicts of interest are most common in multinational hierarchies, and public and health services, where

the organisation style and structure is either inefficient, or irrelevant, to the true purpose of the organisation concerned.

With this in mind, we shall now turn to a brief consideration of classical theories of motivation. Each makes a contribution to the fullest possible understanding of the issues and matters in hand.

■ Major theories of motivation

■ Rensis Likert: System 4

Likert's contribution to the theories of workplace motivation arose from his work with high performing managers; managers and supervisors who achieved high levels of productivity, low levels of cost and high levels of employee motivation, participation and involvement at their places of work. The work demonstrated a correlation between this success and the style and structure of the work groups that they created. The groups achieved not only high levels of economic output and therefore wage and salary targets, but were also heavily involved both in group maintenance activities and the design and definition of work patterns. This was underpinned by a supportive style of supervision and the generation of a sense of personal worth, importance and esteem in belonging to the group itself.

The system four model arose from this work. Likert identified four styles or systems of management (see Figure 3.3):

- **System 1: Exploitative Authoritative**, where power and direction come from the top downwards and where there is no participation, consultation or involvement on the part of the workforce. Workforce compliance is thus based on fear. Unfavourable attitudes are generated, there is little confidence and trust, and low levels of motivation to cooperate or generate output above the absolute minimum.
- **System 2: Benevolent Authoritative**, which is similar to System 1 but which allows some 'upward' opportunity for consultation and participation in some areas. Again attitudes tend to be generally unfavourable; confidence, trust and communication are also at low levels. In both Systems 1 and 2, productivity may be high over the short run when targets can be achieved by a combination of coercion, and bonus and overtime payments. However, both productivity and earnings are demonstrably low over the long run; there is also high absenteeism and labour turnover.
- **System 3: Consultative**, where aims and objectives are set after discussion and consultation with subordinates; where communication is two-way and where teamwork is encouraged at least in some areas. Attitudes towards both superiors and the organisation tend to be favourable especially when the organisation is working steadily. Productivity tends to be higher, absenteeism and turnover lower. There is also demonstrable reduction in scrap, improvement in product quality, reduction in overall operational costs and higher levels of earning on the part of the workforce.
- **System 4: Participative**, in which three basic concepts have a very important effect on performance – the use by the manager of the principle of

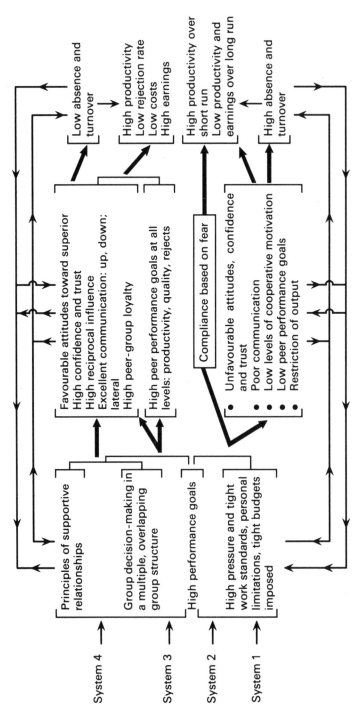

Purpose: to demonstrate the interrelationship and interaction of the variables defined and present a spectrum of organisation and management performance levels

Figure 3.3   System 4

Source: Likert (1961).

supportive relationships throughout the work group; the use of group decision-making and group methods of supervision; and the setting of high
performance and very ambitious goals for the department and also for the
organisation overall. This was Likert's preferred System.

Likert saw the various management systems as having causal, intervening and
end result variables.

The causal variables are independent variables which determine the course of
developments within an organisation and the results achieved; and management
policies, decisions, business and leadership strategies, skills and behaviour.

The intervening variables are those which reflect the internal state and health
of the organisation. These include loyalties, attitudes, motivations, performance
goals and their achievement, the perceptions of all members and their collective
capacity for interaction, communication and decision-making.

The end result variables are the dependent variables reflecting the achievements of the organisation in terms of its productivity, costs, efficiency, product
quality and earnings.

■ Abraham Maslow: a hierarchy of needs

Abraham Maslow was a behavioural scientist whose researches led him to
depict a hierarchy of needs which explained different types and levels of
motivation that were important to people at different times. This hierarchy of
needs is normally depicted as a pyramid (see Figure 3.4). The hierarchy of needs
works from the bottom of the pyramid upwards. It shows the most basic needs
and motivations at the lowest levels while those at the top are created by, or
fostered by, civilisation and society towards.

Maslow identified five key needs:

1. **Physiological**: the need for food, drink, air, warmth, sleep and shelter; basic
   survival needs related to the instinct for self-preservation
2. **Safety and security**: protection from danger, threats or deprivation and the
   need for stability (or relative stability) of environment
3. **Social**: a sense of belonging to a society and its groups, for example, the
   family, the organisation, the work group; the giving and receiving of friend-
   ship; basic status needs within these groups, and the need to participate in
   social activities
4. **Esteem needs**: self-respect, self-esteem, appreciation, value, recognition and
   status both on the part of the individuals concerned and the society, circle or
   group in which they interrelate; part of the esteem need is therefore the drive to
   gain the respect, esteem and appreciation accorded by others
5. **Self-actualisation**: the need for self- fulfilment, self-realisation, personal
   development, accomplishment, mental, material and social growth and the
   development and fulfilment of the creative faculties.

Maslow reinforced his model by stating that people tended to satisfy their
needs systematically. They started with the basic, instinctive needs and then

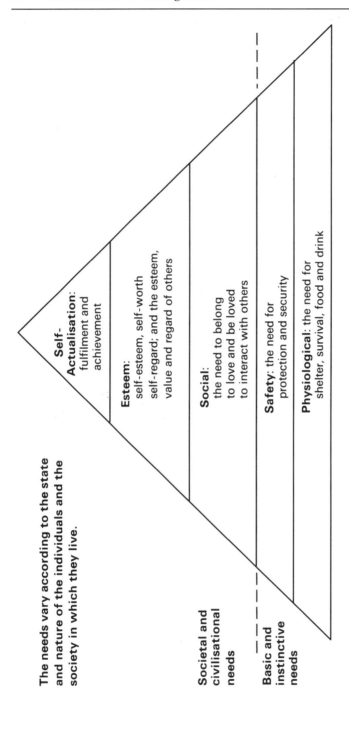

Figure 3.4   A hierarchy of needs

Source: Maslow (1960).

moved up the hierarchy. Until one particular group of needs was satisfied, a person's behaviour would be dominated by them. Thus the hungry or homeless person will look to their needs for self-esteem and society only after their hunger has been satisfied and they have found a place to stay. The other point that Maslow made was that people's motives were constantly being modified as their situation changed, and in relation to their levels of adaptation and other perceptual factors. This was especially true of the self-actualisation needs in which having achieved measures of fulfilment and recognition, man nevertheless tended to remain unsatisfied and to wish to progress further.

Maslow's work was based on general studies of human motivation and as such was not directly related to matters endemic at the workplace. However, matters concerning the last two items on the pyramid, those of self-esteem and self-actualisation, have clear implications for the motivation (and self-motivation) of professional, technical and managerial staff in organisations. There are also implications for the management of all staff in all forms of work.

■ Douglas McGregor: Theory X and Theory Y

McGregor identified two distinctive sets of assumptions made by managers about employees. From this he articulated two extreme attitudes or views and called them Theory X and Theory Y. His thesis was that in practice most people would come somewhere between the two, except in certain circumstances.

□ Theory X

This is based on three premises:

- People **dislike work** and will avoid it if they can. They would rather be directed than accept any responsibility; indeed, they will avoid authority and responsibility if they possibly can. They have no creativity except when it comes to getting around the rules and procedures of the organisation; above all they will not use their creativity in the pursuit, either of the job or the interests of the organisation.
- They must be **forced or bribed** to put out the right effort. They are motivated mainly by money which remains the overriding reason why they go to work. Their main anxiety concerns their own personal security, which they alleviate by earning money.
- They are **inherently lazy**, they require high degrees of supervision, coercion and control in order to produce adequate output.

□ Theory Y

This is based on the premise that work is necessary to man's psychological growth:

- People **wished only to be interested in their work,** and under the right conditions they will enjoy it. They gain intrinsic fulfilment from it; they are motivated by the desire to realise their own potential, to work to the best of their capabilities and to employ the creativity and ingenuity with which they are endowed in the pursuit of this.
- They will **direct themselves** towards given accepted and understood targets; they will seek and accept responsibility and authority; and they will accept the discipline of the organisation in the pursuit of this. They also impose their own self-discipline on themselves and their activities.

Whatever the conditions, management was to be responsible for organising the elements of productive enterprise and its resources in the interests of economic ends. This would be done in ways suitable to the nature of the organisation and its workforce in question; either providing a coercive style of management and supervision or arranging a productive and harmonious environment in which the workforce can and will take responsibility for erecting their own efforts and those of their unit towards organisational aims and objectives.

■ Frederick Herzberg: two-factor theory

The research of Herzberg was directed at people in places of work. It was based on questioning people in organisations in different jobs, at different levels, to establish:

(a) those factors that led to **extreme dissatisfaction** with the job, the environment and the workplace, and
(b) those factors that led to **extreme satisfaction** with the job, the environment and the workplace (see Figure 3.5).

The factors giving rise to satisfaction Herzberg called **motivators.** Those giving rise to dissatisfaction he called **hygiene factors.**

The motivators that emerged were: achievement, recognition, the nature of the work itself, level of responsibility, advancement, and opportunities for personal growth and development. These factors are all related to the actual content of the work and job responsibilities. These factors where present in a working situation led to high levels and degrees of satisfaction on the part of the workforce.

The hygiene factors or dissatisfiers identified were: company policy and administration; supervision and management style; levels of pay and salary; relationships with peers; relationships with subordinates; status; and security. These are factors that where they were good or adequate would not in themselves make people satisfied; by insuring that they were indeed adequate dissatisfaction was removed but satisfaction was not in itself generated. On the other hand where these aspects were bad extreme dissatisfaction was experienced by all respondents.

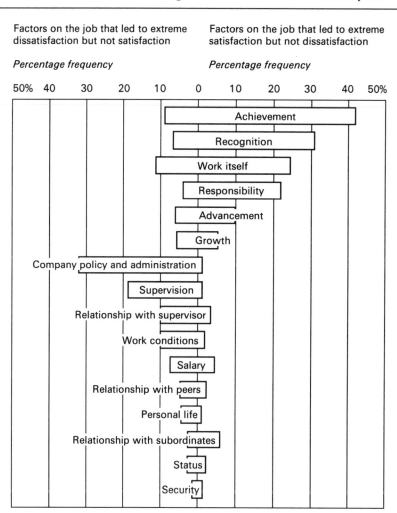

Figure 3.5   Two-factor or hygiene factor theory

Source: Herzberg (1962).

Organisations that failed to provide adequate hygiene factors tended to have high levels of conflict, absenteeism and labour turnover, and low general morale.

The work of Herzberg has tended to encourage attention to such factors as: good and adequate supervision which encourages and extends the workforce rather than restricts it; job satisfaction which can often be increased through work restructuring, job enrichment and job enlargement programmes; and the setting and achieving of targets and objectives based on a full understanding of what they are and why they have been set. Some organisations have also concentrated on removing the dissatisfiers or hygiene factors to ensure that causes of intrinsic dissatisfaction with the workplace and its environment are minimised.

■ Edgar Schein: a classification of people

Schein classified people in four ways:

1. **Rational economic:** people are primarily motivated by economic needs. They pursue their own self-interest in the expectation of high economic returns. If they work in an organisation they need both motivation and control. As they intensify their pursuit of money they become untrustworthy and calculating.
   Within this group, however, there are those who are self-motivated and have a high degree of self-control. This is the group that must take responsibility for the management of others. They also set the moral and ethical standards required.
2. **Social:** people are social animals, gaining their basic sense of identity from relationships with others. People will seek social relationships at the place of work and part of the function of the work group will be the fulfilment of this necessity. The role of management in this situation is therefore greatly concerned with mobilising the social relationships in the pursuit of operational effectiveness and drawing a correlation between productivity and morale; and taking an active interest in the development of the work group.
3. **Self-actualising:** people are primarily self-motivated. They seek challenge, responsibility and pride from their job and to maximise the opportunities offered by it. They are likely to be affected negatively by organisational and management style, external controls, scarcity of resources and other pressure. They will develop their own ways of working, their own objectives and integrate these with those established by the organisation. The inference is that this is strongest among professional, technical, skilled managerial staff; however, all work groups have tended towards higher levels of motivation and morale when given a greater degree of autonomy at work.
4. **Complex:** people are complex and variable; they have many motives, differing and diverse and which vary according to the matter in hand and the different work groups in which they find themselves. They will not fulfil all their needs in any one situation but rather require a variety of activities in order to do this. They respond to a variety of stimuli according to their needs and wants at a particular moment. Schein's view of 'complex people' in organisations is that of a psychological contract, based on mutual expectations and commonality of aspirations. It is therefore a partnership.

■ Expectancy

In essence, this approach to motivation draws the relationship between the efforts put into particular activities by individuals, and the nature of the expectations of the rewards that they perceive that they will get from these efforts.

The expectancy approach to motivation draws a relationship between:

- the expectations that people have in work situations;
- the efforts that they put in to meet these expectations;
- the rewards offered for successful efforts. (See Figure 3.6.)

Understanding individual aspirations and the extent to which work can satisfy these is essential. It is also necessary to recognise the need to balance expectation, effort and reward. If expectations are raised and then not fulfilled, effort declines. If high levels of effort turn out to be unproductive, expectations are repositioned downwards. If the anticipated rewards are not forthcoming, effort declines. The effect of each is always to demotivate and demoralise.

This is clearly centred on the individual. It relates to the ways in which the individual sees or perceives the environment. In particular, it relates to their view of work, expectations, aspirations, ambitions and desired outcomes from it, and the extent to which these can be satisfied at the workplace or carrying out the occupation in question. For example, the individual may have no particular regard for the job that they are currently doing but will nevertheless work productively and effectively at it and be committed to it because it is a stepping stone in their view to greater things – and these are the expectations that they have of it and constitutes the basis of their efforts and the quality of these efforts. This is compounded however by other factors – the actual capacities and aptitudes of the individual concerned on the one hand and the nature of the work environment on the other. It is also limited by the perceptions and expectations that the commissioner of the work has on the part of the person who is actually carrying it out. There is a distinction to be drawn between the effort put into performance and the effectiveness of that effort – hard work, conscientiously carried out does not always produce effective activity; the effort has to be directed and targeted. There has also to be a match between the

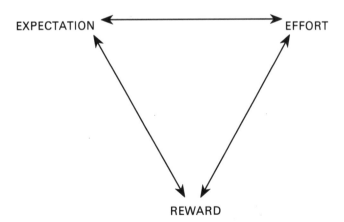

Figure 3.6   The relationship between expectation, effort and reward

rewards expected and those that are offered – a reward is merely a value judgement placed on something offered in return for effort, and if this is not valued by the receiver it has no effect on motivation.

There has consequently to be an understanding of the nature of the motives and expectations of the individual, related to an ability to satisfy these on the part of the organisation if it is to address effectively the issue of motivation. The approach required is therefore to take both an enlightened and specific view of what constitutes job satisfaction (rather than assuming that it exists or exists in certain occupations at least); and an understanding of the processes of perception and the nature of reward in relation to the aspirations of those conducting the work.

The works referred to here constitute the major investigations into the subject of human motivation, both in general and at the place of work. The overall purpose has been to indicate both the importance of the subject itself and the relationship between effective human motivation and effective work performance, and the level of understanding and application required of the subject by those who aspire to manage others.

■ Motivation and achievement

The general correlation between motivation and achievement is a common theme that runs through all of the work to which reference has been made. There are lessons to be learned.

Organisations can and should develop characteristics within their staff to generate in them improved and higher levels of commitment and performance that relate to higher levels of achievement. These characteristics are: activity (rather than passivity); degrees of workplace autonomy; long termism (as opposed to short-termism); self-discipline; self-motivation; and self-awareness. Work conducted by Chris Argyris in the USA concluded that traditional style organisations tended to encourage the opposite of these characteristics (i.e. passivity; dependence; expediency), leading to both individual and corporate frustration and ineffectiveness.

All people, whatever their work, need to have achievements. In recent years the organisational concept of 'the high achiever' has become prevalent. The term implies an individual who regularly completes work to high degrees of quality, output and effectiveness. Such staff require tasks and targets against which their achievements may be measured and regular feedback on the extent to which these have been fulfilled. It is prevalent in task cultures, and high-pressure and output-oriented occupations.

■ Motivation and money

It is stated elsewhere (see Herzberg above) that money does not enhance the intrinsic nature of the work. Indeed in the most extreme cases it will not affect the employee's motivation at all (as with voluntary work, where the driving force is to do with commitment or vocation); while at the other extreme it may simply make working life bearable for a very short period of time (however much one is paid for sweeping roads, the job to be done is still the sweeping of the roads). However, there are additional points to be borne in mind:

1. Wage and salary levels reinforce such matters as **self-image** and the esteem that others hold of the job or occupation. A high salary reinforces the status and responsibility that the job holder is felt to have. A low salary may diminish this. A low salary for a professional person may give the aura of professional commitment at personal expense.
2. Wage and salary levels form the basis of **inter-occupational comparisons** and **expectations**. Wage and salary rises, also, have to be seen in behavioural terms, both against what is 'the going rate', and also against what others in both related and wholly different occupations are getting (or perceived to be getting). If one is at the top of this measure, there will be a tendency towards greater satisfaction than if one is at the lower end.
3. Wage and salary levels reflect the **value** placed upon an employee by the organisation. They also reflect the value and relative value of the occupation range that is carried out in the organisation. They also impart information that relates to the true nature of the work being carried out (for example, a high-sounding job title that carries with it a low salary is likely to mean that the level of work carried out is actually less than the job title implies).
4. **Reinforcement elements** such as bonuses and incentives may also be used by organisations to generate additional output (in whatever terms that is measured), or to reward loyalty. The approach to the management of such payments must be positive and dynamic; such payments should never be allowed to become institutionalised, or their effect is lost.

■ Importance of motivation

From whatever the standpoint, the importance of motivation, and the ability to motivate at the place of work, must be clearly understood by all managers. If these fundamental principles are not adopted, no amount of negativity, coercion or bullying on the part of the organisation, of its staff, will compensate. On the other hand, as we have seen with the Hawthorne example (Chapter 2), the self-perception on the part of the groups of staff, arising from the fact that they were made to feel important, led to great advances in both personal commitment and operational output. Partly, also, because of this approach, the Sanyo plant at Lowestoft, Suffolk, UK, holds an absenteeism and self-certificated sickness rate of 0.2%; and Sheerness Steel Plc, a rate of 0.5%. The commitment of the staff has been engaged.

These lessons should also be seen in the wider context. Many of the lessons to be drawn from the 'excellence' studies (in both the USA and UK), from Japanese business practices, from human resource and industrial relations policies, impinge on the motivation of people at work. The style of leadership and direction, and the aura thus created, also greatly affects motivation and morale.

Finally, all approaches that have as their objective a genuine desire to motivate and generate commitment among the staff, must themselves stem from commitment, belief and value, rather than expediency. If it is the latter, it will simply not work.

■ Groups and teams

Groups and teams are gatherings of people drawn together or organised together and united by common purposes or objectives. These common purposes must be understood by all and subscribed to by them. Ideally they are the overriding issues concerned – where problems and conflicts do occur members subsume their private interests to those of the group.

Effective teams lead to creativity; harmony; improved job and work satisfaction; increased energy; increased motivation and commitment; and dynamism. They tackle tasks that are too large for one person. They bring a 'collective wisdom' approach and intellect to bear on given issues. They are arranged and organised where the matter in hand is very complex or requires a range of expertise not normally found in one person. They also generate and reinforce the critical behavioural factors. They generate a mutual confidence and support among members. They produce a motivation and identity based on team or group membership, additional to any such attributes that the individual may have. They may generate (or be perceived to generate) an elitism, 'a group think', a power of conformity more influential than that of the organisation; this may be in accord with the wider organisation and its purposes or in conflict with it (see Summary Box 3.6).

Teams and groups, and their functions and processes, therefore require both understanding and management if an effective work environment is to be created. The aim overall must be to produce groups that are both positive and productive but which contribute to the overall effectiveness and purpose of the organisation rather than detracting from it or working in competition with it.

It is therefore first necessary to understand that this is a dynamic process. People belong to a variety of groups. They interrelate and interact in a variety of ways, depending on which they are involved with at a particular time. They may bring ideas to one group that they have generated or picked up as the result of being associated with another. People also join and leave organisations constantly, bringing and taking qualities, expertise and characteristics with them.

When constituting groups a balance has to be struck ensuring that there is present both the expertise required and the ability to work together. Part of the process of constituting groups consists of fitting individuals with each other in order to gain productive and synergetic output (see below). The characteristics of members have therefore to be harmonised as well as their capabilities and capacities.

SUMMARY BOX 3.6   High Performance Groups and the Bunker
                   Mentality

With high performance groups or those selected on the basis of excellence or high
status in some sphere there is a short step only from members knowing that they
are always clever and excellent to believing that they are always right.

In extreme circumstances this becomes developed still further into a 'bunker
mentality'. This is where the group becomes so divorced from reality that it
develops its own view of the world which becomes the basis for its investigations,
activities, operations and decision-making regardless of the true nature of the
wider environment.

The phrase derives from the bunker used by Hitler and the other leaders of the
Nazis in the last days of World War Two; rather than come to terms with the reality
of their impending defeat, they created their own version of the world within
Hitler's operations room or bunker.

The motivation of individuals must next be considered. It is not enough that
they have capabilities and expertise to bring that the group requires. They must
also want or need to be a part of the group themselves – there must be something
present in the situation to which all members can respond positively, that
generates in them the desire to energise their expertise for the good of the group.

The generation of an identity for the group must take place. This is the
development of a set of ideas, values, beliefs and norms that transcend the
concerns and aspirations of the individuals in it and give the commonality of
purpose that is required of effective, productive and harmonious groups. Again,
Japanese organisations and others that operate in the same way take a lot of
trouble in the formation of this identity among their staff. It is more endemic
among professional, technical and managerial staff; however, Nissan for
example, spent millions of dollars on training and orientation programmes at
their operating plant in both the UK and USA – a key result of this was the
generation of a strong team, group and company loyalty and identity among
everyone.

■ Groups at work

Groups and teams are formed, constituted, disbanded and reformed over
periods of time for all work purposes, from short-term projects, production
lines, administrative functions, support teams and professional service departments to top management teams and boards of directors. Individuals, as we have
seen, belong to a variety of these in the work environment; therefore the issue of
reconciling the interests and priorities of different groups has to be addressed.

Two critical aspects of groups may be usefully distinguished:

- **Synergy**: the principle that the whole is greater than the sum of its parts; a prerequisite for the effective operation of any group; the principle on which they should be constituted; a focus for the assessment of those who are potential group members.
- **Cohesion**: this is the ability of the group to stick together in the pursuit of the stated purpose. It is manifest in the degree of loyalty and commitment generated among members to each other and to this purpose. It is generated by the combination of behavioural, environmental and operational factors present at the place of work of the group and the extent to which these fulfil the operational and aspirational needs of the group members. This includes: the structure of the group; the structure, style and ways of working; the layout of work; the division of tasks; group size; the technology employed; the work flows; the work pressures; the style of leadership; social factors; the particular rewards to be gained from participation in the group; and the success rate of the group.

Groups may also be identified under the headings of formality, informality and purpose:

- **Formal groups**: constituted and directed for a purpose, to solve problems, develop products, conduct projects, run production lines; these will have formal and organised key results, agenda, constitution and composition. They are also constituted as an expert functional and operational department, unit and division in organisations.
- **Informal groups**: in which the staff organise themselves in ways important or necessary to themselves. This may be for the purpose of professional development or information generation; organisation awareness; improved inter-departmental or inter-functional communication and cooperation; self-regulation and work improvement.
- **Purpose groups**: these are formed either on a coercive, compulsory 'ad hoc' or voluntary basis for specific purposes. Some are distinguishable from the others in that they are often not formally constituted and are expected to meet in their own time, while at the same time addressing work specific issues – quality, projects, inter-unit or inter-departmental dysfunctions or discord, or act as lobbies both internal and external in support of particular initiatives. They may also be constituted as 'think tanks' – the generation of a creative flow of ideas and means of implementing them as part of the change and development processes of the organisation.

The role of individuals in the group must be considered. As the result of belonging, they generate their own identity within it and the organisation (and possibly the rest of the world) will view them as part of it; both aspects may be positive or negative. At a global level this is true of belonging to any organisation; Japanese companies, again, go to a great deal of trouble to foster and formulate the background against which the staff have pride and identity in the company. They understand the needs of the individual to belong, affiliate and identify in a positive way. They also understand the great positive, organisational and commercial benefits that accrue from the successful execution of this.

Individuals also have their own purposes distinct from those of the group, to which consideration must be given. These purposes may conflict, or at least diverge. Managers must understand this and part of the management of the group must be concerned with the reconciliation and harmonisation of these matters.

The group has its own entity, life and distinctive existence. This is self-evident when concerned globally with organisations; it is also true for all effective groups within organisations. It has its own core values, reasons for belonging and commonality and universality of purpose. This also applies to sub-groups within the main group. Mutual trust, honesty, openness and understanding must also be present. This is the basis of an effective group style.

Those who manage groups must also understand the informal networks established within organisations. This is especially true of sophisticated, multi-national organisations, local government, health and public services, where these are often very highly developed. Managers must understand that different groups and professions have conflicting aims and objectives and that individuals who belong to several such groups have to be able to reconcile these differences.

Within this framework also, strong and expert individuals generate their own spheres of influence (whether it be in the formal, informal or work group sphere). These individuals need early identification as their support may be necessary for the successful generation of any group identity and ways of working; indeed, their influence may give it an initial impetus or credibility.

■ The group process

For the effective operation of groups to take place, the group process itself must be understood, managed and maintained. A useful summary of this is the phrase:

Forming – Storming – Norming – Performing

Forming is the initial bringing together of individuals for the designated purpose; the initial meeting; the initial establishment of mutual interests and confidence.

Storming is the first rush of creativity and purpose; the first release of creative energy by the group; the first burst of creative and positive group activity towards the stated purpose; and the first output and initial results.

Norming is the establishment of group operational rules and norms; the development of mutual respect and confidence; it is the development of a group identity; and the further development of the mutuality, confidence and purpose that is necessary to effective operation and successful positive results (see Figure 3.7).

Performing is the addressing of the matter in hand; the obtaining of key results, successes and failures; and the activities devised to ensure a productive and positive purpose to the group.

The four elements are not linear but go on alongside each other at all points in the group's life except for the initial beginning; forming activities will take place as and when new members of the group are introduced; storming as and when the group is given new purposes; performing may be necessary at an early stage in the completion of an initial task.

Two further points should also be considered in the understanding of this process. The first is that of regeneration. That is the means by which the life and work of the group is maintained and developed; this may be conducted by the development of the members of the group by the bringing in of new work and projects to it, the addressing of new spheres of activity and by the bringing in of new members.

It is also useful, secondly, to identify an end phase, or disbanding, which comes into effect when groups finish their productive lives and are to close. This ensures a proper evaluation of tasks and matters carried out. It is also important for those concerned to have psychologically finished with the group and to have let it go in the interest of recognising that this particular phase of business life has finished. This is normally covered by a full debrief of the group or team at the end of its productive life and has the behavioural impact of ensuring that those concerned are not left with feelings of anticlimax or emptiness or unfulfilment; nor with the feeling that the work of the group is not finished. This is a recognition that groups do ultimately come to the end of their useful

- A person seeks to **belong** to peer groups wherever they congregate, including corporate surroundings.
- The tendency toward **exclusivity** exists in open-ended and corporate situations, where people come and go. The formation of groups is influenced by the fact that fellow-workers have been thrown together from the start in unnatural mixes. At a social gathering, groups will drift together and apart without constraint, but in a company, people with different backgrounds and views are forced to work together and form groups. The bigger the company and the wider the range in social (and other) attributes of individuals, the better the chances are that there will be numerous groups with tight-knit and defensive norms.
- When both formal and informal norms coexist, as they do in companies, the informal norms transcend the formal. This leads to what has been called 'shadow organisation', in which the apparent management structure is actually superseded in importance by the mesh of group-norm dictates.
- Individuals will go to extreme lengths to live up to their **peers' expectations**, even doing things that in other circumstances they recognise as going counter to their *own* best interests. They can persevere in this behaviour, however, with the easy rationalisation that 'everybody around here does it'.
- **Norm-imposed habits are lasting**. Even when the original members of a group have disappeared and/or when the norms themselves have lost their original purpose, there will be strong norm remnants, unthinkingly respected by new members.
- **Negative norms** cannot be changed unless the norm-follower is made aware of their existence, because most – if not all – people respect and go along with norms quite unconsciously.

Figure 3.7   Foundation of corporate norms

life and have to be disbanded. This may relate either to the work in hand or to the suitability of the group to carry on the particular task or project – in the latter case, this may consist of handing over the work to a new team so that it can be progressed further.

■ Group components and composition

For groups to be effective a variety of attributes must therefore be present and a range of activities carried out. The different roles and functions that must be addressed consist of: group administration; attention to detail; creativity and ideas; direction and chairmanship and leadership; polishing and completion of tasks; and team and group maintenance.

If some, but not all, of these qualities are present the team will dysfunction – if the members are all creative, for example, the group will generate a lot of ideas but complete very little; while conversely if there is no creativity the group may nevertheless be very strong in its own processes. The end result in either case will be both dissatisfaction and lack of achievement as there will be no actual or material success against which to measure its progress.

Group size must be relevant to the matter in hand. Any pronouncement on ideal size must be seen in this context. Given that, any group of less than five may suffer from a restricted range of qualities and capabilities; while any group of more than nine or ten may create administrative problems, sub-groups and cliques. Difficulties also arise with larger groups in ensuring that all members contribute and are involved; or, in the case of committee and meeting type groups, that they can indeed all get together at the same time.

Group environment must be considered. This consists of its relationship with the tasks in hand; the timescale to which it has to work; its technology; resource constraints; and the quality of outputs that are required. This must also be related to the leadership style of the group and its decision-making processes. The relationship with its environment must include the esteem in which the group is held outside and its general profile and credibility.

The general level of motivation in the group is decisive in the effectiveness with which it carries out its tasks and functions. High levels of motivation result from: group identity; members' perception of the task; the levels of perception of the tasks and outputs of the group from outside it; the timescales, constraints and any time deadlines placed on the group; and the consequences of the group's results. Clearly defined and understood performance standards are necessary to which all group members subscribe. The interaction of group members must be positive and dynamic and related to the matters in hand. This must be managed and maintained by the establishment of ways of working, ground rules and procedures and the application of constraints or sanctions where necessary.

The atmosphere must be suited to the purpose in hand, combining elements of openness, trust and mutuality with task, quality and deadline elements.

In effective groups, conflicts are brought out into the open and dealt with constructively, rather than being allowed to fester. Decisions are reached by consensus and other modes are used only when this is not possible. Ideas are openly and freely expressed and argued out. There is no penalty for dissention or disagreement. Discussion and participation balances the involvement of everyone in the group and their commitment to its purposes with the aims and objectives themselves. The group develops its own critical facilities, designed to ensure a healthy self-questioning and to avoid a group think or bunker mentality.

In terms of the process of establishing the group and building it (both as a group and as a provider of outputs) the following nine aspects must be considered:

- **Management of the task**: setting work methods, timescales, resource gathering, problem-solving and maintenance functions
- **Management of the process**: the use of interpersonal skills and the interaction with the environment to gain the maximum contribution from each person
- **Managing communications**: between different work groups and disciplines and professions, to harmonise potential conflicts and to ensure that inter-group relations are productive and not dysfunctionally competitive
- **Managing the individual**: making constructive use of individual differences and ensuring that individual contributions are both valued and of value
- **Management style**: the creation and adoption of a style that is both positive and dynamic and suitable to the management needs of the situation
- **Maintenance management**: ensuring that administration and support services are suitable to the needs of the group
- **Common aims and objectives**: that are understood, valued and adopted by all group members and that are the overriding common purpose for being in the situation
- **Shared values**: standards of behaviour and attitudes that all members of the group must be able to agree to and in which they have confidence and belief and with which they can work
- **Group and team spirit**: a combination of the shared values, ethics and ethos of the group or team concerned and the extent of the positive identity and loyalty that the members have to each other, to the tasks in hand and to the overall objectives; while its positive contribution to performance is not always fully realised or evaluated, the negative effects of the destruction of group identity or team spirit are often devastating. Group and team spirit must therefore always be positive. This, in turn, gives all those concerned a positive rather than coercive reason for belonging to the group and sense of pride in the work.

For groups to remain effective, monitoring and review processes and activities must be in-built. They must take the form both of continuous processes and activities and also regular formal progress meetings. All groups also benefit from external feedback, monitoring and contacts. These reviews must take account of all the elements referred to here; all contributions to the overall effectiveness of performance of groups; and dysfunction in any of them detracts from the performance, outputs, tasks and purposes, both of the groups themselves and ultimately of the organisation in which they are functioning.

■ Research in the workings of groups

■ The Hawthorne experiments

As we have seen in Chapter 2, this work was carried out at the Western Electric Company of America, during the period 1924–1936. The main conclusions that were drawn concerning the workings of groups were as follows: that work could not be effectively organised without reference to the informal structure and spheres of influence; that work groups would respond positively to any genuine interest taken in them; that group motivation was a process and not an item; and that groups required rejuvenation and regeneration from time to time.

■ The 'Affluent Worker'

These studies were carried out at the Vauxhall, La Porte and Skefco Companies at Luton in Bedfordshire in the 1950s and 1960s. The main conclusions **concerning work groups** here were as follows: the workforce's first and only loyalty was to each other; that they felt no particular identity with the company; that alienation was an inherent feature of production line organisation; that strikes, disputes and stoppages acted as a safety valve to the essentially negative process of group formation in these situations; and that such conflicts and the closing of ranks among the staff were inevitable consequences of this mode of group and work organisation.

■ Volvo

This car company reorganised its work methods from production lines to work groups during the 1960s and 1970s. The overriding reason was to test the hypothesis that both quality and output would rise if staff were able to identify with the whole product and not just their place on the production line. Quality and output did, indeed, initially rise; but the process was deemed to have failed in 1974 because technological advances had been resisted and rejected by the work groups, that had not themselves been maintained, developed, updated and regenerated.

■ Meredith Belbin

Professor Belbin identified a range of attributes and characteristics that the members of groups should have between them if effective group formation was to take place. In essence these characteristics range from imagination, question-ing, creativity, energy and drive; to capacities for hard and painstaking detailed work, methods, steady-state, completion and finishing skills (see Figure 3.8). This work has been developed by both Belbin and others in the building of work teams and groups.

■ Tom Peters

Peters identified the flatness of group structures and shortness of hierarchies in them as prerequisites for their effective operation and performance. Groups with a high degree of autonomy, responsibility, accountability and identity would out-perform those that were over-structured and over-regulated. He also

TYPE	SYMBOL	TYPICAL FEATURES	POSITIVE QUALITIES
Company Worker	CW	Conservative, dutiful, practicable	Organising ability, practical common-sense, hard-working,
Chairman	CH	Calm, self-confident, controlled	A capacity for treating and welcoming all potential contributors on their merits and without prejudice A strong sense of objectives
Shaper	SH	Highly strung, out-going, dynamic	Drive and a readiness to challenge inertia, ineffectiveness, complacency or self-deception
Plant	PL	Individualistic, serious-minded, unorthodox	Genius, imagination, intellect, knowledge
Resource Investigator	RI	Extroverted, enthusiastic, curious, communicative	A capacity for contacting people and exploring anything new An ability to respond to challenge
Monitor-Evaluator	ME	Sober, unemotional, prudent	Judgement, discretion, hard-headedness
Team Worker	TW	Social orientated, rather mild, sensitive	An ability to respond to people and to situations and to promote team spirit
Completer-Finisher	CF	Painstaking, orderly, conscientious, anxious	A capacity to follow-through Perfection

Figure 3.8   Archetype team members
■■■■

Source: R. M. Belbin (1986).

emphasised the high degree of creative energy and synergy as essential for successful group performance. Groups must also be responsive and strong on both staff and customer care, and staff and customer identity and loyalty.

■ The individual

Individuals come into organisations to take up positions and roles within them; to carry them out, develop them and move them on; and to change roles, especially for the better. Individuals also have their own needs and wants, not all of which are easily harmonised or reconciled with the organisation and its demands.

■ Roles

The rest of the organisation will ascribe certain preconceptions and expectations to an individual occupying a particular job. This is their role set or role definition, and consists of a number of factors drawn from a combination of these preconceptions and expectations; the aspirations of the person concerned; organisational and environmental factors; and cultural, situational and social aspects. Into this, the individual then brings and imposes his own qualities, aptitudes, attitudes and capacities. The result or output from the combination of all of these factors is the role performance.

Organisations and certain occupations often insist on a further overt definition or underlining of the roles that are being performed. This gives an implicit or real authority to individuals in dealings (both internal and external to the organisation); and an aura or perception of confidence on the part of those who come to deal with them. A common form of this is the wearing of a uniform – this is highly prevalent in health, emergency and armed services. Other organisations, such as banks and those in the travel industry, for example, insist on staff adopting this form of identification. In manufacturing companies staff may be required to wear overalls and operationally effective and hard-wearing clothing; while there are strong and sound operational reasons for doing this, the behavioural message issued is one of role reinforcement – the members of staff are also making a statement about their own role, as well as protecting themselves from their work environment by wearing these clothes.

Other general manifestations of role are reinforced by job title (see Summary Box 3.7), which may have implications for class, status, power and influence around the workplace. Other aspects are related to and reflected in: whether a person has a company car, their own office, their own secretary, can sign their own letters, can authorise expenditure (and if so, up to how much), whether they must clock on and off, and so on.

SUMMARY BOX 3.7   Job Titles and their Inferences: Role Constructs

Because of their universality, job titles carry strong and distinctive perceptual messages across the whole of society at large as well as within the business sphere. Here are some archetypes:

- **Manager**: is deemed to hold a position of authority and responsibility; to dress in a particular way; to have a good level of income; to have continuity and stability of employment; to have aspirations to be a senior manager or director; and so on.
- **Professor**: is deemed to be clever; to work in a college or university; to have had work published; to be an authority in his own chosen field; to be invited to work on committees; may also be untidy and absent-minded; and so on.
- **Operative**: is deemed to be a wage earner; to work regular hours; to have a wife and family; to like life outside work; to like bars and pubs; to take two weeks' holiday; and so on.

    None of these is intended either to be the truth or even accurate; nor are they designed to generate any debate about the veracity of the qualities themselves. They are simply representative of the ways in which pictures are drawn and built up around people as the result of knowing their occupational role.

■ Role ambiguity and uncertainty

This exists where a definition (perceptual or actual) of the role of the individual is not comfortably or satisfactorily achieved. This is likely to arise from a combination of uncertainties, mismatches and mixed messages related to: the nature of the work that the role holder is to carry out; how this work is to be directed, measured and evaluated; where ultimate responsibility for it lies; expectations related to level, quality and intensity of job performance; prospects for enhancement, development and advancement; levels of pay and reward; and components of the reward package itself. If they are not in accord with each other, if they do not harmonise and match and meet universal expectations, then feelings of uncertainty and ultimately rejection come about on the part of those who have to deal with the role holder (see Summary Box 3.8).

■ Role conflict

This is where the uncertainty and ambiguity develops into the need to adopt more than one role in the same situation. Managers will almost inevitably be subject to this as they both reconcile and carry out the roles of leader, director, confidante, friend, disciplinarian, recruiter, developer and dismisser in relation to their staff. In other situations, work pressures may impose on the domestic or personal life of the job holder – in relation, for example, to pressures to work overtime, stay late, attend at weekends or take work home.

SUMMARY BOX 3.8 Role Ambiguities

People have a great deal of difficulty in handling these ambiguities at all levels; and where two or more conflicting messages are offered all are normally rejected except for one.

Thus the woman who is both a loving mother and a shop-lifter will normally be judged on the basis of one role or the other, but not both.

The man who is both an expert and unkempt will normally either have to change his appearance or lose his expert status.

Customs and border officials tend to stop untidy individuals, or untidy old or decrepit cars at the border crossings where they work; this is because such people **look like** bad people, not because they **are** bad people.

Kim Philby, the Briton, worked as a spy for the USSR for a period of 20 years in the 1940s and 1950s. He was able to get away with it for so long because he came from the same background as those with whom he worked. He was able to survive persistent rumours about his loyalty over this period of time because those with whom he worked could not grasp the basic concept that he might indeed also be a traitor.

■ Role confidence

This represents the relationship between the role holder and the role. It represents also the extent of confidence, pride, joy and fulfilment that the individual has in his role (any role, it is not confined simply to those occupied at places of work). It also reflects the self-worth, self-image and self-esteem of the role holder in relation to his/her role. If any of these are lacking the level of confidence is reduced and the role holder may be expected to move on, rejecting the current role. If there is a serious problem here he may simply leave the role altogether. This may also apply to roles within jobs and occupations as well as to the whole occupation. Such aspects of the role may be rejected for reasons to do with pride, perceived futility of the task, a perceived or real loss of status or prestige associated with carrying out the particular task, and negative associations with the person who previously carried it out. Negative role confidence may also be a general factor or symptom of low morale and absenteeism, as well as fostering neglect of those roles that hold no particular interest for the role holder.

■ Conformity

The last part of this chapter is concerned with consideration of the pressures placed on individuals to accept the norms and values of the organisation in question, and to conform to them.

Much of this will be dealt with at the induction stage. The required standards and attitudes are promulgated then; the norms of the organisation, group and

---

SUMMARY BOX 3.9   Role Acceptance and Rejection

Role acceptance and rejection is usefully summarised as:

- **Rejection**: refusal to accept the role
- **Indifference**: occupation of the role without any form of personal or professional commitment
- **Compliance**: occupation of the role because the individual perceives it to be in their current interests
- **Conformity**: role occupation based on accepting rules and direction but not necessarily interest or commitment
- **Internalisation**: role occupation, based on acceptance of organisational procedures, rules and regulations; and commitment to use the skills, knowledge and expertise in the organisation's best interests.

Increasingly, managers are expected to internalise rather than simply comply. Organisations expect it and it is manifest in the induction and orientation programmes that are put on for such staff. It is related to an increasing general perception that organisations cannot be all things to all people and that they will no longer accommodate or offer the range of tolerance that may previously have been expected or, indeed, present.

Furthermore, a relationship between conformity and business output and profitability can be demonstrated at organisations like The Body Shop, Sony, Nissan and Canon.

---

workplace are made clear, as are its customs, modes of dress, modes of behaviour, attendance patterns, work manners and ways of working and performance measures. The individual has the basic choice of accepting or rejecting these. He may in accepting them do so passively only, or he may fully internalise them (see Summary Box 3.9). As an acceptable minimum there is invariably both organisation and group pressure at least to comply; the penalty for non-compliance is equally invariably that of rejection.

■ Conclusions

The main lessons to be learned relate not only to an understanding of the areas of leadership, motivation, groups and the individual as concepts and subjects in their own right, but also to the extent to which they impinge on each other. They are all interrelated and both the concepts and their application must be seen in this context.

Managers must be able to assimilate all of this and understand the complexities involved, if they are to be able to adapt them in particular situations and use the processes, skills and qualities inherent in them in the promotion of effective and successful business activities.

They must also recognise that which is relevant to particular situations and that which is not. A team performance, for example, may be so bad that the team in question may simply need to be disbanded and a new one formed; no amount of leadership or directive expertise or motivation initiative is appropriate in such circumstances.

Thus, managers must have a full and complete understanding of why this could or might be so, and in order to do this must have grasped the principles outlined in this chapter, their complexities, and the ways in which they interact.

CHAPTER 4

The management of organisations

This chapter is concerned with the organisational aspects and concepts that must be grasped and understood if effective managerial practices are to be constituted and adopted. The chapter deals with the nature and complexities of each in turn; and the interrelationship between them.

There are five matters for consideration:

1. **The structure and culture of organisations**, the ways in which they are designed and put together and given life in the pursuit of the operations that they are to carry out and for which they have been constituted; the ways in which they are to do things; the core values, attitudes, beliefs and ethics that are to prevail as they operate.
2. **The systems of organisations**, the ways in which they devise and develop both core and support ways of working, how these are energised, what their purposes are, what their components are and how they interrelate.
3. **Processes of communication**, effective communication processes are the essential prerequisite to productive harmony, organisational effectiveness, customer satisfaction, stability, permanence and development; and the processes of perception in which humans both limit and compartmentalise the great range of information that is presented to them at all times and in all places.
4. **Processes of decision-making**, the nature of executive choices; the means of doing this to ensure that as far as possible what is executed is both successful and effective (and also dynamic and responsive).
5. **Organisation and employee development**, the means by which organisations and their people grow, extend and improve their qualities, capacities, skills and knowledge. Organisation and employee development also have effects on structure, culture, systems, communications and the decision-making processes, improving capacities in each of these areas.

All organisations at their inception must have their own clear vision, their own 'guiding light' – an articulation of purpose – if they are to be successful. A clear vision for the organisation leads to clarity of strategy, planning, purpose, priorities and motivation; it gives the required standpoint for the channelling of activities and resources in pursuit of those activities; and it is the fountain from which the pride and identity of those who are to work in it flows. It is present in each of the areas to be covered here. Its affects each positively when it is clear; and negatively when it is not.

■ Structures and cultures

Both the organisation form adopted – the structure – and the collective beliefs, values and ethics – the culture – must match the overall purpose of the organisation, in such ways as to ensure the best possible return on investment made; the most effective relationship possible with its markets, customers, clients, and environment; performance; responsiveness and adaptability.

It is necessary to recognise that no two organisations are exactly alike, and that, whatever the similarity in output, product or service, ways of working, shared values, management style, and the relationship with the market, may differ widely.

It is also necessary to remind ourselves at this stage that the business sphere is in a great state of flux. Global influences abound. Concepts of best practice are constantly being updated. Technology is not constant; it is constantly being updated also, and being made more universally available. Rates of product, market and distribution changes are accelerating; as is entry to, and exit from, market and operational sectors. All organisations, in interrelating with these elements, affect their own structures and cultures.

All organisations therefore are different. They have different methods of operation and working, different ways of doing things, different values, attitudes, beliefs and norms – different personalities, in fact. They are as different from each other as people.

It follows from this that structures and cultures vary between organisations; that there is no correct method of organisation, nor set of values to be adopted; but that each organisation must understand the factors that contribute to it, and from this, actively define and design that culture and structure that is most appropriate to itself.

There are ten such contributory factors:

■ Age and history of the organisation

The degree of prominence that it has established, and those elements that are related to age and history: its traditions; its reputation and how this has arisen; its image; its standing in both its business sphere and its local community are involved here. Young organisations will be spending time and resources generating these matters for themselves; while those of long standing will have these elements well established; in both cases they may be 'right' and 'effective', or 'wrong' and 'ineffective', and require managerial understanding, acumen and activity either to develop them further, or to take remedial action.

■ Size of the organisation

And the related elements of spans of control; managerial and administrative structures; information systems; other control mechanisms; and the ways in which organisation permanence is to be achieved. Even for the tiniest of undertakings, some method of recording is required. The larger the organisation, the more orderly and organised these elements will tend to be.

■ The nature of the work

This impinges on both culture and structure, in that people who are highly professionalised, or trained, bring a distinctive set of values with them, which rub against those of the organisation. They require harmonisation, as far as that is possible, in order to resolve potential differences and generate a positive and productive environment. Highly ordered and regulated tasks, and series of tasks, will be mirrored in the organisation of people to carry them out. At the other extreme, projects and innovations may require little formal direction, and leave much to the self-motivation and self-organisation of those carrying them out. Or the matter in hand may be research (medical or technological research, for example) which may take years to come to fruition, and involve a level of investment that accommodates blind alleys, false hopes, and extensive testing and retesting, before a product can be offered on the open market.

■ Technology

The relationship between culture, structure and technology is mainly to do with work organisation. Small-scale activities require a lower and more flexible organisation than those to do with large-scale, permanent, or mass output methods. In the latter case, economies of scale, and the qualities that arise from continuity and performance arise; as do also questions of production and work group organisation and departmentalisation. From this, there are implications concerning alienation, dysfunction, and organised labour and representation, that must be addressed. How organisations and those responsible for designing them, tackle these matters, also bears directly on structure and culture.

The speed at which technology changes or becomes obsolete must also be considered. Organisations cannot seek permanence or stability in an era of rapid technological change or innovation; while where a technology is deemed to have a degree of permanence, a more subtle and organised structure may be devised.

This is affected finally by the levels of investment made in technology, and the returns required. Something that is very expensive with a short useful life puts pressure on organisations to maximise the returns very quickly, before it becomes obsolete; while a ten-year capital programme will require a structure that can exploit fully such a long-term commitment, and permanence as well as effectiveness must be sought.

■ Location

This is the ability to work in harmony with the prevailing local customs and traditions. It may include religious, ethical and social pressures. It is certain to include legal constraints. There are also population size and mixes, and access to services. There will also be standards set by other employers in the area (especially large employers).

■ The environment

In this context, this is the relationship between the organisation; its markets, customers and clients; its competitors; and the wider environment. It includes confidence, expansion, contraction, economic and social factors. States of flux, change and diversity require organisations that can cope with them, respond to them, and indeed affect them.

The related elements of the expectations of the society, its ethics and values, that impinge on the operation of organisations, must also be taken into account.

The degree of stability of the environment must also be noted. Related matters here include threats and dangers of organisation collapse or takeover, loss of markets, and loss of standing or confidence. The overall ability of the organisation to survive and prosper in relation to its environment, and to fight battles with it when necessary, must be considered.

■ People factors

This reinforces the need not only for capable staff, but also for people who can function in the organisation as it is constituted. Relationships can be drawn between the personal characteristics and attributes of status, ambiguity, stability and identity, and their appropriateness to the form of organisation in question. For example, the person having a high desire for a senior-standing title will not get this in a small, flexible organisation, nor will he gain the same measure of order and stability from this organisation, as from a public service or government department. Work can be scaled up or down according to the qualities and capabilities of those involved. Persons of high quality and ability are more likely to be frustrated in stable and permanent organisations than in those which are flexible and dynamic (see Summary Box 4.1).

SUMMARY BOX 4.1   Personal Values

Everyone needs to be aware of their own personal values and value systems so that they may deal pragmatically with any situation that may arise. This awareness allows for any marked differences between individuals or between an individual and the demands of the organisation to be taken into account before action of any sort is contemplated. Value conflicts often arise at places of work. It is necessary to recognise that this does occur, and to take action to formulate a management style that can accommodate it where necessary and reconcile divergent values.

These values may be summarised as follows:

- **Theoretical**: where everything is ordered, factual and in place; it relates to what is socially acceptable and to concepts of fairness, reasonableness and equity
- **Economic**: the pragmatic approach where the achievement of practical, effective and profitable activities is most important; it involves making the best practical use of resources and is result-orientated
- **Aesthetic**: the process of seeing and perceiving beauty; and relating things that are both positive and desirable in relation to all the other senses
- **Social**: the desire to share emotions with other people; and concerns of loyalty, honesty, openness, trust and honour
- **Political**: concerned with the ordering of society and its sub-sections and strata
- **Religious and ethical**: these are the values related to the dignity of mankind, to the inherent worth of people and to the morality of human conduct; such values are also related to the designated and defined religious beliefs and value systems ordered and placed upon parts of the world by priesthoods and faith.

SUMMARY BOX 4.2   Culture's Consequences: Hofstede

The 'Culture's Consequences' studies were carried out in the late 1970s by Geert Hofstede. They covered 116 000 members of IBM staff in forty countries. The aim was to identify basic dimensions of national culture, and their consequences and implications for organisations, especially multi-site and multinational.

Hofstede identified four dimensions.

- **Power-Distance**: how power and influence is distributed; acceptance of unequal distribution of power; access to sources of power, physical and psychological distance from the sources of power.
- **Uncertainty Avoidance**: the presence of order and certainty; the presence of uncertainty and ambiguity; the extent to which either is seen as threatening or disquieting.
- **Individualism-Collectivism**: the extent to which individuals are expected to take care of themselves; the extent to which a common purpose is present, perceived, valued, and adopted.
- **Masculinity-Femininity**: the distinction between masculine values (money, wealth, possessions), and feminine values (care, concern, sensitivity); the priority and prevalence of these.

The IBM staff filled in questionnaires, in which they were asked to mark each dimension as high, medium or low. Results were then produced for each of the forty countries. The main lessons lie in recognising and understanding the prevailing and often deep-seated cultural pressures, and their impact on organisational and individual behaviour. For example, expecting people to act autonomously when their background is in a highly ordered (high power-distance) society is certain to cause stress and conflict; expecting people to adopt feminine values where masculine values are most highly valued is certain to require extensive initial company involvement and attitude formation at the outset. There are implications for all aspects of the management of staff-leadership, motivation, supervisory style, industrial relations. Underlying causes of stress or conflict may also be traced back to mismatches between organisation and social culture.

■ Organisation purpose

This is the extent to which such purpose is clear, articulated and understood; and the simplicity or complexity of goals. Within the overall mission statement, there are also likely to be subordinate aims and objectives which may conflict with the main purpose, and organisations have to accommodate these as effectively as possible.

There are also the effects of those in the organisation on its purpose. For a variety of reasons – shifts in talents and qualities and technologies; new opportunities; or market changes – the organisation may change direction or purpose, acquire new staff and capabilities, divest or reprioritise existing capability and this in itself will affect culture, structure and style.

■ Shared values

A clear set of values or direction offered by an organisation to its people, its customers and its environment, gives a clear sense of identity. Those who identify with them, and adopt them, will come and do business with the organisation; while those who do not, will not.

The adoption of shared values is central to the generation of high levels of commitment and motivation among the organisation's staff, in particular. Recognising that people bring a diverse range of qualities to an organisation is essential. Giving them a clear corporate purpose that is both above individual aspirations, and accommodates them (as far as possible at least), should be a major function of the articulation of shared values. It is also instrumental in articulating the ethical and moral stance that is taken in organisations.

■ Management style

There is a close interrelationship and interaction between this and the work that is done, and the way in which it is done. It is affected overall by the size, complexity, scale and scope of the organisation. More specifically it will be affected by spans of control; hierarchical considerations; degrees of conformity; alienation; the nature of the work; the inherent commitment, qualities and capabilities of the staff carrying out the work; and the expertise and capacities of the managers and supervisors. There are also wider considerations of the coercive–participative spectrum to be taken into account.

■ Archetype cultures and structures

■ Power culture

This is to be found in small pioneering organisations; some political institutions and trade unions; and project groups and certain specific departments both of multinationals, and public and municipal services. This culture depends on the figure at the centre, the source of power. Everyone else involved draws their strength, influence and confidence from this centre, and requires the continual support of it to ensure their prosperity and operational viability.

Entrepreneurs generate power cultures in that they attract those who have faith in them, and who wish to be involved in this kind of organisation; their position is thus dependent upon the success of the pioneer. Such organisations move quickly in response to opportunities, and to the inspiration of the person at the centre.

The main problem that a power culture must face is that of size. As it grows and diversifies, it becomes difficult for a power culture to sustain itself, unless it floats off its peripheral operations, or unless it places in them figureheads directly related to, or in the confidence of, the source of power.

In the longer term, there is also the question of permanence, of what happens when the person at the centre of power passes out of the organisation. In situations where they have generated the ideas, energy, identity, images, production and operational methods, a void is left when they leave or die.

The structural form of the power culture is like a spider's web – the strength of it comes from the centre (see Figure 4.1), and the main relationship between subordinates is with the centre (though they will have parallel relationships also). In the true power culture, the continued prosperity of the subordinate is dependent upon the continuing, confidence in them of the source of power – once this is lost, the subordinate normally has to move away (or is dismissed or marginalised).

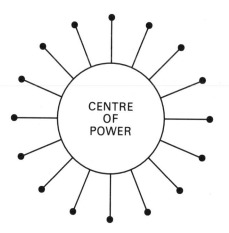

The **key relationship** is with the centre or source of power, hence no joining lines between the 'spokes'

The **key issue** is the continuation of confidence and reciprocity between the two

Figure 4.1   Power culture + structure: The Wheel

■ People/person culture

The people/person culture exists for its people, where a group has decided that it is in their own overriding interests to band together, and to produce an organisation for their benefit. It may be found in certain research groups; a university department; music, rock and jazz groups; family firms, and companies started by groups of friends, where the first coming together is generated by the people involved rather than the matter in hand.

There is little formal organisation or structure. The organisation is based on total flexibility, total interest in the work, total interest in the mutual welfare and benefits of all those concerned (see Figure 4.2).

These organisations normally exist in this format, or from this standpoint, for a short period only. In the interests of permanence and continuity, and prosperity and success, the initial coming together of people must be dovetailed with attention to task, markets, invention and sales.

The **key relationship** is between the people; what binds them is their **intrinsic** common interest. Hierarchy and structure may evolve incidentally; they too will be driven by this intrinsic common interest

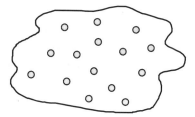

Figure 4.2   People/person culture + structure: The Mass

These organisations achieve permanence only when elements to be found in the other archetypes are present. People cultures may achieve this either by forming their own administration or management function to support the work of the people, or by hiring an agent or management group to do it for them.

These organisations are very rare. However, strong characters or experts may find themselves in more formal organisations, without allegiance to them, as this is the only way in which they can find an opportunity to practise their expertise.

These organisations have little or no structure, except for the relationship with any support or administrative function. The structure form is replaced by the energy, commitment and confidence that members have in each other, and this in turn becomes both the organisational method and control mechanism.

■ Task culture

Task cultures are found in project teams; marketing groups and market-oriented organisations. The emphases are on getting the job completed, keeping the customers and clients satisfied, and responding to and identifying new market opportunities.

These cultures are flexible, adaptable and dynamic. They accommodate the movements of staff necessary to ensure effective project and development teams and continued innovation; and concurrent human activities such as second-ments, project responsibility, and short-term contracts.

These cultures operate most effectively in prosperous, dynamic and confident environments and markets; they may also generate niche activities in these, and create new openings to be exploited. Their success lies in their continued ability to operate in this way.

They fail where these conditions are not present. Effective controls and sanctions are also difficult to devise. Control may be delegated by top manage-ment to group, team and project leaders; but may impose conditions and constraints inappropriate and imperfect to the given situation.

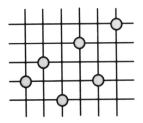

The **key relationship** here is with the task
The form of organisation is therefore fluid and elastic
The **structure** is often also described as a MATRIX, or GRID; none of these gives a full configuration – the essence is the flexibility and dynamism of the form

Figure 4.3   Task culture + structure: The Net

The archetype structure for this is the matrix or net (see Figure 4.3), but this does not give a true reflection of the fluid and flexible nature of the task culture. The format must also be regarded as elastic (rather than rigid) if a full understanding is to be achieved.

■ Role culture

Role cultures are found where organisations have gained a combination of size, permanence and departmentalisation, and where the ordering of activities, preservation of knowledge and experience, and stability are important (see Figure 4.4). Roles are defined and described and ordered, and persons are allocated to them. The role culture reflects the bureaucratic concept (without necessarily any of the negative or pejorative connotations that have come to be ascribed to it in Western business and commerce).

Role cultures operate most effectively where the wider environment is steady, and a degree of permanence is envisaged; where there is a fair element of confidence and prosperity – a seller's market; and where fairness and equity are required – for example, in the delivery of public services.

Such cultures tend to stifle creativity and entrepreneurism in the interests of stability. They also generate frustration among those who wish for a greater control over their aspect of the organisation, or to push beyond their defined role. They also tend to preserve, rather than update, their rules and procedures.

Hierarchical structures derive from the role culture. As well as the division of work, division of responsibility, authority and accountability are present. The

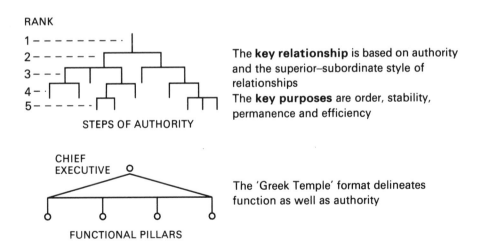

Figure 4.4   Role culture + structure: The Pyramid or Temple

result is therefore a temple structure, which, as in Figure 4.4, may either be in the 'Inca' format, representing a series of steps up; or the 'Greek' format, in which a series of functional pillars supports the organisation and gives it permanence.

■ Social characteristics

These are drawn from a variety of sources and influences. National, regional and local characteristics affect the ability of an organisation to establish its work in the ways in which it desires. There may be strong pressures in different cultures not to work on particular days of the week, or at certain times of the day. It may be necessary to generate a commonality of purpose in order to accommodate and rise above social differences (quite apart from sound operational reasons). It is necessary in any case to recognise the hopes and aspirations of the workforce, and the community from which it comes, as factors that affect the culture of organisations.

Consideration must also be given to concepts of class and status, and the trappings of success, that are important to some people on the one hand; and which, on the other, must be offered in certain measure if people are to be attracted to certain jobs and roles in organisations. Esteem and self-esteem, and respect and self-respect, are general social concepts that have to be recognised over a great range of organisational activities.

This is compounded when those with a high degree of professional or otherwise collective identity are hired; staff from these backgrounds must be provided with ways of working that match their social or expert identity with the requirements of the organisation. This impinges on both culture and structure.

■ Characteristics of Organisation Culture

Organisation Culture is a reflection of 'The ways in which things are done here.' A useful summary is as follows:

LEARNED:	rather than instinctive
SHARED:	rather than individual
CONTINUOUS:	ever developing rather than static or inert
SYMBOLIC:	capable of summary description
INTEGRATED:	changes in one area or group have effects on the whole
ADAPTIVE:	through creativity and imagination, and also training
REGULAR:	using common forms of language and behaviour
VALUES:	advocated by the organisation and expected by participants
PHILOSOPHY:	beliefs, ethics and attitudes
RULES:	organisational guidance and governance
DISTANCE:	the physical distance between members of the organisation; and the psychological distance based on status, trappings and occupational differentials

CLIMATE: the environment, physical layout, technology; internal and external interactions.

■ Culture and structure design

The importance of culture and structure, and their appropriateness to the work of the organisation, is a matter of much current concern. In particular organisations with long traditions of order, stability and permanence (both in themselves and in their dealings with their clients) have struggled to respond to changing requirements, new opportunities, and different priorities.

It is incumbent upon organisations, and their managers, to define and devise the structure and culture that is required for continued and successful operation in the chosen field. For this to be successful, consideration is required of each of the elements outlined above, and management decisions taken, based on a proper evaluation and analysis of each in relation to the nature of work, the market and environment.

Whatever is done must be positive and not simply allowed to emerge by default. The values, aspirations and direction of the organisation must be conveyed, to all those who come to work in it, and all those who do business with it, in its own terms. Concerning staff, this may involve a mutual rejection – organisations will accommodate dissenting staff to the extent that dissent can be harmonised or made productive; to go further requires a dilution of core purpose and values. This remains true even in the pluralist perspective – at no stage is this required to be an 'all things to all people' philosophy.

The organisation's priorities also affect culture and structure, and these must therefore be clearly and accurately articulated. It follows from this that the relationship between sub-systems and support systems must also be clear. This includes control mechanisms, information and communication systems, and support functions (such as finance, secretarial services and personnel).

This is not rigid. The design of organisations and their cultures and structures is not the equivalent of designing buildings. Flexibility, fluidity, responsiveness and initiative are all essential components of the establishment of, and ordering of, the structure of organisations. Stability, too, is an essential element, but this is not equivalent to rigidity. Rather it is the acquisition of those elements that will give a true permanence and continuity in a turbulent and changing business sphere, where the nature of competition is global, and where managerial expertise is constantly improving.

The final element of structure and culture design to be considered is the interrelationship and interaction between the different departments and functions of the organisation, its production and support functions, its marketing, its research and development, and the systems that are introduced to facilitate their operation. These represent the day-to-day functioning of the organisation. They give both permanence and order to structure and culture, and also provide the basis on which they are to be developed for the future.

■ Systems in organisations

It is now useful to consider the relationship and interaction between organisations and their systems, and the effects of each on the other. Systems are devised in relation to the structure and culture of the organisation to make it work and to harmonise the organisational elements, productive and effective activities.

It is useful to distinguish between **main** and **supporting** systems. The main systems are those that are devised to ensure that the core purpose of the organisation is successful and which give life to its front line functions and key activities. Those systems that support this are provided in order to harmonise the work of the rest of the staff in ensuring that the front line functions are provided with the resources and sub-activities needed, both to become and to remain effective.

It is also useful to distinguish the concept of a **maintenance** system. As in operational or technical terms, this should consist of both a system of preventive maintenance and a system of emergency or crisis handling. Preventive maintenance systems are devised to ensure that there is a capacity in the organisation for identifying in advance likely problem areas, organisation and communication blockages and breakdowns, structural and cultural dysfunctions, as well as precise operational and staff management issues; and to support and enhance (rather than detract from) overall organisational effectiveness. Crisis systems are those that ensure that the genuine emergency does not cause complete organisational seizure or breakdown. These should not constitute the managerial norm; a crisis system constitutes the ability to call on resources as and when they are needed. If the crisis approach *is* the organisation's managerial norm, it is very expensive in resource terms as well as stressful and destructive on structure, culture and staff.

In general, therefore, there is a requirement for systems to be well defined, yet flexible and adaptable. Organisations require their systems to work for them and not to be hidebound by them.

At its simplest the systems model is as follows: the conversion of INPUTS via a means of PROCESS into OUTPUTS (see Figure 4.5).

In organisational terms such systems are invariably open. Some of the inputs are either wholly or partially beyond the organisation's control and concern such matters as responding to changes in taste and perception and market activities, as well as more general interactions between organisations and their environment (e.g. boom, recession, social, political and ethical factors).

The systems that are to be found in organisations are specifically concerned with:

- Production, service and the management of operations and projects
- Maintenance functions
- Support functions
- Resource gathering, organising and prioritising

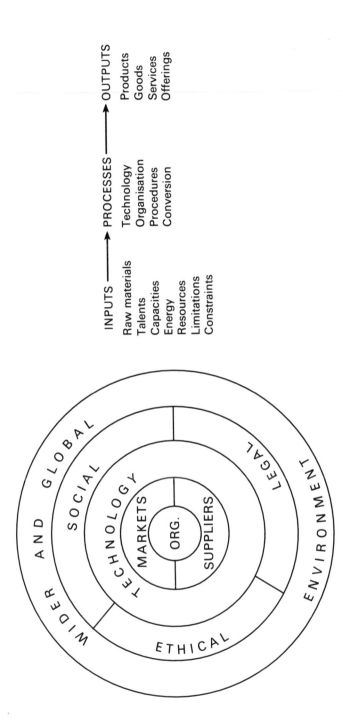

INPUTS ⟶ PROCESSES ⟶ OUTPUTS

INPUTS	PROCESSES	OUTPUTS
Raw materials	Technology	Products
Talents	Organisation	Goods
Capacities	Procedures	Services
Energy	Conversion	Offerings
Resources		
Limitations		
Constraints		

Purpose: to demonstrate and illustrate the range and mix of pressures and effects on the organisation; and to relate these to the requirement for products, goods and services, and the source of these.

Figure 4.5   Organisations as systems

- Systems for the management of, and resolution of, conflicts
- Communication and management information
- Rules, codes of conduct, general procedures, reporting relationships.

There are formal or structured systems developed by the organisation for its greater operational efficiency and effectiveness; and informal systems developed by the staff to facilitate their own individual positions.

These systems may be largely: **social**, to provide for effective interaction between persons; or **technical**, built up and around a production, service or information process in which machinery and equipment feature prominently, as does the staff/technology interface; or they may be a combination of the two.

For the system to operate effectively a number of characteristics must be present:

- **Energy:** required to give the system life and make it work and continue; people are required to see that this happens
- **Returns:** part of the returns on the outputs will be used to ensure the fresh flow of inputs into the processes
- **Steadiness and stability:** most systems work best to a stable flow of work rather than to peaks and troughs; if peaks, pressures and over-pressure do occur steps should be taken to recognise these, address the reasons for them and where possible take remedial or modifying actions
- **Balance:** of input processes and output to ensure a steady flow of work and the avoidance of blockages and bottlenecks
- **Equifinality:** the concept that similar outputs can be achieved from a variety of systems and processes; this is the recognition that no one system will ever be right in all situations
- **Flexibility and adaptability:** concerned with the ability to respond effectively to changes in the environment, markets, perceptions and tastes; and to take advantage of the creative and dynamic processes inherent in them
- **Coordination and control characteristics:** that ensure that the steadiness and balance is maintained.

A number of conclusions and inferences may be made from this:

- There is **no best way** to organise; as the environment changes so the systems must be flexible and responsive
- The environment changes in both **predictable** and **unpredictable** ways; the challenge for managers is to anticipate the unexpected by building requisite variety, flexibility and learning capacities into their organisations
- Due to the relationship with the environment, managers must spend time on **external issues** to manage organisational adaptation and create more desirable contexts for continued operations
- Each input, process, output, cycle changes the nature of the organisation's social and technical resources, presenting an opportunity to strive for **optimisation**
- The environment is **dynamic**, not static or rigid. This allows for limitless opportunities for change to occur; investments in environmental adaptation and transformation are as essential to success as investments in capital equipment and staffing; the more complex and turbulent the environment, the more essential this investment becomes
- Systems are designed for the **long term**; they must be flexible and dynamic if they are to be effective in the long term.

Environmental, technological and social changes are the primary cause and inspiration for organisational improvement. Finally, investment in staff as part of this optimisation process is also essential if the whole is to be creative, progressive and profitable.

■ Communication

All managers *should* be expert communicators. It is essential first that they understand the dimensions of communication.

Communication is all-pervasive and goes on all the time. It is both an active process and also takes place 'in absentia'. Organisations and their managers produce communications of all kinds which are received by their staff and customers and the wider environment; even where these communications are not issued directly, messages are nevertheless perceived by the receivers to have been sent in terms either of neglect, ignorance or indifference.

■ Perception

The first part of the communication process to be understood therefore is that of perception. Perception is both a creative and responsive process; and one by which individuals construct and limit their own unique view of the world. They pay attention to some, and ignore or disregard other, information. How the world is seen counts much more than any true objective reality as this also may simply be a feature of the perceptions of the individual. It is certainly true to say that people both organise and limit the information that they receive; this is their only means of managing and understanding it. Man is by no means a passive receiver of data.

Incorrect perceptions hinder good working relationships and obstruct clear communications. Interpersonal perception can be defined as the forming of judgements by people about other people. The quality of these judgements is vital at the place of work. In the social setting it may not matter so much if perception is in error because the people concerned may choose to relate or not to relate to each other, but in the workplace there may be no such choice. People may have to work with others, irrespective of any like or dislike. If behaviour is perceived by others differently from the way intended the probability of working effectively with them diminishes. The greater discrepancy there is between self-perception and the perception of others, the greater the probability of poor communication and misunderstanding. If an understanding of how information is selected, limited and biased can be developed then it becomes possible to adjust for errors.

Information is received through all senses and is open to interpretation. Whatever is written is also open to interpretation in both letter and spirit.

Whoever is met or spoken to is assessed in the same way. In these situations there is actually so much information available and so instantly that it is necessary to limit it in ways that enable it to be managed, to be given meaning and to be put in context. The basis for this and the concepts that are included in it are as follows.

■ Individual and collective perception

Perception is affected by the individual's own experiences and knowledge of the world. It is affected by socialisation – the interaction between individual and society that provides psychological comfort and stability. It is also affected by the prevailing influences present in particular situations and this includes work organisations.

■ Halo effects

Strong, positive or negative characteristics (often visual or tactile) are either apparent or inferred and the rest of the person's capabilities and personality traits are assumed from this. This is where, for example, a strong handshake given and received at the point of meeting someone leads to an inference that they are a strong character.

■ First impressions

The first impression is the instant positioning of someone or something on the individual's perceptual map. If a strong initial impression is formed, it is very difficult to shift (and this includes both strong positive and strong negative first impressions).

■ Stereotyping

Stereotyping is a development of this. A set of characteristics are assumed in particular categories of people; and particular categories of people are assumed to have these sets of characteristics.

■ Self-fulling prophecy

From this perceptions are developed and rationalised still further, so that people see only what they wish to see and hear only what they wish to hear and edit out

---

SUMMARY BOX 4.3   Perception

- When people exhibit strong and conflicting characteristics, the general response on the part of the rest of the world is to reject or mistrust them, as accommodation and acceptance require an understanding of the limitations of perceptions at the point of meeting and dealing with them.
- A combination of the various perceptual processes is to be found in the 'preconceived idea' and 'pre-judged case'; what invariably happens is that a situation arises where the individual can bring different familiarities and experiences to different aspects of it; they then reconstruct these for good or ill, to the matter in hand, and jump to a conclusion and solution.
- It is possible through the observation of an individual's activity and behaviour, to INFER his attitude. It is NOT possible to prove it; and if this is the overriding requirement of the moment, further action must be taken to overcome these inferences and gain a truer picture.
- The adaptation process is constantly in action. People over-respond to someone who is polite if the last six others that they have met have been rude; the person driving home in a rush from work may fear the wrath of their partner if they are late; if they crash the car in so doing, the driver immediately feels lucky to be alive; the feelings of the person waiting for them change from anger to anxiety and then relief.
- There is the question of 'reconciliation' to be addressed; examples of this include reconciling the brilliant performance of an actor with his own dull personality; the radical politician or religious leader in these roles, with that of next door neighbour or travelling companion; the children's matinee idol who refuses to sign autographs.

  In general, a grasp of the basic principles of perception on the part of those in managerial roles at least enables the questioning of certain supposed 'rules' and 'facts'; it should be part of the process of generating a healthy scepticism and genuinely enquiring mind, when faced with such perceptual 'absolutes'.

---

the bits that do not fit in with this preconceived or pre-perceived picture (see Summary Box 4.3). They therefore come to the logical conclusion that the person with the weak handshake is a weak person because they pick out his other negative characteristics and edit or reject everything else about him.

■ Implicit personality theory

People assume that particular characteristics go together – such as kindness and gentleness; or violence and dishonesty – these are related characteristics with which they may be happy and contented. Different approaches are necessary to accommodate the person who is both kind and violent, for example, or gentle and dishonest. Robin Hood, for example, exhibited all of these characteristics; and this is cloaked in folk heroics to accommodate his violence and dishonesty.

■ Mythology

Most people put a largely spurious rationale on the ways in which they organise this information. Common phrases present are 'in my opinion', 'in my experience', 'in my day we used to . . .', and 'I always ask this question and it never fails'; and so on.

■ Adaptation

This is the definition of 'perception as a continuous process'. Our view of the world is influenced directly by the circumstances and surroundings in which people find themselves. Part of the process also relates to priority levels – what is important now; and what is important for life, work, leisure, and so on.

■ Personal mapping and constructs

In this case what is actually occurring is a process by which people, situations, activities, images and impressions are being fitted into the perceived map of the world in ways which can be understood, managed and accommodated. The information thus gathered is broken down into constructs or characteristics which may be categorised as follows:

1. **Physical**: assumes or infers the qualities of people from their appearance, racial group, beauty, style, dress and other visual images
2. **Behavioural**: placing people according to the way in which they act and behave or the ways in which we think they will act and behave
3. **Role**: making assumptions about people because of the variety of roles they assume; the different situations in which they assume these roles; their dominant role or roles; and the trappings that go with them
4. **Psychological**: whereby certain occupations, appearances, manifestations, presentation and images are assumed to be of a higher order of things than others (part of this is also sociological); this reflects the morality, values and ethics of the society of the day as well as the environment and organisation in question.

This is a basis and outline of perception only. There is no right or wrong. It is a means for understanding the ways in which people perceive, edit and organise the information presented to them from their world including work. Understanding these principles is essential for all those who seek to manage people. There are direct implications for staff management; recruitment and selection; industrial relations; performance appraisal; budgeting and the behavioural aspects of that; marketing and sales; and project management; as well as across the rest of the managerial activity.

■ The communication process

Communication is a process consisting of:

■ Passive communication

Passive communication takes place all the time. In organisations it is worst when it represents a lack of purpose, direction, organisation, management or method in relation to the communications and signals sent out. The style, type and language of communication, through absence or indifference, cause the generation of and reinforcement of attitudes and behaviour related to negativity, alienation, uncertainty and anxiety. Inevitably, there are gaps between what people want to know and what they do actually know and this constitutes the ingredient necessary for the formation of informal networks and a 'grapevine'. It is also very unproductive and debilitating for both morale of staff and organisational performance.

■ One-way communication

One-way communication is where messages are issued by organisations and managers without any regard for those at whom they are pitched. It is widely perceived as being directive or prescriptive. It can also contribute greatly to the process of debilitation referred to above, in that the receivers of the messages will not necessarily perceive in them anything of value and will rather wait either for their own language to be used or a message with more clarity of purpose to be issued to them before actively responding. Examples are edicts from on high; rules, procedures and manuals written without reference to the needs of those who are to read them; operational schedules that have no chance of being completed to time. One-way communication reinforces alienation and psychological distance.

■ Active communication

Active and **two way** communication constitutes the converse of this; messages are issued that everyone can understand and act upon. Language, media and methods of communication are appropriate to both the messages and material concerned and the audiences that are being addressed. It is the basis for effective work transactions, the organisation sets its own modes and styles of communication and does not allow these to emerge or form by default. The staff understand both the wider situation and their own place in it. They understand the changing and developing nature of their environment and business sphere and their changing and developing place within it. Dysfunctional manifestations of bad communication such as low morale are minimal.

■ Distortion of the message

However, it must be recognised that messages and therefore the overall effectiveness of communication systems may be limited by both environmental and operational matters. The senders of messages may filter items out or include elements that have no organisational status. They may bias, skew or distort the messages for their own ends.

The position of the sender may affect the message also. The rest of the staff may not trust them or have confidence in them; or they may be known to have their own axe to grind. They may have been proven false in the past. The position of relative status and authority between senders and receivers may be too wide to have any meaning or too narrow to have any authority; or the sender of the message may have lower status than many of those who are to receive it.

Information overload and use of inappropriate media will also distort the message. What is retained tends to be that according most strongly with the interest of the receiver, whether or not it is important; or that which is most immediate (for example, today's mail, or the last telephone call tend to get acted upon first).

Information as a source of power and influence may also create a tendency for individuals and groups to gather and store information for their own ends and to feed it out in their own way in the pursuit of these ends rather than for the common good.

The length of chains of information and its dissemination also distorts the message as it is passed on; it also contributes (if it is a long chain) to the 'distance' factor and the resulting lack of credibility or lack of impact of the message.

■ Strategic communication

Use of media, channels and networks should therefore be strategically addressed by organisations and their managers to ensure that if the message does not get through in one way it will get through in another. As well as the use of papers, journals, letters, memoranda and leaflets this will include briefing groups, departmental meetings, company and organisation addresses and discussions. It will also include electronic systems, cluster groups, work improvement groups, quality groups, expert groups, status groups and hierarchical meetings of those of the same rank from across departments or divisions. It will include meetings with trade unions and professional and technical bodies. It will include the use of informal networks and even the 'canteen' or 'teatime' cultures that prevail in larger and multi-faceted organisations.

Communication is all-pervasive throughout all human activities, and therefore throughout all organisations. A strategic approach must be devised and adopted by those responsible for the overall direction of the organisation. The presence, use and value of all the processes indicated must be recognised and maximised. The overall purpose must be to create an oil for the organisation, smoothing and making effective in turn its operational processes. It also impinges on all other work systems and work methods; the structure and culture of the organisation; staff management style; and systems for the management of conflict.

■ Oral communication

All managers should be effective speakers. This ability is required for conducting discussions and briefings with the staff; conducting effective telephone transactions and briefings; addressing gatherings, both internal and external on matters to do with the business sphere; conducting effective interviews (selection, grievance and dispute); conducting effective performance appraisals; and organising business activities.

It is also necessary to be able to make presentations to wider audiences as and when required. Any manager should be able to do this; otherwise organisations must, as part of their overall skills audit, be able to identify a panel of speakers both ready and capable of presenting a substantive and credible face of it to the outside world. Both aspects are important – a slick presentation will lack substance and conviction if there is no true content; while the content requires effective delivery if it is to stand any chance of being received, understood and acted upon by the audience. This is of equal importance whatever the matter in hand – and the memory and reputation of any bad or inadequate presentation always lingers long after the event.

■ Written communication

This should always be undertaken with the audience in mind. Accurate, relevant, precise and persuasive writing are all important in different situations and there are skills inherent in this that require identification and development. The end result aimed at should normally be the production of a concise and clear document that the receiver or receivers will understand and be able to respond and react to (in whatever terms that means in the given situation), and that will provide a record of the business that is to be or has been conducted, that contributes to the permanence and development of the knowledge and experience of the organisation.

The objective of the piece must be clear in the mind of the writer as a prerequisite to its success. It should be as brief as possible; if it is necessarily long, a summary should be included. The structure adopted is also important; as well as the use of language, the presentation and delivery must also reflect both the nature of the material being delivered and the expectations of those who are to read it. Finally, it should always be subject to scrutiny (and editing if desirable) before it is sent.

Different formats are both required and expected for: annual reports; quantitative data; journals; committee and boardroom papers; advertising leaflets, papers and inserts; project reports and findings; qualitative data; memoranda; policy initiatives; and complaints and responses to complaints. The structure and presentation of these will also be determined by the audience or audiences intended, and whether these are internal or external to the organisation.

■ Non-verbal communication

Non-verbal communication (NVC) either gives an impression of ourselves to someone else without our saying anything, or else it reinforces what we are saying. This is a simple summary of NVC. The main components are:

- **Appearance:** this may be broken down into the component parts of age; gender; hair; face; body shape and size; height; bearing; national and racial characteristics; and clothing. Each of these items on its own and the combined effect has great implications for: interviewing; public images; creating impressions; advertising; public relations; salesmanship; and presentation.
- **Manner:** this indicates behaviour, the range of emotions, levels of confidence, levels of certainty and sureness (or uncertainty and unsureness), levels of contentment/anxiety.
- **Expression:** after the initial meeting and first impression, facial expression becomes the focus of our attention and we concentrate most of our attention upon it. Again this has implications for advertising, salesmanship and interviewing; and also in face to face situations and interviews.
- **Eye contact:** regular eye contact demonstrates interest, trust, concern, affection, and sympathy. The depth of expression in the eyes generates deeper perception of feelings – anger, sorrow, love, hatred, joy.
- **Pose:** this is either static or active, and is generally used to reinforce the total manner. this has implications in terms of bearing, arm and leg positions; and using different parts of the body as protection, shield or expression. It helps convey the overall impression such as relaxation, activity, passivity, anger, leisure, nervousness and so on.
- **Clothing:** this is also an important carrier of meaning in all face-to-face situations and provides an instant summing up of them.
- **Activity:** this is also important in the emphasis of meaning, and the elements of this are now considered under a separate heading.

■ Activity

□ Touch

This signifies a wide range of perceptions. Consider the difference between different people's handshakes and the impressions that these convey. Touching also reinforces both role and sex stereotypes – the chairman banging his fist on the desk; the woman meticulously rearranging her clothes.

□ Body movement

This may be purely functional and fulfilling requirements, for example cleaning the car; or the movements may be exaggerated, conveying anger or high emotions; or languid, conveying comfort, ease or indolence; or sharp and staccato, conveying forcefulness and emphasis.

□ Positional communication

This may convey formality, for example, two people standing moving little, talking earnestly at a trade gathering or in the corner. Or they may be sitting facing each other across a large desk – this conveys a sense of security and defence to the person whose desk it is and a barrier to be climbed by the other before he can communicate effectively or on equal terms. Or people may sit adjacent at the corner of a desk or table in order to talk intimately. Chat show hosts sit without tables and ensure that their guests do not have recourse to this prop either. This puts the professional at an advantage and ensures that the guest is sufficiently alien to the environment to be subservient to the host. It should also be recognised that people require a certain amount of space around them. In Northern Europe this is about 18 inches around the person. In Southern Europe it is about 8 to 10 inches and touching is a more common feature of NVC than in the North. This is discomforting to Northern Europeans.

□ Other props and settings

The most common are tables and chairs. Other props are used to reinforce advertising or to convey impressions of luxury, casualness or formality in different settings. Settings are designed to ensure that whatever happens in them does so to the greatest possible advantage of the instigator. They may be outdoor or indoor and may be used either to enhance an advertised product, reinforce a position of power, put someone at ease or put someone in the position desired by the setting director.

Broadly props and settings are categorised as familiar, imaginative and fantastic. The latter is implicit or explicit in advertising and entertainment, offering escapism or the promise of something not in fact to be fulfilled. The other two are to be found in interview and other face-to-face business situations. An imaginative setting may often be used (to complete a sale or to do other business, over a meal, for example).

■ Discrepancy in the message

It is important to recognise that the body or setting may convey one message while the spoken words may convey another. This is often noticeable in politicians who, when interviewed on the television, may be uttering bland and pleasant platitudes while their bodies convey great agitation or anger.

■ Society and message

It should finally be noted that NVC (and particularly appearance, props and settings) has conditioned us into to what is expected and what is acceptable socially. We thus do not attend promotion panels unshaven or dressed in a tracksuit. There is no rationale for this other than the expectations of society and those accorded to the particular situation and the consequent pressure to conform.

■ Other aspects of NVC

Other aspects of NVC include: the use of scent and fragrance; the use of colour and coordination of colours (again especially in dress); matters of social or ethical importance (such as smoking); the design of office, production and marketing equipment and furnishings. There are also, as we have seen, non-verbal or parallel messages to be gained from certain overtly verbal communications, whether written or spoken.

This is a summary only of some of the main themes of NVC. It is important, however, first of all in the way that we respond to people or situations that we encounter; and, secondly, in recognising the way in which people will respond to us in the variety of roles and situations in which we find ourselves. We are then able to respond to others in ways which they expect and which lead to productive communication taking place.

■ Use of language

Effective communication only takes place if the language used is correct. Messages have to be put across in ways which the receivers will understand and to which they are able to respond in the ways required. Language also conveys secondary messages and hidden agendas which in turn influence the responses generated. In general, the simpler and more direct the language used, the greater the chance that the message will be understood; and the more complicated or bland the language used, the greater the chance that misunderstanding, resistance or non-response will be generated.

Jargon and organisation or department 'speak' will only be used where all those involved are familiar with it. Otherwise constraints on use of language should be confined by: the levels of intelligence or academic achievements of those at whom it is directed; the occupational spread of those at whom it is directed; and the true nature of the message to be put across.

Language is also used in this way to establish common ground and parameters for the communication process. These processes are called 'codes' and may be found in: industrial relations, sales pitches, recruitment advertising, motivation, instructional techniques and methods, technical drawings, research and development and accounts and budgets. Language is also used externally in the establishment of relationships at organisational level, again for the same overall purposes.

■ Listening

Listening is both a passive and active process. Passive listening may be no more than awareness of background noise; it may also be limited to a general awareness of what someone is saying – 'hearing' may be a better definition of this.

Active listening is both a process and a skill. It is defined as taking a dynamic interest in that which is received via the ears and making a positive attempt to understand what is being listened to, responding to it and developing it. As a skill it is developed partly through the commitment and motivation of an employee or any individual in any given situation; and partly also by the manager or superior of that person developing the listening medium and environment in such a way that it is positive and productive and by motivating the members of staff to generate their own interests in what is being put across.

Poor listening habits cost millions of pounds each year in lost productivity at workplaces. They also constitute a prime reason for breakdowns in relationships both at work and in the wider society.

Research indicates that people only use about a quarter of their listening capacity; that they only use one-tenth of their memory potential; that they forget half of what they have heard within 8 hours; and that they distort what little they do remember; and that such memory is subject to their perceptions and preconceptions.

People who feel they are listened to perform better, work more cooperatively, and have fewer on-the-job problems. In its training literature, the US Sperry Corporation states: 'good listeners think more broadly because they hear and understand more facts and points of view. They make better innovators. Because listeners look at problems in a fresh way and combine what they learn in more unlikely and creative ways they are more likely in turn to hit upon truly innovative ideas. Ultimately, good listeners attune themselves more closely to where the world is going and to the products, talents and techniques it needs to get there.'

Transactional analysis (see Summary Box 4.4, Figures 4.6 and 4.7) has done much to help us understand the 'communication transaction'.

We need also to consider the theories of neuro-linguistic programming (see Summary Box 4.5) on reacting to life situations.

SUMMARY BOX 4.4   Transactional Analysis

Transactional analysis (TA) is a system for the analysis of personal and inter-personal communication and behaviour. It was defined and evolved by Dr Eric Berne whose thesis was that there existed in everyone three quite clearly distinguishable sets of attitudes and behaviours. He called these ego states: configurations of states or frames of mind (see Figures 4.6 and 4.7). These are readily recognisable by things that we say, the ways in which we say them, and the support that we give them by way of body language, gestures and mannerisms.

- **Ego states**
  TA involves using knowledge and skills to recognise ego states; and from this to adopt an ego state that determines whether the transaction is to be effective, ineffective, business-like or a crossed transaction leading to misunderstanding.

  The ego states are as follows: parent, adult, and child. The 'parent' is further modified into: parent nurturing and parent critical. The 'child' is further modified into: free child and adaptive child. Their importance lies in the fact that there is nothing in human communication that cannot be attributed to one of these. People talk and write from different states and it is possible to identify which it is in all cases. From this, a method and choice of response and an appropriate ego state can be adopted so that the transaction proceeds in an effective way.

- **Transactions**
  Transactions may be **complementary** – from adult to adult, parent to child, or child to parent.

  Transactions may be **crossed** – any other variation (parent to parent; child to child; adult to child; child to adult; adult to parent; parent to adult).

  Transactions may be **ulterior** – the message is implied not stated; when this is the case the ulterior transaction is inevitably that which is acted upon (and which the initiator will probably have devised); or the ulterior is that which is intended to be received (for example, when a politician says to his opponent 'I respect your views', what he actually means is 'I do not respect your views').

- **Games**
  Berne also identified a number of games that arise from ulterior transactions. He suggested that people spend a large portion of their time and energy in these games; and that the main reason for this was to gain recognition or 'strokes' – units of recognition. Examples of these games are as follows:

  'Why don't you', 'yes, but.' The initiator states a problem and seeks the advice of others. They offer solutions based on the 'why don't you' which the initiator rejects with 'yes, but'. He ends up feeling self-righteous and thinks 'I know best'.

  'Now I've got you.' The initiator of this game contrives a situation whereby somebody makes a mistake. At the appropriate moment he steps in and confronts the offender who feels bad whilst the initiator enjoys feelings of superiority and dominance.

  'Kick me.' In this game the initiator constantly does things which provoke criticism or punishment; he gets negative recognition which is more important to him than getting no recognition at all.

  'I'm only trying to help.' This is where aid or advice usually unsolicited is constantly being offered. When eventually he is rejected, he can say 'but I'm only trying to help you'.

These are examples of games that Berne recognised that people played in different situations. In extreme cases they became developed into work scripts or life scripts. Scripts represent in TA terms a configuration of the way in which the individual decides how he will lead his life. He makes this plan in response to the range of messages both positive and negative, both critical and nurturing, that he receives from both his workplace and his wider environment.

Ego state	Typical words/phrases	Typical voice tone	Typical behaviour	Typical attitudes
Critical parent	'That's disgraceful' 'You ought' 'You must always' 'Don't ask questions' 'Because I said so'	sneering angry condescending critical disgusted	furrowing brow pointed finger scowling face set jaw pounding on table	moralistic judgemental authoritarian
Nurturing parent	'Well done young man!' 'Splendid!' 'What a lovely boy!' 'Don't worry' 'I'll sort it out for you'	sympathetic warm encouraging	pat on the back consoling touch benevolent smile relaxed	caring permissive supportive understanding non-judge-mental
Adult	'How?' 'When?' 'Where?' 'Let's look at it again' 'It's 6.30'	clear calm enquiring	attentive and aware level eye contact	open-minded interested confident
Adapted child	'I'll try hard' 'Please can I?' 'I can't' 'Please' 'Thank you'	whiny placating mumbling	downcast eyes vigorous head nodding nail biting passive slumped and dejected posture spitefulness taunting	compliant defiant delaying complaining
Free child	'I want' 'Wow!' 'I feel great'	loud fast	laughing with someone noisy crying demonstration of feelings constantly changing behaviour	curious energetic fun-loving spontaneous

Figure 4.6   Some behavioural aspects of ego states

Source: A. Barker, *Transactional Analysis and Training* (McGraw-Hill, 1982).

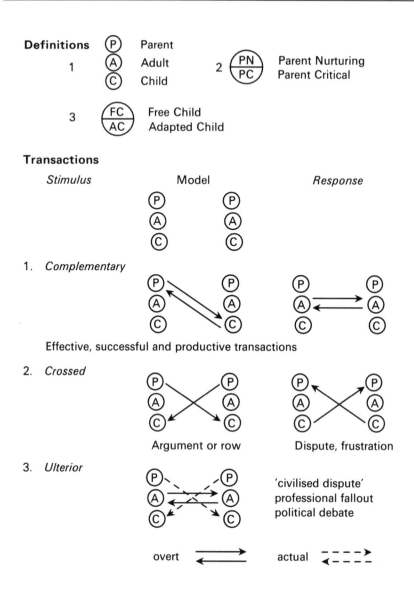

Figure 4.7   Transaction analysis: models

Source: Berne (1984).

SUMMARY BOX 4.5   Neuro-linguistic Programming

Neuro-linguistic programming (NLP) is the title given to the behavioural frame-work and process that provides us with the capacities to use our own resources, intelligence and capabilities more effectively. The process combines the experi-ences of the individual and his perceived view of the reality of the world, and programmes the reactions that he makes to it, developing responses, strategies and behaviour according to the nature of his experience. The experience is acquired through one of two sources – the nerves and senses (the neurology); and through language, both its use and interpretation.

From these experiences and the ways in which they were and are acquired, individuals develop their own programmes to deal with situations that arise and have to be confronted. From an understanding of this, the individual is in a position to devise, adopt, adapt and choose strategies and approaches that enable him to directly and positively impact on a situation in his own chosen way – for example, if you do not want people to look at your head you devise a strategy to draw their attention away from it, perhaps to wear bright shoes and socks so that their attention is actively drawn to your feet.

More widely, the process is adopted to particular situations as they are. The individual is then asked to identify how he would like these situations to be, how he would like to be in them and to identify the internal qualities and resources necessary to achieve this. The personal strategy adopted is then the ordering of these resources into an effective means of handling the situation.

The basis of NLP's success and effectiveness is drawn from the experiences of the individual, often with counselling or expert tuition and help. It is based on the view that high quality of performance comes about only when the individual is confident in himself in relation both to those around him and also to the wider environment. It involves qualities present or potential in the individual and not those that are not; it is thus centred on the individual in question.

It offers improved personal communication, general effectiveness and well-being through the development and use and value of these qualities. Specifically this concerns the uses of and applications of language; self-presentation; clarity of thought and purpose; flexibility; the capacity for the development of relationships at all levels; and the capacity for the development of specific occupational qualities, strategies and approaches to gain and improve operational effectiveness.

■ Decision-making

Decision-making is a constant and integral part of all managerial activities. All managers must therefore be able to take and make effective decisions and understand the processes involved in their implementation. Decisions are taken at strategic and policy level; operational level; and at lower levels concerned with the day-to-day administration and maintenance of group and departmental activities. However, at whichever level the decision is required, there are certain fundamental considerations that have to be made if the process is to be effective and successful. There are different stages which must be understood. If followed, this provides a model for all circumstances in which decisions have to be taken (see Figure 4.8). These are:

■ Problem definition

This may appear obvious but the effects and consequences of a particular course of action will not be fully understood if the issue in question is not accurately and fully defined at the outset. Failure to do this may lead to considerable waste of time and effort as well as resources, as mistakes may have to be rectified later.

■ Process determination

Much of this will depend on the culture of the organisation or department involved. This begs the questions that will have to be considered at the implementation stage of credibility, authority, acceptability and priority.

There is also the question of timescale (see below) to be considered: a long participative exercise at this stage is of value only if the deadline can accommodate it. Similarly, an autocratic or off-the-cuff decision may 'jump the gun' for lack of proper process or without full evaluation of the consequences or costs of following a particular line.

■ Timescale

As referred to above, this is involved heavily in the process determination. It also has implications in a trade-off between information, evaluation and cost. The longer you are able to leave the decision, the better your chances of gaining full or adequate information. However, this also increases the cost of the eventual course of action; again a quick decision may involve hidden extras at the implementation stage later.

It may also be possible to timetable the timescale element; if this is possible the risks involved become minimised if due to changing circumstances the proposed course of action is then either altered or cancelled.

■ Information gathering

The better the information on which it is based, the more effective the decision is likely to be. It is also vital to understand that very few decisions can be made with perfect information; especially when time constraints are involved or there is a prohibitive cost in gathering the information.

The quality of the information is also important and the quality of evaluation, sifting and editing processes are vital also. What those responsible for the

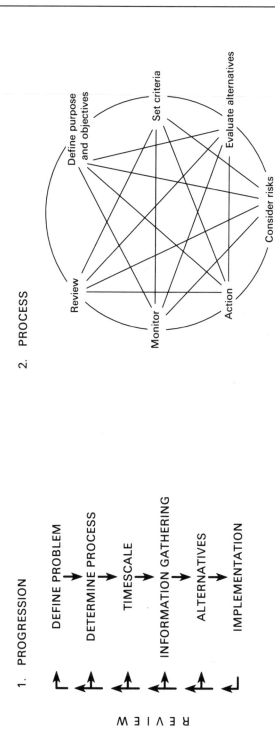

1. PROGRESSION

DEFINE PROBLEM

DETERMINE PROCESS

TIMESCALE

INFORMATION GATHERING

ALTERNATIVES

IMPLEMENTATION

REVIEW

2. PROCESS

Define purpose and objectives

Set criteria

Evaluate alternatives

Consider risks

Action

Monitor

Review

Purpose: to draw the distinction between the two elements of progression and process. The former is a schematic approach; the latter is that from which the former arises, and which refines it into its final format. Effective and successful decision-making requires the confidence that is generated by continued operation of the process.

Figure 4.8   A decision-making model

decision require is as full a compendium and information coverage as is possible on which to base their proposed courses of action. The gathering and evaluation of information therefore itself, requires planning.

■ The alternatives

These are always available – in any situation there is always the option of doing nothing. At this stage the consequences of not following proposed courses of action will also be evaluated. Having understood that, it is also necessary to fully evaluate all of the possible positive steps that are now open as a result of following the previous stages. Possible opportunities will now start to present themselves as well as costings and likely profits and losses, costs and benefits that will accrue.

■ Implementation

This is the point of action. This will be as a result of working through the previous stages of the model with the related implications and considerations.

The decision will in turn affect others and will probably need the assistance of others to carry it out. The action required may require further organisation and planning.

It follows from this that there are wider and more general organisational, environmental and political considerations at this stage; matters of general acceptability and feasibility must be considered.

More generally still, a decision may be taken and implemented on the basis of the intuition of the directorate or senior managers of an organisation, a feeling of what is the correct course of action in the circumstances. This may be in support of the rational model; or it may be in spite of it. Moreover, there may be matters of expediency or short-term advantage, which outweigh (or, at least, are perceived to outweigh) the rational approach. The incremental or progressive model of the decision tree (Figure 4.9) may be valuable here.

Any proposed course of action will have effects on others who should be prepared for this, particularly if there is an adverse element in the decision.

The process is not an end in itself. It will inevitably lead to other courses of action; the action in question must be fully evaluated for measures of success, failure, cost, profit, loss, effects and consequences.

This is a process that, if understood and followed, as fully as possible, minimises the risks and uncertainties of the resultant courses of action. It is not a prescription for the provision of perfect decisions; but rather a means by which both the opportunities and consequences of following particular courses of action and taking particular initiatives may be evaluated.

An incremental or progressive model for the taking of decisions and development of activities

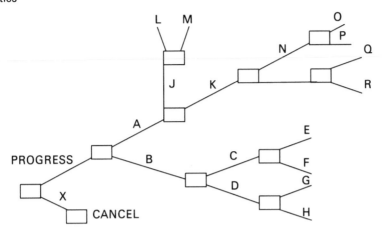

Purpose: to illustrate proposed courses of action, and likely and possible outcomes of them, from a given starting point.

In this particular example, option X – CANCEL – is evidently not on the agenda, as the consequences of this are not extrapolated.

What is illustrated are the ramifications that accrue once the decision is taken to progress; and assuming two positive choices (i.e. other than cancellation) at each stage.

The tree is a useful illumination of the complexity and implications of the process, and of the reality of taking one decision.

Figure 4.9   The decision tree

■ **External factors**

The general objective of anyone in the position of having to take a decision must be to minimise risks, uncertainties and negative consequences and to maximise the chances of success and effectiveness. This should not, and need not, be an excuse for inaction. Nor is inaction always possible. However, it is important to understand that wherever possible decisions should be taken that, if correct, maximise the benefits that are available and that if incorrect, minimise the loss or upheaval that results (see Summary Box 4.6).

□ **Risk and uncertainty**

Broadly speaking the difference between the two is that risk is measurable and insurable while uncertainty is not.

SUMMARY BOX 4.6   The Negative Decision

It is often hard to take this, particularly in relation to an employee request, project or brainchild.

The essence is therefore to keep the transaction both adult and business-oriented. An operational request should **never** be turned down for personal reasons.

1. It must be made clear to the individual that the decision has been well thought out, and is not arbitrary. It must be based on operational logic and soundness and communicated in this way.
2. The word 'NO' should be used, to underline the point.
3. The transaction should end in suggestion or direction towards the positive, and to alternatives, if these are feasible.

No manager should ever hide behind procedural issues or 'niceties of phrase' in such a situation. The employee is entitled to the respect and openness implicit in the above approach.

Broadly speaking also, there is an element of both in all decision-taking. It is reduced only by the quality of the information that is available and the quality of the evaluation of that information by managers. Everything else in the process militates against this. The risks must be recognised and assessed at the evaluation of alternatives stage. One is then able, at least, to understand fully a position whereby, for example, one course of action may lead to greater success with a greater risk of failure, in comparison with another which may guarantee a modicum of success only but minimise the failure should it go wrong. The manager is then in the position of making a judgement on the basis of the soundest information possible.

□ Committees

The success or failure of committees as decision-making bodies will depend to a great extent on the ways in which they work. Marketing and advertising firms, for example, use such groups as brainstorming and creativity groups to generate ideas which then may be fully evaluated at a later stage by groups of managers. On the other hand, public sector committees are very often almost entirely procedural.

The great disadvantages are those of time, cost, responsibility and compromise, particularly if they are dependent on procedures or if there are conflicting vested interests present. Often it is at this point that the 'no decision = no mistake' syndrome becomes evident. The committee consequently becomes a reactive and procedural establishment rather than one which is proactive and dynamic.

□ Broader participation and consultation

This can be most effective particularly when adverse decisions are to be taken. For example, if redundancies are proposed a package agreed between management and workforce is likely to be more acceptable than such a package imposed by management alone or by one manager. Similarly, proposed public developments are more likely to be acceptable if there has been full consultation with all of the members of the public concerned.

However, again there is a danger of a compromise that may fall short of the most basic criteria for success: rather than accepting a collective responsibility it becomes a vehicle for abdicating all responsibility.

At the last resort, however, the decision will ultimately fall on one person (manager, committee chair, or someone else so identified), whose responsibility it will be to undertake and manage the proposed course of action and to evaluate its success, failure and the opportunities and consequences generated by it. The final factor, therefore, in the decision-making process is commitment. There is no point in deciding to take a particular course of action if it cannot be seen through or if there is no collective will to so do. This should be dealt with at the evaluation of alternatives stage and will be one of the factors in such an exercise. With the increasing accountability required of managers, an understanding of decision-making is essential if the manager is going to be successful.

■ Decision-making: other factors

□ Limitations of laws and government direction

These represent national, local and social constraints and restraints. They must be evaluated by organisations to ensure that what is done is not only commercially viable, but also acceptable in the society in which it is to be carried out.

□ Public interest

Public interest is manifest through the general social ethos and consists of dominant public opinions, received wisdom and the activities of pressure groups. This includes such abstract values as freedom, respect for life, respect for the individual, telling the truth and helping the needy; and a more general concern for social values.

□ Eco–socio-political groups

These are more or less organised constituencies which organisations have to consider and which ultimately affect their decision-making activities and policies. They include consumer groups, environmental lobbies, local and public authorities, public agencies such as the health and safety executive, industrial lobbies and pressure groups formed by those whose environment is to be affected by the implementation of the particular decision. Some social values lack institutional voice or political muscle. Some social benefits are defeated by institutional deadlocks. Some powerful groups and lobbies do not represent the public interest. However, they all have voices which must be considered at this stage, and reconciled where necessary.

☐ Public factors

Public factors may also conflict, and frequently do so. Both business and public decisions must therefore take account of this and where necessary reconcile these matters. The decision-making process therefore still consists of the making of choices; in these cases, this also includes matters ethical and choices between the good and greater good of different public services.

☐ Internal factors

This is where the organisation considers those public factors in its internal decision processes and the social implications of its actions and the external groupings it effects as they relate to the staff of the organisation.

☐ External factors

This is where organisations open for discussion the public interests on which they are to impinge. This includes: trade association or trade union activity where there is a specific public interest; discussions with public bodies; discussions and dialogue with pressure groups and lobbies; and involvement in such activities as business in the community.

☐ Organisational adjustment

This is that part of the decision-making process whereby the organisation alters or adjusts its activities in some publicly collaborative way, or makes civic or environmental choices as part of its strategic approach.

There are costs as well as benefits. They include: the time spent in dealing with pressure groups and lobbies; the costs of getting information; costs and time spent on internal consultation and consideration; and the opportunity costs relating to the dovetailing of operational requirements with those of the environment.

There is thus a direct relationship between effective decision-making and the society and environment in which decisions are to be implemented. There are a series of factors that have to be taken into account to ensure that any decision taken is operable, effective and profitable and advantageous for the organisation as well as being acceptable in the environment in which it has to operate.

■ Consultation

Consultation is a behavioural and organisational process, the essential purpose of which is as follows:

1. To gain the commitment of the staff; this is only achievable if the proposal is communicated via all means at the disposal of the organisation and if adequate and full briefings, meetings and discussions are held (see Figure 4.10).
2. To ensure that everyone understands and values the necessity of what is being done. This must include coverage of the reasons and the timescale and progression.
3. To address the needs of groups of staff, and individuals. This includes matters concerning relocation, redeployment, retraining, redundancy, changes in operational or behavioural patterns and organisation expectations. It must also address the ability of staff to continue to get into work, and work their usual hours, and in their usual way. This may include individual counselling.
4. To use the period between the taking of the decision, and the date of its implementation to best operational and behavioural advantage so that, on the day on which the new practice is to start, the transition is made as smoothly as possible.

Consultation is therefore concerned with implementation and understanding. It should not dilute or affect what is to be done, unless the process of consultation itself throws up an operational barrier or caveat.

It may impact on all aspects of work, from major redundancy or relocation exercises, to the introduction of a smoking ban, or the implementation of a small job change on the part of an individual.

Consultation must be fair and reasonable. Normally, such a period will be for at least four weeks; this minimum will relate to relatively minor changes. For a major exercise – a relocation, for example – a period of up to a year may be necessary. A true balance must be struck between the pressures on the organisation and the needs of its staff.

Consultation is an active process, and one which must be led and directed by the organisation. It is not enough simply to give a period of notice of changes that are to happen. Responsibility for gaining the understanding, commitment and support of staff in such matters is an obligation placed on the organisation's top managers; and they must direct it and ensure that it happens in the ways indicated. Tannenbaum and Schmidt (1958) developed a model of how a manager may make a decision (see Figure 4.11) that repays study.

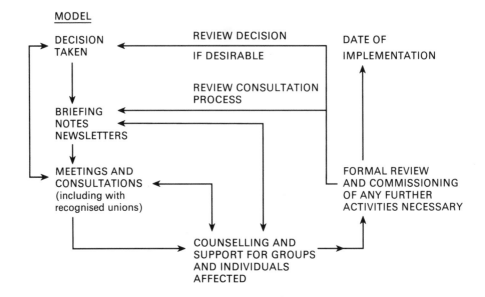

MODEL

To be used for: • strategic, directional, operational, technological and locational changes
              • behavioural and human relations issues
              • solving problems
              • introduction of no smoking, uniform, appraisal and representation policies.

Figure 4.10 Introducing a major or contentious issue: a managerial approach

■ Organisation and employee development

The purpose of studying the concepts of organisation development and the development of employees is part of the establishment of the extent of the organisation's total commitment to its workforce. Various attitudes, strategies and approaches may be adopted by organisations in this area.

The operational reasons for engaging in these activities are more direct, and range from the meeting of certain obligations to the staff to filling gaps in performance levels and to training the next generation of expert staff for the purposes of succession. Employee development activities may also be part of a wider approach to personnel and human resource issues – for example, if an organisation has difficulty in recruiting particular categories of staff, it may adopt a medium to long term strategy designed to produce its own; this in turn will require a steady commitment in this area.

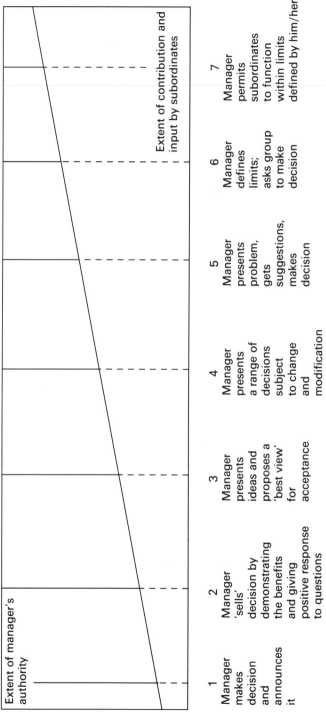

1	2	3	4	5	6	7
Manager makes decision and announces it	Manager 'sells' decision by demonstrating the benefits and giving positive response to questions	Manager presents ideas and proposes a 'best view' for acceptance	Manager presents a range of decisions subject to change and modification	Manager presents problem, gets suggestions, makes decision	Manager defines limits; asks group to make decision	Manager permits subordinates to function within limits defined by him/her

Extent of manager's authority

Extent of contribution and input by subordinates

Purpose: illustration of the autocratic–participative range that is available in organisational and managerial decision-making. It also provides a sound basis for forethought. Certain types of decision will be better understood, and accepted, it they are delivered in particular ways.

Figure 4.11 A decision-making model: the autocratic–participative range

Source: Tannenbaum and Schmidt (1958).

As with other activities, the stance to be adopted must be the subject of top-level deliberations and a strategic decision. From this, there emerges both the employee development strategy itself and also the priority ascribed to it relative to the other business activities.

There are differences in approach to employee development. Some organisations may and do take the view that they will purchase expert and highly qualified staff on the labour market and relegate in-house or organisation-sponsored development activities to a low priority. This is easily achieved when one is purchasing from a large pool of the required expertise; and feasible also when the organisation has sufficient purchasing power, reputation and job prospects to offer to those with rare expertise. In the latter case, however, there is the danger of getting into an auction for this type of expertise and the person attracted to one organisation by the stated combination of reward and prospects may be quickly attracted away by an even better package from another operator in the field.

All organisations should recognise that their staff require development in each of three areas in order to strike the balance between motivation, flexibility, opportunity and organisation purpose and investment:

- **Corporate**: engaging in development activities for the benefit of the continued and future stability and prosperity of the organisation
- **Professional**: in which the requirements to keep abreast of the developments of one's occupation and profession in general, and to be developed and trained in it, are paramount
- **Individual**: in which the organisation has regard for the development and future aspirations of the person concerned
- **General**: the enlargement of the pool of talent and potential available; the generation of positive, flexible and dynamic attitudes.

The balance of the four must be struck. While the organisation's overall purpose and first obligation is to its own aims and objectives, this must include consideration of the wider view. If concentration on the development of employees is limited to organisation needs, their opportunities are restricted to that organisation and there may be problems in moving or transferring them within a public service or divisionalised company.

Consideration must be given to all areas. For many professional, technical and managerial staff it is increasingly an obligation of their continued commitment to, and membership of, their occupational category.

■ Development strategies

Development strategies will therefore stem from the relative priority placed on these activities and, while reflecting this, they will cover the following matters, promulgating policies to the staff on the following:

- The **induction** of new staff and the formation of attitudes and the settling-in process; the initial job training, job understanding and job knowledge
- **Continuing job training** including the usage of the particular technologies, machines and processes that the organisation has available
- **Training and development for the future** over short, medium and long term; this may include career development and succession plans devised by the organisation in conjunction with key staff
- The solving of **problems** relating to human resource operations – performance gaps which cannot otherwise effectively be filled
- The gaining of **qualifications** – academic, professional, technical and vocational – both for the wider purposes of effective staff and organisation development and also because the existence of such qualifications is increasingly required if one is to gain contracted or project type work from multinational and public service internal markets and contracting arrangements
- General policies on the wider and more general aspects of **employee development**; this includes: devising and developing scope for project work; opportunities for secondments and out placements; short-term commissions and activities; and other one-off researches and activities
- There will also be in place general policies designed to reflect the extent to which the organisation will allow individual staff members to exercise their imagination, pursue brainwaves and notions and engage in other **creative** and **developmental** activities of their own and the extent to which the organisation will actively support, sponsor and resource these matters. The final element to be considered is the extent to which the organisation makes available, or restricts access to each, of these opportunities.

The style, language and availability of the employee development strategy and policy also reinforce its actual components and the overall message to the staff of the organisation. Anything that is shrouded in complex terms or highly bureaucratic language, for example, tends to reinforce the impression that the development of employees and the organisation has a low priority. At the other end of the spectrum some organisations both instruct and commit members of their staff to regular attendance on training and development courses and events as a central plank of their terms and conditions of employment. A variation on this is to take potentially qualifiable or part qualified staff into relatively junior positions and to support and sponsor them through their professional studies to full qualification. From the employee's point of view, it is the opportunity to learn the profession from both the theoretical and practical points of view that is to be gained from such an arrangement. They may also be placed in the position of being able to identify matches and mismatches between theory and practice; to gain practical experience of their field as well as a sound basis of knowledge and skills; and to impress upon the organisation the development of their expertise and to indicate both actual and potential qualities. They also receive support (in varying degrees) for the duration of these studies (see Summary Box 4.7).

This approach also extends to technical and vocational qualifications, and undertaking general development activities with an eye to the future. These approaches allow in-house assessment of potential in the specific terms of the

---

SUMMARY BOX 4.7   Professional Studies

There is a wide range of rewards and penalties available for success or failure in the pursuit of professional recognition and qualifications in the UK. From an analysis of a range of students taking the examinations of the Institute of Personnel and Development (IPD) in the South East of England over the period 1988–1994 the following emerged as features:

1. The greatest number of students were drawn from the public services and health service sectors; this was followed by department stores and the retail and distribution sector; and followed in turn by telecommunications, transport and manufacturing. Very few students were offered by hi-tech, mass production or flow production industries, which it seems would rather buy in staff already qualified in this field. Qualifications were becoming of increased importance in public services during the period in question (and beyond) due to the development of internal markets and purchaser provider arrangements.
2. Some students received full sponsorship for as long as it took them to achieve the qualifications (the normal period was 2 to 3 years); some organisations would quite happily keep putting their students forward for as many examination resits as necessary until the student succeeded.
   Other organisations insisted that the students paid their own fees; some reimbursed all or part of them upon successful completion of the courses, while others did not.
3. Some organisations gave students as much time off work as they needed, both in terms of release for classes and also for pre-examination revision. Others insisted that any time taken was either docked from annual leave or made up through flexible working arrangements.
4. Some organisations offered financial rewards and automatic upgrades upon successful completion. Other organisations made successful completion a condition of the continuing right to employment.

---

organisation itself and go a long way towards providing an effective background for the organisation's purpose in employee development.

Some organisations go much further than this, and will sponsor their staff through any course or development activity that the member of staff wishes to undertake.

These organisations take the view that by doing this they are generating expertise, identifying and developing potential and adding to the fund of organisational talent and capacity. It is also cited as being excellent for motivation, morale and retention and part of the payback on the investment is measurable in these terms.

■ Performance appraisal

Any effective approach to organisation and staff development must have as its cornerstone an effective process of appraisal. This will have the purposes of assessing and evaluating past and current development activities and also make a contribution to the future. Performance appraisal at its ideal is a continuing, consultative and participative process conducted jointly by superior and subordinate, that assesses both strengths and weaknesses of current and recent performance and the expectations and aspirations for the future. The process establishes where performance gaps lie and opportunities for progress or solutions based on the development and training of the employee. This process must be the subject of regular meetings and review between employer and employee as a check on progress and as part of the more general approach of development of the employee and the organisation.

The development process and function will ascribe particular obligations and duties in the area to all staff. Part of the function of managers and supervisors will be in the wider sphere of the employees' development – monitoring the employees' progress, coaching and counselling, offering opportunities, propounding solutions to problems, agreeing these, testing and monitoring their implementation. Employees (or certain categories of them) may be required to undergo and accept training and development as part of their commitment to the organisation. Related to this are general departmental obligations to provide the job training necessary to conduct the tasks effectively; complex departments and process functions often have trained instructors working full or part time on these activities.

In devising and implementation these activities, organisations adopt a variety of overall roles in the development of their employees:

- **Administration of training and development activities**: the keeping of records; certification and validation of completion where appropriate; the planning, organising and booking of courses; the promulgation of information
- **The practitioner role**: concerned with the design and delivery of courses (usually in-house); assessment and identification of performance gaps and training needs; the setting of training and development objectives and the monitoring and evaluation of the activities carried out
- **The advisory, expert and consultant roles**: carrying out these duties in relation both to the organisation's directorate and also to the individual divisions, functions, operations, departments and units
- **Resource-gathering roles**: ensuring that any funds or finances that are on offer are gathered in and made available, together with any relevant or suitable public programmes, grants or disbursements
- **Resource management roles**: concerning the volume, usage and allocation of organisational resources in the area; this impinges upon all the other activities detailed here.

It is a complex and wide ranging function, set of roles and mutual obligations. Effectively constituted, the development of the organisation and its employees is instrumental in setting standards of attitudes, values, beliefs and expectations as well as performance. Such development sets specific training standards for jobs and quality. It is the driving force behind the training and development of all staff for both the present and the future. It is also instrumental in setting general standards of motivation and morale among staff.

■ Employee development concepts

In order to complete this view, some fundamental concepts must now be addressed and articulated.

□ Learning style

This is the way in which an individual learns; the preferred learning style is the way in which the person learns best. The learning style is composed of a combination of motivational factors, individual preferences and overall aspirations. It must also reflect the desired material, skills, knowledge, attitudes and behaviour. For example, the individual who does not take to formal instruction may well be prepared to put up with it in the interest of passing the driving test, for which formal instruction is an integral necessity and thus the means to the wider end.

Other factors that have to be considered here are the age, experience and prior qualifications of the trainees; their expectations; and the degree of comfort or anxiety that they feel at the outset of the activities; and the nature of the activities that are to be undertaken.

Work was carried out at the Manchester Business School by Professor Peter Honey in the early 1980s, and four archetype preferred learning styles were identified:

1. **Activists**: who involve themselves fully in new experiences; who are open-minded; and who are fully active both at work and elsewhere; they thrive on the challenge of new experiences but become bored when these become familiar and start to look elsewhere again
2. **Reflectors**: who ponder and reflect on experiences from a wide variety of standpoints; they are thoughtful, meticulous, methodical and cautious
3. **Theorists**: who adapt and integrate disparate facts, theories, observations and experiences and draw coherent conclusions from them; they are keen on principles, models, systems and assumptions; they are uncomfortable with subjective, creative and unproven approaches
4. **Pragmatists**: they measure the success or otherwise of something by the extent to which it works; their approach to a proposal or idea is to put it into practice and to test it; they are essentially practical and problem-orientated; they like to get to the heart of issues and matters and resolve them quickly.

Honey devised a questionnaire to be issued to students at the outset of development activities that had the purpose of assessing their individual balance of each of the four preferred learning styles. Such a basic understanding is useful for a variety of reasons. It enables individuals to form an impression of their own preferred learning style. It enables them to identify the sorts of activities that they are likely to respond to most easily, and those that they are likely to have great difficulty for them. It enables them to identify gaps in their overall learning style and to take steps to develop it in order to respond better to and to gain more from the full range of development activities. It enables course and activity tutors to identify those activities that are likely to hold the greatest and least attraction and benefit for those on courses.

For those who design and implement activities and programmes, a knowledge of this concept is invaluable because it enables assessment of the range of general responses and likely specific responses to be made. Programmes can therefore be designed to fit a particular style (for example, fully participative; or lecture based); or to develop a wider learning style for the student body; or (where it is a general or generic programme) to ensure that the full range of learning styles is addressed.

Appreciation of the concept is also useful for the general manager in that an insight is given as to the possible reasons for the success or failure of particular development activities and courses. It also enables the generalists to make a more informed assessment of the kinds of activities that are likely to draw different measures of success or failure in the future.

☐ Learning curve

This is a configuration of the speed at which people learn things. For simple operations it may be very quick and the curve therefore very steep: for more complex activities a step-by-step approach may be required and the curve will reflect this. Learning plateaux and learning declines may also be identified; the plateaux indicate the present saturation of the trainees, implying that activities should be varied at this point; while declines in the learning curve normally point to one of two matters – either that the learning itself was not effective and is being quickly forgotten or that what has been learned is declining because of the lack of opportunity to follow it up and practise it at the workplace.

Organisations are thus influenced by the approaches taken and by implication the adequacy and effectiveness of the resources ascribed.

☐ Continuous professional development

Continuous professional development (CPD) is the term given in the UK to the obligation placed upon highly skilled, technical or other practitioners to keep themselves abreast of all developments in their chosen field.

It is more highly developed in some areas than others. Part of the practice of medicine (and this applies to the entire range of medical practitioners including nurses, midwives, physiotherapists and radiographers) is concerned with pioneering, testing and developing new methods, drugs, techniques and forms of treatment. This is mirrored in the public's expectations that when they do need medical treatment, they will receive something which is up-to-date, giving them the best possible chance of recovery and return to their usual life.

In the business and management sphere the importance of CPD is becoming ever-more apparent. As the trade of management becomes ever-more professionalised and organised, education, training and professional bodies in the field are both taking extensive trouble to fulfil this requirement for CPD and also insisting that persons attached to them undertake CPD as a condition of their continuing membership or ability to practise. CPD is also a reflection of the acquisition and understanding of techniques and aptitudes and attitudes and values from the entire business world. It further underlines, finally, how essential it is to have high-quality, current and expert management and managers in all organisations.

■ Organisation development

Organisation development (OD) is the generic term given to strategies and initiatives for improving organisational effectiveness through emphases on the capabilities, capacities and qualities of the human resource, and on approaches based on behavioural sciences (see Summary Box 4.8).

OD stems from a corporate commitment to 'doing things this way'. It is an organisation-wide process and endemic and integral to all activities that go on within it. It depends for success on its adoption and absorption across the board in all departments and functions and by everyone at the workplace.

OD depends on the development of staff for commercial success or service quality advancement. It follows from this that there are roles for change mechanisms, change agents and change catalysts and key appointments with key qualities, as well as training and development activities in order to take the organisation in the preferred directions.

The OD process is aimed at changing, forming and developing culture, values, attitudes and beliefs in positive and constructive ways.

The precise nature of the process will vary between organisations that adopt OD as a strategy. In general, the key values and qualities reflect: a measure of

---

SUMMARY BOX 4.8   OD Concepts

Other terms used in the conceptualisation of OD include:

- Continuous development
- Total quality management
- The learning culture
- The learning spectrum
- The learning organisation.

Also any organisation that seeks to offer personal development and learning contracts, accelerated promotion paths and fast tracks, succession planning and an approach designed to grow its own experts and managers must have an active interest in, and commitment to, the overall OD approach.

conformity and the willingness of staff to go down the paths indicated (those that do not must usually either come into line and at least conform, or else leave); obsession with product or service quality; a strong customer orientation; universal identity with the organisation at large on the part of all staff; setting a moral or value-led example and taking an active pride in the organisation and its works on the part of all concerned.

The OD process requires expertise and commitment in its component parts. These are: performance, assessment and appraisal; problem-raising and acknowledgement; openness, honesty, trust; access to information; inter-group activities and cross-fertilisation of ideas; organisation, assessment and evaluation of the development process.

There will be a framework around the OD aspects and activities at corporate, department, divisional, team, group and individual levels (see Figure 4.12). This involves the setting of aims and objectives; devising processes, approaches and strategies; addressing problems and issues; setting timescales and deadlines; and establishing means of implementation, review and evaluation of activities. Alongside this there must be constant process consultation, and attitude, culture and value development activities.

The benefits to be realised are as follows:

- Organisations gain a high level of **commitment**, a strong sense of identity and purpose that rises above any divergent individual aims and objectives
- Organisations set their own **agenda**, **style** and **values** rather than allowing these to emerge
- OD promotes understanding, effective communications and generates a continuing high level of motivation; it promotes harmony between normally or traditionally divergent business and sectoral or functional interests; it promotes **organisation synergy**
- OD provides **niche openings** and opportunities along the way that arise because of the overall approach
- OD generates opportunities for behavioural, structural, role and functional **development** on the part of all concerned, all functions and all departments
- OD promotes and generates a **creative and positive environment** for the approach to, and solution of, problems and blockages
- OD and the techniques related to it work effectively only where there is full corporate commitment. OD is above all a business and managerial philosophy. It is not an adjunct or set of activities to be picked up and put down. It is both a manifestation of, and developer of, the organisation's culture and beliefs. It requires a full level of understanding on the part of everyone in the organisation. There is inherent in OD a universal overall purpose that solves problems and addresses issues from the point of view of the organisation itself, and this is the focus that must be adopted at the outset and to which commitment must be made. Figure 4.13 shows in summary form the criteria for effective, training, development and learning.

All training and development activities should satisfy some of these. The more comprehensive the coverage the more likely it is that effective training will take place. As far as possible such criteria should be pre-stated, reflecting the aims and objectives of the activities under consideration.

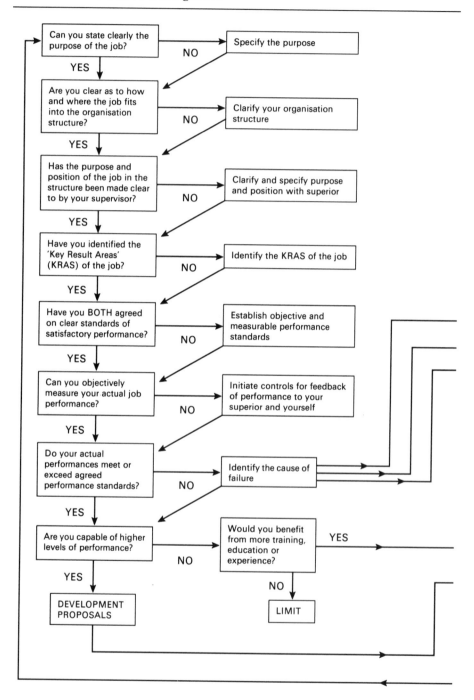

Figure 4.12   Model of the organisation and individual assessment process

Figure 4.12 (continued)

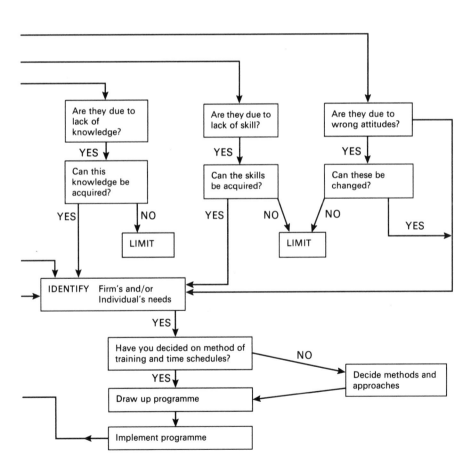

1. Clearly stated aims and objectives and measures of success/failure
2. Motivation of both trainers and trainees
3. Rewards must be perceived or available
4. Benefits in performance terms must be perceived
5. The satisfaction of personal, professional and organisational objectives
6. Training and development must be reinforced at the workplace
7. It must be current and relevant
8. It must have organisational and managerial support
9. It must be planned and planned for
10. It must have priority and importance at the time it takes place
11. It must be part of a total package
12. It must be part of a process
13. It must be evaluated afterwards at regular intervals
14. It must acknowledge preferred learning styles
15. It must meet expectations.

Figure 4.13   Criteria for effective training, development and learning to take place: individual and organisational

■ Conclusions and summary

As stated at the outset, the overall purpose of this chapter has been to introduce and illustrate the concepts and complexities that must be understood as a sound basis for effective management of organisations.

The management of organisations is itself a process. It changes and develops as the organisation itself and its culture, structure and systems evolve and develop. This has implications for the nature and design of both structure and systems that are appropriate and effective to the matters in hand at a given time; they must be flexible and dynamic also in order that changes and developments may be accommodated.

Inherent in this therefore is the necessity to ensure that processes and systems of continuous monitoring and review are present. These address a complexity of matters. Part of their function is concerned with the system of maintenance already referred to; part also to the employee and OD processes. However, they will also be concerned with ensuring the continued effectiveness of, and improvement in, processes of communication and decision-making; and in the maintenance of structure and systems and ensuring their continued effectiveness and suitability.

All of this, in turn, impinges upon the nature, culture and spirit of the organisation. Developments in these related areas in turn develop the prevailing culture, modifying its beliefs and values. This must continue during the process of development to serve the needs of the organisation and its staff and to continue to reflect the nature of activities required if effective business is to be conducted.

The concern of managers with the nature of the organisation in which they find themselves is therefore a fundamental part of the job and integral to any functional or operational success. For, as we shall see, the nature of the organisation in question must be considered if an effective overall management style is to be achieved; if effective and successful functional activities and divisions are to be devised and structured; and if the production and operation's functions are to be both profitable and harmonious.

Summary Box 4.9 tabulates the material and opportunities available in developing organisations and employees.

SUMMARY BOX 4.9   Training Methods and Techniques

- **Classroom:** Lectures, talks, seminars, day-release, block-release, full time study. These are good for demonstrating expectations, cultural soundness and giving regular information and updates. They are limited by spans of attention, the suitability of the material to be delivered in the classroom, the size and composition of the classes themselves and the capacities and capabilities of the teacher.

- **Laboratory and workshop:** For the development of precise, practical and scientific skills and the ability to practise or apply them in safe situations, often having the performance marked or analysed by tutors or observers against the levels and standards of required performance or capability. Limited by group size and the capability of the tutor and observer.

- **Projects:** For the dual purpose of solving a problem and developing the capabilities and experience of the project officer. Limited by the scale and scope of the project and the capability, interest and commitment of the person supervising it.

- **Secondments:** For the dual purpose of developing and broadening the experience of staff and to ensure a regular supply of fresh ideas into different organisational activities and departments. Must be an integral part of the day-to-day operation to be successful or profitable. For the members of staff it should be linked to other activities, skills development and projects with clear targets and objectives.

- **Competencies training:** Specifically targeted at the 'can do' elements of work. Course objectives and, latterly, both vocational and management programmes have been written in this way to refocus and represent the approach to these areas of training and development activity.

- **Open and distance learning:** Whereby the student is given a framework or objectives to work to and sets his/her own agenda, timetable, goals and learning methods within the programme. This is limited above all by the student's own preferred learning style and the quality of support available from the learning provider. Many professions and occupations that aspire to professional status currently require extensive open and self-regulated study.

- **Computer-aided learning**
  Useful in both technical and managerial areas, especially in the areas of decision-making, design, systems operations, and 'what if' type scenario evaluation.

- **Mentoring:**
  Coaching, counselling and other one-to-one relationships with key employees for the purpose of developing them into very high performers. It is extremely time and resource consuming. It requires expertise on the part of the coach, counsellor or mentor; it also requires priority and a long term overall commitment on the part of the organisation to the development of its top quality staff. The candidates must understand the extent of their commitment and have part of their work time blocked off for the purpose of maximising this activity.

- **Role plays, case studies**
  These give the opportunity either to generate a measure of reality or to consider a version of it with a view to recognising, observing and analysing particular behaviour and/or activities. The effective use of each method requires pre-planning, pre-stated purposes and a full measure of evaluation assessment and debrief. Roles may also be reinforced through the use of CCTV for more accurate analysis of behaviour; and of 'what happened next' for greater illumination of deliberations during the course of the activities and the conclusions drawn. Role plays are best used in the generation and development of particular skills, aptitudes and awareness and are also the opportunity for the exploration of related techniques in a challenging but ultimately safe situation.

- **Outward bound:**
  With precise organisation and/or operational purposes defined; generally perceived to be of greatest value in the assessment and development of leadership, strategic and operational characteristics; and in the formation of confidence, trust and mutuality in work groups and teams.

- **Skills updates:**
  These may be technical, for example computer software or managerial; or on leadership, presentation skills and decision-making ability. They depend largely on the calibre of the delegates and their ability to practise what they have learned when they return to work.

- **High-cost seminars and and professional association programmes:**
  The approach in these cases is very different but the end result is often the same, the creation of a forum where persons from similar occupations or organisations can meet and exchange ideas supported by a modicum of structured input, for example from experts in the particular field.

Summary: there is thus a great range of material and opportunities available to all those concerned with the development of organisations and employees. All methods used should relate to the matters in hand, performance gaps and development requirements, and should be viewed as part of a process to be built on and developed in the future (rather than as ends in themselves). The obligations of the organisation, learners and teachers, vary in each situation. The responsibility does not – this remains always with the organisation and teacher.

CHAPTER 5

Strategy

■ Introduction

The overall purpose of strategy is to guide and direct the inception, growth and change of organisations as they conduct their activities. The purpose of this chapter is an introduction to the essentials of corporate policy and strategy; the form that it takes in different types of companies; the variations in strategy between companies, public services and other sectors; the issues involved in devising policy and strategy; and the development, implementation and evaluation of policy and strategy.

A clearly articulated, accurate and understood strategy is at the hub of all successful commercial and public activities; where success is not forthcoming it is often where this clarity of purpose is also not present. Specifically the need for strategy is based upon the overall requirement to manage resources effectively and efficiently. This process has been intensified by requirements for greater accountability in both public and private sectors. There is also a growing realisation among those responsible for directing organisations that these resources must be coordinated and controlled towards agreed policy objectives. Organisations also need to plan ahead in order to ensure that they understand their required direction and are working towards it. Finally, an articulation of strategy is necessary also so that the employees of the organisation know the purpose to which their efforts are being directed.

Corporate strategy is based upon a series and pattern of decisions that determine the organisation's aims, objectives and goals; that produce the plans and policies required to ensure that these are achieved; that define the business in which the organisation is to operate; and how it intends to conduct this business and what its relations with its markets, customers, staff, stakeholders and environment will be.

Operational policies are based on the choices made within the overall strategic view. They are based upon a continuous appraisal of current and potential markets and spheres of activity; the ability to acquire, mobilise and harmonise resources for the attainment of the given aims, objectives and goals; and the actual means of conduct, including philosophical and ethical standpoints and the meeting of wider social expectations.

The focusing and determination of corporate strategy, policy and objectives is a process designed to ensure that the organisation knows why it exists; its strengths and weaknesses; its position in its markets or service sectors is; what it can do and what it should do; what it cannot do and what it should not do; and what its structure and style are to be in order to be an effective and profitable operator in its sector. Ideally, the policies and strategy of the organisation should have relevance to, and be understood by, all its employees. This is essential if individual, group and departmental goals and objectives are to be reconciled with the overall purpose. It is also, as stated above, much better for morale, commitment and the formation of positive attitudes and identity among all staff if they know how their own particular contribution is to fit into the overall scheme of things.

Policies and strategy must also address fundamental operational issues of relevance both in the immediate term and in order to ensure continuity into the future. These are as follows:

- The level of finance and capital required in order for the operation to be established and maintained successfully
- The levels of income, surplus and profit that the organisation needs to make and wishes to make
- The structure of the organisation that is appropriate for those operations to be carried out
- The management style that is to be adopted and the style of leadership, direction and supervision
- The priorities that are to be placed on each of the operations; the markets and sectors in which business is to be conducted.

Figure 5.1 models the sources and development of organisation strategy: Figure 5.2 shows the stages in the strategic planning process.

■ Public policy

Effective public policy is also based on these principles. However, the complexities of this emerge in different ways, and the corner-stone is the reconciliation of the range of matters that are both divergent and conflicting in the area of public policy.

There is the need to provide services for the parts of the community designated as having particular needs and wants. There is the need on the part of politicians to give energy to public policy to meet manifesto commitments, and to reconcile these with keeping taxes down and ensuring the maximum efficiency of public expenditure. Resources have to be targeted at the desired groups in order to maximise their effect. There are also matters of expediency to be considered, such as high-profile success stories. Politicians also have their own aims and objectives to achieve. Consideration must be given to the wider community in which these activities are carried out, and the extent of public acceptance, sympathy and cooperation that is present. The general sympathy in which the particular initiatives are held, the true nature of the demands on the public purse, and the extent to which these are desirable and reconcilable must also be considered. Resources have to be monitored; this is carried out by appointed officials, professionally trained, at the request of politicians.

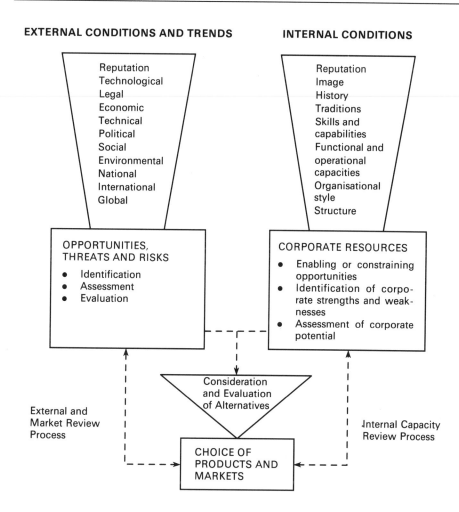

EXTERNAL CONDITIONS AND TRENDS   INTERNAL CONDITIONS

Reputation
Technological
Legal
Economic
Technical
Political
Social
Environmental
National
International
Global

Reputation
Image
History
Traditions
Skills and
capabilities
Functional and
operational
capacities
Organisational
style
Structure

OPPORTUNITIES,
THREATS AND RISKS

- Identification
- Assessment
- Evaluation

CORPORATE RESOURCES

- Enabling or constraining opportunities
- Identification of corporate strengths and weaknesses
- Assessment of corporate potential

Consideration
and Evaluation
of Alternatives

External and
Market Review
Process

Internal Capacity
Review Process

CHOICE OF
PRODUCTS AND
MARKETS

Figure 5.1   Source and development of organisation strategy

Any government has then to reconcile resource constraints with its own perception of what constitutes both the public interest and the national interest, and do this in relation to its own stated aims, objectives and philosophies (if it has any). It has to do this in the almost certain knowledge that there are more demands on public resources than there are resources themselves, and that the demands on these have to be scaled down, ordered and prioritised in the daily operation of public services. For the public sector therefore, municipal, local and national government initiatives translate resources into what becomes the

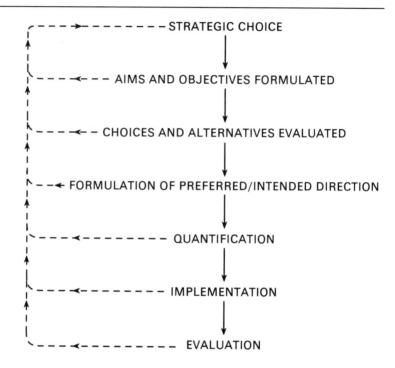

Purpose: the translation of strategy into direction and activity

Figure 5.2   The planning process

designated level of service to be provided and the amounts of finance to be allocated. Structure and style often include the creation of management committees and boards of governors to ensure that what is done, is conducted in accordance with the given objectives of the service concerned.

■ Development of strategy

At this stage there are four basic matters that have to be addressed, whatever the nature of the organisation and its products or services:

- The **true nature** of the product or service, the functions that it serves, could or should serve; how it could be adopted, adapted, extended or improved
- The organisation's main **strengths** and **weaknesses**, whether there are any overriding or dominant strengths or weaknesses; and what the main strengths and weaknesses of the organisation's competitors are
- The **demands** of the customer group for the sectors of society that are to be served

- The **opportunities** and **threats** that exist; the risks and uncertainties that can be identified; and the scope there is for improving the position of the organisation in its markets.

Consideration will also be given to other wider factors – social, economic, political, technological and ethical – that need, or may need, to be taken into account; and the extent to which the organisation is at the mercy of factors that it cannot control.

By way of completion of this section, however, there is a caveat. Most of what has been discussed so far indicates an all-pervasive scientific and rational approach to the conception and formulation of strategy. In reality, there is invariably a strong non-scientific, non-rational element in the devising and evolution of strategy, that either limits the rational, or works against it, or indeed, enhances it.

Consideration must therefore be given first to matters of expediency (the need for a top manager or politico to have a 'triumph' for example); and political, social and environmental acceptability (motorway and airport schemes usually have an unanswerable economic imperative, but are entirely unacceptable in their 'perfect' form to the location required for them). A proposal may also come from a key employee, power player, or over-mighty subject – the organisation may not have the backbone to turn it down, whether it is a good idea or not. Related to this may be waves of inspiration or intuition on the part of top, key or powerful employees, again resulting in the organisation following directions other than those indicated by the rational approach.

The final element of this is to recognise that even if the strategy is rationally devised it may not be possible to control the environment in which it is to be executed. A business loan taken out at a base interest rate of 5%, for example, may be very attractive; however, if the interest rate is variable, and government policy pushes it up to 15%, the loan becomes a burden in normal circumstances. Airline timetables are published giving precise departures and arrivals; in reality they are operable only at the 'whim' (if that is the right word) of the weather!

Thus, the beginning of the strategic and policy formulation process requires a full consideration of the whole sphere of the activities of the organisation from the full variety of different standpoints. The relationship between purpose (strategy) and activities (operations) requires constant attention, and active management.

Consider Summary Boxes 5.1 and 5.2.

■ Internal strategies and policies

In order to achieve all this, organisations will devise related and integrated strategies, and policies and plans for their implementation, that cover all aspects of the operations devised to fulfil the overall strategy.

The following must be covered:

SUMMARY BOX 5.1   The Health Sector

Strategic standpoints adopted by the different players in the health sector are very different. However, their core purpose derives from the same basic human desire – that of 'getting better'.

Emergency services rescue sick and injured people from the scene of their illness or accident. They take them to hospital and arrange for them to be treated. This may or may not be free at the point of delivery; and may or may not be offered as part of the nation's obligation and commitment to its people.

In the UK the National Health Service (NHS) originally sought through a means of generic national insurance to provide a comprehensive and universal health and welfare care to all citizens, again free at the point of delivery.

Insurance companies, private hospitals and patient plans offer a range of health care that is designed in general to diagnose, treat and comfort a series of ailments that is either not available on a welfare or public basis, or which is so available but at the cost of waiting.

Some private clinics also provide treatments in response to civilisational expectations or perceptions, such as fat reduction, wrinkle removal and body contouring.

Each is a particular response to the needs and wants of particular sectors of the public. This may be articulated as: the ability to have any sickness, injury and ailment diagnosed and treated quickly and accurately so that the person concerned is restored to full and active health.

Any operator who aspires to work in this sector must therefore understand this; and the niche operators such as cosmetic surgeries keep this at the forefront all the time. For larger and more complex organisations and activities in such a fundamental sphere of activity it is very easy to lose sight of this core purpose.

SUMMARY BOX 5.2   McDonald's

The strategic corner-stone of McDonald's is this: wherever in the world you find a McDonald's restaurant you are assured of the same quality of product, packaging, service and cleanliness.

The restaurants have a distinctive ambience and design. This has the overall purpose of engendering familiarity, reinforcing the general message. They are comfortable and functional; suitable both for the customer to sit and enjoy his meal and also to be made and kept clean and tidy. The average length of stay of the McDonald's customer is about 15 minutes and the facilities reflect this; the emphasis balances throughput with a level of comfort commensurate with the length of stay.

There is a core range of products offered, though these do vary at the periphery (for example, there is a much greater emphasis on salad bars in North America than Europe). Again this reinforces the message of confidence and familiarity. The company now has outlets in more than half of the countries of the world, all designed and presented in this way and with this core range of products.

The strategy delivers 'the McDonald's promise'. This is a universal content and quality of product together with this concept of familiarity in which the customer may have absolute confidence wherever in the world he chooses his product.

- **Financial, investment, budgeting and resourcing** strategies, concerned with both the underwriting and stability of the organisation, and also the maintenance of its daily activities
- **Human resource** strategies designed to match the workforce and its capabilities with the operational requirements of the organisation; and related policies on ensuring the supply of labour; effective labour relations; and the maintenance and development of the resource overall
- **Marketing** strategies, designed to ensure that the organisation's products and services are presented in such ways as to give them the best possible impact and prospects of success on the chosen markets
- **Capital resource and equipment** strategies, to ensure the continued ability to produce the required value and quality of output, to the standards required by the markets; and to be able to replace and update these resources in a planned and ordered fashion (i.e. including research and development and commissioning of new products and offerings)
- **Communication and information** strategies, both for the organisation's staff and its customers/clients, designed to disseminate the right quantity and quality of information in ways acceptable to all
- **Organisation, maintenance, development and change** strategies, for the purpose of ensuring that a dynamic and proactive environment is fostered; a flexible and responsive workforce; and an environment of continuous improvement and innovation.

■ Vision

Vision is the 'shining light' of the organisation. Vision gives a focus to which everyone concerned can subscribe and aspire, and with which they can identify. It normally arises from the imagination, passion, commitment and originality of those who establish the organisation in the first place, and is translated by the others working in it into the operations that are carried out. It is their view of the world as it could and should be.

It is manifest in many ways, chief of which are the 'values' or 'shared values' of the organisation; elsewhere, these may be defined as 'mission statements' or 'core values'.

A vision must clearly always be positive and accurate, reflecting the highest and true aspirations of the organisation. In particular, staff and customers will identify more closely with the organisation, its products and services, where vision is evident.

Vision is the articulation of a clarity of purpose and direction of the organisation. While most business and organisational leaders and managers are not 'visionaries', the most successful have a clear idea of both the purpose of their organisation, and the directions it is to take in its fulfilment.

Vision is present always in profitable and successful organisations. The International Management Group (IMG), for example, is renowned for the great loyalty of its staff both to the organisation, and to Mark McCormack, the group's creator and founder. Part of the reason that companies such as Sony, Nissan, Canon, IBM and McDonald's run extensive and intensive orientation programmes is to ensure that all their staff subscribe to, and adopt, the organisation's vision of itself in its business.

This is also true in the best public services; again, these are most effective where the persons concerned are sure of the purpose of their part of the service. In the drive to create commitment and improve effectiveness in local government and municipal services in the UK, Europe and North America, public bodies have attempted to articulate this vision to give a measure of focus and identity to both the staff and the community in which they operate. This must increase as such organisations become less protected (as in the UK), and as the services that they carry out are increasingly put out to tender or privatised (a near-universal feature of the 1990s).

■ Core and peripheral activities

■ Core activities

Core activities reflect the organisation's central reason for being. They are the critical part of the organisation's activities, the part without which it would not, or could not, exist. This may be in terms of:

- **volume of activity**: what most people do, or what most resources are tied up in
- **profit and income**: where most of the money comes in from
- **image and identity**: that which gives the organisation its position, status and prominence in the sphere in which it operates.

This has been called 'sticking to the knitting' (Peters); and provided that this is seen in the context of identifying accurately what the 'knitting' truly is, it is as good a definition as any.

Core business also translates into a public sector equivalent – 'core service', in which the central service requirements are identified. This part of the strategic process is successful where each is clear; where the core business, core activity or core service is accurately identified; and where everyone understands what this is, and is committed to it. Consider Summary Box 5.3.

There is a critical relationship to be identified between the organisation type and the core activities undertaken. This is the key to the long-term success of the undertaking, and the way in which it is to be carried out. The structure, shared values, style and strategy must reflect the **core** activities; peripheral activities should be limited to those that this manifestation can support.

■ Peripheral activities

These are the other activities in which the undertaking gets involved. They must not be at the expense of the main or core activities, nor should they be a drain on

---

SUMMARY BOX 5.3   The NHS Reforms

One of the reasons that there have been problems with the UK NHS reforms in the 1990s is that the core purpose and activities of the 'new' service have not been made clear. There is confusion over the range of services to be provided; the priority of these services; the particular types of operations to be carried out; and the nature of the total service to be offered, and to whom.

The problems have been compounded by overwhelming political drives, the proliferation of managerial hierarchies, the generation of administrative super-structures, the introduction of complex procedures, often at odds with those already operating, and the pursuit of the politically expedient by strategically irrelevant 'red-herrings', the chief of which is 'cost per patient'. None of these contributes to the strategic purpose of the service. Each is destructive to the quality of the service, consuming resources that could be used for the treatment of more patients, more quickly, and to higher standards of medical practice.

At no stage during the reforms has the service addressed the question of where its core activity lies. Nor does it have as a priority the promotion of health and the avoidance of hospitalisation.

Only as hospitals (in particular the 'Trust' hospitals) resolve these matters, as they identify what their 'core activities' actually are, will they take steps towards becoming effective operators and service offerers.

---

resources. Rather they should enhance the core activities, or reflect niche or segment opportunities that exist as the result of the core business.

Such activities will nevertheless be essential, expected, and extremely profitable. A hospital is not 'in business' to sell food, sweets, newspapers, books, cards, fruit and flowers; nevertheless it is essential for a variety of operational and social reasons that these activities be undertaken.

Similarly, a car company will invariably make additional parts for the replacement, service and spares sectors; these simply require some form of repackaging or 'differentiation' to generate additional business, in an obvious and profitable area of activity.

■ Risk

The purpose of identifying and studying the components and elements of risk and uncertainty from a strategic point of view is to ensure that anyone in a managerial or executive position understands the full range of issues that must be considered for any situation, in the devising and implementation of strategy, and in the management of operations.

In straightforward and familiar situations this will be a simple process and easily carried out. Otherwise, it requires a full recognition and assessment of a variety of factors:

1. **Sectoral trends**: whether growing or declining, either in size or prosperity; whether this is likely to continue. Factors that are affecting this at present; are likely to affect it in the future; and could possible or remotely affect it.
2. **Substitutes**: what else people could buy or do as an alternative to their current set of activities; what else they might buy or sell or make; where else they might locate.
3. **Social, political and economic issues**: these have become extremely important over the current period. Over this time, the whole range of positive and negative external factors has been brought into play. This also includes ethical and environmental considerations, and the realignment of more fundamental values. The question of doing something (or not) because it is socially acceptable (or unacceptable) is currently an issue for the first time for many years.
4. **Strategic aspects**: relative to the organisation's position in its sector; its preferred direction; its size; its ability to dominate or take control of its niches; the balance of its proactive, steady state, responsive, and crisis activities.
5. **Operational aspects**: in relation to precise goals and objectives especially over the short and medium term, and again having regard to the balance of proactive, steady state, responsive, and crisis activities. This also has regard to levels of resources, staffing, skills and capabilities, available and required, and projections and prognoses of these for the future.
6. **The constitution of the organisation**: its directorate, executive and management. The style and attitude and capability of these, and the extent to which they are stable or changing, or open to reform or takeover, must also be taken into account. This is especially true at present of civil, health and public utilities and services in the UK, which are increasingly subject to privatisation and a profit motive, as well as service delivery.
7. Identification of the **critical requirements of success** of the operation: this is truly dependent upon the executive capabilities of the managers and directors involved in projects. Above all, this part of the process requires a full consideration of the questions: 'What can possibly go wrong?' and 'What is the single most important factor for success?'
8. A **monitoring and evaluating and projection process** that covers the following:

    *   Identification of the best, medium and worst outcomes
    *   Analysis of any critical path or critical incident
    *   Ability to extricate oneself from the situation (or not) and the consequences of this
    *   Assessment of the full range of cost and benefits.

9. Factors **outside the control** of the organisation and its managers.
10. **Behavioural and perceptual issues**: the extent of these in the organisation; their nature; and their influence on strategy and operations.

Within this broad and managerial frame, quantitative, statistical and mathematical approaches may be used to project likely results and possible outcomes. These approaches include:

*   Accounts, profit and loss modelling to assess commercial and cost viabilities; cost apportionment; minimum income levels
*   Statistical modelling, to assess probability and likelihood; averages, frequency and mid-point; standard distribution; the critical path of a given project; time factors; and space usage

- The inclusion of given variables to project changes in circumstances; changes in possible outcomes; and to address the effects of these variables on other components
- Market size and product/service usage projections to infer initial and long-term demand and income.

This is then considered by managers, executives and experts in the light of the real situation in which they must operate. All of this will therefore in turn be limited or influenced by:

- Workforce capacity and potential
- Technological capacity and potential
- Market capacity and potential
- Deadlines
- Particular ways of working
- Where executive power, authority and influence lie
- Key characters
- Local factors and political and institutional aspects
- Particular strengths, weaknesses, opportunities and threats
- Aspects of difficulty, value, frequency, importance and presentation
- The decision-making process
- Culture, values and ethics
- The balancing and accommodation of all these.

The end result is thus that an accurate or informed assessment of the risks involved in any activity or proposal is produced in advance. It does not mean that risks are not taken, but rather that an informed judgement has been made before going ahead. If this is done, a truer range of outcomes can be assessed; more accurate contingency plans can be drawn up; and any future matters arising from the issues in hand can be proposed from a position of relative strength and certainty.

■ Types of strategy

Any business or public strategy must have the following components if it is to stand any chance at all of success:

- It must have properly established **performance targets**, in whatever terms these are to be measured (e.g. income, volume, quality, but set against measurable, understandable and achievable targets)
- It must have **deadlines that are achievable**, that have been worked out in advance, and that represent a balance between commitment, resources and contingencies
- It must have **contingencies** built in, to cover the unlikely, and the emergency
- It considers the **long-term effectiveness** of the organisation.

Outcomes should be pre-evaluated in terms of 'best' – what is the greatest level of success that we can possibly gain by following this course of action; '**worst**' – what is the worst level of failure that can be achieved (if that is the right word) if everything that can go wrong does go wrong; and in between, a range of outcomes under the general heading of 'medium' or 'acceptable'. In particular, the level of bare acceptability of the outcome of a particular strategy should be assessed at the stage of devising strategy.

Outcomes should be extrapolated from each of these positions to try and envisage the following stage of the organisation's activities and the wider implications.

Outcomes should be examined from both long and short term standpoints.

The strategy, and the means of achieving it, must be understood and adopted both by the organisation's staff, and by its customers and clients. Everyone involved within the organisation must be committed to it; it reflects their means of livelihood for the foreseeable future; and also, to an extent, their standing in the community.

Within this context, the following main types of strategy may be defined:.

■ Growth strategies

To be measured against preset objectives, whether in terms of income; market share; sales volume; and new products or services. Required, expected or anticipated measures of growth, and the timescales for this, should be stated in advance. How such strategies are to be supported, financed and resourced, and the implications of this, must also be clearly stated and understood. The staff concerned must know this, and the implications for them.

Acquisitions, mergers and takeovers: are all variations on the theme of growth. Again, these approaches must be against preset objectives, and with the overall view to enhancing the profitability and/or quality of the business (see Summary Box 5.4). In support of this, what may actually happen is to introduce the organisation into new geographical areas, to increase the sectoral position; it may also help to defend and protect the organisation's own position.

Such activities may also include the acquisition of suppliers and distributors and sources of raw materials; this is known as 'vertical integration'.

They may additionally represent niche opportunities, the ability to get into new and profitable market sectors, to purchase the client list, resource or base of a competitor, or parallel operator.

■ Retrenchment

This is the withdrawal from niche or peripheral activities; the sale of assets; the concentration on the core activity. It need not have negative connotations; for example an organisation may sell off its lorry fleet, and lease lorries, at the time of credit squeezes and high interest rates. On the other hand, where there are negative connotations, effective retrenchment will have the overall purpose of

---

SUMMARY BOX 5.4   Acquisitions Example: Sony and Matsushita

In 1989 the Sony Corporation paid $3.4 billion for Columbia Pictures, a Hollywood TV and film studio. In 1990, Matsushita paid $6.1 billion for MCA, the American music, video and entertainment company.

The lessons to be drawn in both cases stem from an assessment of the strengths and direction of the organisation in question. In general, any growth, diversification or acquisition strategy will be based upon an estimation of what the new business will bring to the existing one and how this will strengthen both the overall portfolio and its operational capacities.

Thus the rationale behind each was that they had expertise and capabilities in electrical and electronic technology that could usefully and profitably be translated into the new spheres, that there would be returns on the amounts paid measurable in commercial terms. The acquisitions would also lead to new market opportunities in the USA and in the entertainment sectors, and would give each of the companies a further foothold and reputation in the West.

Both decisions were criticised at the time as being acquisitions for their own sake, pushed on by the desire of the company's ownership to gain a stake in a glamorous and high-profile industry, and by companies that had more cash than they knew what to do with. There was also perceived to be a competitive element between the two organisations – and especially their Chairmen (Akio Morita of Sony and Konosuke Matsushita of Matsushita).

---

protecting the core business and the certain markets (in so far as there are any), at the expense of the niches in which the organisation has been operating.

Retrenchment activities in public services are very often the cause of crisis, because there has to be every attempt to maintain the level of service against a declining budget provision.

Retrenchment activities must also be carried out against preset aims and objectives, and with a defined purpose and planned outcome.

■ Diversification

This is where organisations take the conscious decision to move into new markets and activities, very often in spite of the fact that there is no particular expertise in the new chosen field. Expertise in the new field, and the assimilation of its modus operandi, must be acquired by the organisation, if it is to be successful.

In practice, most effective and successful diversification strategies follow the vertical integration patterns, moving into new sectors that are clearly indicated by the current core business (for example, the Murdoch organisation moved into satellite television; it had no particular expertise in television or satellite technology but, looked at from a different standpoint, was a major player in mass media and communications). Consider Summary Box 5.5.

SUMMARY BOX 5.5   Virgin Airlines

The move by the Virgin Group into the business of airline operation, from music, video and record distribution, was spectacularly successful; but to do it required extensive research, projections, expertise acquisition, and market understanding on the part of what was hitherto essentially a chain of shops. There were certain assets perceived by the Group, of which it could take advantage as it moved to become an airline also – a large customer base, strong UK image, reputation for quality, and public confidence; however, these were qualities that had, in practice, to be refashioned by the new airline for itself. Moreover, any failure on the part of the new venture would have had serious consequences for continuing and future confidence in the rest of the group's activities.

■ Price leadership

The organisation in this case sets out to gain the reality and the reputation of being the market player with the lowest prices, and to ensure that everyone who purchases from the organisation knows this. This will not be entirely at the expense of quality; products and services still have to be good enough to attract people to purchase in the first place.

Some price leadership activities are spectacularly successful, such as the sale of petrol by British and European supermarket chains. Supermarkets in Europe and North America do adopt 'pile it high, sell it cheap' strategies, but this is generally limited to certain products within the state; similarly, 'Do It Yourself' chains will generally have some products at good prices for the consumer. The concept is thus most widely developed as 'loss leadership', rather than as price leadership. The IKEA furniture chain, however, is making attempts at present to expand across the countries of the EC, on the premise and image that all its prices are low, and represent better value than the indigenous competition.

■ Differentiation

This is the offering of a homogeneous product on the basis that it is somehow different from the other offerings by other competitors. Strategies designed to differentiate must create a strong image, identity or association; they must relate the product to a lifestyle, set of values, or status that the customer desires.

Thus, margarine is sold on the various bases that it is: healthy; slimming; tasty; sunny; svelte and sexy. Petrol is: high-tech; reassuring; reliable; clean and environmentally friendly; the petrol station is also a gift shop and grocery store. Cosmetics are colourful; sexy; and also environmentally friendly. (This concept is expanded in Chapter 6, as part of the discussion of the marketing mix.)

Prices, in differentiated strategies, may also be brought down to give an impression of a good-value purchase. Price may itself conversely give an impression of an opulent lifestyle (as, for example, in the leisure wear and trainers sectors of the clothing markets). This is carried to its extremes in the 'luxury goods' market; there is a widely held perception that there is a price **below** which it is impossible to sell fragrance, perfume and aftershave, for example, because of the extreme associations of lifestyle and image that go with them.

■ Focus

This is where the firm selects a much narrower or more specialised market sector, and concentrates exclusively on it. This sector may be defined in a variety of ways (see Chapter 6); the 'focused' strategy will pick its niche, assess its viability, and set its targets. Possible targets may include: the supply of a critical component for a larger industry; coverage of a particular geographical area; coverage of a particular income segment or population segment; domination of a particular technological niche.

Taking one example of what is a large and expanding sector, that of video tapes: particular focuses may thus be:

- Video tape cassettes, essential to the continued well- being of the home entertainment sector
- Video tape cassettes of a particular running time, because consumers want a choice of running times
- Video tapes to be supplied to the manufacturers of the cassettes themselves
- The central points without which the tape cassettes cannot work; the plastic casing, which is required in particular formats to complete the cassettes; the cardboard boxes; the shrink-wrapping; and so on.

Each of these is carefully focused. Any organisation that wishes to operate in such a sector must decide the nature of the focus that it wishes to adopt. Any of the items included in the example are clearly areas in which the conduct of profitable business is possible. Consider Summary Box 5.6.

■ Market domination

Strategies aimed at market domination normally adopt and adapt components from each of the above to ensure a dominant position. Domination may be by sales volume, assets, income derived, largest number of outlets, or outlets in the most places (or a combination of some or all of these). It may also arise as the result of being the majority supplier (i.e. holding more than 50% of the market); the largest single player, though with less than 50%; or one of an oligopoly of operators (in some countries and sectors, this may be organised into a cartel, though this is illegal in many sectors and many countries).

SUMMARY BOX 5.6   Generic Strategies: M. E. Porter

Porter (1981, 1985) identifies three generic positions from which all effective and profitable activities arise. These are:

- Cost Leadership: the drive to be the lowest cost operator in the field. This enables the absolute ability to compete on price where necessary. Where this is not necessary, higher levels of profit are achieved in both absolute terms and also in relation to competitors. To be a cost leader, investment is required in 'State of the Art' production technology and high quality staff. Cost leadership organisations are lean form, with small hierarchies, large spans of control, operative autonomy, simple procedures and excellent salaries and terms and conditions of employment.
- Focus: concentrating on a niche and taking steps to be indispensable. The purpose is to establish a long-term and concentrated business relationship with distinctive customers, based on product confidence, high levels of quality, utter reliability and the ability to produce and deliver the volumes of product required by customers when required. Investment is necessary in product technology and staff expertise. It is necessary to understand the nature of the market and its perceptions and expectations. It is also necessary to recognise the duration of the market, where developments are likely to come from and the extent to which these can continue to be satisfied.
- Differentiation: offering homogeneous products on the basis of creating a strong image or identity as stated in the main text. Investment is required in marketing; advertising; brand development, strength and loyalty; and outlets and distribution. Returns are generated over the medium to long term as the result of cost awareness, identity, loyalty and repeat purchase.

Porter argues that the common factor in all successful strategies is clarity and that this stems from adopting ONE of these positions. Organisations that fail to do this, do not necessarily fail themselves; they do however fail to maximise and optimise resources. They lay themselves open to loss of competitive position from those who do have this clarity. They tend towards a proliferation of management systems and processes that dilute effective efforts.

Source: Porter (1981, 1985).

In practice, it is rare to find massive majority dominators of sectors, though British Airways handles about 70% of internal British air traffic by passenger volume; otherwise domination in this way is limited to gas, electricity, water, and telecommunications. Oligopolies may be found in media, newspapers, oil and cars among others.

■ Measurement and evaluation

This process, in general, will be carried out against the preset aims and objectives of the particular strategy; quantifiable where possible, areas of particular success or shortfall will be apparent, contributing to the organisation's expertise in the field and ensuring further improvement in the strategic and planning processes for the future.

Beyond this, evaluation is both a continuous process, and the subject of more formalised regular reviews at required and appropriate intervals, thus setting a framework against which the strategy is to be judged.

Some specific questions can also be posed and answered:

1. The extent to which the strategy is **identifiable**, clearly understood by all concerned, in specific and positive terms; the extent to which it is unique and specifically designed for its given purpose
2. Its **consistency** with the organisation's capabilities, resources and aspirations; and the aspirations of those who work in it
3. The levels of **risk** and **uncertainty** being undertaken, in relation to the opportunities identified
4. The **contribution** that the proposed strategy is to make to the organisation as a whole over the long term
5. Market **responses** and **responsiveness**.

These questions can be answered as part of both the continuous evaluation and the regular review process.

■ Implementation of strategy

The determination of strategy is therefore a combination of the identification of the opportunities and risks afforded by the environment; the capabilities, actual and potential, of the organisation, its leaders and top management; and issues of ethical and social responsibility. Turning this into reality effectively, in both business and public service activities requires, first of all, a commitment to the given purpose that is sustainable. It requires both functional and structural organisation, coordination, control and direction systems relevant to, and supportive of, the given purpose. Aims and objectives must be set, monitored and reviewed; these also must be relevant to the purpose in hand, and assessable for both success and failure, in the long, medium and short term. Review processes must be included as part of the strategic establishment, with the ability to activate both fine tuning, and crisis and emergency management aspects (see Figure 5.3).

Within this broad framework, a series of particular activities must be undertaken:

● **Key tasks** must be established and prioritised, effective decision-making processes drawn up, and systems for monitoring and evaluation of strategic process devised
● **Work** and **workforce** must be divided and structured to a combination of functional and hierarchical aspects, designed to ensure the effective completion of the tasks in hand; this must include relevant and necessary committee, project coordination, working party, and steering group activities

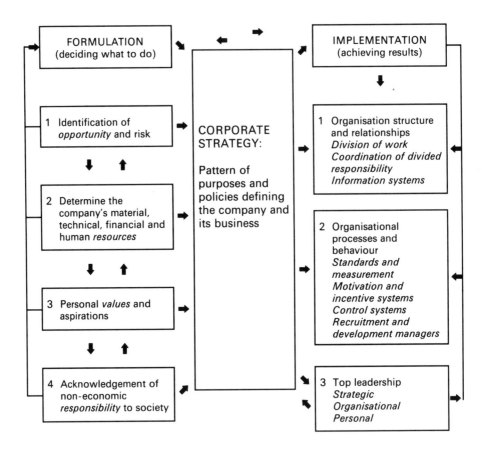

Figure 5.3   The implementation of strategy

- **Information** and other management systems must be designed and installed; control and constraint systems must be a part of this, to include financial, human resource, production, output and sales reporting data
- Tasks and actions to be carried out must be **scheduled** and **prioritised** in such a way as to be achieved to given deadlines; as well as establishing a background for precise work methods and ways of working, scheduling provides the basis for setting standards against which short- and medium-term performance can be measured
- **Actual performance** can, and must, be measured against forecast, projected or budgeted performance; customer and client responses. Performance may also be judged in comparison with other operators in the same market place
- **Human resource** (HR) **policies** may be assessed for their effectiveness and quality, relevance and suitability to the work in hand, and particular HR difficulties; they may also identify wider issues of conflict, communication blockages, disputes and grievances, and their causes

- HR **management techniques** that have been adopted may also be measured for effectiveness; these will include payment and reward systems, rule-books, methods of performance appraisal, and staff training and development for all levels
- The creation of a **corporate culture** that is both relevant to current ways of working, and that can be developed in such ways as to maintain harmony and a positive and productive environment for the future, must be undertaken; this must extend to induction, orientation and attitude-forming activities.

The commitment of the organisation's leadership and directorate, both to the strategy and the components for its implementation itemised above, is a dynamic and continuing process, consistent with the aims and objectives, and also the style and structure adopted for their achievement. Consider Summary Box 5.7.

■ Evaluation of strategy

We have consistently and continuously seen that any process of evaluation must have the following components if it is to be effective. It must be made against preset aims and objectives; it must be in both global and operational terms; it must be in both long and short term time frames; and it must be a continuous process, with the additional purpose of identifying and preventing and managing positive failure and crisis on the one hand, and additional opportunities for positive and profitable activities on the other (see Figure 5.4). Within this broad framework, however, other matters have to be considered.

■ Criteria for assessment

Criteria for assessment should be clear and understood by all concerned.

They should cover the widest possible operational spectrum. They should not be in terms of short-term financial gain or immediate cost advantage. This always gives an incomplete picture, and organisations that pressure their managers or staff in these directions inevitably do so at the expense of long-term investment, or long-range interest, product and service research, modernisation or technological development.

SUMMARY BOX 5.7 'Post It'

The 'post it' pad was invented by an employee of the 3M company in the USA. He sang in his local church choir and he wanted markers for his hymn book that would not fall out of the book when it was lifted up.

The pads were first popularised within the company itself through the enthusiasm of the employees and their constant use of them for the myriad of purposes to which we now all put them.

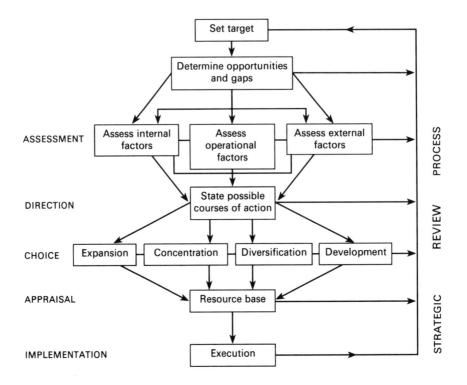

Figure 5.4   The monitoring, review and evaluation of strategy and direction

They should be in terms that coordinate and integrate all organisational, divisional and departmental activities – human resource, marketing, production, sales, research and output. They should be translated into compatible terms for all organisational levels and activities.

They should identify global, organisational, operational and individual issues and concerns, in such a way that those involved can both take advantage of those opportunities that present themselves, and also signal any immediate or potential causes of concern.

The question of 'who evaluates' must also be answered. Both overall and departmental objectives must be set and met; therefore those responsible in both areas must have importance in the evaluation processes. Top management, above all, must retain familiarity with specific outputs from particular departments. As well as the overall view, they must be prepared to recognise specific operational issues from this more detailed aspect, and from this, take any remedial action necessary. This should be built into both management information systems and reporting relationships up the hierarchy.

This has emphasised the importance of universality of understanding of strategy and direction at all levels of the organisation. It is difficult, if not impossible, to give any true measure of success or failure, if those doing the assessing are not clear what is being evaluated. Also, a shared interest at all levels in the problems to be overcome helps to make the communication, reporting and evaluation systems themselves more effective and precise.

Consideration must again be given to the non-rational, non-scientific elements. This will include coverage of the expedient, the politically-driven activity, the brain-child of the powerful member of staff.

As any strategy unfolds, side benefits and spin-offs become apparent; indeed, this is an attraction in the commissioning of projects and product developments. Defence equipment manufacture has always led to technological advances that have other uses –radar, for example, used to detect hostile craft in times of war, is used, among other things, to allow aeroplanes to fly without fear through cloud and fog; and is used by fishing fleets to locate shoals of fish.

This process also invariably leads to new applications being found for existing technology – the digital watch is a by-product of the development of the pocket calculator.

Finally, major sectoral projects bring technological advances in their wake. The Channel Tunnel project has generated a wealth of expertise in geotechnology, construction and tunnelling equipment, and railway technology, as the result of its commission.

Such benefits are expected to accrue from any course of action undertaken, and each sector has its own equivalent. While there is a strong rational imperative at the core of successful strategy formulation, implementation and evaluation, it is essential to have regard to the wider elements as indicated.

■ Ready-reckoner strategic analyses

These are introduced here to enable the assessment and compartmentalisation of particular activities in the ways indicated. They require short and intensive creative discussion or brainstorming activities on the part of those undertaking the analysis. The issues thus raised can then be rigorously assessed, evaluated and prioritised; accepted or rejected; or used as the basis for further research and analysis.

Strengths, weaknesses, opportunities, threats: SWOT analysis

The purpose of SWOT analysis is to help organisations learn, clarify issues, identify preferred and likely directions (see Figure 5.5).

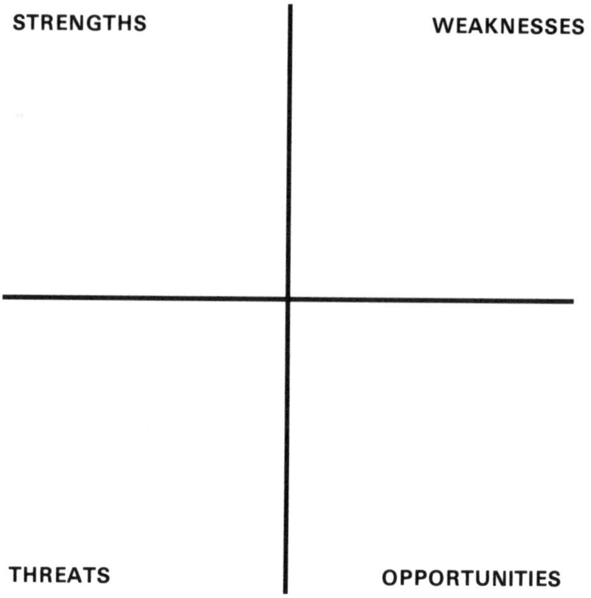

STRENGTHS	**WEAKNESSES**
THREATS	**OPPORTUNITIES**

The method by which the ideas are generated and compartmentalised is a creative group discussion, OS, 'brainstorming'. The end result of this is a list of items under each heading.

From this a full discussion and development of the idea is concluded.

There are no 'holds' or 'taboos' in a SWOT analysis: the purpose is to be creative, not restrictive.

Figure 5.5   SWOT analysis

In this activity, issues are raised, highlighted and categorised under four headings:

- **Strengths**: the things that the organisation and its staff are good at and do well; that they are effective at; that they are well known for; that make money; that generate business, and reputation
- **Weaknesses**: the things they are bad at, or do badly; that they are ineffective at; that they are notorious for; that make losses; that cause hardships, disputes, grievances and complaints; that should generate business, but do not; this aspect requires a degree of candour
- **Opportunities**: the directions that they could profitably go in for the future, that may arise because of strengths or the elimination of weaknesses
- **Threats**: from competitors; from strikes and disputes; from resource and revenue losses; from failing to maximise opportunities or build on successes; this also includes matters over which the organisation has no control.

Opportunities and threats are representations of the external environment and its forces. The information thus raised and presented is then developed, researched or investigated further. It can be done for all business and managerial activities, and to address wider global and strategic issues. It is an effective means of gathering and categorising information, of illustrating or illuminating particular matters, and for gathering or articulating a lot of information and ideas very quickly.

▊ Social–technical–economic–political: STEP analysis

The purpose of STEP (or, sometimes, PEST) analysis is also to help organisations learn, but the material arising is much more concerned with the analysis of the wider strategic situation, and the organisation in its environment:

- **Social**: the social systems at the workplace, departmental and functional structures, work organisation and working methods; externally this considers the relationship between the organisation and its environment in terms of the nature and social acceptability of its products and services; its marketing; and the regard with which it is held in the community
- **Technological**: the organisation's technology, and the uses to which it is put, and the potential uses of it; and the technology that is potentially available to the organisation and others operating in the given sector
- **Economic**: the financial structure, objectives and constraints (e.g. budgets and budgeting systems) at the place of work; externally this considers the market position, levels of economic activity, and commercial prospects and potential of the products and services offered
- **Political**: the internal political systems, sources of power and influence, key groups of workers, key departments, key managers and executives; externally, it considers particular considerations in the establishment of markets, by product, location, ethics, and values.

Again, the information thus raised can be further analysed and evaluated. It establishes in more detail the wider background against which particular product or service initiatives are to take place; and raises wider issues or concerns that may in turn require more detailed resource and analysis.

▊ Industry structure analysis

This is based on Michael E. Porter's 'five elemental forces of competition'. In this analysis focus is directed at each of the five distinctive elements that are present to some extent in all sectors. Again, the purpose is to clarify the position of the organisation in its chosen sphere of operations and also to signal any likely or obvious issues for concern. The five elements are:

1. **The industry competitors**: the nature and extent of rivalry among those organisations currently operating in the field and the implications of this for the future (for example, reduced profit margins where price wars occur; reduction in capacity where there is over-provision)
2. **Suppliers**: the extent to which they dominate the sector either through the supply of a key, critical or rare component; their ability to integrate forwards into the market itself; the range of choice of suppliers available; and the ability to use alternative supplies; the overall bargaining position of the suppliers
3. **Buyers**: the extent to which they dominate the sector either because they purchase high volumes from it, or because they control the final outlet of the product in question; their ability to integrate backwards into the market itself; the number and type of operators in the buyer group; and the ability to generate and supply alternative buyers; the overall bargaining position of buyers
4. **Potential entrants**: the extent to which organisations operating in other sectors have product, technology and staff capacities to gain entry to the sector in question; and the extent and nature of the entry barriers that surround the sector (entry–exit barriers are discussed below, pp. 166–7)
5. **Substitutes**: the extent to which the organisation's product is a matter of choice on the part of the buyer; the extent to which equivalent benefits can be gained from a product that is similar (but not the same).

(An industry structure diagram is given in Chapter 6, p. 172.)

■ Competitor analysis

This involves an assessment of the other players in the field. It considers the initiatives that they may themselves take to promote their own strategic advantage and also to measure their likely responses to such initiatives on the part of the organisation in question (see Figure 5.6).

The components of a competitor analysis are:

- The strategy of the competitor, its driving and restraining forces
- Its current business operations, capacities, strengths and capabilities
- The assumptions held about both the competitor and the industry itself
- A detailed profile of the competitor, its current satisfaction with its current position; its likely moves and responses to moves; its position in the market; its under- or over-capacity.

This constitutes a detailed discussion to be devised and conducted by sectoral, corporate, strategy specialists and experts and to be used as the basis on which both offensive and defensive strategic moves are made. Presentation to an organisation's top management and directorate will normally be limited to the matters arising, the results of analysis, the conclusions and recommendations drawn from a detailed competitor analysis.

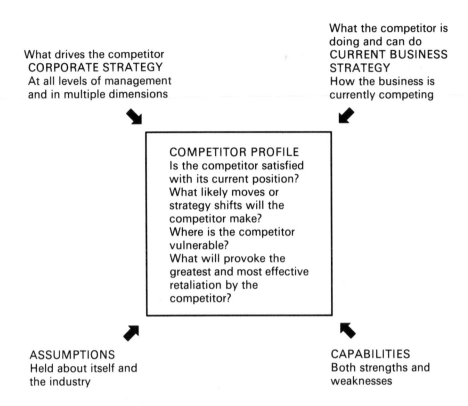

Figure 5.6   The components of a competitor analysis

■ Ethics and morality in management

Of all aspects of management education, training and practice this is the area that suffers from greatest neglect. Part of the reason for this is the term used – 'ethics'. The danger is that the matter becomes intellectualised, that it generates academic debate and discussion without having any noted relevance to real organisations and their real objectives. In addition to this there is a traditional resistance from executives of previous generations, who perceive a softness in presenting a caring and concerned organisation.

■ Standards of behaviour and activity

This may be summarised as 'the way we do things'. This is manifest in the relationship between the organisation and its customers, clients and community and the ways in which these are carried out. One of the reasons that the *Herald of Free Enterprise* sank in 1987 was that the company that operated it could not agree on a basic standard of operation that ensured that the bow doors were closed before the ship set sail. It was not considered important enough. Elsewhere there is a discrepancy in the attitudes of the community in Cumbria in the UK to the BNFL Nuclear Reprocessing Plant. The organisation is the major local employer. There is, however, also a 'dark area' concerning the extent of the environmental and social pollution that may be taking place. Much of this would be dispelled by the availability and presentation of honest information and a definite ethical stance.

■ Dealing with the public

This is reflected in the ways in which customer complaints, queries and approaches are handled; the prevailing and perceived attitudes that are apparent in the relationships between the organisation and its clients and locality. It is also reflected in the view that, if at all possible, people will not deal with organisations that are, or are perceived to be, unethical or dishonest.

■ Dealing with the staff

This concerns the state of industrial relations at the workplace, and the overall approach and attitudes adopted. Traditional 'conflicts' in industrial relations are a major stumbling-block to effective business not only because of the dissipating and divisive essence of such disputes, but also because they reinforce a general attitude and internal business ethic. In extreme cases, this is entrenched in tradition, folklore and industrial mythology and requires major investment either to manage or to change. Part of current management thinking has been concerned with taking a much more enlightened view of workplace relations and the establishment of standards of 'right and wrong' in dealings with the staff; and some call this 'ordinary common decency'.

■ Corporate citizenship

The overall concept of corporate citizenship concerns the wider position of the organisation in its community, its markets and its environment. In this context there are roles as employer, from the standpoint of providing employment, income, investment and sponsorship in the community. There are roles as organisation also from the standpoint of non-polluter, provider of high quality goods or services, general benevolence and setter of wider community and social standards and expectations.

■ Leadership qualities

In this context leadership qualities consist of honesty, openness, trustworthiness, sympathy, empathy and identity. This is not to say that there is anything soft about this – Mark McCormack, Mary Kay Ash, Alan Sugar and Anita Roddick have all taken strong ethical stands and are very competitive business people and directors, running highly profitable organisations (see Summary Boxes 5.8 and 5.9). They create positive responses rather than a vacuum. They generate great loyalty and commitment. They illustrate the relationship between developing a strong business ethic on the one hand and highly profitable and effective organisations on the other.

The concept of 'ethics in management' is much more widely understood, accepted and adopted in the USA, Japan and parts of mainland Europe than in the UK. In the latter, in particular, there is a cultural resistance which has to be overcome. Additionally, there is a prerequisite need for the leaders of both business and public services in the UK to recognise and understand the direct relationship between high ethical standards and high levels of organisational performance.

Figure 5.7 models the effects of social/political considerations on strategic choice and direction.

SUMMARY BOX 5.8   Body Shop

The concept behind the 'Body Shop' range of cosmetics and skin cleansing products was the ability to produce and offer goods based on the use of natural plant and herbal resources drawn from all across the world. The ethical stance taken in support of this was based on concern for the environment. The company manifested this in using materials that Anita Roddick had seen being used all around the world, either for cosmetics or for cleansing or for medication purposes, rather than those industrially produced using chemical processes. Packaging was also kept to a minimum for each of the products and this remains true today. In certain sectors, especially among the educated middle classes of Europe, Australia, New Zealand and North America, there was a swing towards health foods, a healthy lifestyle and an enlightened consumerism in the 1970s, and Body Shop, which opened in 1976, reflected this. It also sought to contribute directly to environmental improvement and restoration by putting both funds and resources into projects that aim to achieve this. It further insists that Body Shop staff work on such projects in their own time as part of their terms and conditions of employment or franchise holding.

Body Shop is a quality organisation that has enjoyed commercial success since its inception. In this context it represents an excellent example and configuration of the balance and combination of business vision, business acumen and an ethical stance in the formulation of a successful and profitable undertaking.

SUMMARY BOX 5.8   P & O Ferries: Dover–Europe

The P & O Company took over Townsend Thoresen, a car ferry operator that plied between Dover, France and Belgium, at the beginning of 1987. It immediately faced problems – the Zeebrugge disaster of 1987; and the seamen's strike of 1988. P & O had therefore to reconstitute and re-launch the ferry services from the port of Dover to France and Belgium virtually from scratch. This was devised, determined and conducted as follows:

1. **Image**: The company changed the colour scheme of the ships, replacing the distinctive orange, white and green scheme of the previous owners of the ships with its own dark blue and white. The distinctive P & O flag was adopted as the logo and focus of attention and was painted on the funnels of all ships. The ships were all renamed – they are all 'The Pride of . . .' Dover, Calais, Kent, Brugge and Burgundy; a very positive approach. The freight ships that they operate give an alternative message – the names used on these are all prefixed with the word 'European'.
2. **The ships**: The ships were specifically designed for operation on this route and to be manoeuvrable in the confined spaces of the ports of Dover and Calais. In appearance they are also very distinctive and the organisation has made a feature of this in its marketing and promotional activities.
3. **Facilities**: These have been emphasised as being suitable to a great range of tastes and requirements. A club or business class is now on offer, having regard to the coming on stream of the Channel Tunnel, with its express through passenger trains aimed at business travellers; this provides exclusive facilities for this niche. A range of restaurants, waiter service, cafeteria, coffee and burger bars is available. Exclusive facilities are provided for lorry and coach drivers. The whole impression generated is that of a combination of high quality and excellence of facilities whichever particular niche the member of the travelling public happens to fall into.
   Other offerings on board ship include a cinema, computer and video games, duty free shopping and children's play areas.
4. **Service**:
   (a) **Volume**: The company operates up to 60 return crossings per day. This may rise; this will depend upon continued increases in traffic volumes between Britain and mainland Europe and the company's stated desire to operate a shuttle service whereby a ship would leave each port either when it was full or at the end of every stated period of time, whichever came sooner. The company currently has five ships on the route.
   (b) **Capacity**: The ships as stated above were all designed with this particular route in mind. They are able to accommodate up to 2,500 passengers per crossing in a variety of combinations – tourists, business, coach and package parties, lorries and heavy haulage, and other commercial.
   It should be noted that during the depth of the UK recession of 1992 total traffic volume carried between Dover and the mainland nevertheless increased by 11%.
   (c) **Staff**: All staff complete an extensive induction and orientation programme and periods of job training. The emphasis is on the satisfaction of customers and the quality of service required and expected in order to achieve this. Attitudes, behaviour, standards of dress and appearance are clearly defined. Smart yet functional uniforms are worn by all staff, giving both identity and confidence.

(d) **Staff relations**: These were reformed in the period following the seamen's strike of 1988 and 1989. The trade union (RMT) was de-recognised by the company; work and shift patterns were altered; the numbers of crew members per ship were reduced; and a much greater flexibility both of rostering and occupation was determined. The organisation stated that its purpose in doing this was the necessity both to compete with the Channel Tunnel and to improve the efficiency and effectiveness of the services as they developed and extended in the period following the integration of the single European market.

The strategic purpose behind all this is complex. P & O first of all desires to be the major ferry operator in the single European market. It needs to be able to compete with the Channel Tunnel as the potential of its operations is realised in the mid- to latter part of the 1990s and beyond. It desires also to set standards of service, reliability, confidence and quality that underline its strategy.

The process in which the company engaged in transforming the nature, quality and style of its services between Dover, France and Belgium took the best part of three years to achieve. What is in place now is a distinctive, profitable and high quality service, equipped to compete with the Channel Tunnel and versatile enough to take advantage of any new market opportunities that may be afforded to it on its routes, both in operational terms and also accommodating any increase in volumes of traffic generated by the continued development of the European market.

■ Conclusions

The devising of corporate policy and strategy must both identify and reconcile a complex range of matters if it is to be effective. This chapter has attempted to illustrate the main issues.

Devising and implementing strategy is a continuous process, one that is subject to constant analysis, evolution and review. It must be clear and strong enough to give a universally understood clarity of purpose; but this must not be mistaken for rigidity. All organisations must combine this with the qualities of flexibility, dynamism, opportunism and responsiveness if they are to survive into the future.

Strategy has also to be seen as operating in different ways over different time periods. A strategy articulated for a period of up to a year may be very clearly defined, easy to assimilate and follow and something to which everyone can subscribe; and the same may also be true to an extent for a period of between one and two years. In relation to the business sphere and wider environment however, anything projected over a period longer than this requires careful and constant evaluation and re-evaluation at all times. The nature of this environment makes it extremely difficult to predict anything that may happen anywhere in it, or even what its nature will be in, for example, five years' time.

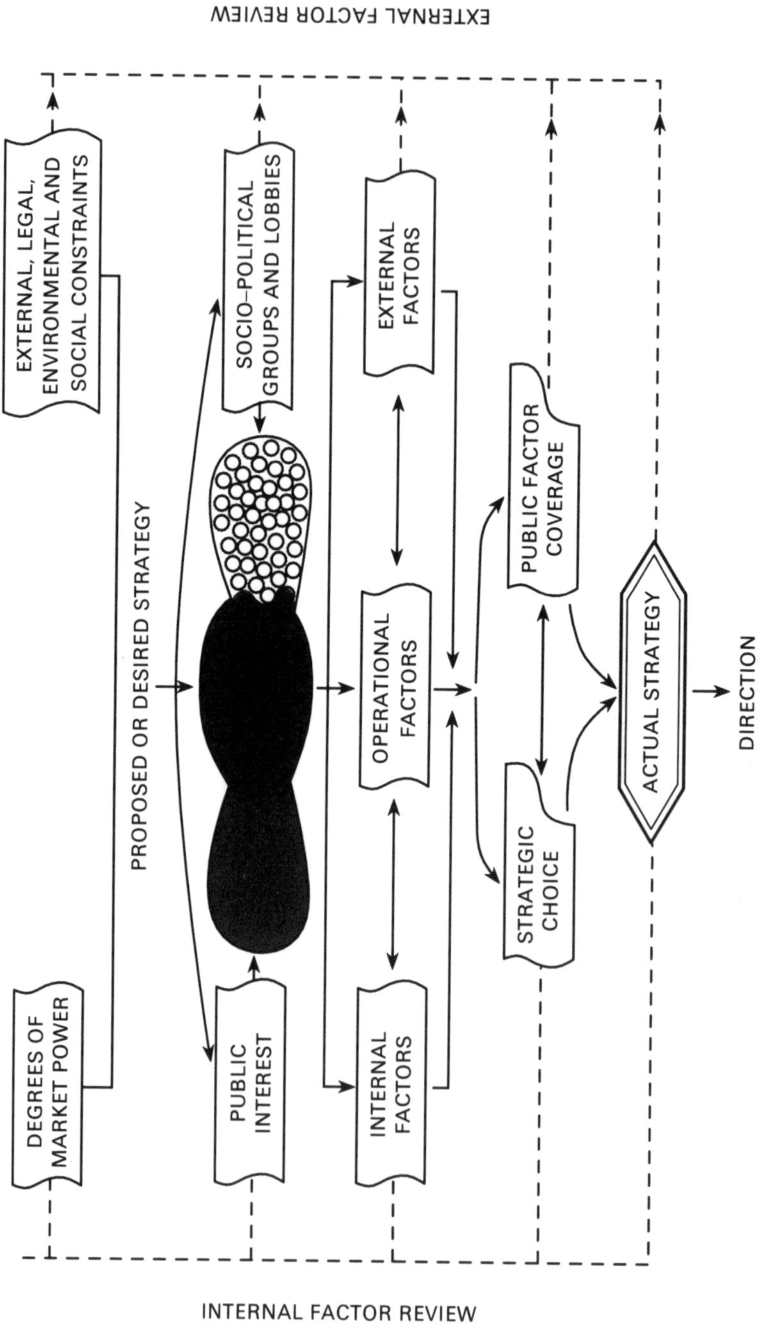

EXTERNAL FACTOR REVIEW

EXTERNAL, LEGAL, ENVIRONMENTAL AND SOCIAL CONSTRAINTS

SOCIO–POLITICAL GROUPS AND LOBBIES

EXTERNAL FACTORS

PUBLIC FACTOR COVERAGE

PROPOSED OR DESIRED STRATEGY

OPERATIONAL FACTORS

ACTUAL STRATEGY

DIRECTION

DEGREES OF MARKET POWER

PUBLIC INTEREST

INTERNAL FACTORS

STRATEGIC CHOICE

INTERNAL FACTOR REVIEW

Figure 5.7   The effects of social and political considerations on strategic choice and direction

Consequently, the best and most valuable use of long-term plans and strategies is as a guiding light; they should be used to illuminate the pathway chosen, rather than as a set of rigid directions that are to govern the organisation for the period stated.

CHAPTER 6

Marketing

The purpose of this chapter is to introduce the background and concepts needed for an understanding of marketing and its importance in the business sphere. In addition, there are related aspects to do with both the internal management of organisations, and the presentation and delivery of proposals, initiatives, and ideas, that must also be understood. There is a fundamental business relationship between a product, invention, or service, and the way in which it is presented both to the world at large, and to market sectors in particular, that is critical to overall commercial success.

■ The marketing process

Marketing is the competitive process by which goods and services are offered for consumption at a profit; this definition should be seen in the broadest possible terms. It is about building a reputation and making sales for cash and profits in particular markets. It involves gaining credibility and reputation in order to establish an effective and cooperative working relationship. In public service terms, it is about ensuring that all those who are entitled to the service, who want it or need it, get it in ways that are acceptable and relevant to them.

There is a requirement to generate images, reputation, confidence, positive attributes and continuing effective business relationships in order to ensure successful and productive activities.

The fundamental concept of marketing is thus that all business activities are in some way the relationship between oneself and one's clients. Marketing takes the view that the most important stake holders in the organisation are the customers, and that keeping them contented and satisfied, and returning for repeat business, is the first concern of the staff. Marketing activities are thus central to the function of everyone in the organisation, in the development and execution of systems, structures and style in support of this.

The marketing role is universally carried out. Every interaction between the organisation, its staff and its environment, has some input on the relationship between them. Additionally, when members of an organisation address a school prize-day, or appear to give a point of view on the television, they contribute to the marketing of that organisation. When members of an organisation are in trouble with the police, or involved in an affray or other problems, they are also contributing to its marketing. Some organisations take this several stages further, clearly establishing the wider standards of behaviour and deportment that they expect of their staff, whether or not they are at work, and may discipline or dismiss the person concerned for bringing the organisation into disrepute.

In support of this, organisations devise marketing strategies, and also carry out a range of activities designed to assess and satisfy customer needs and wants. They gather market intelligence; conduct market research and obtain customer responses. They organise product packaging, promotion, sales and distribution. They generate product awareness through advertising, image formation, differentiation, promotions, sales methods and techniques, and presentations.

At this stage it is also useful to note that the customers and clients of an organisation may be different from the consumers or users of a product (for example, parents usually buy childrens' toys and clothes, and they thus have to be convinced of their value; while in organisations, technologists will assess production technology, finance staff will fund it, and workforces will use it).

Finally, purchasers of goods and services buy them for the value benefits and satisfaction that they afford, rather than for their own sake (although possession of an item for its own sake may afford satisfaction).

■ Marketing strategies

As stated in Chapter 5, all strategies adopted reflect ultimately the strengths, capacities, inclinations, technology and size of the organisation in question. Within this broad constraint marketing strategies fall into the following seven categories:

- **Pioneering or 'first in the field'**: opening up new markets or new outlets for existing products, new products for existing outlets; taking an original and distinctive view of the marketing process and devising new methods and campaigns
- **'Follow the leader'**: the great benefit of being second in the field is to learn from the mistakes and experience of the pioneer and can take informed judgements about the nature of the involvement to be taken on based on their experience; or it may be that the second organisation can see opportunities that were not exploited by the first
- **'Me too' or 'all-comers'**: where the market is wide open, entry to and exit from it are relatively easy, where the products and services in question are universal or general and where there are many suppliers but where there are more buyers than suppliers
- **Supply led**: where the product is produced because the organisation has complete faith in it and knows that once made it will be able to be sold at a profit
- **Technology led**: whereby the organisation finds itself in a particular line of business because it has at its disposal a particular type of technology which can be turned to productive and profitable advantage in a variety of sectors
- **Staff led**: because of the skills, qualities and preferences of the staff of the organisation that happen to be gathered together and where the products or offerings reflect these (very prevalent in the small business sphere)

- **Market led**: where the organisation looks first at a range of markets, then assesses their requirements, and finally decides which of these it can most valuably and profitably operate in and fill (see Summary Box 6.1).

The organisation may also adopt its commercial position based on a strong moral or ethical stance. This in turn becomes the initial strong or overriding attraction of clients to the business and gives a firm additional impression (usually of honesty and integrity) in addition to its commercial and business capabilities.

Marketing strategies may be offensive or defensive. Offensive activities seek to make inroads into the competitive position and client base of others. Defensive

---

SUMMARY BOX 6.1   The Leisure Wear Sectors

The provision of products for the leisure wear sectors of Europe, Australia, New Zealand, South Africa and North America constitutes the ultimate in fast-moving consumer goods. The benefits that accrue to the customer from their ventures into this area are to do with image, impression, distinctiveness, lifestyle, identity, the imitation of film, pop or sports stars, and personal esteem and comfort. Having gained all this for themselves, they wish to be held in positive and popular esteem by their peers, and to carry a wider label of status and prominence in the society in which they live. Niches for leisure wear may therefore additionally be identified by:

- **Age**, which ranges from birth virtually through to death and is often very precisely targeted in the areas in between. For example, the teenage (13–19 sector) can be configured at each of these ages, any combination of them and also pre-teen (8–12) and post-teen (early 20s and even beyond)
- **Sex** and **gender** and **sexuality**, and associated images
- **Location**, regional, local and national variations on the particular products; this is compounded by that which is perceived either to be a leading location or one to be avoided at all costs
- **Branding**, the quest for distinctiveness mirrored in the desire and ability on the part of the consumer to wear the badge and distinction with the given qualities of pride, identity and esteem and to gain the esteem, real or perceived, of others
- **Transience**, the new is not new for long. The moment the next distinctive offering comes along the previous one is first *passé* and then obsolete.

This must be reflected in both strategies and ways of working adopted by companies that seek to operate in this field. Marketing and market research are everything in the establishment of the profit range and profit base. Staffing policies will mirror this, drawing upon a range of qualities and levels of commitment that represent expertise, familiarity, understanding and the ability to forecast in the area and to produce new, effective and targeted products quickly. Design is a critical facility in such companies. Marketing strategies concentrate on the differentiation aspects and use all media sectors, both mainstream and niche in the pursuit of this. The leisure wear sector is saturated yet entry and exit barriers are low, affording plenty of opportunities in a business area in which the consumers of the entire world wish to participate and which they will participate provided that they have sufficient disposal income. This is the strategic base from which all players in this sector must operate.

and responsive activities are taken with the object of at least preserving the original position in response to the offensives of others.

■ Segmentation

In the UK the main approach to this is social.

Marketers categorise society by means of 'social segmentation'. Based on the occupation of the head of the household (usually the male occupant), society is categorised as follows:

A Aristocrats and upper middle class, directors, senior managers, senior civil and public servants
B Middle class, lawyers, doctors, senior managers
C1 Lower middle class, teachers, nurses, doctors, engineers, technologists, managers
C2 Skilled working class, including some engineering and technology activities
D Working class
E Subsistence, including the underclass and unemployed

Clearly, this is not exact – the conclusion of some occupations in more than one category is deliberate and illustrates the imperfections present. It is, however, a useful means of defining society for the purpose of understanding and evaluating it for a variety of reasons. In marketing terms, it enables a relationship to be drawn between sectors of the population, and income, tastes, aspirations, spending patterns, product and service purchase and usage, and related matters. It is also universally recognised in the UK.

Segments may additionally be defined by age, sex, status, aspiration, values, location, occupation, and expectations. These are then underpinned by image, identity, differentiation, branded and visual qualities and presentation. This is done to identify the types of buyers; the class of buyers; the size of the customer base in given niches; the balance of quality that buyers expect; the value of the product relative to other items available for consumption; patterns of spending among the members of the niche or sector, and the extent to which they use credit, credit cards, cash, or cheque books; their propensity to spend and save; ease of access to product and after-sales outlets; ease of access to facilities and services; the frequency with which a given item is to be used.

This identifies, to a good degree of precision, the area, style, content, and emphases of particular marketing campaigns, to ensure that activities are directed where they will be most profitable.

■ The competitive environment

Competition always exists where there is choice. The market is the environment in which competition take place. Markets may have any or all of the following features.

■ Degree of captivity

The market can be captive, because consumers have to buy from the suppliers; or entirely fluid, where anyone can supply the market, and the consumer can go to anyone for supplies.

■ Expanding, static, stagnant or declining

This can be in sales, financial and volume terms; in terms of numbers of customers; in terms of reputation or product or service offered; in terms of product or service demand (which may nevertheless not be satisfied, as with the increasing demand for health services in Western Europe, the UK and the USA).

■ Ethical and non-ethical

In whatever terms this is measured, social, religious, environmental and civilisational. Ethical aspects also include the use of animals for product research; sexual images in advertising campaigns; exploitation of cheap labour; working in areas where employment legislation is lax or non-existent; and environmental pollution. Each of these factors has either direct or indirect effects on organisational marketing.

■ Entry barriers

These may be very high, making entry to the market, and the ability to compete in it, very difficult. Such barriers consist of levels of capital investment; staffing volumes; technology; market location; protectionism and size; legal constraints; economies of scale; access to distribution channels; the loyalty of customers to those organisations supplying substitute or alternative products; and the costs incurred in switching from the current to the proposed activities, or of starting up and making entry as the first initiative of a new business. They may also be very low, if the products, buyers and markets are easily accessible, and the production technology freely available.

Barriers must also be regarded from the point of view of those firms currently involved in the market – their ability to defend their position, or to engage in their own activities devised to prevent the entry of new competitors. They may possess substantial financial resources, and also more nebulous perceptual advantages to do with image, confidence, quality and reliability, which any organisation wishing to break into the market would first have to overcome. Because of its position and reputation also (apart from any reasons to do with size and influence, or financial resources), an existing player may be able to cut its prices low enough and for long enough to force a new competitor out.

This last point was a factor (by no means the only one) which enabled British Airways, TWA, and Pan Am, to exclude Laker Airways from the highly lucrative transatlantic air routes. When Laker entered as a small but cut-price operator, the other, larger, carriers were able to reduce their fares and hold them down long enough for Laker to have to leave the market.

The final entry barrier to be considered is the value of, and access to, information pertaining to the sector. Command of information is itself a critical factor in establishing and maintaining a customer and client base; and lack of information will normally fatally affect the ability of an organisation to operate in the field.

Entry barriers vary between sectors; they must be considered at the outset of any marketing initiative. They may, after assessment, be seen as very low, offering no resistance to the potential entrant. Finally, the question of 'behavioural' entry barriers must be considered – the organisation considering market entry may have to compete with very strong existing perceptions or preconceptions about the organisation; on the other hand, existing players in the market may have very strong images or customer loyalty which any new entrant may first need to overcome.

■ Exit barriers

In considering the competitive environment, it is necessary also to look at both the opportunities and constraints on withdrawing from a particular market or markets. These may also be seen in terms of capital and investment costs – the organisation may have tied up resources in the long term, and take a tremendous economic loss in withdrawing. There may be staffing implications, redundancies, re-deployment and retraining, which have to be accounted for in advance of any proposed exit. There will be operational and behavioural considerations to be taken into consideration. Withdrawal from one market, or the abandonment of one opening, may cause a more general loss of reputation, that may in turn affect the performance of other products in other markets. There may be wider considerations of reportage and media interest to take into account, which may contribute to the problems concerned with exit and withdrawal.

■ Legal constraints

Most markets and sectors have specific legal regulations and constraints, quite apart from the wider considerations of the laws of the country concerned. Governments may also regulate the operations of organisations by the requirement to obtain licences for particular activities; and to operate to given legal minima in employment, marketing and production practices; and in the setting of quality standards for certain products and services.

This also extends to imitation and copyright; organisations have the right not to have their pioneering or profitable ideas stolen and represented as a genuine article by an imitator.

■ Differentiation

This is the process of distinguishing between the offering of the same (or substantially the same) product by different companies, in distinctive ways, to generate an impression of real choice of product. Consider Summary Box 6.2.

SUMMARY BOX 6.2   Butter

Butter may be offered for sale as salted, slightly salted, unsalted, low-fat, or 'virtually-no-fat'. There exists a measure of difference between each, though it is slight enough for the process of differentiation to be invoked.

Butter may also be British, American, French, German, Dutch, and New Zealand – so that 'difference' is devised on lines of nationality.

Butter may be supermarket/own brand; proprietary; paper or foil-wrapped; a deep yellow or nearly white – the differences are now even less marked.

Finally, butter may be (and is) associated with media advertising images that represent identity with a particular lifestyle; health; 'the country'; monetary success; and fun.

Differentiation generates a great amount of promotion, packaging, advertising, media initiative, design, and creative activity. It is the foundation for campaigns concerned with generating and maintaining expanding markets, niches and product identities for consumer goods; food and drink; package holidays to particular destinations; household and electrical appliances; cars (within present parameters of size); washing and washing-up powders and liquids. The approach used to do this consists of presenting the products in the given media in conjunction or association with the desired related images. The images used in Western Europe, the UK, USA, Australia, New Zealand and South Africa, are: sex, glamour, value, youth, luxury and opulence, health, sunshine, brand names and slogans, style, designer labels, space, time, speed and reliability. They are related in turn to the expectations of those who seek to be in the position of progress and shaping and influencing their part of society – thus the consumers of ready-meals are very often portrayed as power-dressed with a job shaping the world's destinies.

The images will reflect the aspirations associated with the buyers and users of products that market research has identified; the items referred to above are presented and utilised in different ways according to the sector of the population involved.

For example, the image of 'glamour' is related in different ways across a range of products and services. The promotion of the Rover 400 series of cars in Western Europe is related to a glamorous suburban and rural lifestyle carried out by senior executives. The advertising of air travel by international carriers is related to the glamour and luxury of first class travel, with supporting images of high quality food and service.

■ Other factors in competition

□ Luxury goods

Goods designated as such carry extremes of meaning and impression, above all in terms of price and value.

An excellent example of this is the scent/perfume/fragrance sector, where the product is offered entirely on the basis of the lifestyle, luxury and opulence with which it is associated. There is a clear correlation between price and value, and the market has established this to such an extent, that as the price of particular offerings has risen, so has demand. Such items are also often bought as gifts and therefore state a value on the relationship by both giver and receiver. Indeed, if the price came down, it would be seen to cheapen and devalue the image, and sales would reduce.

□ Good value

At the other end of the spectrum, there are thriving niches based on the offering of items of a certain quality at low or cheap prices – 'price advantage'. Food supermarkets in Europe and North America have made very successful and profitable business over long periods following marketing policies based on the twin premises of 'value for money', and 'volume sales on low or minimal margins'.

The main rider to this is that any image generated has still to be positive, and if it is not it will not do effective or profitable business (almost) no matter what the price advantage. People want to be offered cheap prices on the basis that they represent good value, and not on the fact (however real it may be) that they cannot afford anything else. People require quality and positive identity even where prices are low. It is notable that both sales and reputation of Japanese cars and electrical goods improved in Europe and North America in the 1970s and 1980s, when they moved from being both low price and low quality, to low price and high quality; and sales have continued to rise as the price of the goods has risen, because the quality has remained high.

Good value as a marketing concept must be seen in this context. In the purchase of satisfaction, buyers and consumers are drawn towards positive images and association, quality and value, whatever the price (and any other economic factors) may be.

□ Rivalry

This is the process by which a company establishes its position in the sector, using the marketing tools and techniques at its disposal – price competition, differentiation, advertising campaigns, image formation, identity generation, and sectoral battles. The factors affecting rivalry intensity are as follows:

- The number of **competitors** in the sector; especially where there are many companies of equivalent size and capacity in the sector, and the products and services are undifferentiated – there is no particular brand loyalty or identity, or at least this is not the overriding factor
- **Sectoral growth** where growth is slow or steady, companies which wish to expand will precipitate marketing wars. Related to this is the expectation of high rewards to be gained by the 'winning' player or players. Where growth is rapid there is a threat of entry when existing players cannot cope with increased demand
- **Exit barriers** where exit barriers are high, companies may remain in business in the sector even if they are not making profits because the costs of total withdrawal are greater than continuing to produce. Companies facing this, use it as an opportunity to seek other markets, sectors and niches; and also to engage in wider marketing activities with the purpose of differentiating its products and services, generating new images, identity and loyalty to them. Where exit barriers are low, companies normally withdraw.

The mixture and balance of these elements changes as the sector and market environment concerned changes, and as the marketing activities of **all** players in it have effect. Ultimately, there will be company collapses, shake-outs, mergers and takeovers, as the weaker players go to the wall, and the stronger seek to consolidate their positions.

□ Buyer groups

These have the greatest influence where they are in the position of being able to force down the price to be paid to suppliers; or to demand higher quality, volume or service from the supplier group. They may also play one supplier off against others.

The power and influence of the buyer group depends on the following:

- If there are few entry barriers or critical switching costs on the part of potential suppliers, especially to do with capital or legal constraints; in such cases, buyers are able to approach anyone they choose.
- Where products are undifferentiated, where there is no brand loyalty, buyers also have greater influence.

The level of profit in the buyer group's business is also critical; and where this is low, there is great pressure on the sector to lower its costs.

The relative centrality of the purchased product in question to the overall performance of the buyer group is also important – if a poor or basic standard item can be sold effectively on to its customers by the buyer group operators, then a pressure commensurate with this tends to be exerted on suppliers.

Finally the buyer group may have the potential to integrate backwards and establish its own suppliers (often by buying up the particular companies).

□ Supplier groups

These exert pressure on participants in a sector by raising prices or reducing the quality of products and services offered. They squeeze profitability out of any sector unable to recover its costs through price rises.

The supplier group is powerful if, above all, it is dominated by a few companies, and is more concentrated or organised than the sectors to which it sells (such as oil, which is dominated by the major multinationals of Shell, BP, Texaco, Aramco, and Gulf).

It is powerful if the product is central to the expectations of buyers or if it is differentiated and the buyers' customers have brand identity or loyalty; or if the product is central to the needs of the buyers' clients.

It is powerful if there are capital or cost or legal elements in the entry barriers faced by potential or putative entrants to the sector. It may also pose a threat of forward integration into the business of the industry itself, by establishing its own relationship with the ultimate clients and consumers of the product or service.

Suppliers' groups may not be dependent on any one sector for continued existence, but may be able to switch sectors easily, generate new markets for the products and services in question, and ultimately find new applications for existing production technology.

Figure 6.1 models the five elemental forces in the competitive environment.

■ The organisational standpoint

The approach of an organisation to its marketing efforts and initiatives is based on the answers to a range of matters and issues that must be determined and decided at corporate level. This involves evaluation and analysis of the following:

1. The true nature of the **products** and **services** on offer; the functions that they serve; the benefits and attributes they afford to purchasers; the potential or additional functions that they could also serve
2. The true nature of the **market** or **markets** in which the product and services are offered; considerations of expansion, contraction, stagnation, growth, maturity, saturation and decline; assessment of the state of product and service life-cycles

3. (a) The true nature of the **organisation's** capabilities, strengths and weaknesses; and an assessment of what truly distinguishes it, and its products and services, from the competition

   (b) The true nature of the capabilities, strengths and weaknesses of the organisation's **competitors**, and assessment of what distinguishes each from the others in the sector

   (c) The identification of the **relative advantages** of the organisation over its competitors

4. (a) Assessment of **opportunities** and **potential** in the markets and sectors in which business is currently being conducted, and an assessment and continuing investigation into potentially new areas; the overall purpose here is to identify areas where new, more profitable and better business could and should be carried out

   (b) Assessment of the **wider concerns** of the market, the ways in which business is conducted; wider environmental, ethical and moral concerns, and the ways in which these should be addressed and tackled; and the ways in which they interact with each other.

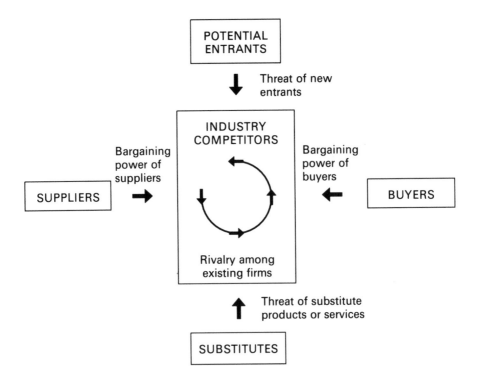

Figure 6.1   Five elemental forces of competition

Source: Christensen (1987). Used with permission.

■ Internal marketing

This is the application of the wider principles and practices of marketing to in-organisation activities. Rather than overt and profitable business, the results are translated as follows:

1. Credibility and confidence of particular departments, in relation to their interaction with others: creating a positive or productive working environment, and inter-departmental harmony and mutuality and trust; dependence of one department or function on another for its expertise is well-founded; the results of inter-departmental cooperation are positive and productive
2. The ability to approach internal functions for expert and high-quality advice, service, support and direction, in the knowledge that this will be forthcoming
3. Internal marketing also creates the aura, harmony and general mutuality within which the organisation works; it is a contributor to the motivation of individuals, and the morale of the total organisation; it helps in the setting of modus operandi, performance standards, attitudes and values
4. Management style, the relations between different levels of staff, the identity with and adoption of the purpose, vision and core values of the organisation, also owe much to the organisation's ability to market itself to its staff.

■ The marketing mix

The concept of the marketing mix came about as the result of research at Harvard University in the 1930s and 1940s. This identified key variables in archetype marketing programmes and activities.

The easiest definition of the marketing mix is in terms of the 4Ps:

- **Product:**   variety, branding quality, packaging, appearance and design
- **Promotion:**   advertising, sponsorship, selling, publicity, mailshots
- **Price:**   basic, discounting, credit, payment method, appearance
- **Place:**   coverage, outlets, transport, distribution and accessibility.

Marketing mixes arise from combinations and interactions of each of these elements. Consumers of products and services – offerings – will normally hold one of the elements more important than the others. In turn, the forces and pressures of the markets in which the offerings are made also reflect their relative importance.

There are legal and ethical restraints placed on marketing activities in the western world. In general, spurious or misleading claims may not be made for products, nor should misleading impressions be deliberately fostered – apart from anything else this is very bad for repeat business. Actual products must reflect the reality or impression given by both promotion and packaging. Products must also not be harmful or detrimental to their consumers; minimum standards of performance, manufacture, quality and safety have therefore to be met.

We will now consider each of the 4P elements in turn.

■ Product

'Product' in this context is the term habitually used to describe anything that is offered to a market sector for consumption, and includes commercial and public services. The product mix is the range of products offered by an organisation. This is determined by the matching of the organisation's capabilities and capacities with the markets and niches to be serviced and by the scope and scale of its operations. People buy the benefits that they expect to accrue from a product rather than its features. Organisations therefore sell those benefits. McDonald's and Coca-Cola are well known examples of this. They have created both strong and wholesome images for their products and the desire in their market sectors to be associated with this image. To the consumer, the items are not merely food and drink but part of a way of life with which they wish to be associated.

□ Quality and durability

Product quality and durability must be considered. The two are not mutually exclusive (a disposable syringe is only to be used once but it has to work that once). There is also no point in offering a highly durable product to the stated market sector if that is not what the sector wants. (Fashionable shoes and clothes, for example, are offered to some sectors on the basis that they are today's style, and that they will become obsolete when the next design comes along). Consider Summary Box 6.3.

□ Branding

Branding gives credence and confidence, especially where the brand is well known. The consumer is content with what is offered and comfortable with the appearance of a name on the product. Ford, General Motors, Renault, Volkswagen, Fiat, Toyota – all give messages of confidence and reliability. They are all major companies in their industry.

□ Packaging

Packaging is used both to present the product to its best advantage and to protect it up to the point of consumption. It is instrumental in reinforcing the identity of, and with, the product. Many soap powders, for example, now come

---

SUMMARY BOX 6.3   Lycra: Quality, Durability (and Flexibility)

This is an excellent example of the way in which a general product has grown into different markets.

Lycra is a highly elastic versatile man-made fabric, the properties of which have been known for a long while; however, its commercial exploitation and maximisation was fully realised only in the early to mid-1990s. It was originally used for the manufacture of grid iron football trousers, tracksuits and cycling shorts – clothing that fitted the wearers exactly, clung to their body and limbs and thus did not chafe when the body and limbs were moved. Indeed, the cycling shorts were popular among cyclists because they actively prevented the limbs from chafing against the bicycle saddle.

Variations were and are being developed for use in the whole sporting and athletics range and lycra shorts are now also worn by association footballers and rugby players both for prevention and safety and also to give thigh muscle support.

The use of the material in other clothing is also being realised. As well as its comfort and ease of wearing it is also very easy to wash and keep clean; it is warm in winter and yet light and comfortable in summer. It does not crease easily and therefore has what is (perceived to be) an inherently smart appearance. Its potential is being developed in the realms of evening wear, high fashion, and working clothes; and is also being offered across all age ranges.

---

in smaller boxes as a kindness to the environment – and this becomes part of the advertising and promotional campaign.

☐ Product benefits

The benefits of the products should be seen in their widest context. The full offering often includes after-sales service, spare parts, help and emergency lines, call-out facilities and product advice and familiarity sessions for those who are to sell the product. Marks & Spencer, the UK department store, offer a money-back guarantee or the ability to exchange one product for another that will be of greater satisfaction and benefit to the customer (the company is consequently a favourite for the purchase of Christmas and other presents). Mail order catalogues normally offer a 'no quibble' returns service at the expense of the company. Companies that sell computer systems for industrial, commercial or public service use normally include staff familiarisation as part of the total package offered, together with problem-solving services. Consider Summary Box 6.4.

☐ Product ranges and portfolios

This is the total range of organisations' offerings. Ideally, the confidence and reputation of each feeds all the others. When one product is perceived to be bad or unreliable, it is likely to have a knock-on effect on all of the others. One excellent product normally allows others in the range to gain at least some credibility and reputation, even where these are not as strong or as well respected (see Summary Box 6.4).

One way of looking at portfolios and ranges is to classify products as:

- Those which are advertised
- Those which sell
- Those which make money.

Another way is the 'Boston Group' matrix (see Figure 6.2).

The need is for a balanced portfolio. All products can be classified under each heading. It is a useful easy ready-reckoner, a quick way of mapping the organisation's products.

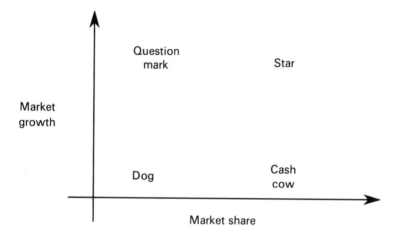

Cash cows: High share of low growth market; today's breadwinners; the main source of income.
Stars: high share of high growth market; today's and tomorrow's breadwinners from which future cash cows will come; normally need high investment and support to maintain position.
Question marks: low share of high growth market; tomorrow's potential breadwinners; not all will succeed.
Dog: low share of low growth market; normally only kept if they have some distinctive positive deature.

Figure 6.2   The 'Boston Group' matrix

☐ The product life cycle

All products have a beginning, a middle and an end (see Figure 6.3). The concept of product life cycle defines more precisely these stages and identifies the points at which specific marketing initiatives and activities might usefully be generated.

SUMMARY BOX 6.4   Ford

The Ford Motor Company offers a range of models and 'models within models'. These include the Fiesta, Sierra, Tempo, Escort, Granada, Mondeo and a range of vans and pick-ups. The Fiesta is offered as: small and large engine; limited edition, diesel for Europe; XR2; 3 door and 5 door. The Escort is offered with all of these and also as a cabriolet (soft top or convertible).

This reflects the ability of the organisation to differentiate even using the most automated and sophisticated of production techniques; its ability to identify precise niches, even those that will take perhaps a few hundred cars a year only from an organisation of this scale, size and technology; and its ability to present a range of offerings from which the different consumers may make their choice.

The company follows this with a range of warranty services; guaranteed maintenance at a Ford dealer; guarantees on parts for a number of years; finance plans for the purchase of the cars; accessories, in-car entertainment and clothing. Ford have:

- **Products to advertise**: the RS1600 Series; the Cosworth Series; the XR2 and XR3 Series
- **Products to sell**: Fiesta, Escort, Granada, Mondeo
- **Products to make money**: extended warranties, finance plans, accessories and service contracts

The company supports all of this with extensive advertising, distribution, promotion and distinctive branding. The primary aim is to ensure that whichever model is bought both the specific benefits to the customer and the overall general confidence that goes with the Ford name are both purchased and protected.

There are four stages:

- **Introduction**: the bringing in and bringing on of the new product; this is the culmination of a period of both product and market research, the point at which the offering in question first comes on to the market
- **Growth**: this is where the product takes off and its true potential (rather than that projected by research and modelling) begins to become apparent; sales and demand both rise where this is successful; unit costs decline
- **Maturity**: the product is now a familiar and well-loved feature on the market; people are both happy and confident with it, unit costs are low. The last part of the maturity stage is that of saturation; this is where the company seeks to squeeze the last remaining possible commercial benefits from the item before it loses its commercial value
- **Decline**: where the product is deemed to have run its course and no more value or profit is to be gained from it, it will then be withdrawn from the market. Marketing interventions are made at each stage to ensure that the product potential is maximised. The product must take off so that the full range of benefits to be gained from consumers of it are realised by the sector at which it is aimed; then as it reaches maturity initiatives are taken to breathe as much new life into it as possible using the whole range of promotional and

advertising media; very often this means one advertising campaign too many before the product declines.

Products may also be rejuvenated through re-packaging, re-presentation and changing the quality or value emphases.

Summary Box 6.5 relates product strategy to the stage in the product's life cycle.

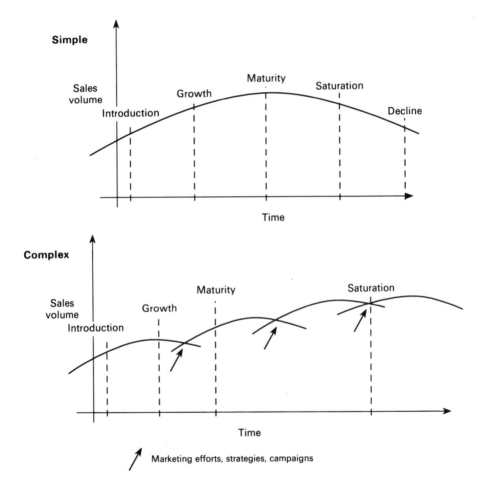

Purpose: the model indicates the regeneration, renewal and extension of the profitable life of the product concerned and its relationship with successful marketing activity.

Figure 6.3   Product life cycles

SUMMARY BOX 6.5   The Growth–Share or Product Portfolio Model

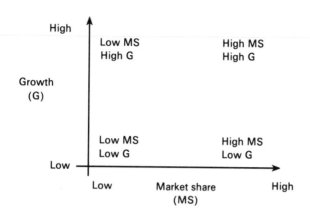

The model assumes that organisations have a range of products or offerings, and that these will be at different stages at a given point in time.

There are four quadrants in the model, for the assessment of products, and the basis for taking marketing decisions in relation to them.

The model provides a means of assessment of the portfolio, and indicates more general or strategic implications (for example, whether the 'low-low' configuration of a product should signal its divestment, or whether it is worth generating or regenerating).

■ Price

Organisations set price levels that enable them to generate sufficient income to keep shareholders and any other stakeholders happy and contented. They must further set prices to ensure that sufficient income is generated to ensure continuity of operations and to provide sufficient general cash flow to meet the needs of the organisation (above all, it must be profitable). Price therefore normally covers at least variable costs (the costs of production), and also makes some contribution towards the organisation establishment.

The price of an item must reflect both the willingness and capability of the customer to pay. If one is offering in niches where the customers and consumers are always paid by cash (as distinct from cheque or credit or debit cards or finance plans) then prices must reflect the volume of cash carried and must be sensitive to the competing demands on it. Summary Boxes 6.6, 6.7 and 6.8 demonstrate crucial aspects of price setting.

Price thus reflects the range and complexity of offerings made, the relationship with the consumer and the degree of choice that the consumer has. Price

---

SUMMARY BOX 6.6   Legend of the Razor

The legend of the razor has a series of lessons for all who aspire to management. It illustrates most vividly the difference between selling an organisation's products and the provision of customer benefits and satisfaction. In apocryphal terms the razor cost £1.00 to make, but customers would only pay 20p for it. However, the razor blade cost 0.1p to make but customers would pay 10p each for them.

A distinction is therefore drawn between offering a razor for sale and the ability of the customer to shave. If the organisation concentrates on the razor it is not possible to conduct profitable business. By concentrating on the 'shave', however, and additionally ensuring a steady and continuing supply of blades, profit is made on the offering to the customer's continuous satisfaction.

SUMMARY BOX 6.7   Airline Tickets

People travelling on the same airline flight will almost inevitably have paid widely differing amounts for their seat.

The offerings by the airline are: first class; business or club class; tourist and economy class and charter. However, the variation in price will depend on a much greater number of matters:

1. **When** the ticket was purchased: airlines give discounts for purchases well in advance or right at the last minute (standby)
2. **Where** it was purchased: through travel agent, discount house (bucket shop), at the airport, direct with the airline; or which country it was purchased in, and what currency was used
3. **Who** purchased it: and whether it is a corporate or personal expense
4. **Why** it was purchased: for business, pleasure or holidays
5. **Other factors**: especially concerning whether the trip is part of a package holiday, fly-drive or reciprocal arrangement with an hotel chain, for example.

Airlines arrange their schedules with the prime purpose of ensuring that their planes travel as full as possible as often as possible. The price range thus ensures both a variety of offerings and also many sources of passengers. More importantly from their point of view, they thus maximise their chances of achieving their prime purpose.

---

also impinges upon the areas relating to the desired market share for the product on the part of the organisation; prices being offered by the competition; and the prices of substitute goods. There may also be particular revenue targets required by the organisation. However, large and complex organisations generally have a measure of flexibility in this area; for example, they can offset possible losses on one product through great gains on another. In such cases price will be seen as a component only of a wider marketing strategy.

Organisations need a measure of flexibility in the determination of price that will enable them to respond to any competitive moves elsewhere in the market.

SUMMARY BOX 6.8   The 99p Syndrome

The first use of price as a means of marketing in itself is ascribed to Marks & Spencer Plc of the UK in the 1970s. Instead of charging £5, £10 (or 5 or 10 local units of currency) the amount is reduced by one currency unit, to £4.99 or £9.99.

There is a strong perceptual message inherent in this which must be considered at this stage. The customer receives change as well as the goods or service that they desire, assuming that they pay with the single currency unit. The message that they consequently receive is that they are paying less than a particular amount for the product. In addition, the price is related to the note value of the currency where possible – £4.99 is related to the UK £5.00 note, for example and 99p to the £1.00 coin.

The price label thus becomes a feature of the presentation of the product or service itself, and becomes incorporated into the mainstream marketing activities generated.

N.B.: It is also said that this acts as a check on the integrity of both staff and customers. It is very unusual to pay the exact price if it is so presented. It means that the staff have to use the till. It also means that the customer must be given a receipt.

The activities of competitors, both offensive and defensive, therefore have an important bearing on pricing decisions; this may be instrumental in allowing or restricting one's abilities to move one's prices as one desires.

Finally, it is necessary to consider what is actually included in the price of an item or commodity. For example, when a car is bought the consumer achieves personal transport and mobility. However, the price paid may also include the concept of the 'lifetime of the car', including regular servicing, after-sales arrangements, emergency cover, insurance policies, finance plans that cover the purchase of the car as well as the other accessories that may go with it. In addition, a relationship with the garage or dealer may be bought that takes all the worry out of motoring provided that you continue to patronise the establishment, to have the servicing and after-sales conducted by them and possibly also to replace the car through them in a period of years hence.

From a marketing point of view, therefore, there is a context in which the arriving at and arrangement of the price of a commodity has to be seen. There are financial cost and contribution elements that must be considered (these are dealt with in Chapter 10); in marketing terms there is a much wider picture that has to be seen.

■ Promotion

This is the combination of methods used to generate public awareness, identity, confidence, desire and conviction in a product and ultimately its adoption and usage by the general public (see Summary Box 6.9). The methods used in the pursuit of this are: advertising in all mass media including newspapers, television

---

SUMMARY BOX 6.9   Health Care Promotions

Promotions in health care sectors are all pervasive. They range from notepads and pens issued by drugs and medical equipment companies to the medical equipment itself. Anything provided by the companies carries their logo and other distinctive identity marks. It is all provided in hospitals, clinics and doctors' surgeries. The returns to the companies come from prescriptions and other drugs recommended by general practitioners to their patients; this practice is endemic across the entire western world.

According to Eric Clark (1988), 'doctors are subject to the most intense sales promotions and pressures in the community. As much as 25% [of the sales effort] may be spent on promotions. In the United Kingdom each doctor is the target for over £5,000 worth of promotion a year . . . which falls better into place when another is added – the £58,000 worth of drugs that the average British GP prescribes each year'. This is a graphic illustration of the size of the market that is to be tapped and the nature and extent of promotional activity that can be both contemplated and afforded by those seeking business from the health care sector.

---

and radio; sponsorship of events, other products and activities; sales calling by organisational representatives to generate new business and general awareness and to maintain and service existing business; brochures designed to generate the image required of the product and to demonstrate the features and benefits that its consumers are perceived to require; product placement, by which producers of films, brochures, magazines, novels, stories and television series are per-suaded to adopt distinctive brands of product such as cars and clothing to be used and worn by their heroes and heroines, thus assisting in the generation of positive images and high level identity; other publicity features such as general awareness-raising articles, news items and general interest stories, featuring particular products and services; and price, which may also be integrated into the promotional campaign adopted.

□ Image and identity

The most important aspect of any promotional campaign, whatever media it is decided to use, is the decision about what to say to prospective customers and the precise image and identity that is generated. Promotional activities concentrate on increasing customer familiarity with the product or service in question; informing customers about the features, benefits and qualities of the product or service; indicating any distinctive advantages that it has over competing or substitute products or services; differentiating between the product or service in question and any near equivalent; establishing its overall credibility and consumer confidence in it; encouraging potential customers and maintaining the current customer base.

Promotional methods adopted in the pursuit of custom will depend upon the number of customers; their location; other niche considerations; their spending habits; and their expectations; accurate assessments of these are arrived at as the result of marketing research. In general, within these constraints, the promotional campaign will set out both to familiarise in broad terms and also to generate a particular identity for the product in question among the potential consumers (see Summary Box 6.10).

These elements constitute the ways in which promotional effectiveness is measured – that is, the extent to which the general awareness of the product and its benefits has been aroused; and the nature of and identity with the images promoted in the market sector. Finally, in this case reference should be made to the fact that there are both offensive and defensive promotional activities. Offensive promotional activities are those where the organisation seeks to promote its own products and the benefits of them to consumers at the expense of the other players in the market. Defensive promotional activities are those engaged in in response to the offensive promotional activities of competitors. Summary Boxes 6.11 and 6.12 demonstrate the extent of marketing activity that underpins promotions. Summary Box 6.13 shows how perception of image and brand loyalty are concerned.

☐ Internal promotion

Internal promotion is the means by which confidence and awareness of the organisation's products and services is generated among its staff; this includes in particular any new product or service that is to be offered. It is greatly

---

SUMMARY BOX 6.10 Drink

No set of products carries a greater concept of image than drink. When they buy, drinkers become associated with all the dreams and illusions that the advertising and promotional agencies have built up around the brand. The famous drink brands themselves are testament to this. They are all household names – Coca-Cola, Pepsi, Heineken, Bacardi, Guinness, Southern Comfort. Moreover, they have all gained a verbal currency in both the English and other languages of the West. Thus for example, Bacardi is not a type of rum but has its own identity and uniqueness.

These images and concepts of identity are developed using the whole range of media available. The pictures used are always of exotic locations; overt sexuality; health and fitness; opulence (in the use of domestic and hotel settings, for example, as the backdrop against which the products are promoted and illustrated). They exude an inherent wholesomeness and honesty, a statement that the promise contained in the advertisement about the product will be delivered.

Marketing and promotional campaigns thus concentrate on the images and aura as much as on the product and its benefits to the consumer; and on keeping these images up-to-date. Campaigns therefore use backcloths that keep the universal and positive images going but change the human stars regularly to ensure that they are currently fashionable.

SUMMARY BOX 6.11   Soap Powder

In the UK the soap powder industry is dominated by two major organisations, Reckitt & Coleman and Lever Brothers (Unilever). The generic offering is the ability of the customer to wash clothes to a high degree of cleanliness that makes them suitable for wearing in public again.

The packaging and differentiation activity that goes into this is quite remarkable; it is in itself a multi-million dollar business. Distinctive packaging is carried out with the following purposes:

- Generating distinctive brands and brand loyalties (e.g., Persil, Daz, Bold)
- Demonstrating a cost advantage (e.g. Bold again, it has the advantage of being an all-in-one cleaner and conditioner of clothes so the customer needs only one product and not two – i.e. a conditioner as well)
- Identifying supermarket own brands as well as the named brands (again usually with a price advantage)
- Differentiating in the following ways: big and small packets – the advantage of the small packet is 'environmental'; this has, however, to be balanced against the perception that the larger packet is better value for money
- Refills that come in plastic bags, again with environmental advantages, real or perceived
- Odour-free and perfumed powders to be used according to taste
- 'New person' approaches – even men and boys can use the washing powder effectively
- 'Working person' approaches – that allow (usually) the woman of the house to give the impression of both holding down a job and fulfilling her domestic obligations and responsibilities
- Traditional approaches that fix the obligation firmly on the woman of the house to come up with bright, clean and fresh clothes for her family (consisting of one husband, one son and one daughter).

This last was the central feature of the initial promotion of the Radion brand (Reckitt & Coleman) and was extremely successful. This portrayed the woman of the house in a stereo-typical role. Her responsibility was to provide bright, clean, shining and fresh smelling clothes for the man and children in her life; her obligation and responsibility was clearly demonstrated as lying in this area by the style of promotional campaign adopted. The packaging used for the product was red. The underlying tone adopted for the product in general was traditional.

The product generated a multi-million pound turnover for the company, becoming a very successful offering in this market. This success was due to the promotional and packaging activity, style and image indicated above.

---

advantageous at the inception of a new product and when it is being brought on to the public mainstream to have the organisation staff using it and demonstrating confidence in it as part of the general process of awareness raising.

For example, as we saw in Summary Box 5.7, the post-it note was invented by an employee of the 3M company. The employee sang in a church choir; and initially he wanted a slip of paper with which he could mark the places in the

---

SUMMARY BOX 6.12   Storylining

Product storylining is a promotional instrument peculiar to the UK. For years PG Tips, the brand of tea, has been promoted through the use of a group of monkeys in a variety of comedy sketches; indeed, this is so central to the promotional activities and the consuming public has such a sense of affinity with it, that the company that owns the brand (Brooke Bond) has felt unable to sanction any departure from it.

Storylining has been adopted by other brands in their promotional activities with varying degrees of success. The two most distinctive, successful and long-running are for Oxo gravy (which has followed an archetype family as it has grown and prospered for ten years); and for Nescafé Gold Blend instant coffee, developing a relationship between a glamorous couple who live next door to each other over a similar period of time. The series has made national figures out of the pair of actors used (a new couple have been introduced late in 1993), and a novel telling the story of the characters is now for sale. The series has made national figures out of the actors, and a novel telling the story of the characters was a national bestseller in 1993 and 1994.

All this is in the generation of sales of universal British consumer goods – tea, coffee and gravy.

---

hymn book but which would not fall out of the hymn book as it was moved or carried around. He thus devised the small slips of paper with the sticky strip. The product was given an excellent initial impetus through its adoption by the staff of the 3M company who were the first people to use it for the myriad of purposes now adopted.

The other feature of internal promotion is specifically concerned with internal markets that may be found to exist in new-style public services, local governments and health authorities of the kind promulgated by the UK in the 1990s. Such arrangements may also be found between divisions of multinationals and other agglomerate corporations. In either case a key feature of the internal promotions mechanism will be the generation of, and maintenance of, business confidence. In the style of public services indicated in particular, if this is not forthcoming the purchasers of particular facilities may be at liberty to seek a better provision from outside the organisation.

■ Place

The fourth element of the marketing mix is place; getting the products and services to the customers and clients. This means knowing who they are, where they are, how they want the products and services delivered, what the nature and level of their expectations are, and how these may best be satisfied. Part of the creative process involved in marketing is concerned with both meeting this requirement on the part of the customer and also generating an expectation that if they do go to a particular place then this particular need will be satisfied.

SUMMARY BOX 6.13   Customer Perception

Research conducted by the tobacco industry in the 1980s demonstrated that brand loyalty was almost entirely based on image and identity rather than the taste of the product. Tests were conducted on those who stated categorically that they only liked their own brand. Smokers could not differentiate between their own brands and others of equivalent strength and similar tobacco when they were not given the packet from which to choose.

This also applies to soft drinks; tea and coffee; bread, cakes and biscuits; butter and margarine.

People are also more positively disposed towards any of these products if they are told that it is of their preferred brand, whether it is or not.

Source: Clark (1988).

The concept of place derives much from the segmentation process (see above). The other main feature here that must be considered is that of location. This reflects the nature of distribution networks, especially those concerned with getting the product or service to the point at which consumers buy it or take delivery of it. There is thus currently a propensity among organisations operating in Western Europe and North America to locate on the edge of towns in order to have convenience of access to road distribution networks. Organisations that use railway, sea and air distribution will consider the rest of their own specific marketing mixes in relation to this.

The question of location also relates to the production and operation philosophies that are concerned with the traditional view that an organisation would locate near the sources of raw materials if the items that it produced lost weight during the production and manufacturing processes; and that conversely they would locate near the markets if their processes resulted in the products gaining weight.

Location also reflects any sectoral or regional demands or desires or constraints. Hitherto, for example, there has been an expectation that each community would have its own school, its own library, its own hospital; these have become limiting factors in the offering of education and health services. The same is true for certain sports facilities. There thus becomes an onus placed on those responsible for organising, providing and managing these services and constraints within which they have to work. If this is not the most efficient or effective way of providing the service, then part of the process of changing it must include a raising of the understanding required of the public – promotion of the benefits of the new proposed arrangement. People will go along with this if they see and understand that it is in their best interests to do so, and if they can see the benefits that will accrue to them.

This has been achieved by the supermarket and shopping mall sectors in Europe and North America. A whole process of behaviour and expectation reform has been completed in the pursuit of this. People now go to out-of-town mega-stores in the UK and France; and to shopping malls in North America. The benefits of ease of access and 'everything under one roof' have been successfully demonstrated to those niches of the population that use them. Those responsible for the hypermarkets and the generation of business for shopping malls took steps to understand the nature of the requirements of those that were expected to use them, what products and services they would require from them, and designed a consumer environment where both could be satisfied. It has had a major impact upon the location of commercial activity and those who continue to do business in the centre of towns have had to consider much more precisely the attractions of their particular location to the consumers that continue to come to them.

The other matters that concern the 'place' element of the marketing mix are principally to do with the nature and style of distribution adopted. The product or service in question may go straight from the organisation to its customers; conversely, it may go through a highly sophisticated channel of distribution. Whichever it is, it must be borne in mind that the key requirements on the part of the customer of flexibility, responsiveness, ease of access and general convenience remain the key to conducting continuing and effective business.

■ Varying the marketing mix

As stated at the outset of this section, the precise nature of individual marketing mixes will depend upon the product and the ways in which it is to be offered in the particular sectors; and the rationale for this depends upon the key marketing strategies and standpoints adopted by the organisation. Organisations may seek to vary their marketing mixes in the interests of generating or regenerating new business initiatives; for example, organisations will bring down the price of commodities that are nevertheless sold on a quality rather than a price-sensitive basis if by doing so they consider that an advantage can be gained; conversely a manufacturing organisation may release its products for sale in a supermarket, thus trading off the exclusivity of its product in return for the ability to generate a much wider accessibility and acceptance.

■ Marketing research and development

The purpose of such research is to identify and maximise opportunities that the product and marketing mix of the organisation affords. Essentially, this combines the need to seek alternative outlets for products and the technology that the organisation has at its disposal with that of finding out what customers' wants and needs are. Initiatives can then be proposed and generated with the view to satisfying these needs; and in the devising and initiating of further business opportunities.

The process undertaken is concerned mainly with an understanding of the capabilities and capacities of the organisation on the one hand and the requirements of the market and environment in which business is conducted on the other; this will address matters concerning general levels of confidence on the part of the market, customers' purchasing power, their needs and wants, their priorities and any other seasonal aspects, and relate these to the capabilities and capacities of the organisation. Other factors to be taken into account will include a more general assessment of the market and the products in question, the extent to which these are in expansion, decline or stability (see pp. 000, 000); research will include competitor analyses and the extent to which alternative and substitute products are available in the broadest sense; it will consider the reputation of the organisation in question from a universal and general standpoint, as well as in the particular case of its own relationship with its own market sector. Customer assessments will also be conducted in order to gain a general understanding of their motives, desires, preferred images and identity with the particular product or range of products that is to be offered. Finally, modelling activities will need to be commissioned or conducted by the organisation with a view to assessing the extent of the profitability or effectiveness of the range of activities in question. Marketing research and development is thus an integral part of and critical to the success of wider strategic aspects, and critical to the determination of the organisation's future direction and instrumental in the determination of its success.

■ Corporate citizenship

This concept was introduced in Chapter 5.

In the context of marketing it deserves a further brief mention. Part of the total marketing activity is the ability to present an image, to both the markets served and the local community in which the organisation itself is located, of wholesomeness and a high ethical stance. As an example, the initial push of the Eurotunnel organisation in the South East of England in the mid-1980s was to gain a general acceptance of the project at this level. It succeeded to a great extent through the generation of an aura both of positiveness and of openness and by the enthusing of the schoolchildren population with a pioneering and exciting vision of the Channel Tunnel and the opportunities that it will bring to their generation.

■ Public relations

The public relations or PR function is to ensure that the marketing wheels are kept oiled and that the organisation's marketing machine works smoothly and positively in order to fulfil the purposes for which it was designed. It has a maintenance function that mirrors the operational equivalent (see Chapter 10); planned PR concerns the identification in advance of suitable initiatives and items that will generate good publicity and placing them in the media where they will have the greatest positive effects; there is also remedial PR, which is where the organisation has to take responsive or other creative action to put right something that has gone wrong or to address a negative story concerning it that has appeared somewhere in the media.

Overall, therefore, PR is conducted at the interface between the organisation, the environment and the community, its customers and clients, and the media, in order to maintain, preserve, and improve positive and effective images and relationships; to build confidence and credibility; and to resolve problems when they arise.

The importance of the positive approach to PR cannot be overstated. When problems do occur, the organisation must accept responsibility for any 'repair' or remedial action necessary, whether it was at fault or not. Inability to do this is always seen in a negative light, and is often offensive to both customers and the wider community.

The issuing of brochures and information about the organisation is also part of the PR function. Again these must be designed and drawn up with the readership in mind – presentation, language and images used must be in the terms of those who are to receive them.

Similarly the handling of the press, television and radio must be conducted in ways that ensure that an overall positivism is maintained, and that when problems arise, the last and most enduring note of the story is of the progress that is now to be made.

Organisations will also engage in the placement of stories favourable to themselves, in the media, and in those parts of it where the greatest benefit to them will accrue. This is both as a counter to those occasions when problems do arise, and also as part of the more general process of building confidence, positive images, and an aura of 'good corporate citizenship'.

Organisations may also engage in more general customer and market liaison activities as part of their PR effort. This usually takes the form of sending staff on high-profile and sectoral seminars and conferences, and taking stands at trade fairs and exhibitions. Part of the effort of the sales force may also be simply to ensure that customers (and potential customers) are kept aware of the organisation's continued existence and activities. The sponsorship of events also contributes to this general effort.

Finally, organisations engage in positive PR in relation to their staff and to this end they run sports and social clubs, welfare facilities, and staff newspapers, newsletters and other publications for internal consumption. There is also a strong element of this aspect of PR inherent in the nature and conduct of personnel policies.

Large and complex organisations set great store by this. The removal of a corporate customer or regular order, for example, may cost millions of dollars even to a multinational, and the presence of a PR department and activities to

---

SUMMARY BOX 6.14   A PR Master Stroke

An estate agent in Sandgate in Kent once sold a house to a customer in a notorious landslip area. The purchase went ahead; and the house subsequently fell into the sea. The customer sued the estate agent and the story was a nine day wonder in the local press. The estate agent, the subject of bad publicity, was nevertheless able to turn this to his advantage through a PR master stroke. This was that he was insured against such contingencies and that people could continue to deal with him in the utmost confidence even though this had happened, in the sure and certain knowledge that even in such an extreme case as this there would be no penalty to the customer.

---

respond to such matters and to avoid this happening is considered well worth having. Consider Summary Box 6.14.

■ Conclusions

Marketing has therefore to be seen as having the following managerial characteristics. It permeates the entire organisation and all its activities. Without a marketing stance, the organisation has no reason for existence. This also extends to the provision of public services; in absolute terms the consumers or users of these public services are the clients of the public service organisation.

Marketing is at the core of the strategic purpose of the organisation. Without a clear purpose of the nature of the operations that it is going to conduct and the business that it is going to be in and the markets in which it is going to operate, the organisation will have no impetus or clarity of direction. Further to this, there is a range of organisational and managerial activities that have to be conducted in the effective and successful devising and implementation of marketing initiatives.

Marketing is an all-pervasive business concept. It is there to ensure that what is done is both effective and profitable. Any activity that is undertaken should be in accordance with the strategic aims, the technology, the capacities and capabilities of the organisation, its staff and resources. It is also concerned with seeking and generating improvements in the organisation's business activities. It provides the impetus for the devising, development and implementation of new products and services. It is concerned with seeking new business opportunities in fields with which it is familiar and also in new areas. Marketing sub-strategies, plans and objectives will be devised in the pursuit of this.

Effective marketing is also concerned with the gathering of effective and suitable information concerning the organisation's products and their impact on customers, competitors, suppliers and the market place and environment at large.

The final part of marketing activity is that which is concerned with the continuity of the organisation; it is the generation of and bringing on stream of a steady supply of new products, suitable in both operational and quality terms for the markets in which the organisation operates or seeks to operate. More generally, organisations will seek to identify market opportunities, design and devise strategies, and then to implement and develop them. Marketing is thus both a process and a reflection of the corporate state of mind in relation to its business as well a combination of functional activities and expert and specialist understanding.

CHAPTER 7

Human resource management

The purpose of this chapter is to introduce the student to some fundamental concepts in what is an ever-developing field of importance in the management sphere. Peter Drucker finds the question of Human Resource Management (HRM) to be so crucial and central to the role and function of the manager, that he questions the need for personnel departments at all – this work should be done by **every** manager, and **every** manager should have expertise in this area.

■ Introduction

In general, the concept and basis of HRM has moved from welfare concerns and a moral or enlightened attitude to the staff and workers of organisations, through highly structured and highly staffed corporate and department personnel functions, to 'resource management', where it currently rests, and from where it is likely to develop.

The current regard for HRM has, initially, the disquieting connotation that the human resource is to be exploited, in the same way as land, capital, technology, and information. However, if this is seen in a context of responsibility and obligations on the part of the organisation, its managers and its staff; the necessity to maintain and develop the resource (as with any other); and to see in true terms the requirement to gain a return on the investment in the human resource (and all that **truly** means), it sits easier from the moral standpoint, as well as making sound managerial sense.

Effective and successful HRM is a highly cost-effective, even profitable, aspect of management.

The main areas of activity are as follows:

- Formulating HRM policies and strategies
- Devising a staff management style that sets the approach and standards of employee relations
- Providing the means – rules and procedures – for the implementation of those policies
- Analysing and packaging work into jobs and occupations
- Providing a service function, maintaining and improving management of staff at the workplace
- Planning for the required staff; recruiting, motivating and developing

- Setting performance standards for everyone; providing the means of measuring and appraising performance; supporting performance with procedures and practices
- Devising and implementing fair payment systems
- Providing and implementing strategies for change that address the organisational and 'human aspects'.

Organisations have general obligations to their staff. There is a general duty of care. There are also legal and ethical requirements. In the UK and EU there is extensive legal protection for all workers. There is also a direct correlation between the ways in which the human resource is addressed and approached and organisation success and failure.

The management of the human resource is thus becoming recognised as an area of high expertise, and one in which a fully effective and direct contribution to business performance and business profit is to be made. It follows from this that there are skills and knowledge that can be taught, and which must be learned, by those who are to practise in the area; that, finally, HRM is increasingly regarded as a universal, rather than a specialised, aspect of management.

■ Corporate aspects

Human resource strategies and policies are designed and devised to meet the operations and undertakings of the organisation. They reflect overall aspirations; business strategies and policies; direction; technology; skills, knowledge and expertise. They need to meet the aspirations of those who carry out the work. They address the formation of the required culture, attitudes, values and beliefs. They define the 'aura' and 'ethos' of the organisation. They set out the desired type of employer and define the management style. They establish the standpoints to be taken on specific issues as follows:

- Work analysis and staff planning, recruitment, selection, assessment, succession and promotion
- The style of HRM to be adopted and fostered in the everyday dealings with and between staff
- Industrial relations, representation, rules, regulations and procedures
- The approach to the health and well-being of the employees
- The approach to be taken to safety at the workplace
- Employee development, work methods and practices
- Pay, remuneration and benefits
- Employee services, job analysis, design, improvement and enrichment
- Personnel specification
- Performance standards establishment, maintenance and appraisal
- Human resource maintenance
- Attention to discipline, grievance and disputes
- The assumption of responsibility for ensuring levels of performance

- The content of induction and orientation programmes
- The basis on which opportunities are offered to individual employees
- Evenness and fairness of treatment of employees across the entire organisation, as well as within individual departments and functions
- Health and safety and occupational health
- Attention to workstation design and improvement
- Attention to work development, enhancement and enrichment
- Attention to organisation and staff development. (See Figure 7.1.)

AREA OF WORK	STRATEGY AND DIRECTION	PERSONNEL OPERATIONS
Work design and structuring	Principles, approaches, departmentalisation, organisation structure	Job descriptions, work patterns, work structuring
Staff planning	Systems appraisal, design commissioning	Systems usage
Recruitment and selection	Standpoint (grow your own, buy in from outside)	Training of recruiters and selectors, recruitment and selection activities
Induction	Policy, content, priority	Delivery
Use of agencies and external sources of staff	Principles, circumstances	Contacts and commissions
Performance appraisal	Purpose, systems, design, principles, aims and objectives	Systems implementation, training of appraisers and appraisees
Pay and rewards	Policy, levels, mix of pay and benefits, package design	Assimilate individual staff to policy
Occupational health	Policy, content, design of package	Operation of package in conjunction with functional departments
Equality	Standards, policy, content, context, ethics	Policy operation, monitoring of standards, remedial actions
Industrial relations	Standpoints (conflict, conformist), representation	Negotiations, consultation, participation, staff communications
Discipline	Policy, procedure, practice, design, standpoint	Implementation of policy and procedure, support for staff, training of all staff

Table 7.1 *continued*

Grievance	Policy, procedure	Implementation of policy and procedure, training of all staff
Training and development	Priority and resources	Activities, opportunities, accessability
Dismissal	Standards of conduct, examples of gross misconduct	Operation of disciplinary procedures, operation of dismissal procedures, support and advice

Human Resource Management is divided into strategic and directional activities; and personnel activities. The role and function is:

- policy, advisory, consultative, supporting, a point of reference;
- personnel practitioner;
- establisher of policy content;
- establishing standards of best practice;
- creator of personnel activities;
- monitor/evaluator of personnel activities.

Figure 7.1   Human resource management summary

■ Equal opportunities

Equality of treatment, opportunity and access is an issue of attitude, or corporate state of mind. It is a fundamental prerequisite to the creation of organisation and operation effectiveness. Managers and organisations must first overcome the tendency to compartmentalise people by race, gender, religion, marital status, disability, age, location, postal address, non-essential qualification, school background, club membership, hobby and interest, etc. They must take the opposite standpoint of isolating the qualities essential and desirable to carry out a job. They must view people in terms of their potential as staff members, as contributors to the success and prosperity of the organisation. Without this, true equality of opportunity cannot exist.

There is also a question of basic human decency, that requires that all people be treated the same. This is a social as well as organisational concern. For organisations, all activities, management style, policies, practices and procedures, publications, advertisements, job and work descriptions, person specifications are written in ways that reinforce this. This emphasises, formulates and underlines the required attitudes and beliefs.

These standards are based on operational capabilities alone. Anyone, including managers, adopting a negative approach or attitude to equality of opportunity or who victimises, harasses or bullies members of their staff, must be subject to organisation discipline.

Offering equality of opportunity to all sectors of the workforce is both cost-effective and profitable. By concentrating on (discriminating against) certain sectors of the population on operational grounds, organisations greatly limit their prospects either of making effective appointments or of maximising the human resource.

The lead therefore, comes from the top of organisations and the attitudes filtered down to all the staff. Organisational equal opportunities policies must be clear, unequivocal and easily understood by all concerned. They must be valued and adopted at all levels and in all sectors and departments. A genuine adoption of the principle of equality for all constitutes excellent marketing to the human resource of the organisation. Staff are known to be valued for their capabilities. It also underlines any high moral or ethical stance taken in other business and organisational activities.

■ Staff planning

This is a dynamic and continuous process of which all managers should have a good understanding. This is because of the increasing complexity of organisations and activities; legislation; the availability of required expertise; technological changes and advances; labour turnover patterns; the structure of the workforce; the changing nature of labour markets; imbalances between skills available and required; the nature of core and peripheral workforces. All of this is increasingly an expected and integral part of the task of any manager in every functional area and activity.

The key elements involved are as follows:

1. **Work analysis** to order jobs and occupations in ways that are interesting, rewarding and fulfilling to the individual, and profitable and effective to the organisation
2. Assessing the **staff/manpower mix**, by each of, and a combination of, the following criteria: age; length of service; jobs held; promotions; sex, race, ethnic origin; skills and knowledge and expertise in different categories; flexibility and transferability
3. The balance between the **supply** of labour, and **demand** for labour overall, by location, and by the elements of the manpower mix given above; and the reconciliation of this supply and demand
4. **Future projections** for staff, based on accurate and informed projections of business activity and the HRM activities that are implicit in this
5. **Manpower information and computer systems**, and the information that they contain; managers are concerned not so much with the content and components of these systems as with the conclusions, use and value of the information
6. **Constraints**, especially resource constraints and those imposed by budget considerations and other operational factors. These include location and any consequent implications for the nature and type of workforce; the history and traditions of industrial and commercial activity in the area in question; and operational constraints that may be imposed by ways of working and industrial relations agreements.

The key results of these activities are as follows:

■ Workforce profile

The ability to 'build' a full and useful profile of the workforce using the criteria of age; qualifications; capabilities and capacities; training and qualifications held; full and part-time job holding and patterns; equal opportunity considerations of race, gender, disability, government deployment programmes and schemes.

This is essential if effective HRM policies are to be devised and implemented. There are implications for upsizing (taking on of additional staff); downsizing (lay-offs and redundancies); and rightsizing (matching the size and scope of the workforce with the range of work to be done). It has implications for skills and technological obsolescence, staff regeneration and development and the creation of a dynamic, flexible and responsive organisation.

Organisations managing their staff planning in this way are likely to be much more flexible and capable of responding to production and customer demand, and market shifts (see Summary Box 7.1).

SUMMARY BOX 7.1   Mitsubishi

Mitsubishi, the Japanese manufacturing and heavy industry conglomerate, transformed itself from being a major shipbuilding organisation into a major manufacturer of cars. It was able to do this without a single lay-off or redundancy because of the approach it took to its workforce. Because the people working for the company were used to continuous retraining and redeployment, it was able to make the transformation from one industrial sector to the other successfully and effectively.

■ Skill match and mismatch

This is the ability to build skills, knowledge and experience profiles of the workforce, identify matches, overmatches, undermatches and mismatches, and use this as the basis of informed effective remedial action and the ability to recognise that these change with implications for redundancy, redeployment and retraining initiatives.

■ Turnover analysis

This is the ability to establish why people leave the organisation and/or its component departments; the nature of these reasons, whether positive or negative; the extent to which they remain within or outside the control of managers. This can later provide the basis for the redesign of work; the assessment of acceptable and unacceptable levels of turnover (either overall or, again, in sectors, departments or occupations); and other matters that are implied or indicated, such as those to do with reform or improvement of staff management practices, the work environment, or patterns of work.

■ Staff recruitment/planning

Three things are vital here:

- Difficulties, and the nature of such difficulties, in recruiting particular types of staff; people with particular skills and mixes; people in and from particular locations and occupations
- The ability to identify the problems, negative issues, bad job and operational features, both across the organisation and in particular departments and occupations within it
- The ability to identify the attractions and positive aspects of the organisation and its work, both as a whole and in particular departments and occupations.

The ability to assess staffing strengths, weaknesses and problems being faced by the organisation and its managers emerges from effective staff planning and information systems. Accurate proposals, either for building on strengths, or for the resolution of negative issues are then drawn up, based on real data rather than 'received wisdom' or preconceptions.

■ Behaviour and expertise development analysis

Three things are again vital here:

- The ability to recognise individual potential and from this, to take action to prepare people for career paths and a long-term productive and effective future
- The ability to identify negative patterns of behaviour on the part of groups and individuals and to take remedial action based on hard evidence
- The ability to identify particular patterns of strikes, disputes, grievances, accidents and emergencies, and to take corporate remedial action based on hard evidence.

■ Succession

It also enables organisations to successfully and effectively address problems of succession – a good flow of talented people into key, senior and executive positions as they become vacant. All organisations should have a succession policy (even if it always recruits such staff from outside, this should be the subject of corporate assessment, evaluation and decision).

This policy will in general recognise the appraisal, development, and organisation-specific human resource activities required. The widest and most positive approach to succession is necessary. This must include opportunities for variety and diversity of work as well as promotion. Long-term career and certainty of promotion is no longer possible (or desirable) in present-day organisations.

There are also elements relating to equality of opportunity; qualities, aptitudes and capabilities; and industrial relations. General organisational aspects concerning motivation and morale must be remembered – organisations that progress talented people to their limits encourage others to follow on.

The main requirements in the establishment of effective staff planning policies, and HR information systems, is the value placed on them. At best they are central to the effectiveness of managerial activity and a key requirement in the gaining of effective returns on investment in the workforce.

Fitting the work to people: fitting the people to work

This process is abbreviated to FWP–FPW (see Figure 7.2).

It requires an understanding of the critical elements of the job, and the critical skills, knowledge, attributes, qualities, attitudes, behaviour, expertise and experience necessary to carry it out. It requires an understanding of the kind of people who are likely to hold these qualities. It requires an understanding of the extremes of the job – those elements that are brilliant and attractive and that consequently ensure applications from people who wish only to carry out those parts of it (or who are qualified only to carry out those parts of it); and those elements that are boring, dirty, dangerous or else require personal displacement (for example, working away from home for long periods of time).

FWP–FPW produces effective work and job definition, and people both capable and willing to work. It is essential therefore that it draws attention both to work attributes and also to wider elements such as work methods, style, environment, present and future opportunities and constraints. This need not be long and complicated. It should not be neglected however. At its simplest it represents a quick checklist and aid to thinking. It also represents the first and most important step in the devising of recruitment strategies. If this first stage is not right, the rest of the process is also flawed.

Pay, remuneration and reward

Effective systems of payment or reward must meet a variety of purposes and considerations. They must reward productive effort, expertise and outputs in whatever terms that is measured. They must provide an adequate level of

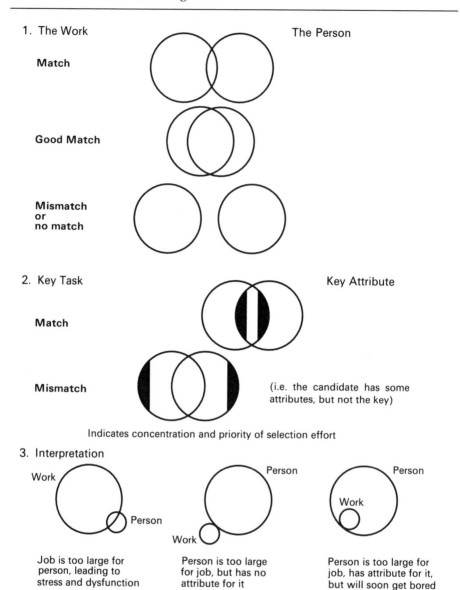

1. The Work   The Person

   Match

   Good Match

   Mismatch
   or
   no match

2. Key Task   Key Attribute

   Match

   Mismatch   (i.e. the candidate has some
                                                  attributes, but not the key)

   Indicates concentration and priority of selection effort

3. Interpretation

   Work   Person   Person   Person
        Person   Work   Work

   Job is too large for   Person is too large   Person is too large for
   person, leading to   for job, but has no   job, has attribute for it,
   stress and dysfunction   attribute for it   but will soon get bored

Purpose: indicates requirement to define personal attributes in relation to the job
   In all organisations, the process must be **validated**. The relationship between key tasks and key attributes must be related to effective performance.
   It must also be **reliable**. Any test used to predict performance from the process must demonstrate the quality concerned, and relate it to performance, in all circumstances.

Figure 7.2   **Fitting the work to people: fitting the people to work**

income on a regular basis for those receiving it. They must motivate and encourage. They must meet the expectations of those carrying out the work. They must be fair and honest to all concerned.

Rewards based on targets must be achievable. Rewards based on quality of performance must be measurable in some way. Specific payment systems such as commission, bonuses or merit increments should be clearly understood by all concerned. The criteria by which performance is to be measured is clearly spelled out. As long as objectives and targets are met, payment must be made.

For some occupations, this is very straightforward. The sales executive working to a commission based on sales volume or income from sales has a clear ready reckoner against which he/she will be paid.

For others, it is not so clear. Performance-related pay schemes for office, administrative, clerical, executive and professional staff have often fallen short of expectations because the criteria against which performance was to be measured were never made clear or fully understood by those concerned. In such cases, the scheme actually demotivates those affected, and falls into disrepute and discredit.

Those devising payment systems must also understand the motivations and expectations of the job holders, and either meet these as far as possible, or else understand the consequences of not meeting them. In general terms, these factors will consist of a level of income; consistency, stability and security; and a match between achievement and reward. Workforces have become used to annual pay rises to compensate for the loss of purchasing power due to inflation. Professional, clerical and managerial staff expect to receive incremental rises in addition to this.

Bad and unvalued payments and reward systems cause instability and labour turnover of their own accord. A major consequence of a bad system is extreme demotivation and demoralisation. This is true for whatever is wrong with the scheme – if objectives are not achievable or if they are achievable but the rewards are not forthcoming; and if the pay or pay rise does not meet expectations.

Finally, it must be remembered that while all payment systems should aim to provide motivation to the job holder, no amount of money will make a boring job interesting, but merely more bearable. Similarly, it is possible to offer intrinsic benefits in inherently interesting or fulfilling jobs, where there may be constraints on a reward package based purely on salary.

Components of a wage, salary or reward package

We can isolate five elements here:

- **Payment**: annual, quarterly, monthly, four-weekly, weekly, daily. Commission, bonus, increments, fees. Profit, performance and merit related payments (see Summary Box 7.2).

- **Allowances**: attendance, disturbance, shift, weekend, unsocial hours, training and development, location and relocation, absence from home.
- **Benefits**: loans (e.g. for season tickets), pension (contributory or non-contributory), subsidies (on company products, canteen, travel), car, telephone/car phone, private health care, training and development, luncheon vouchers.
- **Chains of gold or super benefits**: school holidays (teachers); cheap loans

---

SUMMARY BOX 7.2   Profit and Performance Related Pay: Ground Rules

The basis of any such scheme must be to relate as precisely as possible the rewards to staff with the effectiveness and success of their work. This is best achieved as follows:

1. The scheme must be believed in, valued and understood by all concerned
2. Targets must be achievable. They must neither be too easy, nor too difficult. Their purpose is to balance effective effort and effective output
3. Targets must be set in advance. If they are achieved, payments must always be made
4. The aim is to reward effort and achievement on the part of all the staff whatever their role or occupation
5. The language and presentation of the scheme should be positive and aimed at 'rewards for achievement'. The scheme's rules should not be couched in bureaucratic phraseology.

Notes

- Profit and performance related pay are not a means of cutting wage and salary bills. The purpose is to reward effective efforts not to penalise them. Profit and performance related pay normally increase wage and salary bills because people normally work much more effectively when their efforts are distinctively targeted.
- Effective profit and performance related pay ensures that all staff are focused on the purposes for which they are supposed to be working, and that they also assume a positive stake in operational success.
- Profit related elements: the allocation of percentage, or proportion, or amount from the surplus generated by the organisation to the staff. The means by which this is to be allocated should always be made clear in advance of any actual award in the interests of both fairness and confidence in the scheme. Some organisations offer shares and equity in the organisation to build staff commitment, public confidence and the market value of the organisation. Others offer cash bonuses. Cash bonuses should reward all on an equitable basis. This is often best achieved through giving everyone an equal percentage of their annual salary.
- The relationship between profit, ownership, commitment and pay is a constant theme of the 'Excellence Studies'. In the UK, the Bell-Hanson report of 1989, researching 113 publicly quoted companies, found that profit-share companies outperformed others by an average of 27% on returns on capital; earnings per share; and profit and sales growth.
- Those assessing profit and performance related pay, and those being assessed, must have full confidence in each other.

(banks); free/cheap travel (railway, shipping, airlines); pension arrangements (for older or longer-serving staff).

- **Economic rent**: high rates of pay for particular expertise (especially scarce expertise or that which is required at short notice).

This is very complex, and the mixes adopted by organisations in the devising and implementation of reward strategies for different staff categories cover a variety of aims and purposes in response to particular situations. The overall general objective is, however, to address the following:

1. **Expectations**: all systems must meet the expectations of the job holder to a greater or lesser extent if they are to be effective at attracting and retaining staff in the required occupations. (See Summary Box 7.3.)
2. **Motivation**: within the constraints illustrated above, all payment and reward motivates to a greater or lesser extent; the levels of reward offered to particular job holders also carries implications for the nature, complexity and commitment to the work in hand that is required on their part.
3. **Mixes of pay with other aspects**: much of this relates to expectations also, for example, in the UK, the offer of a company car to professional and managerial staff is still very attractive, in spite of the diminishing tax advantage.
4. **Occupational aspects**: part of the reward package may include the provision of specialist or expert training and equipment.
5. **International variations**: these relate to the mix of payment and other benefits in the total reward package; in the UK, there is a wide variety of components; in Switzerland, on the other hand, only 2% of managers receive a company car, preferring instead (collectively) a higher level of salary.

■ Job and work descriptions

For all staff, these should be drawn up in broad terms rather than trying to define every last task that an employee may at some point be required to carry out. The use of phrases such as 'to work as directed', or 'as required by the company' is perfectly legitimate, and above all give maximum flexibility and scope to what is an organisational tool, and not a straitjacket or restrictor. Required attitudes, behaviour and approaches to the job can also be written in the same way – 'to work to the required standard', or 'to follow normal organisation practice'.

This is far removed from the very specific and task-oriented descriptions previously devised for all kinds of jobs. At their most detailed these actually enshrine restrictive practices and demarcation lines, and have a very debilitating effect on both the workforce and the work itself. Very often the subject of collective workplace agreements, such job descriptions have proved very difficult and expensive to change.

■ Job and work evaluation

The overall purpose of job and work evaluation is to assess and evaluate the nature of the work to be done in a particular job; the key tasks to be carried out,

SUMMARY BOX 7.3   Mass Production Work

Food processing technology devised in the 1960s and 1970s enabled meat and vegetables to be dried and preserved for long periods of time. It enabled ice-cream and yoghurt to be produced very cheaply en masse, for distribution through supermarkets. It also became possible to produce a great variety of fizzy drinks for mass markets. However the work itself, consisting mainly of watching the products being processed, and either picking out samples for testing, or clearing up blockages when they occurred, was extremely tedious and debilitating. For example, those who watched peas being freeze-dried frequently complained of nightmares (with the peas as the central feature). The only HRM activity then in use was the rotation of staff between the different production lines. Each quickly became equally disaffecting, and it thus was impossible either to motivate or retain the staff for more than very short periods of time. The food processing companies used therefore to concentrate their efforts on having a steady influx and supply of labour, rather than addressing the possibilities of reanalysing or redesigning the work that needed doing. Consequently, a substantial part of the cost advantage of mass production and the technology was being lost in the constant pursuit of a pool of staff, and in staffing problems arising at the workplace.

The ways in which work is arranged and organised impinges on rule-books, work practices, departmentalisation, divisionalisation, industrial relations, selection, training and development. If work is boring, there will be high levels of disputes, absenteeism, self-certificated sickness; high levels of managerial time and resource used up in the operation of procedures; and over-supervision of such things as time-clocks, work sheets, and meal breaks. It also has great effect on the total atmosphere or aura of the place of work, and 'canteen cultures' can easily take hold.

This form of work is both physically and mentally debilitating as well as expensive. It has caused industrial and production organisations to seek alternative methods and patterns of employment and approaches to mass labour work.

The Hawthorne experiments (see Chapter 2) demonstrated as part of their findings that work, in itself mundane, could nevertheless be conducted much more effectively by strengthening the personal and group identity of those carrying it out, while at the same time ensuring that management control was not lost to any potential informal system. The lighting experiments referred to in Chapter 2, and the effects on both the experimental and the control group, underline this.

The Sony Corporation recognised this in the late 1960s. It went to a lot of trouble to remove some of the negative pressures inherent in the work, by instead creating a positive atmosphere and culture of 'value of the workforce'. By giving this, Sony removed the need for time-clocks and any other form of supervision of arrival and departure times. Washrooms and toilets were kept clean, and absenteeism was reduced. Part of the process involved the instillation of personal responsibility for work, quality and achievement in **all** members of staff.

and the balance, difficulty, value, frequency and importance of these; the subordinate tasks to be carried out, and the marginal tasks also, measured against the same criteria. Skills, qualities, capabilities and attributes are matched up, and a market value placed on them, with particular weightings as necessary or desirable. Jobs are then placed in a ranking order for the organisation, matching them up against grades, job titles, salary scale or scales; in large or complex organisations, these may be clustered according to staff, budget or capital responsibilities; spans of control; key results or objectives; flexibility; progress and innovation.

Public and multinational organisations spend a lot of time and resources on job evaluation, and many have permanent job evaluation panels and committees. The main organisational criteria essential to the success of any scheme of job evaluation are to do with fairness and equity of treatment for all staff and grades and occupations; clearly publicised and preset criteria for the evaluation process; acceptable to and understood by all; the opportunity for representation and appeal; speed of operation; and the ability of the organisation to communicate all of the evaluation process, and specific findings on individual jobs, in clear and unequivocal terms.

■ Person specification

The person specification identifies the skills, knowledge, attitudes, behaviour, qualities and attributes required either on:

- Individual bases for those who are to occupy key positions or bring particular expertise to organisations; or
- A universal basis for groups of staff to ensure rigour and precision selection.

These qualities and attributes should be classified and prioritised in such a way that they can be tested (if at all possible), observed (if testing is not possible) and inferred (if that is the only course available at the time or within the organisation).

It breaks these requirements down into understandable and manageable chunks, and it enables a clarity of thought about the issue among managers who are often not experts in the field.

■ Recruitment and selection strategy

■ Attracting candidates

This is achieved through advertising, the use of agencies and specialists, internal opportunities and offers, and word of mouth. It requires the consideration of when, where and how to advertise; the style and content of the advertisement; and which particular outlet is suitable for the candidates in question.

Whatever is chosen, the process of induction and attitude formation in the eventual new employee starts here, so the initial image and standpoint created must be that which is eventually required.

This is especially true where potential employees have already been customers and where they will have formed preconceptions and impressions. This extends in particular to transport; insurance; health services; national, municipal and local government; communications and media organisations.

■ Applications

The purpose of getting people to apply is to give the organisation enough background information to enable a **preliminary** judgement to be made as to their suitability for this job. It will not give a **final** judgement – this will be done by the selection process. Applications to work come in one or more of the following formats:

- **Application forms**: information comes in a standard and complete format
- **Curricula vitae**: the candidates' own version of their lives and achievements. They are most useful when read in conjunction with application forms and may give or indicate qualities and experience not apparent or asked for on the form, but which nevertheless will be useful
- **Telephone applications**: normally very dubious, both for acceptance for interview and rejection. In particular, an unproductive conversation is no measure at all of a potential candidate's unsuitability – the conversation may have been limited by anything, from conflicting pressures to a heavy cold
- **Pre-screening by agencies**: removes this burden from the manager, but it is limited by the agencies' perceptions of the nature of the candidates, and ultimately the new employee required. This is true whether it is a technological or executive 'head-hunter' that is involved, or a labour or secretarial agency.

■ Selection techniques

The main techniques available are as follows.

□ Tests

1. **Skill and aptitude tests**: assessing the nature and degree of capability and skill; assessing degrees of potential. Skill and aptitude tests indicate capability, not willingness or commitment
2. **Personality tests**: indicating the presence (or otherwise) of particular personality traits in the individual, and that can then be related to those required for the carrying out of the job that have previously been isolated as important
3. **Psychometric tests and questionnaires**: are tests of habitual performance, designed to measure a combination of personality characteristics, values, behaviour and interests, and again, relate these to those deemed necessary in the job holder. **Note**: personality and psychometric tests do not predict job performance
4. **Intelligence tests**: to ascertain the IQ of an individual.

Any test that is used must have pre-stated, measurable, inferable, or observable aims and objectives. Candidates who undergo any tests set should do so (as far as possible) under the same conditions, and following any specific test rules. The tests must be **valid** – that is, they must measure what they purport to measure; and they must be **reliable** – that is, they must produce results that are stable and consistent. They must be free from social or cultural bias. Finally, they only measure what they purport to measure – they only assist in the selection process if they have been properly and precisely targeted at some part of it.

☐ Exercises

The overall purpose of setting up particular exercises is to be able to observe or infer aspects of individual performance. Some of those used are as follows:

1. **In-tray exercises**, used in managerial selection processes to identify or infer the ways in which the candidates prioritise, make decisions, and work under stress
2. **Case studies**, designed to indicate or infer the analytical processes of the candidate, and (possibly) also their decision-making methods
3. **Particular skills and aptitudes** required, such as group interaction (whereby the candidate is placed in a group situation and his approach, behaviour and modus operandi observed); or presentation skills (whereby the candidate is asked to conduct a short presentation to a panel, with the purpose of assessing his capability in this sphere).

☐ Interviews

Selection normally includes an interview (or series of interview). For some occupations, this may constitute the entire process. Part of the purpose of interviewing is to meet expectations, on the part of both organisation and candidate, and to conduct some of the process of mutual familiarisation.

Beyond this, again, the interview (or series of interviews) must be conducted with precise purposes and aims and objectives in mind; in order to meet these, the interview (or series) must be structured; the same questions asked of each candidate, and the same weighting put on each answer.

Interview processes are structured to ensure that the best possible result can be gained in the circumstances. The role of all those involved in interviewing is clearly defined at the outset. Selection interviews work to preset structures with given aims and objectives. For best results this is based on an accurate and rigourous person specification.

At the end of the process, a set of data has been gathered on each candidate. This enables the candidates to be compared on an equivalent basis.

The overall measure of the success or otherwise of selection processes is the regularity with which they produce effective and successful appointments. All recruitment and selection is therefore subject to continuous monitoring and review. This should include all aspects – successful sources of candidates; effectiveness of different media; effectiveness of testing and interviewing. (See Summary Boxes 7.4 and 7.5.)

SUMMARY BOX 7.4   Assessment Centres

Assessment centres involve devising a combination of the different selection methods outlined for the purpose of identifying as precisely and as accurately as possible the qualities and capabilities of the candidate or group of candidates who are to be assessed.

Assessment centres therefore have the advantage of producing a much greater and more detailed profile of the candidates. Skills, knowledge, attitudes and behaviour can all be observed in a greater variety of situations and in much greater depth.

Assessment centres may be conducted over half a day, one day or even two days, depending on the nature of the appointments being made and the complexity of the centre itself. They are consequently expensive in themselves, and returns are required on them in terms of the accuracy and effectiveness of the appointments made as a result. Those assessing and observing the candidates must also be briefed and trained in advance.

The content of the centre will reflect at all times the qualities that the candidates are required to exhibit, and effectiveness will therefore be measured in terms of the quality of the staff thus appointed. They have their greatest merit in the assessment and appointment of expert and executive staff where the consequences of a bad or inappropriate decision may be extreme; and where conversely every step is taken to ensure that all the qualities required can be tested, observed or at least inferred over the period of the centre.

SUMMARY BOX 7.5   A Note on Panel Interviews

These are constituted for a variety of reasons – the ability of many key staff to see and question the field of candidates; the ability to form a comprehensive range of opinions about them; and to meet organisational expectations and often requirements, especially in the making of public appointments. In the latter cases representatives of the relevant authority or its board of governors are also often present.

Care has to be taken in the composition and constitution of such panels, and the structure to be adopted for the actual interviews. Care must also be taken to assess in advance the roles and responsibilities of each panel member in the selection process and their expectations of it and from it.

The purpose of constituting a panel must be kept at the forefront of its activities. The panel members must abide by the self-discipline required of them in the pursuit of this. At no stage must it become a competition between panel members with the aim of getting their own preferred candidates accepted at the expense of the others.

■ Reviewing the process

This should be carried out at the end of any selection process. For non-key or unskilled appointments this need not be intensive or take very long – even on these occasions, however, it should be done and may serve to identify particular issues or difficulties (and also strengths) in the process conducted.

For key and other professional, technical and managerial appointments, a full review should be conducted. It should not necessarily be a complex or lengthy process, and again may simply serve to confirm a highly successful recruitment exercise resulting in the hiring of excellent and top quality members of staff. Identification of that which was done well in the circumstances should nevertheless be carried out so that these lessons can be learned and assimilated and the same highly expert approach taken by all in the making of such appointments in the future.

Problems and other such matters arising from the process must be reviewed and evaluated to see where they occurred and why this was so, with the view to taking remedial action that ensures that they are avoided or improved upon in the future. Matters that have occurred that were outside the remit or control of those responsible for the selection process should also be considered at this stage if they impacted on it (for example, matters such as the enforced absence of a key figure in the process due to illness, and any other items that fall under the headings either of 'lucky' or 'unlucky').

■ Induction

The purpose of induction is to get the new member of staff as productive as possible, as quickly as possible. This consists of matching the organisation's needs with those of the individual as follows:

1. Setting the **attitudes** and **standards of behaviour** required, ensuring that new employees know what is expected of them, and that they conform to these expectations and requirements; it is most important that the organisation assumes absolute responsibility for this, rather than allowing employees to set their own standards, or for these to emerge by default
2. **Job training and familiarisation**, mainly to do with the ways of working required by the organisation, and ensuring that these are matched with the new employee's expertise; and establishing the required standards and methods of work
3. **Introductions** to the new team, work colleagues, and other key contacts as part of the process of gaining confidence, understanding and mutuality of objectives required for the development of effective working relationships and environment
4. **Familiarisation with the environment**, premises, ways of working, and particular obligations on the part of the employer; ensuring that the new employee understands their position in this environment; emergency procedures and health and safety.

Commitment is vital. Many organisations go to much trouble to ensure that this is adequately and effectively completed, recognising the returns on an excellent and well-resourced induction process in the production of a highly motivated and committed workforce.

The induction process will have been started in general terms by any vague impression that the new employee has picked up of the organisation; it will have been further reinforced if, for example, he has been a customer or client of it. Any correction of these impressions must also be addressed as part of the induction process, which will also be reinforced by the ways in which the selection process is conducted.

■ Measuring performance

Performance measurement is conducted for the organisation, departments, divisions, groups and individuals. To be effective and successful, it must be conducted in the following ways:

- It must be against **pre-set** and **pre-agreed aims and objectives**, fully and clearly expounded and understood by all concerned. These should additionally (where there are more than one), be given priority and deadlines for achievement; such performance targets should be realistic and achievable – if they are not, they will be ignored; if they are too easy, they set a wider agenda for the lowering of performance standards
- It is a **process**, consisting of both a series of regularised formal reviews, at which targets and objectives are to be assessed for success and failure; and a continuous relationship between appraiser and appraisee, that ensures a mutual and continuing confidence on the part of each in the other
- It must be **flexible** and **dynamic**, and part of the wider process of ensuring that the organisation's strategy and purpose
- It must be a **participative process** between appraiser and appraisee, to ensure that the wider behavioural objective of mutual commitment to any aims and targets is achieved. It must be believed in and valued by both appraiser and appraisee
- **Formal reviews** should take place at least every 3–6 months. If they are more frequent than this, they tend to impose on the continuing process and relationship that should also be present. If they are less frequent, it becomes very difficult to conduct an adequate or genuine review of what has been done.

Within this framework, particular organisational appraisal schemes may seek to: provide merit pay awards; identify potential; identify training and development needs; identify job–person mismatch; identify organisation development prospects; identify poor and sub-standard performance; be a vehicle for other remedial action.

Appraisal schemes fall into disrepute for the following reasons: that they are not believed in or valued; they do not contribute to the wider success of the organisation; they are bureaucratic or mechanistic; that it is the scheme and its paperwork that are important, and not the process that should be completed; that the reviews are too infrequent, or (in practice) missed altogether; that what is promised in them (e.g., pay awards, training, promotion) is not delivered in practice.

They also suffer from performance criteria being identified in general terms only. This leads to inconsistency in application and unfairness (and perceived unfairness) in the award of merit pay rises and places on training courses; while at the other end of the spectrum, individuals may be picked up for poor performance on the same uneven basis.

There is, and must be, a basis of mutual understanding, openness, trust and honesty inherent in the process if it is to succeed. If staff are asked to declare shortcomings in their recent performance, and if this is then used as a stick with which to beat them, they will simply not do it.

It follows, therefore, that there is a necessary body of skills and knowledge required of the manager in the conduct of effective performance appraisal. Communication, articulation, target and objective setting, counselling, support, trust, dependency and assertiveness, are all clearly necessary; and they will also be required to be translated into dealings with frustrated and recalcitrant employees in particular situations.

Finally, the control of the appraisal process must always rest with the manager, and while agreement of objectives with the member of staff is desirable, this should never be at the expense of a diluted or sub-standard performance.

Maintenance factors in human resource management

The basis of this approach is that the human resource requires maintenance in the ways equivalent to other aspects and resources of the organisation if it is to be maximised and optimised.

The basic concept is not new. Its beginnings may be seen in the work of Cadbury and the Human Relations School (see Chapter 2). The lessons to be drawn were based on the premise that direct positive interventions led to improved work performance; and that a lack of such interventions led to performance decline. Some of this activity came under the heading of 'welfare'; other aspects arose from a moral, ethical or even religious belief that this was the right way to treat people; while others again related the religious aspect to obligations to generate wealth, both for profit for the organisation and the greater good of society. Current issues are: work design; occupational health; personal health.

■ Job design

This is design both in terms of the formation of attitudes and standards at the workplace to which employees are required to subcribe; and also in the division, regulation and allocation of the work itself. Both are undertaken with the intention of generating a greater measure of positive commitment and a reduction of workplace alienation. This may involve job rotation and progression schemes; and project work, secondments, fixed term, action learning type placements also. Related to this is the ever-increasing obligation on employees to maintain and improve their skills, knowledge and technical expertise in the interests of continuing organisation, effectiveness, profitability and prosperity. On the other hand, the expectations of those at work have also changed, and part of the job design process increasingly includes improving the *quality* of working life. Consider Summary Box 7.6.

■ Creative approaches to employment patterns

This involves a much greater awareness and willingness on the part of organisations to relate the hours of work that they offer to the non-work commitment and aspirations of potential staff members. This means having regard to the use of flexitime, annual hours and other flexible work patterns; job sharing; working away from the organisation and especially allowing staff to work at home and providing them with the means and workstations to do so; and the devising of shift patterns especially to fit around those with primary responsibility for looking after young children. More widely, organisations may

---

SUMMARY BOX 7.6   Stress

Stress may be either positive or negative. It essentially consists of the amount of pressure present in a given situation in which the individual finds himself. The sources of stress are occupational, role, organisational, hierarchical, social and personal; and stresses on the individual result from an imbalance of these. There is, in particular, a growing awareness of the links between work and stress and other illnesses such as nervous exhaustion, executive and professional burn-out, heart conditions and high blood pressure. The manager's role in this is therefore three-fold: to recognise it as an issue; to prevent stress among staff; and to recognise it in himself and take steps to limit it.

Good occupational health schemes thus have stress recognition and the ability to treat the symptoms and manifestations of it as a central part of them. The ability of organisations to accept and recognise the condition, to treat it where it occurs and, above all, to engage in practices and a style of management that prevent it from arising as far as possible is an essential contribution to the maintenance of the human resource.

offer career breaks – extended periods of time off for employees in which they may go to do other things. Organisations may also offer 'returner schemes' pitched primarily at those who have had lengthy periods of time out of work, usually for the purpose of bringing up a family; the returner scheme tackles the issues of familiarisation, confidence building and personal and professional comfort that are the concerns of anyone coming into any job after a lengthy break. Such schemes also provide specific job training and re-training as necessary and desirable. Organisations may also underline their commitment to these creative approaches, through the provision of nursery facilities for very young children; canteen facilities that are open all day so that all work patterns are accommodated; and through the adoption of general ways of working and general attitudes at the workplace that place the same intrinsic value on all members of staff regardless of their own particular pattern of work.

These matters are all interrelated and together constitute a greater attention to the needs of the workplace human resource. A positive approach to the maintenance of the human resource has also been demonstrated generally to have positive effects on morale and motivation and reductions in accidents, sickness and absenteeism. There are also anecdotal connections at least between the adoption of a positive approach to human resource maintenance and organisation success, effectiveness and profitability. There is also evidence that the converse is true – that alienation, demotivation and low morale are most prevalent where the human resource is not maintained. Current thinking, priorities and initiatives have arisen out of the assessment of these examples in business terms and the relationship drawn between success and the practices of successful organisations. This is again the result of increased awareness; it represents the state of the art/science/profession at present; and it gives a springboard for the further development of the human resource maintenance function.

■ Occupational health

Organisations are increasingly assuming responsibility for the good health of their staff and taking positive steps and making interventions that are designed to ensure this. This consists of determining that the employee is fit and healthy when he or she first starts work and that this continues throughout the period of employment. For those who have persistent or regular time away from work there may be included assessments by company medical staff as well as the employee's own doctor. This may require the employee, moreover, to take medical treatment at the behest of the organisation, as a precondition of continuing to work for it. Occupational health schemes at the workplace are, in the best cases, particularly strong and valuable in the early diagnosis of jobspecific illnesses and injuries. They also provide a valuable general source of medical knowledge by which the organisation may assess the overall state of their workforce's health.

Particular matters related to the workplace have come to the fore and gained recognition and currency. Major issues of which any manager should be aware are:

- Stress, its causes and effects and techniques for its management
- Repetitive strain injuries (RSI) which are caused by continuous use of certain muscles or the carrying out of certain activities – for example, continuous keyboard working and process work
- Back injuries caused either by bad lifting practices or a continuous bad back posture
- The effects of VDU screens on eyesight
- Industrial and commercial heating and lighting and the relationship between these and eye strain, coughs, colds and other minor but recurrent ailments
- Smoking, both active and passive, and the effects of it on all staff (both in relation to health and also more general concerns as odours) (see Summary Box 7.7)
- Alcohol abuse (see Summary Box 7.7)
- HIV and AIDS, and the implications for particular workplaces and occupations (see Summary Box 7.8).

■ Industrial relations

Industrial relations – or employee relations, employment relations, staff relations – is the system by which workplace activities are regulated, the arrange-

---

SUMMARY BOX 7.7   Organisational Approaches to Tobacco, Alcohol and Drugs

These are dealt with because they are current, high profile and contentious issues.

Organisations should make clear the stance to be adopted on each, giving a clear lead to managers and staff. Whatever the outcome it should reflect organisational requirements, and not simply be allowed to evolve unmanaged. Organisations may set any standard that they wish on each of these issues (provided that they also conform with the law).

Organisations that wish to exclude smoking from their premises may do so. In the implementation of this, they should consult with staff, and offer counselling and support to those who have to fundamentally change behaviour. They will follow the consultation process and timescale referred to elsewhere.

Staff who have addiction problems should be supported by organisations; they should be offered counselling, rehabilitation and reference to medical authorities except in the rare cases where this is impossible.

There is a moral as well as an operational imperative in this, that is increasingly being recognised as part of the organisation's total commitment, ethical stance and wider obligations to its staff. Levels of support for members of staff through programmes and periods of treatment will be directed at both treating the matter in hand and also rehabilitating staff, getting them back into productive and effective work.

SUMMARY BOX 7.8   AIDS: Acquired Immune Deficiency Syndrome

Over the near future, organisations are inevitably going to be required to adopt a direct and positive stance in regard to the matters of AIDS and the HIV virus. This must cover the matter from all angles. It must include blood tests for potential members of staff, if necessary, as part of regular check-ups and other occupational health matters. It must include a continuing obligation to those members of staff who contract the virus while working at the organisation. It must include reference to customer contact; covering both clients and staff who have the virus.

The overall purpose is to ensure that all those who work in the organisation, and all those who deal with it, know where they stand in regard to this issue. In addition, the extent and nature of the organisation's precise obligations are thus at least defined for its own purposes, in an area where the extent and coverage of the law is not yet clear.

Operationally, there are problems of organisation and staff insurance that have to be addressed. From a cultural and perceptual stance, there are issues concerning the mystique, legends, and levels of knowledge of the matter that must be considered, with the purpose of generating understanding, enlightenment, and a suitable and effective way of working.

---

ment by which the owners, managers and staff of organisations come together to engage in productive activity. It concerns setting standards and promoting consensus. It is also about the management of conflict.

Much of this has its roots in the economic and social changes of the industrial revolutions and the urbanisation of the nineteenth century; the inherent conflict between labour and the owners of firms; the formation of collectives, combinations of groups of workers to look after their own interests; and the demarcation lines and restrictive practices that some occupations and trades were able to build up. The influence of these traditions remains extremely strong, particularly in long-established industries such as factory work, transport and mining. However, in recent years there has been a serious attempt to change the attitudes of all concerned in this field, and to generate a more positive and harmonious ethos. Companies and their managers have come to recognise the importance of positive industrial relations and the contribution that they make to profitable and effective organisational performance; some trade unions have seen this as an opportunity to secure their future, and to attract new members. Other unions have lost their influence because of the great numbers of jobs that have disappeared in the sectors which they represent.

Three distinct approaches may be clearly identified.

- **Unitarism**: which assumes that the objectives of all involved are the same or compatible and concerned only with the well-being of the organisation and its products, services, clients and customers. The most successful of unitary organisations (e.g. McDonald's, Virgin, IMG) set very distinctive work, performance and personal standards, to which anyone working in the company must conform. This is also inherent in the Japanese approach to the management of the human resource.

- **Pluralism**: admitting a variety of objectives, not all compatible, among the staff. Recognising that conflict is therefore present, rules, procedures and systems are established to manage it and limit its influence as far as possible. This is the approach taken especially in public services, local government and many industrial and commercial activities, where diverse interests have to be reconciled in order that productive work may take place.
- **Radicalism**: the view that commercial and industrial harmony is impossible until the staff control the means of production, and benefit from the generation of wealth. Until very recently, this was a cornerstone of the philosophy of many trade unions and socialist activists in industry, commerce and public services.

■ IR strategies

IR (industrial relations) strategies ultimately depend on the industrial or commercial sector concerned, or whether it is public or government serviced. One of the following positions is normally adopted.

- **Conflict**: the basis on which staff are to be dealt with is one of mistrust, divergence, irreconcilable aims and objectives; disparity of location; divergence and complexity of patterns of employment and occupations; professional, technical, skilled and unskilled staff In such cases as this, the IR strategy will be devised to contain the conflicts, and to reconcile differences; and to promote levels of harmony as far as possible.
- **Conformity**: where the diversity of staff and technology may be (and often is) as great as in the above scenario, but where the IR strategy rather sets standards of behavioural and operational aims and objectives that in turn require the different groups to rise above their inherent differences.
- **Consensus**: where the way of working is devised as a genuine partnership between the organisation and its staff and their representatives The consensus position in IR is rare in all but the simplest and smallest of organisations (and may not exist even in these).

■ IR, staff and the organisation

Whichever is adopted, there are common threads. Organisations must understand the nature and strengths of the types of staff that they employ. They must recognise that there are divergences of aims, and different priorities that must be resolved if effective and profitable work is to take place. The nature of IR and related staff management activities will vary accordingly, but at the outset all staff whatever their occupation must form an identity with the organisation that is both positive and complementary to its purposes. Boundaries of performance and behaviour requirements must be established in order that these purposes are achieved effectively and successfully. Issues to do with the nature and style of workplace regulation and staff representation must be resolved. Above all, IR and staff management must be seen both as continuous processes and an area for constant improvement. If designed and conducted effectively by the organisation, it will constitute a major return on the investment made in the workforce as a productive entity.

Whichever IR strategy is adopted must, therefore, be supportive of, and complementary to, the wider aims and objectives of the organisation. This will extend in some measure to the capabilities and qualities of the workforce; but ultimately the workforce must be harmonised to the needs of the organisation. Effective IR strategies start from this point. They may have regard to staff who, for example, are highly trained or professionalised; however, the overall direction of IR will seek again to match these with organisational requirements. Where staff have a very strong group identity – because of their profession again, or because of sectoral traditions or a long history of unionism, for example – the organisation must work to ensure the harnessing and commitment of this to its own purposes.

The inability of organisations to do this can be seen across the whole range of industry, commerce, and public services. In the latter, major conflicts have arisen between the 'professional' commitment to client groups – teachers to pupils; doctors and nurses to the sick; social workers to the disadvantaged – and the management by organisations of these staff. IR in these situations is largely ineffective because of the inability of organisations to direct their professional staff in ways universally understood as effective; and because of their lack of regard for, or ability in, IR matters. It has been compounded by the perceived conflict of objectives between service managers and service professionals. Finally, at no stage have professional people generated an identity with the service organisation that remotely touches that which they have with their profession.

Boundaries are established by organisations as follows:

- Standards of performance required
- Standards of ethics, behaviour and attitude
- Parameters of industrial relations activity and where those parameters end
- Procedures for the management of disputes, grievances, discipline and dismissal
- Consultative, participative and communication structures
- The precise forms of workforce representation including the recognition of trade unions
- The desired aura of workplace staff relations.

Note: the **aura** is the backdrop or general impression created. The aura is reflected in the nature and numbers of accidents, disputes and absences at the place of work; it may also be indicated by rates of turnover and labour or problems with particular staff categories.

Whatever standpoint is adopted, it is important that both managers and staff understand it so that they can identify their mutual expectations. Needless disputes are kept to a minimum, as long as everyone understands the position of everyone else.

Figure 7.3   **Boundaries of industrial relations**

Industrial situations are traditionally no better. IR in coal mining across the world has been so bad that miners have adopted loyalties to anyone other than the mine owners. In the UK, the focus of coal mining is the Union, which provides welfare, leisure and recreation facilities; support for families in case of death or injury; representation at disputes; and a lobby for increased investment in safety and technology. Endemic throughout hundreds of years of coal mining, the result has been that the first and only loyalty of the staff has been to the Union; at no stage has any managing organisation, either private or nationalised, been able to provide an identity equivalent to this (nor is there any real evidence that they have tried). Rather they have taken the view that conflict is inherent, and have sought to devise 'safety-valve' IR strategies, to ensure as far as possible that when conflict does blow up it can be contained without serious disruption to the work in hand. (See Figures 7.3 and 7.4.)

The strategy adopted will be supported by staff handbooks and rule-books; the procedures used and the ways in which these are promulgated; and any formal structures that are devised and put in place. These are in turn, underlined by the nature of staff representation, induction and orientation programmes, and day-to-day work practices. (See Summary Box 7.9.)

■ The framework of industrial relations

The framework of industrial relations is **tripartite**, that is, there are three main parties involved. The parties are government; employees, their representatives and trade unions; and employers, their representatives and associations. Each has distinctive roles.

- **The structure of the workforce**: operational aspects; dispersion; departmentalisation and groupings; particular ways of working
- **Staff management aspects**: of core and peripheral work groups; specialist sub-contractors, consultants and advisors; those on fixed term or fixed project contracts
- **Balancing** and **reconciling** a great mixture of conflicting and divergent elements in the basic interests of organising and maintaining effective working methods and ensuring fairness and equity to all
- Balancing **harmony** and **contentment** with commitment, drive and organisation purpose
- The establishment and provision of **standards** and **sanctions** for the enforcement of rules
- **The capability of managers**: one of the greatest advances in the field has been the recognition of the qualities, aptitudes and attitudes necessary for the promotion and maintenance of effective and harmonious IR; and the training of managers and supervisors in the field.

Figure 7.4   Other considerations

SUMMARY BOX 7.9   Problem-Solving in Industrial Relations

A strategic approach to specific IR matters will be adopted by organisations and their managers. As well as briefings for staff, and training for managers in IR skills and knowledge, organisations will take an approach to the management of workplace conflicts based on answers to the following six questions:

- What is the likelihood of a dispute occurring? If it does, how long might it last? What are the wider consequences to ourselves, and to our staff?
- If it does occur, can we win it? What are the consequences of winning it? What are the consequences of losing it?
- If it does occur, what costs are we going to incur? As well as financial cost, what of the questions of PR, media coverage and local feelings in our community? Is this a price worth paying?
- What happens when it all settles down? How will we interact and work with the staff afterwards? How long will any bad feeling last? What are the wider implications of this?
- What other ways are there around the matter or dispute in hand? Are we able to use these? What are the pros and cons of going down these alternatives, vis-à-vis a dispute?
- What are the behavioural and psychological aspects that surround this issue? If we win, what will be the effects on the workforce? And on managers? Are there questions of morale to be considered? If we lose, would loss of face be important? How could we save face, if that were to arise? What would be the response of the workforce and its representatives?

From consideration of the matter in hand this way, and by establishing the answer to these issues, the answer to the critical question emerges:

- Why are we seeking, entering, or preparing to enter, into this dispute?

This approach will form the basis of any strategic consideration of any conflict, or potential conflict, whether global, organisational, departmental, or divisional; or at team, group or individual level.

■ Government

The government is the single major universal influence on IR everywhere. It invariably is the single largest employer responsible for the pay, terms and conditions of employment, of the civil service; the armed services; the police; the emergency services; local government and services; nationalised industries and utilities; health and social services. As dominant employer, it sets standards of employment and IR practice that others will be expected to follow; and there is great scope for setting 'model' terms and conditions. Major public activities (especially large hospitals, government functions, nationalised industry premises) are often the dominant employer of a locality, directly affecting what others have to pay to attract staff to work for them.

Government make employment and industrial relations laws, as with everything else, and set the standards and boundaries of practice. They also establish codes of conduct, codes of practice and employement protection and encouragement policies. They may also set contract compliance rules, requiring anyonewishing to tender for government contracts to adhere to particular standards of practice. Governments may also use the military police and emergency services in terms of industrial strife to keep essential services open and maintain the general national quality of working life.

Governments codify all aspects of workplace relationships – the rights and limits of trade union activities; the rights of individuals at the workplace; the rights of organisations and their managers; equality of opportunity; the right to strike; and the right to work.

■ Employees

The interests of employees at places of work are looked after by trade unions, staff associations, some professional bodies, and the individuals themselves. Over the years the greatest single influence has been trade unions. (See Summary Box 7.10).

Trade unions were first established to protect the interests and standards of living of persons working in particular sectors. A variety of definitions have grown up, and unions may be classified as:

- **Industrial unions**: all members are from one industry (e.g. mineworkers; steelworkers; railway workers)
- **Skilled or craft**: in which all the members have completed a course of training or apprenticeship (e.g. electrical; engineering)
- **White collar**: for example, the civil service and banking unions
- **Local government**: as a distinctive sector
- **Professional**: representing such groups as teachers and nurses
- **Technical**: representing managerial and research staffs
- **General**: representing the unskilled and semi-skilled.

In recent years, trade unions in many parts of the world have lost influence and reputation as the source of much of their power and membership, the manufacturing and primary sectors, have declined. New jobs created have been in the assembly, service and retail sectors, where no traditions of unionism exist. Legislation has been enacted to ensure that proper procedures are followed before strike action or other disputes take place. Governments have reduced the national influence and reputation of the unions by setting their own IR agenda, and by covering the widest possible range of employees' representative bodies. Finally, automation and technological advance has eliminated most of the demarcation distinctions between occupations, and the move is now towards multi-skilling and the flexible workforce.

Unions have therefore had to seek new or redefined roles. They have returned from national lobbies to effective action at individual workplaces on behalf of

---

SUMMARY BOX 7.10   The Donovan Commission

Part of the review of the Royal Commission on Trade Unions and Employers' Association (the Donovan Commission of 1965–67) was to define for the first time what the real roles of unions were. In summary, the findings were that unions:

- Bargain for best possible wages, terms and conditions for members
- Lobby for improved share in national wealth for members
- Influence government policy, legal framework on behalf of members
- Lobby for social security for all
- Lobby for full employment, job security, wage levels, cheap housing for the poor
- Bargain nationally, regionally, locally, industrially, for organisations and individuals
- Represent members at disputes and grievances and for any other reason according to need

Source: Donovan (1967).

---

individuals and groups of members. They have engaged in cooperative agreements with organisations, including productivity, training and no-strike arrangements. They have gained benefits for members such as advantageous rates for personal and possessions insurance, and health care. They have engaged in mergers and membership drives in order to maintain and improve on the levels of influence that they have.

■ Employers

The third party to the framework is the employer, represented by employer and trade federations and associations, individual companies and organisations. The influence of employers is currently at its highest level, and rising, on the conduct of work place industrial relations though (as with the unions) the employers' lobby has declined at national level.

The function of the employer in IR is to set standards of staff management, attitudes, behaviour and performance for the organisation or company; to set terms and conditions of employment, and pay levels and methods; to act in a fair and reasonable way towards all employees at the work-place. They may take part in national arrangements to set minimum standards for the sector concerned. They may choose to recognise trade unions or not. They will make representations to government on their own behalf, through their associations and federations.

In recent years, the area of IR has become recognised for the first time as an area of profitable and effective activity. Managers are now being trained in the skills of staff relations and problem-solving. Great emphasis is increasingly emerging in the devising of human resource policies, the tone and style of staff handbooks, the attitudes and approaches to staff and workforces. Companies are looking at fresh and creative approaches to HRM issues, and staff and IR management problems.

The final element in this framework is the recognition that all parties concerned act and react in the provision of national and workplace IR. Two 'systems' may be distinguished:

- The 'formal' system embodied in rule-books, procedures, negotiating and consultative committee activities and constitution
- The 'informal' system, manifest in the behaviour of the individuals concerned in given workplaces.

The two may diverge; for example, nationally agreed pay scales may be 'topped up' at local level due to particular staffing difficulties.

■ Collective bargaining

Collective bargaining is the traditional process by which agreements between employers and employees, or their respective representatives, are made. Agreements may be at national, regional, local, sectoral, or plant and unit level. This may involve very senior and highly trained personnel at sectoral or national levels, and elected lay representatives at local levels.

Two separate strands can be identified: the **substantive**, or what is to be negotiated; and the **procedural**, how it is to be done, and how procedures and other regulatory instruments are to be used.

Collective bargaining is based on mistrust and conflict – that is, that there is a fundamental divergence of interest between employers and employees. At stake, initially, therefore, is a basis on which the two can agree to cooperate together at all. This is made more difficult or extreme where there exists a long history and tradition of workplace conflict. Collective bargaining is a strategy and structure for the management of this conflict.

Summary Box 7.11 shows the ritualised nature of labour relations and bargaining.

Much of the process is therefore stylised and ritualised, and anyone who wishes to operate it effectively must understand the importance of this. The purpose must be to use the instruments and the language involved to gain workplace agreements that at least contain conflicts that are inherent.

■ The bargaining framework

There is a broad bargaining framework to understand (see Figure 7.5):

SUMMARY BOX 7.11   Behavioural Theories of Labour Relations

Walton and McKersie (1965) distinguish four inter-related processes:

- **Distributive bargaining**: The resolution of conflicts of interest. This is the classical collective bargaining process. It concludes a consideration of the costs, benefits and opportunities afforded by each side of an industrial dispute; the ability and strength of each party concerned; and the bargaining position, tactics and postures to be adopted. The process consists of presenting the opponent's standpoints and likely responses to particular moves; the use of tactics which influence the opponent's perceptions; the manipulation of the opponent's perceptions of his own position of strength, either by changing his views of the value of his own demands or by changing his view of the unpleasantness or unacceptability of the other side's proposals; presenting the costs of the dispute to one's own advantage; setting deadlines, 'final deadlines', 'final final deadlines', and so on; and manifesting all of this in a degree of commitment that is necessary to ensure victory in the dispute. Finally, in such a situation it may or may not be necessary to demonstrate that one side has won at the expense of the other; in such cases, forms of words and other face saving formulae may need to be devised.
- **Integrative bargaining**: This is the process by which common or complementary interests are found and is the means by which problems are resolved in a way that is in the interests of all parties concerned. In this way, both sides gain; the purpose therefore is not to conduct a dispute but to find means of resolving it in the interests of all concerned. The confrontational postures and stance indicated above do not form part of integrative bargaining. The process adopted rather uses a problem-solving model – that is, the identifying of the issue or matter of concern; searching for alternative solutions and extrapolating their consequences; and from this, choosing a preferred course of action.
- **Attitudinal structuring**: This is the process by which each side influences the attitudes of the participants towards the other. In this situation attitudes are formed and modified by the nature of the orientation that each party has towards the other and towards the matter in hand. This may either be competitive, whereby the parties are motivated to defeat or win the other over to their own point of view; individualistic, in which the parties concerned pursue their own self-interests without any regard for the position of the other; or cooperative, whereby each party is concerned about the other as well as its own position. An extreme form of this may be a form of collusion, whereby the parties concerned form a coalition in which they pursue a common purpose, possibly to the detriment of other groups within the organisation.
- **Staff relations**: The final matter to be considered here is the form of intra – organisational style of staff relations, that is concerned to maintain a balance and equilibrium about the organisation; and to prevent issues from arising that affect this balance. The main part of this process is to ensure that people understand the true nature and strength of their own position; to ensure that people's expectations are met; and to ensure that the two are compatible.

Source: Walton and McKersie (1965).

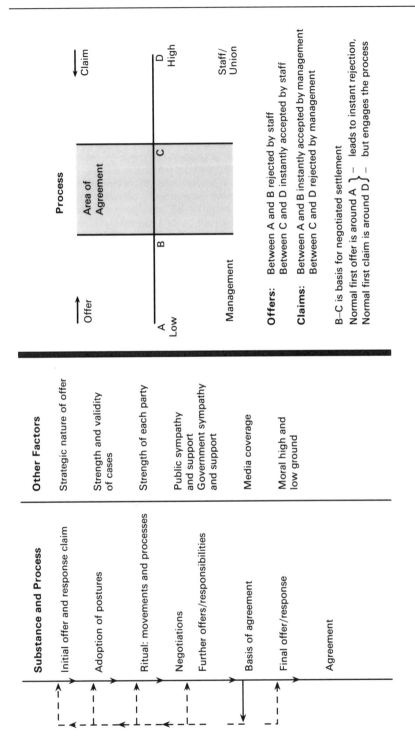

Figure 7.5   The collective bargaining process

- The **first offer or claim** is always made on the basis that it will be rejected (if for any reason it is accepted straight away, it generally causes resentment rather than instant satisfaction)
- There then follows a process of **counter-offer and counter-claim**, with each party working its way gradually towards the other
- The content of the **final agreement** is usually clearly signalled before it is made; and the basis of what is genuinely acceptable to each party is signalled also
- Serious disputes occur either when one side is determined *not to settle*; or when there is a genuine **misreading** of the signals
- Settlements reached are normally couched in **positive terms** in relation to all concerned, to avoid the use of words such as 'loss', 'loser', 'climb-down' and 'defeat', which have negative connotations for anyone associated with them, and tend to store up resentment for the future, and polarise attitudes for the next round of negotiations.

The following standpoints in the bargaining process may be usefully identified:

- It may be necessary to settle with one group or part of the workforce, at the expense of others
- It may be possible to resolve problems to the satisfaction of all concerned
- It may not be possible to satisfy everyone
- It may be necessary to take a hard initial stance to try and persuade the other party to revise its expectations.

Part of the function of the process is also to structure the attitudes of each party towards the other, and to try and build impressions of honesty, trust, openness, firmness, reasonableness and fairness, as necessary. A fundamental credibility must also be established.

■ Objectives of bargaining systems

Within this context, collective bargaining systems have three specific objectives:

- To provide the means for agreeing the price of labour
- To provide a means of industrial governance, and workplace rules and regulations
- To provide a means for controlling the stresses and strains inherent in any work situation.

■ Formal and informal bargaining systems

There are both formal and informal systems to be considered. The former is constituted with agenda, objectives, purposes, outcomes, deadlines and time-scales; the latter is the means by which the former is oiled, and consists of corridor meetings, contacts and networks that enable the formal system to function. Public services, municipal and local authorities, and multinational companies tend to have both sophisticated formal procedures, and highly developed networks also.

■ Work organisation traditions

There are histories and traditions of work organisation to be addressed also, either through the reformation of bargaining activities, or through the effective management of a wide range of employees' representatives and multi-unionism. All this has its origin in the differentiation of occupations, demarcation, restrictive practices, and barriers to occupational entry, devised by groups of workers to protect their trades and give them a measure of exclusivity; and allowed to grow by employers, partly because their need for staff was overwhelming, and partly also because they had no alternative to offer.

■ Employee expectations

Finally, there are employee expectations that have either to be met, or understood and dealt with. In the immediate past, employees have expected an annual percentage pay rise and improvement in conditions, devised partly to offset the effects of inflation: the 'annual pay round' is a feature of the industrial West. There have also arisen concepts of 'pay leagues', whereby a given occupation would offer terms and conditions of employment in relation to other occupations – to alter these 'leagues' generated resentment on the part of those occupations which perceived themselves to be moving down the 'table'. Closely related to this is the general concept of the 'going rate' for a job – the anticipation that, by joining a particular occupation, a known range of benefits will be forthcoming.

■ Multi-unionism

A large part of traditional IR has been taken up with the reconciliation of differences between trade unions. This has occurred not just between occupational groups within organisations, but also within them. Multinational corporations, public and health services carry vast, complex and sophisticated industrial relations superstructures consisting of committees, sub-groups, working groups and ad hoc groups that all have to be managed and harmonised by the IR managers and departments concerned. Moreover, they arrive at working practices which the functional managers in the organisations must adopt and respond to.

The complexities of multi-unionism have been compounded by the tradition of setting nationally agreed terms and conditions, wage levels and trade union policies (see Summary Box 7.12). A feature of organisational approaches to IR has been to attempt to reconcile these. A variation of this has occurred (in industry rather than services) where national minima have been agreed across the board and then top-ups offered by employers in relation to their difficulties or otherwise in attracting and retaining staff. This phenomenon is known as 'drift' in wages and conditions and is a key feature of local collective bargaining arrangements.

■ Recourse to arbitration

This is open to managers at all times in their attempt to resolve disputes at the workplace. Arbitration is available whether these disputes are individual (between a manager and a member of staff) or institutionalised (between an organisation and a union or body of employees). Used effectively, it represents a means of resolution that is both considered and subject to internal scrutiny and which may also have the benefit of acceptability on the part of all because a third party has arrived at the conclusion.

Arbitration is not in itself a universal means of problem-solving. It can only be applied where all other approaches have failed, or when there is an issue of presentation concerning the means of delivery of a decision.

It is not an industrial relations policy. Regular recourse to arbitration encourages extreme positions on the part of those in conflict so that any middle position recommended by an arbitrator is as favourable as possible. Internal credibility is lost. Continued recourse to arbitration leads to the frustration of those who can, and would, resolve their own problems and this leads to the loss of IR skills, expertise, aptitudes, and therefore control.

Recourse to arbitration thus becomes an additional tool to be used by managers when the context and situation requires. Its use and value will be pre-evaluated in the light of these situations, the advantages and disadvantages weighed up by managers when they decide on whether to go to arbitration on a particular matter or not.

SUMMARY BOX 7.12   Multi-union Illustrations: UK

- The teaching profession in the UK is served by the following unions; National Union of Teachers, National Association of Schoolmasters and Union of Women Teachers; Association of Teachers and Lecturers; Professional Association of Teachers; National Association of Head Teachers; and Deputy Heads Association. Some are more specific than others; however, there is nothing to prevent a head teacher from continuing to belong to one of the generic unions.
- A State Registered Nurse (RGN) may choose to belong to any of the public service unions. However, his/her qualification will be endorsed by the Royal College of Nursing, a recognised trade union as well as a professional body.

■ Conformism

Conformist IR requires the subordination of divergent and conflicting interests at the workplace, in the interests of pursuing common and understood aims. These are set by the organisation in advance of any staff agreements. The stance normally taken is that the organisation must be successful, effective and profitable, and that the purpose of IR (like all other workplace activities) is to contribute to this.

For the approach to be truly effective, overwhelming obligations rest with the organisation and its managers. Standards are preset and prescribed, not the subject of negotiation. Areas of managerial prerogative, matters for consultation, and aspects open to negotiation, are all clearly stated. Conformity leaves much open to consultation, but very little to genuine negotiation.

Procedures are quick and direct. Managers seek to solve problems and promote harmony. Conflicts of interest between groups are kept to a minimum. Disputes (especially those to do with pay and conditions) are resolved within given deadlines. Staff identity with the organisation must be strong. The position of trade unions (and any other staff representative bodies such as staff associations) is clearly defined and limited at the outset. The basis of any agreement is set by the organisation. The union or representative body is invited to work within it. If it feels unable to do this, it will not be recognised.

■ The single union agreement (see also Appendix: *The Sanyo Staff Handbook*)

This is the approach to IR highly regarded especially by Japanese companies operating in the West. It is a conformist approach. The IR agreement is made between the company and one trade union, along the conformist lines indicated above, with the overriding concern of streamlining and ordering workplace and relations, to ensure that their operation is as effective and ordered as any other business activity. Pre-designed and pre-determined by the organisation, such agreements are normally limited to a single site or operational division.

Invitations to tender for the rights to representation of the staff are issued to a range of trade unions. The unions then normally present the benefits that accrue to the organisation of dealing with them. The organisation will hear all the presentations, and then decide on one union, which it will recognise, and which will then represent all the staff.

It follows that the groundwork for this must be very carefully carried out. There are problems of acceptance on the part of managers, who may not be used to dealing with a particular trade union; and on the part of the staff also, who may have no previous affinity or identity with it. There are also problems of acceptance on the part of highly organised occupational groups for the same reason; and on the part of those unions that are not to be recognised.

To be effective and successful this strategy for the management of IR must have the following attributes:

■ Attributes of single union IR

- It must mirror the **philosophy, ethos, style** and **values** of the organisation concerned; there must be commitment to it and a willingness on the part of the organisation to resource and underwrite it all.
- Managers and supervisors are trained in the **procedures** and **practices** of IR, the ability to manage staff on a basis free from inherent conflict, and the ability to solve rather than institutionalise problems when they occur.
- **Wage levels** tend to be at the upper end of the sectoral scale, and will also be good in relation to other variables such as regional considerations and the ability to compete for all categories of staff in both the sector of operations and the locality where work takes place. Wage rises are never backdated.
- There is **one set** of procedures, terms and conditions of employment only, operated by the organisation, in conjunction with the recognised union. The procedures themselves, together with the rest of the IR policy, are devised and drawn up by the company and the union invited to participate on preset terms. The IR sphere is not a matter for joint negotiation or agreement.
- The union represents **all members of staff** at the workplace and there is no other IR format. Staff are encouraged to join the union but are not compelled.
- **Disciplinary and grievance practices** operate from the standpoint of resolution and prevention of the matters in hand, rather than institutionalisation. They are aimed above all at getting any recalcitrant employee back into productive work in harmony with the rest of the company as quickly as possible. Where recourse to procedures is necessary, these also are designed for maximum and optimum speed of operation. The purpose here is to prevent any issue that may arise from festering and getting out of control. Summary Box 7.13 shows the single union no-strike agreement between Sanyo and the EETPU.
- The **disputes procedure** is normally that of binding pendulum arbitration (see below) and represents the final solution to the matter in hand. It is only invoked at the point where an official dispute would otherwise take place; there are cultural as well as operational pressures that ensure that this gets used as rarely as possible.

This style of IR is above all designed to be a business-like approach and arrangement, designed as part of the process of ensuring the success, continuity and profitability of the organisation. As such it is integral rather than an adjunct to it.

■ Single table bargaining and agreements

Single table bargaining is a variation of the single union agreement. The principles, practices and approach are the same. All staff are on the same basic terms and conditions. Representation is allowed from more than one union, and is conducted from the one central standpoint. The advantage is that, within the broad constraint, it gives a measure of choice to the individual member of staff in the matter of representation.

SUMMARY BOX 7.13   Single Union No-strike Agreement between Sanyo (UK) Ltd (Lowestoft) and the EETPU

- The standpoint in the first section of the agreement is that of a business venture and the contribution of industrial relations to success, continuity and business profitability.
- The parameters of industrial relations and the extent and limitations of the union's involvement and influence are clearly defined.
- Consultative and participative meetings are to take place on a regularised and formalised basis; matters for consideration are prescribed (though there is an in-built flexibility).
- The standpoint of grievance and dispute, and disciplinary handling is clearly stated. The full operation of procedures for these should be kept to a minimum; where they are necessary they should normally be fully invoked and the issue resolved after a maximum of two weeks. Rights of representation and appeal are clearly indicated.
- The pendulum arbitration procedure is clearly stated.
- The final paragraph reinforces the tone of the agreement in which the necessity for industrial action in any form is precluded and which again restates the business nature of the agreement.

See Appendix for full Sanyo (UK) Staff Handbook details.

■ Pendulum arbitration

This is the term given to the instrument in most common use in this situation, which is invoked only at the point where a strike or other industrial action would otherwise take place.

An arbitrator is appointed by agreement of both sides to the dispute. The arbitrator hears both sides of the dispute, and then **decides** wholly in favour of one party or the other. Someone therefore always wins (and is seen to win); and someone always loses (and is seen to lose). The concept of pendulum arbitration is based on this – faced with the prospect or possibility of losing a dispute, each party will wish to resort to the negotiating table once again to resolve the differences. In particular in Japanese companies, there are strong cultural pressures on managers not to get into disputes, and not to lose them if they do.

Pendulum arbitration normally represents the final solution to any dispute, against which there is no appeal; this is clearly stated in handbooks and agreements in which this is the instrument for the resolution of disputes. Those entering in to it agree to be bound by the outcome before the arbitrator hears the case.

■ IR without unions

If industrial relations is to be conducted without unions, the reasons why people join unions must be removed. Trade unions grew to prominence in organisations to represent the employees' interests, to serve particular groups, and as a brake on the worst excesses of management that led to a quality of treatment across the whole of the business sphere that by any standards, commercial or ethical, was unacceptable and untenable. If this arises once unions have been eased out or de-recognised (or in a new organisation where there is no intention to have them in the first place) the staff will simply join up again *en masse*. So an approach to IR that precludes the need for outside representation is essential.

This normally consists of adopting a benevolent, consultative and open mode of general communications, corporate attitudes to the staff and an enlightened general attitude as the cornerstone of the IR and staff management approach. Operation of procedures and practices must be fair, and perceived as such. Pay, pay rises, working conditions and other operational matters are consulted upon through works, organisation councils and staff associations.

Responsibility for the style and tone of industrial relations rests entirely with the organisation. Staff adopt the desired corporate attitudes, values and aspirations.

■ The single status concept

This concept is based on an ethical stance that all employees should be treated equally, and that the same fundamental terms and conditions of employment are to apply to all. There is, in these situations, a single staff handbook applying to all. Terms and conditions, and elements of the contract of employment, on such matters as holiday accrual, hours of work, the provision of staff facilities, working clothes and safety and protective wear, are the same for all. Participation in such things as profit-related or merit award payment schemes involves everyone.

Behavioural issues reinforce this. Everyone is addressed in the same manner regardless of occupation. The work of each employee is valued and respected. Differentiation between groups and categories of employees is on the basis of work function only; there are no exclusive canteens, or car-parking spaces.

■ Flexibility

Related to single status is the concept of the 'flexible workforce'; that is, where everyone concerned is both trained and available for any work that the organisation may require of them. Staff normally will be made to understand, when they first join, that they may be required to undertake duties away from their normal or habitual occupation. In the wider interests of staff motivation, organisations will endeavour to do this on a positive rather than coercive basis. Nevertheless it is a fundamental departure from traditional specialisation, demarcation and restrictive practices.

Implicit in this are obligations on the part of employees to accept continuous training and development as part of their commitment to the organisation – and this applies to all categories and occupations.

■ Works councils

Many organisations have established Works Councils in recent years. This is akin to having a board of directors looking after the employee (rather than shareholder) interests. Representatives are drawn from all departments, divisions and functions, as well as any recognised trade unions.

■ IR procedures

These are written and promulgated for the purpose of regulating workplace activities – discipline, grievance, disputes, health and safety, internal opportunities, equality.

They are used by managers, in their pursuit of and operation of these aspects of work. They are for guidance, and only where something requires precise operation (such as a safety procedure), or there is a legal restraint (such as with discipline), should they be strictly adhered to. Their purpose otherwise is to set standards of behaviour and practice at work; this also has implications for the more general standards of decency, ethics, and staff treatment that are established at the workplace. Procedures also indicate and underpin the required attitudes, and let everyone know where they stand. More generally, they define the scope and limits of the influence of the workplace. Above all they have to be understood and followed by all concerned; as long as they meet any legal requirements, organisations and their managers must follow what they promulgate.

Procedures should always be in writing, and state to whom they apply, and under what circumstances. They should be written in the language of the receiver, so that they are easily and clearly understood and followed. The best induction programmes will contain both coverage and explanation of them, so that new employees know from the outset where the boundaries lie, and what the expectations and obligations under them, on the part of both themselves and the organisation, are.

Procedures should be reviewed and updated regularly, and when they pass from currency they should be changed to reflect this. Staff groups and any recognised trade unions should always be consulted on the introduction, use and application of procedures and any changes that are made. Ultimate responsibility for both the standards that they set, and their design and implementation, must always remain with the organisation.

Summary Box 7.14 briefly compares UK IR practice with that adopted in the USA and Europe.

■ Conclusions

The general level of understanding and appreciation required of the managers if they are to be truly effective in this field is clearly deep and complex. They must create the basis of an harmonious, productive, working environment so that

---

SUMMARY BOX 7.14 Comparative Industrial Relations

It is relevant to draw attention here to the uniqueness of the UK IR system and its divergence from others. This is especially true of the trade union movement. Until 1993, all UK trade unions took at least a collective standpoint and most were overtly socialist, at least in their leadership. The Labour Party was originally founded to represent the interests of the unions in Parliament; the major stakeholders in the Labour Party remained the trade unions. Only now is this relationship being seriously examined for the first time.

The other quirk specific to UK trade unions is their sectoralisation and specialisation. The titles – National Union of Teachers; Rail and Maritime Trade Union – define spheres of influence and interests. They are drawn from a tradition of demarcation and specialisation and, again, this is only being examined for the first time in the last decade of the twentieth century, where there are moves afoot among certain sectors to refocus their outlook.

This is to be contrasted with unions elsewhere. In the USA they are professional lobbies. They work in the same way as any other such lobby to promote and defend their interests – through the media, political representatives and on industrial, and commercial councils and committees. They are neither as universal nor as institutionalised as in Europe and the UK, neither do they carry the same influence (indeed they have lost credence and influence in the wake of corruption scandals in recent years).

In the countries of Europe, unions adopt a much wider brief than their UK counterparts, representing 'public services' or 'the car industry', for example, rather than a particular occupation or sub-section of it. They also adopt a much wider variety of stances and affiliations ranging from communism and socialism to conservatism, christian democracy and roman catholicism.

Finally, a much wider view of IR is taken. This ranges from conflict (e.g. France, Italy) and concentration on welfare benefits as much as wages (e.g. Holland); while others adopt the stance that a productive, harmonious and profitable undertaking is good for everyone including their members (e.g. Sweden, Germany).

---

effective work can be carried out. Employee motivation must be maintained. The managers must establish formal, semi-formal and informal chains of communication with workforce representatives (if there are any) and with employees at large.

They may have to bring a range of skills to bear in the day-to-day handling of staff matters. Negotiations, dealing with disciplinary and grievance matters, handling disputes, and other problem solving activities may have to be undertaken. They may have to balance conflicting demands and may only be able to resolve one issue at the expense of another.

Managers may be fortunate enough to be able to conduct HRM in an atmosphere of positivism and industrial harmony. Conversely they may constantly be working in an atmosphere where mistrust is endemic and outright conflict is just below the surface. In such circumstances, the best strategy may simply be to move from problem to problem if by doing so the manager can at least ensure a modicum of output. The ability to make any progress and shape a more positive and effective future for them in such circumstances will stem from an understanding of the status quo in the first place. Beyond that, a full appreciation of the principles outlined here and a commitment to change from the organisation in question together with a clear vision of what that change should be are essential for such progress to be successfully enjoyed.

Moves towards full workforce flexibility have also been made and the concept is now familiar and understood. However, it is not yet fully implemented in public services or the multinational sector. The full human resource and wider managerial implications have also yet to be thought through fully. Many organisations are still enmeshed in a great array of differing terms and conditions of employment, complicated working arrangements and restrictive practices and these are maintained at the expense of operational effectiveness.

There must be a universal commitment to the development of all employees. As the value of this becomes more widely recognised and the benefits can be seen to translate into increased profits, service quality and organisation stability, flexibility and continuity, so the profile and priority of these activities will rise. Alongside this must come a greater awareness of the purpose and benefits of effective performance appraisal and the wider relationship between the efforts of staff and the prosperity of the organisation.

A general appreciation of the traditions, history and background of IR is also essential if the managers are to understand both the current general state of IR thinking and also that of their own organisation in particular. These traditions are underpinned by mythology, legends and folklore that still engender great pride in certain sectors of the population; this mythology has its roots in real grievances, deprivation and a style of entrepreneurship and management that was very often entirely unacceptable by any standard against which any such practice would be measured in the world of today.

This helps in an understanding of the behavioural and procedural niceties of bargaining activities, and also ensures that their importance in the conduct of IR is not underestimated. In traditional, long-standing and public UK institutions, both staff and unions are comfortable with this way of doing things; taking a little time to ensure that the processes and structures are adhered to may repay dividends in the early, ultimate resolution of conflict or negotiations. It also helps in the understanding of the scale and scope that any intended reform of IR practice must address. It is not enough simply to cut out the behavioural and procedural aspects, as these provide the format in which IR practice takes place. If such reform is to be carried out, either globally or at the workplace, in relation to these traditions, an entire new system of IR must be devised and implemented. That way, any uncertainty, mistrust and conflict inherent in piecemeal tinkering with the status quo is avoided.

Finally, this history explains the attraction to organisations of both the single union and non-union approaches. Both have a ready-made model and set of principles to work from. Both have been demonstrated, tried and tested elsewhere with a marked degree of success and effectiveness in certain circumstances.

As a field of study and of managerial practice, human resource management is developing all the time. There exists now a much more universal understanding of the principles of human resource management, how these should be applied and what they are supposed to achieve. More widely, it is recognised as a business activity, a key function that contributes both to the effectiveness and the profitability of the organisation. In line with this, organisations are now setting their own HRM agenda rather than relying on traditional ways of doing things.

■ Appendix: Sanyo Industries (UK) Ltd: Staff Handbook

AGREEMENT

THIS AGREEMENT is made the tenth day of June 1982
BETWEEN:-

(1) SANYO INDUSTRIES (UK) LIMITED
of Oulton Works, School Road,
Lowestoft, Suffolk NR33 9NA

(hereinafter referred to as "the Company")

(2) THE ELECTRICAL ELECTRONIC TELECOMMUNICATIONS AND PLUMBING UNION
of Hayes Court, West Common Road,
Hayes, Bromley, Kent BR2 7AH

(hereinafter referred to as "the Union").

The Company and the Union have agreed to enter this Agreement for the purpose of recognising various mutual and other objectives which is in the interests of both parties and of the employees of the Company to achieve and accordingly the Company and the Union have agreed the following matters:-

1. (1) The independence of the practices and procedures laid down in the respect of the factory premises at Oulton Works, School Road, Lowestoft ('the Establishment') from time to time
   (2) The non-federated status of the Establishment established by this Agreement
   (3) Each of the terms and provisions of this Agreement is dependent upon the observance of all the other terms and provisions, individual provisions cannot be acted upon without consideration of all other relevant provisions in the Agreement
   (4) For the duration of this Agreement the Union shall have sole recognition and bargaining rights for all employees covered by this Agreement

2. In order to achieve the above objectives it is agreed that:-

   (1) All aspects of the Establishment and its operations will be so organised as to achieve the highest possible level of efficiency performance and job satisfaction so that the Company shall:-
   (i) be competitive and thus remain in business
   (ii) provide continuity and security of employment for an effective work force

(iii)   establish and maintain good working conditions

(iv)   establish and maintain good employee relations and communications by supporting the agreed consultative negotiating grievance and disciplinary procedures set out in this Agreement

(2)   Both parties accept an obligation to ensure that the Establishment will operate with effective working methods with the best utilisation of manpower and without the introduction of wasteful and restrictive working practices and this objective will be achieved by:-

(i)   the selection, training, retraining and supplementary training of employees, wherever necessary, to enable such employees to carry out any job

(ii)   the maximum co-operation with and support from all employees for measures and techniques used in any area to improve organisation and individual efficiency and to provide objective information with which to control and appraise the performance of individual employees and the Establishment

(iii)   the maximum co-operation and support from all employees in achieving a completely flexible well motivated work force capable of transferring on a temporary or permanent basis into work of any nature that is within the capability of such employee having due regard to the provision of adequate training and safety arrangements

(3)   Both parties recognise that the well-being of the employees is dependent upon the Company's success and that the high standards of product quality and reliability are essential if the products produced at the Establishment are to become and remain competitive and that therefore the maximum co-operation and support must be given to measures designed to achieve maintain and improve quality and reliability standards.

3.   The following matters have been agreed in connection with the Union:-

(1)   Employees will not be required to become union members but the Company will encourage all employees covered by this Agreement to become a member of the Union and participate in Union affairs and in this connection the Company will provide a check off arrangement for the deduction of union subscriptions

(2)   Union representation will be established in the following manner:-

(i)   The number of representatives of the Union together with the constituencies which they will represent will be agreed between the Union and the Company

(ii)   The representatives will be elected in accordance with the Union Rules by union members in each constituency

(iii)   Each such representative ('the Constituency Representative') will be accredited by the Union and the Union will then send details of the credentials of such representative for approval to the Head of Personnel who will confirm such approval with the Union and thereafter inform the appropriate line management concerned of the appointment

(3)   The elected representatives will elect from amongst themselves a senior representative ('the Senior Representative') in accordance with the Union Rules

(4)   The Senior Representative will be responsible for controlling and co-ordinating the activities of the Union in accordance with the terms and conditions of this Agreement and within the Union Rules and Regulations and will ensure that each elected representative shall have a working knowledge of the Union Rules and Regulations and in this connection in conjunction with the Personnel Department of the Company the Senior Representative shall ensure that the representatives shall have a comprehensive understanding of the industrial relations procedures and practices of the Establishment and of general industrial relations procedures and practices and it is agreed that all communication between the representatives and the full-time official(s) of the Union will be made through the Senior Representative

(5)   Each elected representative must be employed in the constituency which he represents

(6)   The Company will provide adequate facilities to ensure that all Union elections and ballots of members shall be carried out in secret and by the use of voting papers and not by way of a show of hands

4. It is agreed by the Company and the Union that all matters of difference should wherever possible be resolved at the source of such difference as speedily as practicable and it is the intention of the parties that all such matters will be dealt with in accordance with the agreed procedure and in this connection:-

(1) Where a matter relates to an individual employee covered by this Agreement such employee must in the first instance raise the same with the supervisor who will then be given the appropriate time necessary to resolve the situation PROVIDED ALWAYS that:-
  (i) if the employee is not satisfied with the solution proposed by the supervisor then the employee may request the services of the constituency representative to reach a solution with the supervisor
  (ii) if the constituency representative and the supervisor shall fail to reach agreement then the constituency representative will discuss the matter with the Department Manager or his representative
  (iii) if after careful deliberation a satisfactory solution cannot be found then the constituency representative shall be entitled to raise the issue with the Senior Representative who will then decide if the grievance should be discussed at a higher level of management within the Company and the services of the Personnel Officer may then be called upon if is considered that this will help to resolve the matter
  (iv) failing such resolution discussions will then take place between the Senior Representatives of the Company normally including the Head of Personnel together with the Senior Union Representative and the constituency representatives on the Joint Negotiation Council ("JNC") referred to in Clause (5) below
  (v) in exceptional circumstances the services of the National Officer of the Union may be requested to assist in the matter either by the Union or by the Company and in such circumstances the Company will arrange an appropriate meeting to be attended by senior representatives of the Company and the Union as well as the National Officer or the Full-time Official

(2) Insofar as differences shall arise in connection with issues of a Departmental nature then the procedure shall commence with a meeting between the constituency representative and the Department Manager or his representative

(3) In the case of an issue concerning the Establishment or the Company as a whole the matter will commence on the same basis as is set out in Sub-Clause (iii) above

5. The Company and the Union will establish a Joint Negotiation Council ('JNC') for the purpose of providing a forum through which discussions regarding improvements to employment conditions and other major matters can be discussed and in this connection:-

(1) The JNC will consist of representatives from the Company including the Head of Personnel and Senior Company Representatives and on behalf of the Union the Senior Representative from Production/Warehousing one constituency representative from Administration.

(2) Discussions regarding substantive improvements to employment conditions will normally be held on an annual basis during December in each year and such discussions will not include changes arising as a result of promotions transfers or changes to job content which can be implemented at any time as agreed

(3) Matters agreed by the JNC will constitute one of the terms and conditions of employment for each employee covered by this Agreement

(4) The Senior Representative will be given appropriate facilities to consult with Union Members Constituency Representatives and the Full-time Official or National Officer of the Union to enable the Senior Representative to conduct a meaningful collective bargaining exercise

(5) All claims on behalf of Union Members must be made in writing by the Senior Representative to the Head of Personnel who will convene the appropriate meeting of the JNC

(6) It is recognised by both parties that whilst discussions are taking place all business and negotiations discussed at the

JNC will remain confidential to its members and the Company recognises its responsibility to ensure clear communication to employees of the results of such discussions and negotiations and in this connection the Head of Personnel will be responsible in consultation with the members of the JNC for announcing the details of any offer to be made to employees following such discussions and negotiations as aforesaid

(7)   In exceptional circumstances the services of the National Officer or the Full-time Official of the Union may be requested by the JNC and in such circumstances the Company will arrange an appropriate meeting to be attended by representatives of the Company and the Union and the National Officer

6. In addition to the JNC the Company will establish a Joint Consultative Council ('JCC') and the following provisions shall apply thereto:-

(1)   The membership of the JCC shall consist of the Head of Personnel (as Chairman) and appropriate members of the Company's Senior Executives and the Senior Representative together with one constituency representative from each of Production, Engineering and Administration and a further constituency representative on a rotating basis as a co-opted member and in addition the Managing Director of the Company shall act as President of the JCC and shall attend meetings from time to time

(2)   The JCC shall meet on a monthly basis for the purposes of discussing issues of a mutual nature and one week prior to each JCC meeting the Personnel Officer will publish an Agenda agreed with the Senior Representative who will be responsible for submitting items for discussion on behalf of the Union in time for such items to be included on the Agenda

(3)   Items to be included for discussion at JCC meetings will include:-
  (i)   manufacturing performance
  (ii)   operating efficiency
  (iii) manufacturing planning
  (iv)   employment levels
  (v)   market information
  (vi)   establishment environment
  (vii) employment legislation
  (viii) union policies and procedure
  (ix)   level of union membership

(4)   Following each meeting of the JCC the Head of Personnel will be responsible for communicating to all employees the nature and content of the discussions and in this connection the Company and the Union recognise the need to conduct meetings of the JCC in constructive manner for the benefit of the Company and all its employees

7. In the event that the Company and the Union shall be unable ultimately to resolve between themselves any discussions or disputes they may jointly agree to appoint an arbitrator and in this connection:-

(1)   The Arbitrator will consider evidence presented to him by the Company and the Union and any factors that he believes to be appropriate

(2)   The Arbitrator will decide in favour of one party
(3)   The decision of the Arbitrator will be final and binding and will represent the final solution to the issue

8. DISCIPLINARY MEASURES
It is in the interest of the Company and its employees to maintain fair and consistent standards of conduct and performance. This procedure is designed to clarify the rights and responsibilities of the Company, the Union and employees with regard to disciplinary measures

Principles
The following principles will be followed in applying this procedure:

8.1 In the normal course of their duties, the Company will make employees aware of any shortcomings in performance or conduct. This counselling stage is separate from the disciplinary procedure as such
8.2 When the disciplinary procedure is invoked, the intention is to make the employee aware that the Company is concerned with their conduct or performance and to assist the person to improve to a satisfactory level
8.3 When any disciplinary case is being considered, the Company will be responsible for fully investigating the facts and circumstances of the case
8.4 The procedure will operate as quickly as possible, consistent with the thorough investigation of the case
8.5 The employee will always be informed of any disciplinary action to be taken

and the reasons for it, indicating the specific areas for improvement

8.6 Normally the formal procedure will commence with the issuing of the first formal warning, however, the disciplinary procedure may be invoked at any stage depending on the seriousness of the case

8.7 Each formal warning will apply for 12 months. Should the employee improve their conduct or performance to an acceptable level and maintain the improvement for the duration of the warning, this will result in the deletion of the warning from their record

9. DISCIPLINARY PROCEDURE

The stages of the disciplinary procedure as follows:-

9.1 *First Formal Warning*
A formal warning at this stage represents the outcome of investigation and discussion into an employee's conduct or performance. If a first formal warning is issued, the individual concerned will be advised to this effect both verbally and in writing by the Company representative conducting the hearing, indicating the duration of the warning (which will be 12 months), the reasons for the warning and the specific areas for improvement

9.2 *Final Warning*
If there is no significant and sustained improvement in the employee's conduct or performance, then the next stage of the procedure is the final warning. If a final warning is issued, the individual concerned will be advised to this effect by the Company representative conducting the hearing, both verbally and in writing, indicating the duration of the warning (which will be 12 months), the grounds for the warning and the specific areas for improvement

9.3 *Dismissal*
If there is no significant and sustained improvement in the employee's conduct or performance during the period of the final warning, then following thorough investigation by the Company, the next stage of the procedure will be the dismissal stage. This stage will also be invoked in cases of gross misconduct (see Establishment Regulations). If an employee is dismissed he will be advised in writing

of the principal reasons for the dismissal, and the notice periods which will apply to him

9.4 *Union Representation*
At all stages of this procedure and consistent with the circumstances of the issue the Company will ensure the involvement of the appropriate constituency representative. When, following careful investigation, disciplinary action is contemplated by the Company and the union members concerned will be afforded the services of the Union constituency representative

10. APPEALS

Appeals against disciplinary action will follow the procedure as outlined below

10.1 All appeals will be in writing by the Senior Representative within two working days after the disciplinary action shall have been taken by the Company

10.2 The appeal will be made to the Personnel Officer who will arrange the formal appeal hearing within two working days of the appeal

10.3 The appeal will be heard by a Senior Personnel representative and a Senior Manager of the Department concerned who has not been involved in the case

10.4 The appeal will be conducted on the employee's behalf by the Senior Representative accompanied by the Department representative

10.5 The employee appealing, his Supervisor and other appropriate employees may be called to give evidence if is thought their involvement is essential to the outcome of the hearing

10.6 The decision of the hearing is final. It is recognized that the Union may wish to discuss the matter as a collective issue

11. INDUSTRIAL ACTION

The Company and the Union undertake to follow the procedures agreed to and recognise that this Agreement provides adequate and speedy procedures for the discussion of Company related affairs and the resolution of problems and as such precludes the necessity for recourse to any form of industrial action by either the Company the Union or the Employees.

Signed by

M. SADA

N.T. SALMON

duly authorised for and on behalf of
SANYO INDUSTRIES (UK) LIMITED

SIGNED by

R. SANDERSON

L. CHITTOCK

duly authorised for and on behalf of
THE ELECTRICAL ELECTRONIC
TELECOMMUNICATIONS AND PLUMBING
UNION

Dated this 10th day of June 1982.

Source: Sanyo (UK) Ltd. (1982). Used with
permission of Sanyo Industries (UK) Limited,
Oulton Works, School Road, Lowestoft,
Suffolk NR33 9NA

CHAPTER 8

Operations management

The main purpose of studying operations management as a distinctive element is to identify, the range and complexity of activities, and the combinations of the concepts, techniques, skills and knowledge referred to throughout the book, that are necessary to direct and organise productive efforts. Successful operations management requires clear strategy, effective marketing and human resource management. It also requires attention to investment, technology and financial aspects.

These matters are relevant to all operational aspects, though their emphasis will vary between organisation types, as well as the nature of business being conducted, whether it is: production; technology; commercial services such as banking, insurance, travel, tourism; sales and retail; health care (commercial or public); central, local and municipal government. These matters and elements all impinge on each other, but may be usefully identified under the broad headings of location; facilities; work design and measurement; levels of activity; reliability, safety; production types and categories; creativity and innovation; schedules and timetables; purchasing and supplies; maintenance management; and systems of coordination and control. We will consider each in turn.

■ Location

The question of location must first be addressed. This depends on an assessment of the demand for the products or services; the ways in which it is envisaged that they are to be delivered; the ability to gain the 'raw materials' or inputs (in the widest possible sense) and get them to the location; and matters to do with distribution, transport and delivery to the markets themselves. This requires further assessment if multi-site operation is envisaged. It may be further complicated by the sheer size and scale of the operation – delivering social or education services, for example. Both public and commercial services will tend towards the perceived necessity of being accessible to, and a focus of, the communities that they serve. The final consideration at this stage will concern the speed, quality, reliability, and modes of delivery of the products or services that are envisaged.

There are certain more specific matters to do with location that also bear consideration. Traditionally, industry would tend to locate near its markets if the production process **added** weight to the products; and at the source of materials if the processes **detracted** weight from the products. Consequently, certain areas became known for specific industrial and commercial activities. They were left very exposed when production technology or materials changed, and the question of relocation became both feasible, and technically viable. Consider Summary Box 8.1.

There are matters of access also. Communities, for example, expect to have their own schools, social, health and hospital services, as well as products and services offered commercially. A match has to be made between these expectations, and questions of investment, finance, economies and dis-economies of scale. Banks perceive the necessity to maintain a presence in all areas as part of both their operations and marketing activities, and there are competitive elements to this. There is also a potential 'snowball' effect; the bank that has no direct presence in a given community will lose business to the banks that have – and the same applies to all commercial activities.

■ Transport and distribution

It follows from this that the movement of products and services, the speed of movement, the modes and methods used, must also be considered at the point of deciding on location. This includes wider questions of access to motorway, airline and railway networks, in the case of industrial and commercial products. Supermarket and DIY chains have also moved to edge-of-town and out-of-town

---

SUMMARY BOX 8.1   Co-Steel Sheerness Plc

This is a small steel manufacturing company. It is situated on the north coast of Kent, UK, in the town of Sheerness on the Isle of Sheppey. It breaks all the rules of operations management. It is not located near to the sources of its required inputs – ore and energy fuel. Nor is it located near to its markets. Road access between the organisation and the wider world is by a single bridge linking the Isle of Sheppey with the mainland county of Kent. There is a sea ferry terminal in the town of Sheerness which links with Vlissingen, Netherlands, eight hours away.

The company is both successful and profitable. It concentrates on its inherent strengths rather than bewailing its weaknesses. The top managers of the company have generated a culture and way of working that transcends the operational issues outlined here that have to be faced.

The company has created a conformist culture. This is based on high quality and customer satisfaction. It is reinforced with staff policies of organisation and continuous development and a philosophy of continuing improvement. This has been championed by the director of human resources, Hugh Billot, who is the architect, inspiration and energy behind this.

The company has won national operations, human resource, training and development and Prime Minister's awards in the UK. This has been championed by the director of human resources, the architect, inspiration and energy behind this.

locations in the interest of providing a wider convenience of access to a greater number of people. By providing a total facility, including cafeteria, car parking and toilets as well as a comprehensive coverage of the stated product range, such stores have removed trade from town centres, and have forced those who continue to conduct business there to reappraise their own location and operations mix.

■ Staff

The ability to staff the undertaking at the preferred location must be considered. There is the problem of the volume of staff required. Matters to do with the skills, knowledge and aptitudes prevalent among the potential workforce will also be considered; and more general questions of the prevailing beliefs, attitudes, and values of a given location, region, or town, or of those who used to work in a now-dead industry, may also be important.

Japanese companies locating in the UK have taken complete responsibility for staffing aptitudes and attitudes. In the cases of Nissan at Washington, Tyne and Wear, and Toyota at Derby, the companies have recognised the existence of a potential workforce, and have invested heavily in pre-selection, pre-training and the pre-formation of the required attitudes and values. In effect, they have 'designed' their workforces.

The lesson to be drawn from this in terms of operations management is the assumption of the widest responsibility for the staff and their effective contribution to the undertaking. Whatever the nature of the work, it is clear that there is an extensive obligation to the staff who are to carry it out, on the part of the organisation, if effective operations are to be achieved.

■ Facilities

The scale and scope of facilities must be addressed, in the context of their suitability for the plant, equipment, technology and ways of working required for the particular undertaking. General elements are also important where there is a general public interface; or even more specifically where direct dealings with customers are an essential part of the undertaking, and where that public expects certain modes of delivery (again, such as supermarkets and banks). The range of facilities will also extend to the accommodation of the workforce, and must include rest and staff rooms and car parking; and may also include medical provision, staff restaurants, and trade union facilities, depending upon the scale and scope of the undertaking.

The ways of working of the organisation and the design and layout of the work to be undertaken must specifically be addressed. The purpose of this is to establish the nature of premises that will be suitable for the business to be conducted, and to assess matters of efficiency, effectiveness, space usage, work flows, and support functions. Opportunities, costs and benefits that accrue from a range of alternative facilities and premises, and ways of organisation, will be assessed. The end result desired is a choice of facilities based on a strategic assessment of all of these matters, and one which has regard also to the wider questions of flexibility to expand or contract; effective use of space; potential or possible alternative ways of working and technological updating; matters concerning location and distribution; and matters concerning staff.

The purchase of equipment and technology will be appraised and conducted from the same standpoint. As well as its capacities, matters concerning its useful life; its costs, depreciation and replacement; and its user-friendliness in relation to the capabilities and capacities of the staff must be evaluated.

Appraisal of facilities must consider the sub-systems and support activities that the organisation decides are necessary to ensure an effective overall operation. This includes administrative and support functions, reception of raw materials, storage and stores policies, and marketing and sales activities. There is also the wider question of the intrinsic nature of the working environment to be considered, and while this may initially be viewed as a cost or a charge upon the undertaking, successfully addressing it may generate much more in returns in terms of reduced labour turnover and increased identity and motivation on the part of the staff.

The choice of facilities will depend ultimately upon the appraisal and balance of all of these elements, ensuring that the result is an effective, productive and profitable working environment that people will wish to attend and work with pride and commitment, and which is stable and efficient over a long period of time, while at the same time having the capabilities of flexibility and responsiveness to opportunities.

■ Design and measurement of work

The process of measuring work is complex, and it is essential that those who do it understand this. Work measurement comprises considerations of timescale, task complexities, repetitions, varieties and rotations, human maintenance time, flexibility, and pressures. This is to be balanced against the organisation's inflow of work, orders and activities. It is possible to itemise tasks and their components and to build profiles and patterns of tasks into both individual and group jobs and activities. Wider considerations to do with the work environment, intrinsic job factors, and questions of motivation must also be considered. Finally, the capacities of production and operations technology will be assessed, and both 'perfect' and 'real' flows of work quantified.

From this, patterns of occupation, skills, knowledge and aptitudes emerge, that are to be related to the work in hand. Matters of attitudes and values, identity and alienation, will also be addressed, and will impact upon the standpoint and design of human resource and industrial relations policies; and the style of supervision and management to be adopted.

The mix of the volume, quantity and time pressure must also be considered. Where the quality requirement is high, methods of measuring work must accommodate this, either in the pre-setting and pre-testing of equipment; or (where the human content is critical) in the allowances to the operatives in their own work time and scheduling to ensure this.

Any 'average', 'perfect', or 'ideal' work flow has therefore to be seen in this context. It is possible, for example, to identify a range of customers passing through a given bank till, or supermarket checkout, over a period of time. What cannot be done from this, is to draw a measure of absolute productivity.

On average, a till may serve twenty customers an hour; in a given hour, it may serve three complex customers, or 100 that are straightforward. Similarly, a production line may output sixty television sets in an hour; care must be taken when reading into it, that this also constitutes one set per minute, or 480 per eight-hour shift. It may represent this, or it may not, but such conclusions will only be reached after a strategic, rather than a mechanistic, appraisal of the situation.

There are thus qualitative as well as quantitative aspects to be considered in the design and measurement of work, which must in turn be the subject of supervisory and managerial assessment if it is to be fully effective. If this wider context is appreciated, then methods of work measurement and design will be much more truly and accurately constituted. Only when it is approached in this way, can more specific aims be ascribed to the design and measurement of work that are to do with maximising efficiency, eliminating waste, achieving optimum cost-effectiveness, improvement and optimisation of staff and equipment, improvements in working methods, and overall improvement in production and productivity.

■ Levels of activity

These may usefully be defined for the purpose of generating an overview and basic understanding of the components of operational activities. We need to consider five here:

■ Steady state

The day-to-day activities of the organisation, its core business and purpose, the ways in which most things are done most of the time. Contained within steady-state activities are the standard and usual organisation of work; implicit within it are matters of culture, style, ethos, modes of management and supervision, technology, skills, aptitudes and attitudes. Steady-state activities normally have the major and lasting impact on the organisation, its continuity, constitution, policies, reputation and prosperity.

■ Innovative

Most organisations engage in research and development (R&D) activities, prospecting and opportunity seeking to some extent. The ways in which these are conducted will normally reflect the innovative capabilities present in the organisation, any potential or under-utilised talents or technology, the creativity and imagination of key staff, abilities to identify and exploit new opportunities, and the widest possible understanding of the abilities of the organisation.

■ Crisis

All organisations must be able to accommodate and respond effectively to the genuine emergency, but crisis management must never become the normal way of working. It requires a recognition of the full range of possibilities that can go wrong, and the likely or actual frequency with which they do. From this, effective management techniques will be devised to ensure the minimum lasting impact, and the most effective resolution possible, that arises from any emergency. It also enables assessment of those matters over which the organisation has no control.

■ Policy

These activities constitute the *raison d'étre* for top management. They are concerned with ensuring that the organisation continues to operate effectively, and recognising early any possible negatives (or crises) with a view to taking preventive action.

Policy activities are also concerned with wider environmental, market, technology and general business assessments, and the match and mix of each in the pursuit of profitable activities. There may also be constraints to be accommodated in the form of legislation, loss of market to a competitor, or loss or change of public taste and perception.

■ Pioneering

This is the development of the 'policy' and the 'innovative' elements. Much of the background to pioneering work will be confined to creative (and in itself unprofitable) speculation and discussions; from this, possibilities may arise, and from these, certain more concrete concepts and ideas of potential value to the organisation, or which could potentially be exploited by it, may become apparent.

From such a background emerge the new ideas, the range of possibilities, that generate the next range of products, services and offerings (see Summary Box 8.2). The extent to which organisations will make commitments in the pioneering field will depend upon very 'hard' elements such as appraisal of investments made. It may be limited to organisational cluster or brainstorming sessions; or it may provide a limited range of grants or rewards to employees at the development stage if they do have an idea – they may be given scope and facilities to develop it, in return for a pre-agreed royalty if it becomes successful.

This is quite distinct from organisational R&D activities, which are part of the organisation's commitment (fixed cost and investment) to its own future. At its best, pioneering is an opportunity afforded by organisations to all people as one of the means of identifying talent and potential, gaining and encouraging commitment, and improving work methods. More generally, it also underlines positive approaches to quality improvement. It also provides an outlet for employee creativity and invention.

■ Reliability

The nature and concept of 'reliability' varies from sector to sector, and between operational elements. There are general considerations to be made, however. There must be an overall understanding of what the operational sector understands by 'reliability'. There is a competitive component to be understood. This occurs in the global aspect (e.g. an English electronics company must overcome,

---

SUMMARY BOX 8.2   Product Success: the Sony Walkman

This product is a world leader. It has generated its own universal identity, and was instrumental both in transforming the operations of the Sony organisation, and in raising its public profile. It has also created the £60 million per annum personal entertainment industry.

None of the components of the product were original, but rather the adaptation of existing items and concepts – the transistor radio; the earpiece; transistorisation and miniaturisation; batteries; and audio cassettes. There was the concept of providing personal and private entertainment that people could use in public places. Finally, it was necessary to generate public awareness, to familiarise the concept, and thus generate demand.

The product concept has since been developed and extended to include compact disc television, and radio provision. Once expensive and exclusive to Sony, equivalent products are now produced by all the electronic companies of the world. At 1996 prices, these products are now available for as much as £300 for deluxe models; while a basic personal radio may be purchased for as little as £3.

or at least come to terms with, the universal perception of the reliability of Japanese products if it wishes to operate in the sector). It also occurs in local situations where local rivalry and competition may take place between similar operators (e.g. a key feature of successful, local and small building firms is their reputation for reliability).

Customers expect reliability. They expect deadlines to be met, products to work, and services to deliver what they purport to offer. In commercial terms this is straightforward. The same expectations also extend to health services – there is an expectation of accurate diagnosis and treatment of ailments, illnesses and injuries. 'Reliability' has connotations of length of wait for service and treatment, and the effectiveness of the service and treatment in its widest sense (if one seeks medical advice for one ailment, and another is found along the way, there is an expectation and requirement that this will be treated at the same time).

'Reliability' also refers to the quality of the human aspects of operations. Customers and potential customers require confidence in the supplying organisation and its staff. Organisational presentation must therefore exhibit those qualities of perceived expertise, modes of presentation, and technical know-how, that constitute 'credibility'. These reinforce initial feelings of reliability and form the basis of a continuing positive business relationship.

Only when these conditions are satisfied is there any purpose in addressing the technical or intrinsic qualities of the products or services on offer. There is no value in having the greatest, most advanced product range in the world, if potential customers have no belief, faith or confidence in it.

■ Safety aspects

Products and services offered to the public at large must also be healthy and safe as far as is reasonably practicable. In the EC and North America, there are standards of materials usage and design which must be met. This ranges from the avoidance of sharp points or edges on products on general sale, to the proscription of certain chemicals and elements in certain processes (e.g. some pesticides may not be used on certain crops; some colourings may not be used in food processing).

Best practice always requires an approach based on **prevention** rather than **cure**. Where accidents and emergencies do occur, however, inquests and inquiries are often held to ascertain the true causes, and to draw lessons that have the overall objective of ensuring that it never happens again. Organisations are generally required to have adequate and effective accident reporting methods and procedures in place, and to notify a variety of statutory bodies according to the nature of what has happened; where it has happened; whether it was kept internal to the organisation, or caused damage to the world outside; and who was affected.

High-profile coverage of workplace disasters normally affects general feelings of confidence. In the worst cases, the integrity of the entire range of activities – even the industry itself – may be questioned. (See Summary Box 8.3.)

A large part of good health and safety practice constitutes the adoption of positive and effective attitudes and ethical stances. It reflects a wider concern for both workforce, customers and the community. Lack of attention to health and safety invariably indicates a much deeper operational malaise.

SUMMARY BOX 8.3   Disasters: Bhopal, Chernobyl, Seveso

Major industrial disasters can invariably be traced back to a lack of genuine concern and integrity at some stage of the operational process. This in turn meant that neither production systems nor the human elements were correctly designed in the first place, nor were they capable of being sustained in the long term.

- **Union Carbide**: the Union Carbide plant at Bhopal, India was built in the 1970s to standards and constraints specified by the then Indian Government, rather than to those required as absolutes by the chemical industry. The result was that safety systems and procedures were not adequate to prevent disaster, whether or not they conformed with the law, and 2,500 people lost their lives after a toxic gas escape which, because it was heavier than air, effectively flooded the town around the works and people suffocated as the result.
- **Chernobyl**: Chernobyl was a nuclear disaster that occurred near Kiev in the Ukraine in 1986. Ninety people died in the immediate explosion and fire. Thousands more subsequently suffered serious and fatal illness from the radiation spread afterwards. The entire area will be polluted for centuries. The problem was caused by a lack of both preventative and emergency maintenance. It was compounded by insufficient attention to the limitations and finite useful and safe life of the technology; and institutional unwillingness and incapability of recognising the real nature of the operational management commitment as the result of being in this industry, in this location, at this time.
- **Seveso**: the Seveso disaster occurred near Milan, Italy in 1972 when a large agrochemical plant blew up. It brought a cloud of poison dust down on the town and rendered large areas uninhabitable. This caused leukemia and all sorts of other cancers among the population immediately; and the long-term effects included very high proportions of children born in poor health or with deformities. Parts of the town had to be completely evacuated for months to enable a proper clean-up to take place. The problem was again traced back to system and technology design and capability. In this case, it was compounded by a lack of inspection, quality assurance, testing and analysis at all stages, especially at the inception of the project.

In none of these cases have there been any successful prosecutions. All of the organisations at the time claimed that this at least proved their integrity, if not their competence. However, the long-term effects were measured in each case in terms of loss of confidence in the sectors; loss of employee, public and customer confidence; as well as financial disaster. They would each have been avoided if the management of operations had been based on absolute integrity and understanding rather than short-term expediency.

■ Legal aspects

There are various legal duties and obligations for organisations to establish premises and work methods that are (as far as is reasonably practicable) healthy and safe. It is a derived requirement of this that organisations accommodate any actual or potential hazards at the workplace by ensuring that employees have access to safety clothing and equipment; that they are fully trained and briefed in matters to do with health and safety; that standards of operation encompass best practice in regard to these; and that potentially dangerous or hazardous machines are adequately guarded and provided with cut-outs and emergency switches. Any process that uses hazardous, toxic or potentially lethal components must be isolated from those working on it. They in turn, must be provided with all protection necessary (and often legally stated) to ensure, as far as possible, that they derive no harm from their occupation. Provision must be made at the workplace for the isolation of, and supervision of, designated restricted stores and equipment.

This must be underwritten by safety policies that reflect the general approach and attitude to the health and safety at work of the employees and the organisation itself. The policy will consist of a concise general statement and organisational arrangements which are to be distributed to all employees for their reference. This is underpinned by a more detailed account or collection of documents which pertain to particular activities at the place of work. The policy sets the general standpoint and attitude adopted to the promotion of safe and healthy working practices. It is clear from this that overall responsibility for health and safety at the place of work rests at the top management level. However, all individuals at every level have a joint degree of responsibility to ensure that their own aspect and work environment is kept as far as possible both safe and healthy. The policy will identify any instruments for monitoring and assessment – such as safety representatives and the election or appointment of safety committees. This may also include training for both managers and operative staff. Finally, particular hazards will be indicated, as will the requirements to wear particular types of clothing, use particular types of equipment and follow particular procedures in dealing with particular hazardous or potentially unsafe situations and practices at the place of work. This includes the storage, handling and usage of restricted or supervised goods, chemicals and other equipment.

The work environment must be organised in such a way as to be healthy and safe as far as possible. This includes:

- **Temperature** levels; proper training and clothing must be provided for those who have to work in extreme heat or cold
- **Lighting**, which must be adequate to work without strains on the eyesight of the workforce
- **Ventilation** of all work premises, where necessary through air-conditioning and filtration procedures

- Suitable and sufficient **sanitary accommodation** for all, including separate conveniences for each gender, and the disabled; and related provisions of washing and drinking-water facilities
- **Machinery** must have guards and cut-outs in-built, and training be given in this usage and operation; these guards must be maintained in an effective state, and not be removed during operations
- **Offices** must also be **maintained** in a safe way: telephone and computer wires must not be left trailing; fire doors must not be propped open or locked shut; passages and corridors must be clear and unobstructed
- **Floors, stairs and passages** must be soundly constructed and maintained, and railings put on stairs and raised walkways
- Specific **training** must be provided for all those who are required to lift **heavy weights**; or to work with **toxic** or **dangerous fumes or substances**
- **Records of accidents** must be kept; all accidents which result in fatality, loss of limb, or absence from work of more than three days must be notified to the Health and Safety Inspectorate
- **Toxic and hazardous substances** must be kept locked; access to them must be via designated persons only.

In many places employers are now required to assess health and safety risks to their employees and anyone else affected by their work activity. Employers are obliged to:

- Take measures to prevent significant risks and to protect employees against them
- Appoint competent staff with health and safety responsibilities
- Provide employees with health and safety information and training
- Set up emergency procedures and train employees in them
- Cooperate with other employers if they share the company's workplace.

In many parts of the world there are regulations governing the provision of, and use of, work equipment. Adequate instruction and training must be given to all employees.

Manual Handling Operations Regulations require employers to carry out a risk assessment for manual handling operations in order to reduce injuries as far as possible.

Workplace, health, safety and welfare regulations rationalise and codify the existing legislation. They establish employers' responsibilities for lighting, heating, ventilation, workstation suitability, seating and other ergonomic factors; safety; and toilet facilities.

■ Production types and categories

It is useful now to distinguish these because they have implications for the organisation and management styles, and methods to be adopted in the design and definition of the operations themselves.

■ Jobbing or unit production

Most production organisations have the capacity for single or specialised jobs. In larger organisations this may be limited to the production of prototypes or prestige models, or linked closely to new products research; in smaller organisations this will represent the main way of working. Resources are gathered together in order to produce limited volume or unique items in response to orders. To be a successful specialist organisation a variety of conditions must exist. The workforce must be flexible, adaptive and innovative as well as responsive. Quality and attention to detail will normally be endemic features of work. Scheduling will also be flexible and responsive. Deadlines will normally be set by the customer unless the work is highly specialised.

Manufacturing is expensive in such situations; on the other hand the nature of the product will normally make it less price sensitive than more universally or mass produced items.

The wider concept of specialisation may also be extended to non-manufacturing sectors. The basis of such activities as specialist holiday companies, exclusive restaurants, some publishing, limited editions of ceramic and glass figurines, postage stamps, is the same as for unit production.

■ Mass production

This was first used at Ford and was based on the 'scientific management' principles of F.W. Taylor (see Chapter 2). Work was broken down into the simplest possible elements and the workforce stood alongside a moving production line performing their tasks or fitting their parts to the cars as they moved slowly past each work station. In such ways large volumes of a standard unit were produced, each indistinguishable from all the others. Automated and electronic production lines, and electronic methods of control and standardisation have now refined production to a much greater extent and genuinely identical products are now produced.

Mass production requires high levels of investment in both production technology and the premises to house it. It also requires managerial investment in production scheduling and related activities at both beginning and end of the production processes – storage, input, output, marketing, sales and delivery – commensurate with the product volume being completed. There are implicit in this strategic decisions to be considered – investment appraisal, technology purchase, long-term forecasting, market and sales volumes – before such production is undertaken.

Once mass production methods are installed, up and running unit costs become low and control straightforward. Work methods are standardised, and production is efficient, long term or long run for best returns. There is also plenty of scope for the organisation of work, whether this be into autonomous groups, work teams or through job rotation methods.

■ Process and flow production

Related to mass production in scale, but applying to oil, petrol, chemicals, plastic extrusion, steel and paper is process or flow production – the output of commodities in a continuous stream or flow. Again capital, technological and process costs are high. Input has to be planned in order to ensure continuity, often permanent and invariably for months at a time. However, the processes, once installed and instituted, are often fully automatic and running costs are minimal.

The greatest charge on either a flow or mass production system is when they are shut down. Levels of capital investment require that they run for as much of their useful life as possible. If they are not producing, either because of the lack of input materials or because of industrial accident or dispute, the charges on the capital have still to be borne without the benefit of output providing a return on this investment. Many steel and chemical processes cannot be shut down without substantial to the production technology.

The principles of mass and flow production are also translated into the provision of both public and commercial services. Capital costs are high and the scheduling of services is pre-designed, in hospitals, health care; education; social services; package holidays; postal services; banking, insurance and finance; and mining and quarrying. The greater strain on resources is when there is no usage of them or when they are not taken up or when they do not match demand.

■ Batch production

Somewhere between the specialisation of jobbing and the economy of scale and capital investment requirements of mass flow production comes batch production. A 'batch' is defined as being a quantity large enough to require a measure of technology and investment and capital output and yet small enough to have its own distinctive identity. Effective batch production combines standardisation of production with the ability to respond to customer requirements and the flexibility and dynamism on the part of the organisation which goes with it.

Batch production is to be found in the components and supplies sectors, sourcing other manufacturers, certain foodstuffs, limited edition and differentiated cars and clothing, some building materials, and retail drugs and medicines.

Again, the concept of batch may be translated away from production situations into both commercial and public services. Mid-range, medium volume holidays packages are 'produced' in this way, balancing availability, price, location and date. Particular educational initiatives may be devised to meet short or medium term or specialised needs again – combining the elements of investment, direction and flexibility and again pitched at particular sections of the community (for example the disabled, those with educational or learning difficulties).

An impression of the relationship between the scale of the undertaking and general prerequisites for success can be drawn. There are considerations of flexibility and responsiveness, and permanence and volume that must be balanced and taken into account. There is also the question of return on investment that must be seen from the production, operations and general management standpoint. Concepts of unit, jobbing, batch, mass and flow production and their relationship to scales and types of operation and undertaking are useful and valuable background for all those coming into, or working in, the great variety of organisations indicated.

■ Production capacity

Whatever the form of production capacity undertaken, attention has always to be paid to the following:

- **Production equipment and technology,** which must be commissioned, designed, installed and used so as to ensure that there is always a steady stream of products and outputs to the required quality and volume. In some cases this means having equipment specifically designed and commissioned for particular jobs; in others this will mean the use of generic or flexible technology that can be adjusted to suit a variety of purposes as and when necessary. The onus is on those responsible to ensure that what is required is available. This means ensuring in turn, that a realistic and practical view of the nature and volume of demands on the organisation is undertaken in the first place. It also means reconciling the balance between getting adequate returns on the technology (all other things being equal), with having both the flexibility and the spare capacity to undertake special activities when required. These include special orders, opportunities for new market and new activity entry, a creative and enlightened view of the business of the organisation, and the capability to produce and pilot new products
- **High quality staff,** capable of using the technology to its full capacity in all circumstances. This in turn means attention to workstation and work environment design and training in the understanding, use and operation of the equipment itself. The organisational view must be that this is an absolute commitment; and this is to be transmitted to the staff so that they are in no doubt that they also are committed to being trained in the full, effective and continuous use of the equipment.

■ Automation

There are two major benefits of production automation:

- **Accuracy.** The first is that products can be designed and produced to much greater detail, much more accurately and with much greater uniformity than previous manual systems. This applies to all aspects of production processes – design, quality, volume, scheduling, maintenance and inspection.

- **The human factor**. Automation removes tedious, repetitive, alienating and debilitating jobs from humans and places them in the hands of machines and robots. The human function then becomes concerned much more with the setting, monitoring, inspection and maintenance of equipment and production. At its best, this has created opportunities for work enlargement and enrichment. Those who were previously concerned only with a tiny or specific part of the process can now be involved in all the aspects indicated above (with the possible exception of design). It is becoming ever-more usual for production workforces to assume responsibility for quality control; and in many cases, they have become the points of reference for customer enquiries and complaints. This in turn, reduces or even removes altogether the need for costly administrative systems and especially quality control departments and functions. It also reduced the need for public relations functions to deal generally with customer complaints. There is a psychological and behavioural drive inherent in this on the part of the workforce to get the product right.

The benefits of automation are to be found in all areas related to the output of products and services. Computer-Aided Design (CAD), Computer-Aided Manufacturing (CAM), automatic controls on production volumes, robotics and flexible manufacturing systems all contribute to the ability to produce better quality products and increased volumes more quickly. Each of these also contributes to the capability to reduce the time between each of the stages (see Figure 8.1).

From a production and operations point of view, the product cycle may be represented as follows:

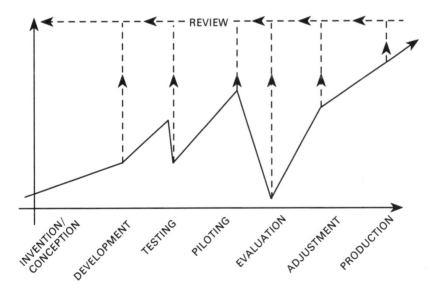

Figure 8.1   The product life cycle

■ Creativity and innovation

It is essential that creative and innovative attributes are present if organisations, their departments and their staff are to progress and develop. However, some occupations, business sectors and organisational and management styles and structures lend themselves better to this than others.

Attitudes to failure must be considered. Waste of time or energy is not to be tolerated. An enlightened view of what waste and failure is essential. Any activity or approach that is to be taken with the view of progressing and developing the organisation, solving its problems, bringing new ideas, products, projects and initiatives on stream, creating fresh approaches to current or commonplace activities with a view to being part of the 'theme of constant improvement' is encouraged, fostered and nurtured. Where the activities fail or fall short of their stated purpose, they will be reviewed for lessons to be learned.

The concern is to foster energy, enthusiasm and drive and a personal as well as professional commitment to the work in hand and its development. This can only be achieved if the style and attitudes indicated are created as part of the general approach to the management of the organisation, unit or department concerned.

Summary Box 8.4 shows how performance indicators can form the basis for an organisation's agenda, capitalising on its strengths and minimising its weaknesses.

■ Research and development

Part of the function of production and operations management is concerned with ensuring that a flow of new ideas, products and offerings is available. This takes various forms. It is concerned with the generation of the genuinely new and pioneering product and product concept. It is concerned with adapting existing products in new ways for new niches; and adapting existing components in new ways to form new products. It addresses the capacities of the production technology and processes, looking for ways in which this could be better or further developed. It considers the products and offerings of other organisations, and looks at ways in which these could be exploited, without infringing copyright or patent laws.

The research and development strategy needs to be decided, that includes levels of investment, scale and scope of activities, means of evaluation, and relationships with production and marketing outputs. The research and development operations require management and direction that balance the desire for new products and offerings with the consumption of resources and other operational priorities.

New products must be reconciled with the current portfolio of offerings, strengths of the organisation, and wider perceptions of it in the environment.

SUMMARY BOX 8.4   Measures of Success and Failure

These may be compartmentalised as follows:

- **Strategic**: related to successful and effective performance over the period of the lifetime of an organisation
- **Operational**: related to the success and profitability of the products and services of the organisation; product mixes and portfolios; productivity and output
- **Behavioural**: related to the perceptual and staff management aspects of it; the extent of or lack of strikes, disputes and absenteeism; and the general aura of well-being or otherwise
- **Confidence**: the relationship between the organisation and its environment; its backers; its stakeholders; and (for public companies) stock exchanges
- **Ethical**: the 'ways in which the organisation does things' and their acceptability or otherwise in their markets and community.

They form the basis of an agenda for the analysis of organisational performance, and help to pinpoint its strengths, weaknesses and concerns.

The approach must be flexible enough to encourage diversity, without detracting from current strengths.

To complete the picture, all potential products and services must be the subject of wider assessment, to ensure that what is proposed fits in with all aspects of the nature and level of activities. If it is decided to proceed down a particular line in support of a new product, it must have both the support of the staff, and be complementary to the organisation's current range. If the new product is to replace an old one, the process must be a check that this is indeed so. If it is to tap into an hitherto-unexploited sector, the same criteria, of confidence and feasibility, will also have been tested.

All organisations evaluate their research and development activities for effectiveness – the regularity, frequency, and volume of new and successful and effective products and offerings, in relation to the nature and levels of investment made in them.

■ Schedules and timetables

The purpose here is to ensure that, whatever the matter in hand, it is completed to time while meeting quality and volume constraints. This remains true whether items are being produced or whether 'production' concerns delivery of public services or the sale of commercial services.

Managers will work out in advance notional completion times for particular initiatives from their inception or placement of the order, through the process and its mechanisms, to the point of job completion. This will generally be undertaken at the one end from the 'perfect' standpoint – when everything goes as well as possible; and at the other when everything that can go wrong does so. This gives the boundaries within which an order can be fulfilled and forms the basis of offering the given product or service.

■ Meeting deadlines

If the organisation is constantly losing business because it cannot fulfil orders quickly enough for customers, fundamental appraisal of technology, work methods, work division and organisation must take place. There is a perceptual consideration to be accounted for here – it is much better to give a long deadline and deliver early than a short one and deliver late.

All managers must recognise the range of matters that can (and do) prevent deadlines from being met. The organisation itself, its structure and culture, its chains of command, may simply not be able to respond quickly enough to deadlines promised to customers by sales staff; or on the other hand the order may be placed or received in ambiguous tones. An order received by one department may not be processed to the production or operation function. The sales function may promise delivery of an order in good faith only to find later that the items in it are out of production, manufacture, print or whatever (or if the item is a package holiday for example, to find that the destination is no longer used).

Matters of quality and reliability must be addressed in relation to the production/output processes, as well as the product (in its widest sense) itself. Defects in either will lead to delay or dissatisfaction or rejection on the part of the customer. This may be exacerbated by poor raw materials and inputs or faulty components. Production processes, equipment and technology must also be considered in this light – in terms of total output, flexibility, response to one-offs, important or urgent orders, and in terms also of the effect that any varying of schedules will have in mainstream operations. At the other end of the spectrum, there may be teething troubles with new technology, equipment or work practices.

Problems and potential difficulties in distribution and delivery methods must be considered. In particular, where motor vehicles are to be sent out on to crowded roads, delays are endemic, and schedules must take account of this, striking a balance between meeting the customer's needs while not building too much slack time into the distribution method. Similar approaches need to be considered in relation to rail, sea and air transport, and postal services.

Delays may also arise as the result of working with sub-contractors. Their particular part of the process may itself have been delayed for reasons beyond control; or a bad sub-contractor may have been chosen to do the work.

Delays occur, especially in public works, where both officials and politicians ask for changes in specification at short notice, without any regard for the consequences of them, or indeed any true knowledge or appreciation.

The whole aspect of delivery, delivery failure, and delay must therefore be thoroughly considered. It is extremely complex and there are implications for both management style and levels of investment.

■ Schedules and timetables

The starting point for the definition of a schedule is earliest point at which all the materials, resources, equipment, technology, staff, information and supplies can be gathered together for the particular purpose stated (without having other conflicting pressures on them).

Proper running timetables, charts, work flows and other processes will be devised, taking as their starting point the commencement date indicated above. Each element will include the maximum and minimum completion periods referred to above and a model that can be established for the whole job. This then forms the basis of the working arrangements and work methods.

As the work progresses the actual timetable will be completed alongside the model. The two can then be compared. If it is a regular job, mean, medium and mode job times can be established and used as managerial information for the more accurate scheduling of production and as an informed basis for negotiations with clients. It identifies the most likely blockages to progress and also those that can be controlled and those that cannot. It provides a daily record of progress, a step-by-step measure of the job completion process measurable again against the projections made earlier. It acts as an early warning system for potential hitches, problems and crises.

All schedules will be related to precise targets and sub-targets along the way so that work appraisal may take place at regular intervals and after critical activities.

There will also be built into the scheduling process elements of progress chasing. Essentially this conducts the twin functions of general monitoring of progress to a given point in time; and an appraisal (and resolution where possible) of where particular activities have fallen behind schedule. Any deviations from schedule are thus identified early and the maximum opportunity is afforded to put them right.

■ Purchasing and supplies

The standpoint here is to ensure that all materials required are in place when necessary, while at the same time striking a balance between this and taking up an inordinate or uneconomic amount of space in storage.

The elements for consideration are consequently: cost; storage charges; frequency and reliability of sources and deliveries; and the flexibility or otherwise of production scheduling.

■ Sourcing

Sources of raw materials will be assessed on the balance of these and, above all, not merely on cost. There are managerial and operational decisions to be taken on the placement of orders and the components of the contract which go into these. Beyond this, matters to be considered include the ability to get extra deliveries when required, especially at short notice; the interrelationship, if there is one, between the suppliers and any competitive elements that exist between them; reliability, as defined by the organisation that is being supplied; any considerations of quality; any competitive tendering or contract compliance requirements; the critical nature of the particular supplies; and the relationship between the organisation and its suppliers. This last is particularly important where there is a dependence on one supplier of a rare, essential or expensive component.

■ Purchasing strategy

This is based on balancing the expense of storage with the consequences of production loss if a component is not delivered for any reason. Space, however expensive, may be used for storage if a balance or stock of a particular component is more important than this cost. This is especially true where the full costs or implications of downtime or production loss are examined. Organisations may at the other extreme insist on an instant response from the supplier as the precondition of placing orders, again with the same regard to downtime. When the supply of a key component is rare or unreliable, organisations buy up as much as possible when it is available and stockpile.

Consideration will also be given to the balance between the retention of stocks and the permanence or otherwise of specifications and designs. If a client changes any of these the organisation may find itself not only with the charges incurred on expensive storage space but also those that arise from the possession of obsolete or dormant items.

From this it is clear that an essential part of the purchasing and stores remit is a broad knowledge of the organisation's sphere of operation; likely, actual and potential innovations and changes; changes in specification, quality and materials to be used; and the shifting requirements of clients. The purchasing function will constantly research the field, seeking out potential (alternative) sources of supply.

There are behavioural aspects to be considered also. An organisation may be prepared to bear the price of stockpiling in return for the comforting knowledge that particular components are there as and when required. Organisations must have confidence in suppliers, in the regularity and reliability of deliveries if they are to place their faith in 'just in time' deliveries or frequent inflows rather than stockpiling.

The next element is the nature of the organisation's business and that of the supplies received. It may be impractical either to stockpile or to receive regular deliveries; the nature of the supplies may dictate which is to occur. Or, the supplies may come from a major and universal supplier of the common product which has its own ways of working and which can impose these on the markets with which it deals. The receiving organisation must either be a major purchaser or else conduct business in relation to these ways of working. There are also certain goods which have to be stored under legally stated or regulated conditions or with limited access or under constant supervision. Storage premises and facilities must be designed and built to the required standards.

■ Just in time

The just in time (JiT) approach to purchasing is attractive because it removes the need to use expensive premises for the storage of components and supplies. JiT is based on the ability to engage in relationships with suppliers requiring regular (daily and in some cases, many times a day) deliveries to be made. This form of supply has always been the norm in the fresh foodstuffs industry always. It has now been extended into all industrial and commercial areas and many public service activities also.

When they are delivered, supplies go more or less straight into production areas. As long as it works well and supplies can be more or less guaranteed, JiT is both efficient and effective. Its success depends entirely on the reliability of the suppliers. In practice, it also depends on the ability and willingness of the supplier (or suppliers) to vary the volumes, normally at short notice, to cope with sudden upflows and downflows in production.

JiT contracts require careful consideration. As well as regularity, they need to ensure both quality and volume of components and supplies. There is a question of contract length and notice periods, reconciling flexibility, certainty and continuity and bearing in mind that both supplier and purchaser have to be effective in their own right as organisations. Finally, specifications for both supplier and purchaser may change at short notice and this too must be capable of being accommodated.

■ Dominance and dependency

Dominance and dependency is a behavioural view of the relationship between purchaser and supplier.

Suppliers tend to dominate the relationship when they are the key or major source of a particular component or material or when they are the only organisation able to respond to the specific needs in the ways required of a purchaser. It also occurs where they control a rare and much sought after primary source of raw materials.

Purchasers tend to dominate the relationship when they are the major user of the materials or components. It also occurs when they are a sufficiently large customer that the loss of this business would be a threat to the well-being of the supplying organisation.

In the short term on either side, an advantage may be gained through dominating the relationship. In the longer term, whichever side is dependent, will seek to reduce its dependency.

Suppliers seek alternative outlets for their products and alternative uses for their technology. Purchasers seek alternative sources of components and may also re-design their offerings to avoid having to use the particular components or materials.

An enlightened and above all, managerial view of the situation is required if a long-term and satisfactory relationship is to be engaged. This stems from recognising that there is a mutual dependency over the long-term and that any advantage that may be gained in the short-term from the ability to dominate is certain to be nullified at some point in the future.

The end result must be a system of controlling the organisation's inventory that strikes the balance between all the elements indicated, contributing both to the effectiveness of the workflows and to the maximisation of the resources put into it.

■ Maintenance management

The core purpose here is to ensure that all resources and equipment are in a state suitable for use when required and to provide a swift and effective remedy when things break down or go wrong. It is thus essential that maintenance activities are planned and scheduled and organised in the same way and from the same standpoint as anything else.

Two distinct factors emerge from this: that of **planned maintenance** and that of **emergency response**. Planned maintenance requires the ordering and rescheduling of activities designed to prevent things from going wrong – indeed it is often called 'preventive maintenance'. By conducting regular audits and checks of equipment signs of wear and tear can be detected; parts that are beginning to wear out can be replaced before they break down or cause malfunction; equipment that is reaching the end of a production or operational period can be planned to be out of productive action while it is being remedied.

Planned maintenance requires adoption as a concept and strategy on the part of the organisation as a whole and its operations and production directors. It thus becomes a fixed cost and an essential element in the devising and ordering of schedules. It is bound up in the agreement of deadlines for delivery of products with customers.

There are presentational and behavioural aspects to be overcome. When a machine has not actually broken down, pressure grows to sacrifice a maintenance period in the interest of extra production, especially if it is a short run only. Such a situation requires its own assessment when it arises. 'Perfect' maintenance schedules require that this is only done to accommodate the true windfall opportunity or emergency. Maintenance strategies, like any other, are designed as part of the assurance of permanence and stability, and must be seen as such.

Maintenance activities must be seen in their wider sense also. Schedules, methods, packaging, presentation and the human resource all require maintenance, as do work methods, job design, communications and staff and departmental management activities.

Emergencies and breakdowns do occur, however; and they also have to be managed. The first and most important step is to keep breakdown to a minimum by the adoption of a maintenance strategy aimed at prevention. Beyond that the maintenance function must be able to accommodate such breakdowns without either risking work overload or having expensive staff, equipment and other resources idle. Strategies for the management of emergencies must therefore be flexible enough to deal with a 'worst case scenario' and this will be assessed in terms of projected volumes of emergency work, repairs and replacements, duration and timescales and possible downtimes and the costs of these. Balances of repair of existing equipment and replacement of it will also be struck.

■ Systems of coordination and control

Operational systems, procedures and processes must be sufficiently well defined to give a direct purpose to the task management, and flexible enough to be improved where necessary, thus increasing the effectiveness in which the task in hand is addressed and also giving the means of rectifying any errors or blockages.

It follows, in turn, that systems devised to ensure that this is successful, are dependent upon feedback gained from processes of monitoring, review and evaluation. If this information is to be effective itself, the operations systems must be capable of accommodating it and using it to best advantage.

Managerial systems of coordination and control must also be in place with similar properties – again, this constitutes the combination of flexibility with clarity and decisiveness of purpose and direction. Such systems reflect the precise nature of the operations in question, the consequent nature of the inputs, processes and outputs and means of assessment of effectiveness that relate to them.

These are, first, concerns relating to the nature and inherent dynamism, volatility or stability of the market and environment; and likely changes and future directions. Other matters for understanding and analysis at this stage concern the relationship between the operations of the organisation and its stated goals, aims and objectives; the composition and constitution of specialist functions and degrees of specialisation (and the nature of that specialisation); and systems for the harmonisation of inter-departmental activity and the resolution of operational conflicts. Only through an understanding of this as the basis of the complexity of operations management is a grasp of the true nature of the management of production and service processes possible.

■ Project management

This is the branch and aspect of the management of operations that is concerned with the completion of projects, something that is an identifiable entity in its own right, that has its own place in the continuity of organisational operations, and that requires the acquisition, organisation and combination of resources for this specific purpose. The project itself may greatly vary in scale and scope. 'Projects' in this sense range from the construction of world famous landmarks such as the World Trade Centre, CN Tower or Sidney Harbour Bridge, to the installation of electronic information systems or the commissioning of a brain scanner at a health service hospital, and to the development of any new product or service offering (e.g. the invention and development of diet coke was a project that has now become a product).

Whichever it is, it will have specific objectives that it is designed upon completion to meet. It will have precise specifications to which it must conform – in terms of cost, quality, volume, deadline, timescale, technology, durability and performance. It will have a defined date for completion and very often also a stated starting date. Funding, investment and budget limits will be placed on it – it is very unusual for there to be no constraints in this field (though some projects are more amenable for a variety of reasons to cost and deadline overruns than others).

Summary Box 8.5 outlines the environmental and situational factors that impact on project completion.

■ Measures of project success and failure

These reflect the aims and objectives assessed and defined at the outset of the project; they will be subject to variation and modification as the work has unfolded along the course of its completion.

In general terms, projects will be measured in relation to:

- **Timescale**: whether the deadlines were achieved and if not, the reasons for this
- **Budget and financial performance**: and the reasons for variances in these
- **Acceptability**: of the finished item to those who commissioned it, and again the reasons for this (especially if it is not acceptable)

SUMMARY BOX 8.5   Operations and Projects: Environmental and Situational Factors

---

The management of all operations and projects requires the adoption and utilisation of the principles and practices illustrated, if they are to be successful. Part of this process of adoption and utilisation must involve the recognition of the precise nature of the environment and situation in which the work is being carried out.

- **Economic mixes**: all sectors have their own distinctive economic mixes. For example, the finance industry pays high salaries. The defence research and production sectors are extremely cost-flexible, because of the nature of the work, the nature of the competition, and the commissioning process (invariably by government wishing to gain or preserve a military position). The health research sector is similarly pressurised by tendencies to overrun on cost, though this is less critical than defence.

  These are extreme examples deliberately taken to demonstrate that each sector has its own economic mix. 'Health Economics' and 'Defence Economics' are both distinctive fields of study and expertise in their own right.

- **Returns**: all sectors have their own norms and expectations, in terms of finance and timescale. They are mirrored in both the expectations and the confidence of those backing operations and projects. What is an acceptable return in one field is not therefore a universal measure. For example, Concorde was built at (almost) any cost, to demonstrate the reality of a supersonic airliner. The Channel Tunnel was completed at (almost) any cost, because it then becomes a lasting facility. Returns on food sales of 1% – 2% are acceptable in the particular sector in the United States of America and France, but do not measure up to the expectations of the same sector in the UK, which are 7% – 10%.

- **Schedules**: again, all sectors have their own balance between the actuality of the product or project, and the delivery of it to time. Some new product developments have deadlines imposed by the nature of the sector, and competitive moves in it: in early 1993, all the major European car companies launched a new and distinctive model (not all of the same size, or for the same sector or niche); there was thus a mutual pressure on each, and consequences for failing to deliver.

- **Staffing**: in general, staffing operations must consider the traditions and influences that have impacted on the sector, even if the desired cultural and attitudinal factors referred to elsewhere are to be fully and effectively implemented.

- **Limitations**: the main matter is time. Major projects that are commissioned, that have a lead time of years, are to be delivered to a world that will almost inevitably have changed out of all recognition. Defence projects commissioned in the West or the Communist Bloc in the period 1985–90 will be delivered to a world in which the Cold War no longer figures. Information and computer technology projects must be stable enough to be substantial, researched and tested; but flexible enough to be able to respond instantly to developments elsewhere in the industry.

- **Resources**: normally projects are commissioned on the basis that adequate resources are available and this forms part of the contract agreement. It does happen that resources subsequently become cut or limited for some reason. When this occurs, it is normally in the interest of both contractor and client to take steps to resolve the matter.

- **Technology**: some projects require the invention and development of their own technology before they can be commenced. Tunnel boring machine technology used on the Channel Tunnel is an example.

Each must be weighed, weighted and balanced by those who are to commission work, and those who are to carry it out. The balance to be struck is that between the nature of the sector, the factors outlined here, and absolute measures of profitability, effectiveness and delivery and completion.

- **Effects** on the organisation (or organisations in the case of joint ventures) that has agreed to carry out the work; these will be seen in terms of general changes, cultural effects and special effects upon the rest of the work (e.g. the extent to which one project is dominating the whole of an organisation)
- **Side effects and spin-offs**: opportunities, inventions and openings that occur as the result of carrying out the main project.

■ Background and basis of the management task

From the overall concept of project management and from the ways in which success and failure are to be measured and judged, comes the full implication of the enormity and complexity of the management task concerned. The general starting point will be when tenders are invited for a particular activity, whether on the basis of open competition or by selective invitation.

Whichever it is, the result will be at this stage, the meeting of the project commissioner with those potentially responsible for completing and delivering the project.

■ Groundwork: terms of reference and constraints

Initially, the terms of reference will be drafted and discussed, and this includes deadlines, resources, cost, volume, quality and delivery date. Feasibility studies, projections, pilot studies, extrapolation and 'what if' exercises may be undertaken at this stage. Any misconceptions and misunderstandings about the nature of the work to be carried out should be ironed out. Any necessary external constraints within which the work must be carried out will also be identified at this point – these include such things as public enquiries, political and social opposition, resistance from sections of the community and pressure groups – and any awareness-raising or other marketing related activities assessed.

From this, a variety of more specific measures emerge. There is normally a pre-project process that must be gone through which may, in itself, be very complex (e.g. those activities which will require public enquiries or new

---

SUMMARY BOX 8.6   M25: The London Orbital Motorway Project Assessment

This was conceived in the 1970s with the twin purposes of providing a route for long distance traffic that kept it out of the centre of London, and to increase its speed and therefore efficiency.

It was necessary, at the outset, to limit its size to three lanes in each direction to take account of political and social lobbies and pressures. It has become necessary since, to increase this to four lanes in each direction; it will undoubtedly be necessary to increase capacity in the future, either by widening it again, or through the construction of a completely new project.

In this context, therefore, the following lessons should be drawn.

There are certain projects which require full commission if they are not to fail. In these cases, whatever is planned cannot be diluted in order to satisfy a lobby, and still remain successful and suitable. For example, this motorway attempted to satisfy political, environmental and settlement lobbies, as well as handling the required volume of traffic. It has failed on each count.

It follows from this that matters relating to the greater good, in all possible and necessary ways, have to be considered from a strategic point of view. It is also necessary to articulate accurately the purpose and planned outcomes of such projects. These must also be presented in ways that attract public support rather than repel it.

In this particular case, finally, work will have been carried out at least three times, rather than just once.

SUMMARY BOX 8.7   *Concorde*

Concorde was developed in the 1960s as an Anglo–French joint initiative that was going to show the way forward to universal supersonic airline travel.

As a project and product it fell far short of this success. It did not succeed in generating this measure of supersonic travel; the only supersonic airliners currently in use remain the eight *Concordes* each of British Airways and Air France.

In marketing terms, however, it has been turned to great advantage. *Concorde* is both a monumental technological achievement and a highly photogenic flagship for the two airlines and the two nations. Furthermore, the service developed around it is designed to be first class in every sense. As well as the speed of travel the quality of facilities and service, hospitality, food and refreshment is very high. All those who travel by *Concorde* are made to feel especially important, part of an elite. The aura thus generated is similar to that which surrounded the 'pullman' class on the railways in the early to mid-twentieth century.

---

technology or inventions or developments), and require the commissioning of sub-projects and other activities in related fields (see Summary Boxes 8.6 and 8.7). This may in turn lead to full pilot and feasibility activities. An 'all things being equal' timescale is devised, as the basis for further definition and as an archetype of the way forward that both commissioner and commissionee envisage. And all things being equal, a resource bank can be defined, outlining the source and nature of resources, their scope and scale, the timescale over which they are to be required. The extent to which this will impinge on other activities of the organisation's concern will also be assessed at this stage.

At this stage an idea of the cost of activities and of the project as a whole will start to emerge based on the size and scope, scale, complexities, technology, volume and quality of staff concerned, pressures and opportunity costs to be borne by the organisation, any risks that are to be encountered as well as the global aspects of deadlines and quality of the finished project (and volume aspects, if there are any).

The end result of this process is the assessment on the part of the project commissioner of the capabilities and capacities of those tendering for the work in the above terms. From this, precise terms of reference for the project and an accurate working brief accommodating all of these factors and constraints will be drawn up. Precise and formal bids will then be invited from interested parties. These companies will mirror this activity in terms of their own capacities and capabilities and the other constraints within which they have to work. They will then make a bid for the work based on this assessment.

The terms of reference, on the one hand, and the commissioner's bid for the work in response to this, on the other, form the hub of the contractual arrangements between the two parties.

■ Inception

At this stage, schedules, deadlines and timetables in support of the overall schedule, deadline and timetable for completion will be worked out. These relate to all resources – staff, skills, finance, technology, equipment. Resource and activity inter-relations are defined. The interaction between different activities is defined and modelled. Particular problem areas or areas of greatest pressure and difficulty are assessed in advance, as are likely periods of relative tranquillity and straightforward progress. Critical paths and other network progressions will be drawn up also; essential, critical, non-critical and sub-activities will be defined. These will all be published and promulgated; actual progress will be measured and evaluated against them.

■ Customer liaison

More general matters relating to the management of the project must also be addressed. A rationale and mechanism for flows of information must be worked out in advance and pre-tested for effectiveness and flaws. The last thing that any project manager needs is to have to deal with misunderstandings that have arisen because the interface with the customer is inadequate. The general format additionally normally consists of a series of regular meetings with a set, yet flexible, agenda and pattern of attendance in order to ensure that both sides understand each other on a continuing basis. It is also normal to establish a hotline for the resolution of genuine emergencies.

The process of customer liaison is to ensure that the inception, development and completion of the project is effective and successful. The process itself must therefore be designed specifically for each project. The formal part of it consists of regular performance updates and reviews, resource utilisation and a check and measure on actual progress in relation to that which was planned and envisaged.

In certain public projects it may be necessary to develop the liaison process into a non-executive but highly authoritative steering group, because of the requirements or demands of the commissioning bodies, for example where these are municipal health authorities or instruments of national, regional and central government.

■ Project assessment

As the result of these activities a reasoned and accurate impression of the project is arrived at. The terms in which this will be measured include its complexity overall, any particular special requirements, from whatever angle, the preferred structure of the project and the ways in which this is to be achieved, the risks inherent, particular technological requirements, particular budget constraints to be imposed or required of particular aspects of it. Any complexity or sophistication of planning activities required as the overall results of the rest of the assessment will thus become apparent.

■ The project manager

In its own way, therefore, the overall task of the project manager is as complex and critical as that of the chief executive. Indeed, the project manager may be seen as chief executive for the particular activity, and for its duration.

In particular, the project manager must have strong personal attributes of energy, enthusiasm, drive and commitment. Project managers cannot expect others, especially those working for them, to be committed to it if they themselves are not. Externally they are the champions of the project in dealings with both its commissioner in particular and the outside world in general.

They must be innovative and creative. The complexity of the task will inevitably require this. They must make trade-offs between conflicting demands and pressures, having both the foresight and occupational acumen to do this effectively without losing sight of the ultimate purpose.

They must have controls, but these must work for them. Reporting systems and other management information systems are there for illumination, as a general aid to problem-solving, and from which to learn (so that future issues can be minimised or avoided altogether). Project systems are not an end in themselves to become the subject of intensive and interminable inquests.

This remains true even for something as extreme as a bad accident. An organisation that incurs this during the course of a project should of course accept responsibility where this is due. It should above all use such an event as the means of improving its processes, procedures, behaviour and attitudes; and thus to ensure that it never happens again.

The overall managerial view to be taken is to look to the future – a positive adaptation of 'what is done is done'. This does not imply any complacency about the past, but rather a respect not a preoccupation with it. The global view is that of making progress towards the ultimate goal. The project manager is thus adopting and matching the strategic view and imposing it on the project, rather than acting with a narrow supervisory perspective.

■ Problems during the project

If the whole process is effective, a balance of the capacity to avoid problems (by recognising where they potentially lie and taking pre-remedial preventative action) with the ability to solve them quickly and effectively when they do arise is necessary.

The articulation of the strategic and global approach of the project manager is part of this. The qualities and attributes that are inherent in adopting this approach – those of flexibility, innovation and clarity of purpose – facilitate this. This will be underlined in the reality of the operations by the commitment, enthusiasm and drive of the project manager in the situation, and the stake that s/he has both personally and professionally in the success of the project in hand.

The process of management and the continued use and development of these qualities and attributes feed off themselves. The managers responsible for a series of projects are thus likely to have highly developed qualities of strategic awareness, enthusiasm, scheduling and problem-solving awareness. Each project in which they are involved develops and fosters these aptitudes still further. There is also developed a variety of approaches to what may be generally the same sort or type of issue; this variety has its roots in the different circumstances, nature and requirements of the project in hand rather than the project itself.

For example, a labour dispute on one contract may be resolved instantaneously by a short meeting between the project manager and the aggrieved party; while on another it may linger because a member of a steering committee may also need to be consulted before the issue can be resolved. In each case, the only right solution is the one that adopts both content and process to get the issue resolved and the work truly back on course; the really effective project manager is the one who recognises the different approaches necessary to resolve what is overtly the same problem.

More generally, the installation and generation of these capabilities and capacities constitutes effective development of the innovative and creative faculties of all managers. This helps to break organisational and procedural straitjackets and to develop the most costly and critical part of the human resource into a successful and effective body of staff.

■ Project management and the human resource

The particular requirement here is the combination of the human resource for the stated purpose. Some members of the project team will be permanent, others temporary; others will be drafted in at regular or frequent or rare intervals. The project managers' role here is to ensure that what is done in this sphere is effective. Managers must be able to mobilise and activate specialist contributions when required. They must be able to generate a project identity and team spirit and harmony among such disparate elements so that when they are working, they are doing so with the full measure of commitment.

Managers must recruit and bring on board the right people for the task – both in terms of aptitudes and attitudes required. They must be able to motivate them to work together and in productive harmony for the period of their involvement. They must be their driving force, helping them to make effective contributions and decisions that move the project as a whole forward. They must stimulate in others the required flexibility of approach. They must maintain close liaison with all staff, both specialist and generalists, both skilled and multi-skilled, ensuring that their contribution is, and remains, effective. They must in-build swift and effective remedies when situations arise where this is not so.

For large and complex projects and for those areas where they are not specialist themselves, managers must be able to delegate. This again means selecting persons not only of capability but also those in whom the project managers can place full confidence for their particular activity. Ultimately they are responsible for seeing that the work in question is carried out successfully.

An effective decision-making process and communication forum is also essential in the generation and maintenance of effective project teams. These combine both the understanding and clarity of purpose required with the overall aim of the project and the nature of the members of the team, so that what is done is both effective and subscribed to by all concerned. A task-orientated, professional ethic must be generated as a prerequisite to this. This is in turn both essential to mutual confidence and also part of the process of building it. Reporting relationships on the team must be adequate, without being cumbersome, or again an end in themselves. The project managers need these facilities as a check on progress and for coordination purposes and to provide early hints and warnings of problems. The general ability to manage the human resource in these ways and in relation to the nature of constraints of the particular project is thus critical to its success.

■ Project monitoring

This is conducted in relation to the project plan devised in the first place and the following matters must all be covered, whatever methods are adopted. The defined timescales must be evaluated, and this must cover the overall and sub-times. The same is true for costs and budgets. Other matters concern the volume and quality of work, and their relationship with cost and time elements. Flaws in both planning and operational processes will become apparent, providing reasons for remedial action and, where necessary, rescheduling, redesign and reallocation of resources. Performance of different elements of the project will be measured against their own aims and objectives and for success and effectiveness in whatever terms these are to be assessed.

Monitoring must be carried out in effective and suitable ways; and if part of the process of necessity includes stakeholders' representatives, then this must also be accommodated. What is ultimately required is a vehicle for the illumination of progress (or lack of it); for the identification, prevention and solution of problems; an early warning system; and the means to more effective performance in the future. The past will be dwelt on, as stated above, only where it is an integral and critical part of this.

Benefits of the project management approach

The approach taken is designed to ensure that the whole project is carried out effectively and that progress along the way can be monitored and reviewed.

There is a great range of benefits that accrue to organisations both from conducting projects and also from adopting the project approach to management (that is the utilisation of an equivalent set of criteria in its day-to-day operations). First and foremost it develops innovative, creative and committed managers, able to perform effectively in a wide variety of situations. Alongside this it provides a vehicle for the measurement of resource effectiveness, maximisation, optimisation and waste – the opportunity for full accountability taken from a strategic rather than administrative standpoint. There is inherent in this the capacity for the development of effective planning, organising and estimating capabilities on the part of the organisation and its staff. This comes about from both the extent of the involvement in projects and the range and diversity of them, and becomes both an organisational and professional expertise. The quality of the organisation's planning activities can also be assessed as there are pre-stated models, networks and schedules against which the actual work is to be carried out.

A structure of project management is developed which in itself must be flexible. This in turn tends to promote a flexible and responsive ethos within the

---

SUMMARY BOX 8.8   Joint Ventures and Other Cooperative Efforts

This is where two or more organisations come together for a stated business purpose or project. The reasons for this relate precisely to the situation. In general, they are a configuration of the synergy principle (see Chapter 2); and related to business reasons to do with the pooling of expertise, sharing of risk, building of confidence and playing to specialisms and strengths that make the joint venture a sounder approach than an attempt on the matter in hand by an individual organisation.

In this context, and from an operational and executive standpoint, there is a requirement to establish a commonality of purpose among those drawn together from the different organisations in the joint venture. What is necessary is the reconciliation of organisational rivalries and propensities for conflict through means of focus on the precise purpose of the joint venture. Within this, it is also necessary to reconcile the often differing and divergent sub-objectives that the individual organisations have for becoming involved in the first place. This is exacerbated if one organisation is the senior partner or another has been brought in simply to fulfil a small but critical part of the project. Qualities of trust, harmony and openness between organisations that may be competing for work elsewhere may need to be fostered. Reporting relationships, lines of communication, and management structure and style have to be adopted that achieve all of these matters and provide a basis for positive and harmonious activity. Any network planning or project scheduling is complicated by the need to reconcile inter-organisational as well as operational factors. In summary, the 'project approach' is complicated by the need to create both a distinctive identity and clarity of purpose within the situation as outlined and implied. This will be underwritten by a form of contract at the point at which the work is commissioned and the venture agreed.

It follows from this that a full situational as well as operational assessment requires completion at the planning and pre-agreement stages. A balance has to be struck between ensuring and insuring one's own position in the joint venture and the promotion of a positive and harmonious approach. Forms of limited liability may be drawn up as part of this process or an umbrella organisation or distinctive configuration created. It also follows that the length of the commitment as well as the breadth, depth and nature of it requires setting out. Part of the legal format may apply penalty clauses if any part of the timescale is overrun by one of the parties to the joint venture.

Above all, from a managerial stance the joint venture must have its own distinctive entity and identity, management style and culture – that is, the focus for all those who are working in it for the duration of their time with it. This is necessary in these situations as in all operations and projects and for the same reasons – to give positive direction, clarity of purpose and reason for being there to all those concerned that both transcend other loyalties and accommodate them in this pursuit.

---

organisation at large. Summary Boxes 8.8 and 8.9 examine joint ventures as a means of project organisation.

Any evaluation of projects will also go into more general reasons for success or failure. These include the separation of those factors that are in the organisation's control from those which are not; and in particular concerning

---

SUMMARY BOX 8.9   Joint Ventures: Examples

1. British Airways and US Air generated an agreement that allowed or guaranteed connections between the flights of the two companies and a mutual through-booking system that allowed customers to book from anywhere to anywhere on either or both of the networks operated by each airline. In operational terms it enabled British Airways passengers to book through to the 300 US destinations that they have no access to but that US Air does; and US Air passengers to book through to anywhere on the British Airways global network (especially in Western Europe) that they have no access to but which British Airways controls.
2. Transmanche Link (TML) was formed by the five UK and five French construction companies which agreed to build the Channel Tunnel. It gave distinction of identity in accordance with the project itself; it provided a vehicle for the harmonisation of a ten-company joint venture; and a focus for finance. It also gave a means of interface between these organisations and the project commissioners (Eurotunnel). It also is a stated organisation for those involved with the venture; as such it provides the distinctive loyalty and identity referred to in Summary Box 8.8.

---

any environmental, political or social pressures that may have come to bear. This is also part of the learning process for the organisation and its managers, especially in periods of change or turbulence. From the whole process and approach comes the ability to assess whether a particular aim or objective was met or not, and the reasons for this.

■ Conclusions

The nature and complexities of operations and project management outlined in this section should serve as an illustration of the managerial tasks necessary in these activities. They cover all manufacturing and service activities, and all forms of project work – construction and engineering projects, urban regeneration, power stations, irrigation schemes, transport and traffic activities (such as highways, motorways, bypasses and the channel tunnel) – such projects have their own external and distinctive entity, life and manifestation, often bringing work, resources and inward investment to the communities in which they are located.

They also cover academic and commercial research, medical research, computer and defence projects (see Summary Box 8.10). Such activities normally trigger off research and development initiatives all of their own, and sub-project, related and contributory activities and the teams that go with them are generated in response to the main matter in hand and in support of it. Such projects and activities inevitably have a 'blossom' effect – that is, that due to their very nature and complexity inventions, technological advances, new

SUMMARY BOX 8.10   AZT: Commercial and Social Drive

The prevalence of the HIV virus, and its increase among the populations in all societies of the world, has generated intense and highly pressurised activities among pharmaceutical companies to find an immunisation, vaccine or other treatment for those who have contracted AIDS, and to prevent the onset of full attacks.

The Wellcome Company produced AZT in response to this. Huge levels of investment were generated, and initial results among users of the drug were encouraging, in spite of the fact that it had side effects. The drive to get it on to the market came from the usual areas of the need to get returns on investment; to be a market leader' the importance of winning this particular race; and the generation of confidence among investors. It was reinforced by the social drive of finding a 'cure' for the particular virus and disease, and the demands of those with it.

The case for AZT is not yet proven. If it does eventually prove successful, both the organisation and society will benefit enormously. If it fails, there is a commercial and social loss that has to be borne by the organisation alone.

SUMMARY BOX 8.11   The Channel Tunnel Project: Measures of Success
and Failure

The Channel Tunnel is an excellent example of the difficulties and complexities that have to be considered in the assessment of the overall success or failure of business operations.

We have stated already that aims and objectives must be set for any undertaking, as criteria and measures and assessors of success and failure. In the case of the Channel Tunnel, these may be defined as follows, as absolute measures:

- **Deadline**: initially March 1993, now December 1993 – March 1994
- **Cost** – at £10 billion ($14 billion), over the twice the original projection of £4.5 billion.
- **Cultural and political aspects**: the Tunnel is completed, and there now exists a land link between the UK and France.
- **Infrastructure**: the link is made; the fact of the link is not yet fully exploited; the motorway links to it are mainly in place; the rail link is completed in France but not the UK.

There are clear, wider considerations to be taken into account. All projects, product developments, and operation commissions have associated and derived benefits, and opportunities that are both envisaged, and also that become apparent along the way.

In the particular case of the Channel Tunnel, these are as follows:

- **Technology**: there have been demonstrable advances in design, information, geotechnical, and construction technology; in the particular matter of tunnelling and mining advances in technology, there is a body of experience for translation and assimilation at the next similar project or undertaking.

- **Organisation**: there is a rich body of knowledge, practice and experience on which to draw, and from which to learn, in the formation of structures, cultures, and systems, on which to base the completion of mega-projects.
- **Financial structures and sources**: and the variation, merits and demerits of both the approach taken, and also possible alternatives.
- **Operational aspects**: these plainly remain to be seen, and have to be related to the infrastructure that serves the project; in general, these will be measured in terms of content and volume of traffic; percentages of capacity usage; and returns on the levels of investment.
- **Targeting**: of completion and sub-completion dates, the lessons to be learned from this, and the consequences of overruns on these, and their implications for other mega-projects.

Finally, there is the fact of its completion, the success of the achievement itself, the realisation of the dream and vision of making a link between England and France.

The actual objectives, derived benefits, and their implications, are the basis on which a managerial assessment and judgment can, and should be made. The example given, and the points raised, form the basis of an agenda for the consideration of any such project.

---

opportunities are made or come to the fore. Summary Box 8.11 considers such issues in relation to the Channel Tunnel.

Projects may be developed because there is a ready and known market or use for that which is envisaged as the outcome. This is especially true of defence activities again, and also research commissions concerning drugs, medicine and health care. Pressure is on companies operating in this field and university research departments also to find the means of curing AIDS, motor neurone disease, muscular dystrophy and cancers, to give but a few examples (see Summary Box 8.10). There is a mutual and precise meeting place identified between the wants of the customer and the commercial opportunity because of the nature of the field in question.

A similar approach is taken also to the development of new products and new niches for existing products. This consists also of the coordination and combination of resources, schedules, staff and their expertise, but in response to a real or perceived market opportunity rather than in pursuit of a more distinctive entity.

Finally, the 'project management approach' is perceived as being highly beneficial both for organisations at large and those who work within them, developing as it does a range of qualities related to flexibility, experience, dynamism, pride and achievement in a wide variety of situations; there is current received wisdom in the fields of operations and project management, that if one can manage effectively and successfully tasks and activities of this nature and complexity, then one can manage anything.

CHAPTER 9

Quantitative methods

The purpose of this chapter is to introduce and outline the importance, use and value of the quantitative tools and methods that are available to the manager, and to indicate and illustrate their uses in different situations.

From the point of view of the manager, it is the ability to interpret and use statistical and financial data (rather than being a specialist in statistics or mathematics) that is important. It is this standpoint, therefore, that is taken.

As well as the ability to use and analyse material thus gained, there are behavioural and perceptual issues which must be addressed, and these are indicated also. The chapter additionally focuses on the particular quantitative, mathematical, statistical, financial and accounting elements that are important to the manager, and of general value in the identification of the 'complete management task'.

The importance of this basic understanding is thus critical to the manager, providing a quantitative basis for the evaluation of situations, and a sound basis for qualitative decisions. Gathering information and producing accurate statistics and other figures is not therefore an end in itself. It is the use to which these are put that is important.

■ Statistics

This is the discipline which deals with the preparation, collection, arrangement, presentation, analysis and interpretation of quantitative data. The discipline can be divided into the study of probability (or mathematical statistics); and descriptive statistics, which deal with the compilation and preservation of data to provide information on which to base decisions, and to assist in forward planning and forecasting.

■ Primary and secondary data

Data can initially be categorised as primary or secondary data:

- **Primary data**: is that obtained direct by organisations and individuals through observation, surveys, interviews and samples, and using methods and instruments drawn up specifically for the stated purpose.
- **Secondary data**: comes from other data sources, such as official statistics, provided by government sources and sectoral data gathered by employers' associations and federations, and marketing organisations.

▪ Uses of data gathered

The use of secondary data always involves taking information that others have gathered, and interpreting and analysing and using it for purposes different to those which the original gatherers designed or intended. There may also be variations in definition or coverage which have to be taken into account.

The decision to gather primary data, or use other sources, will depend on the nature of the information required, the availability of it from sources other than primary, the range and coverage of it, the field of enquiry and its size and scope, the accuracy of the data required, and the date or deadline by which it is required. It will depend also on the purpose and aims of the enquiry to be made and the uses to which the information is to be put. Finally, the reconciliation of all of these points may not be easy (for example, where wide-ranging, precise data is required urgently).

The data thus gathered is then classified into groupings, or classes, with a common element, for the purposes of analysis, comparison and evaluation.

As far as the manager is concerned, the main purpose of this gathering and assessment of data is to provide background information that is accurate and quantifiable. This is a basis in turn for accurate planning, forecasting, projected activities, and decision-making in whatever the discipline involved; or at a strategic level, to provide a sound basis for accurate general direction.

It is useful, therefore, to identify the different statistical sources, methods and techniques that are available to managers in organisations, and their particular uses in this context.

▪ Sources of information and data

The manager will consult six main sources:

- **Government statistics**, highly publicised in the media, and useful as general indicators of the state of the national, business and economic confidence, direction and activity, and the direction that it is likely to take in general over the foreseeable future.
- **Sectoral statistics**, produced by trade federations, employees associations and professional bodies, for the support and enlightenment of member organisations, and to contribute their knowledge and awareness of the global aspects and overview of their own sectors; this may contribute in great measure to policy formulation in particular sectors, in the setting of minimum and maximum wage, price and output levels, for example.
- **Market research organisations** hold data on vast ranges of issues which they promulgate and sell on a commercial basis to those requiring it; the main initial value of this is to indicate the general state of business, and range of business opportunities that may be available, again as a prelude to organisations either conducting or commissioning their own future investigations.
- **Local government** holds a wide range of general data on the composition, social state, occupational range and population structure of those who live in the UK; this is published in general terms by local government and municipal departments, and again is a useful precursor to more rigorous investigation.

- **Public enquiries** and investigations generate a great amount of information concerning particular initiative (e.g. on urban development, by-passes, power stations, etc.) that are often a useful initial point of reference for those planning to go into similar ventures in the future.
- **Organisational statistics**, gathered internally for specific purposes (see Summary Box 9.1).

SUMMARY BOX 9.1   Organisational Statistics and Management Information

This may be classified as follows:

- **Human resource management**: wage levels (individual, departmental, divisional, functional total); staff turnover (overall, individual, departmental, divisional, functional or occupational); absence and absenteeism levels (individual, departmental, divisional, functional and total); strikes and disputes; levels of disciplinary and dismissal activity; grievances and other staff problems; ability/inability to recruit; qualifications and capabilities; training and development records; identification of potential; succession; variety of work and experience; total experience
- **Public relations**: nature and volumes of complaints; sources of complaints; nature and volumes of media inquiries; general requests; dealings with the community and its institutions – schools, colleges, evening classes, clubs and societies; nature and volume of organisational coverage in the community and media; proportions of time spent on general public relations activities; proportions of time and resources spent on specific issues
- **Marketing**: market assessment information; gathering of marketing information; use of information; information for using and evaluating the effects of marketing campaigns; effectiveness of the targeting of marketing activities; effectiveness of general marketing activities; effectiveness of the total marketing position
- **Sales**: by product; by product cluster; total range of product; by outlet; by location; volume and quality; demands for returns; after-sales demands; the number of times that guarantees are invoked; complaints; blockages
- **Production**: deliveries; product output volumes; product to market; time factors; quality factors; volume factors; number of complaints per site/factory/batch/unit/production run/location; blockages; supplier factors; distribution factors
- **Financial**: total costs; cost breakdowns – by site, division, department, function, location, occupation; fixed costs; variable costs and causes of variability; marginal costs; budget and budgeting processes
- **Administration**: staff records; financial records; budget usage; balance of activities; technology usage; technology lifespan; technology obsolescence; replacement programmes.

From this it is apparent that there is a vast range of information available for the organisation's use. The effectiveness of this use depends on both the organisation's ability to gather and store this information, and on the capabilities of individual managers to identify what they want, when they want it and to evaluate it in particular situations.

■ Presentation of data

Data must be presented in ways that are easily and readily understood by those on the receiving end. This is true both in the generation of overall impressions, and in the presentation of precise findings. The method of presentation must take into account the relative interest and capability of the audience, the time that is to be spent on it, and the purpose for which it is being presented.

It is essential that this is understood at this stage, because statistical surveys and information systems now hold, and can generate, vast amounts of data on all aspects of business in relatively short periods of time. The data is of value, however, only if it can be understood and assimilated. For this to be effective, presentation must be in 'audience-friendly' or 'user-friendly' terms, meeting their expectation as well as getting the required message across.

There are five main methods available (see Figure 9.1):

- **Tabulation**, where data is presented in tables devised against two or more axes or criteria
- **Bar charts**, a more visual representation of tables, and usually presented against two axes or variables
- **Pie charts**, where the data is represented in a circular or 'pie' format, with the slices representing the quantities or percentages given
- **Graphs**, on which data is plotted, also against two variables (e.g. dates and volume; timescale and sales figures)
- **Pictures (Pictograms)**, such as the use of a small picture of a person to represent a small number of unemployed, and a larger picture to represent an increase in the figure recorded.

■ Accuracy of data

The accuracy of any data depends on the way in which it was gathered, the quality of the actual data gathering, and any rounding at the end of it. If a survey took a sample, rather than dealing with everyone or everything concerned in a particular activity, the results may indicate particular conclusions very strongly, but they will only be **proven** if the entire sector is surveyed. If there is a flaw in the statistical methods used, or if the wrong questions are asked, the results will also be flawed, and inaccurate. Finally, rounding of numbers is widely used and has also to be seen in context and as a limitation – balance sheet figures for multinational companies are given to the nearest hundred thousand pounds, or even million pounds.

Social survey and market research organisations consequently go to a lot of trouble to make their surveys both valid and reliable, through the establishment of proper objectives; the design of questionnaires and other survey instruments; the provision of high-quality and rigorous training of surveyors; and the recognition and promulgation of limitations on the research to be carried out. Any findings, analysis and conclusions are thus seen in context.

(a) Tabulation

YEAR	SALES £	PROFIT £
1986	3430	114
1987	3560	119
1988	4740	240
1989	5862	650
1990	4711	350

(b) Bar chart

(i)

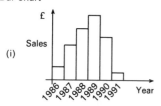

(ii)

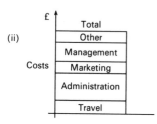

(c) Line graph

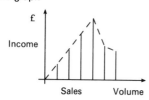

(d) Scatter diagram

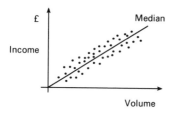

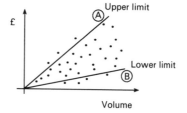

(e) Pie chart

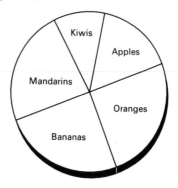

(f) Pictograms

Car sales

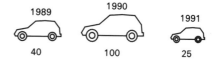

Unemployment

Figure 11.1   Presentation of data

SUMMARY BOX 9.2　Statistics and Proof

Taken in isolation, statistics are used to prove everything and anything. In the wider context, they seldom prove anything especially in the managerial sphere.

Example: government statistics

Government statistics are used by politicians in support of their own vested interests. For example, one political party may say that 'crime figures are at an all time record high'. The other responds with 'spending on policing and prisons is at an all time record high'.

Or, one party says that 'the economy is growing at the fastest rate of any in the world/western world/civilised world/EU/third world' – without taking into account or making clear that the lower the base from which measurements are taken the higher the percentage growth rate is certain to be.

Product portfolios

The legend of the razor (see Summary Box 6.6, Chapter 6) must never be forgotten. In practice the ability to buy satisfaction is what draws customers and consumers to organisations. If organisations withdraw given items because they do not of themselves make money, they may find customers going elsewhere; and they will consequently lose sales of items that are profitable.

This also applies to the concept of having product ranges that can be divided into: those that are attractive and presentable, and those that make money and sell. A mathematical approach to sales figures in isolation would 'prove' that, in many cases, the attractive product was a loss maker. This again, has to be seen in the context that withdrawal of the attractive product would adversely affect sales of the main consumer offerings.

This is a useful illustration of the shortcomings of the use of statistics in isolation from context; and of the managerial approach required if understanding is to be achieved.

These lessons should be translated into the business sphere and its related managerial activities. The disciplines of accuracy of data and information gathering hold relevance in those management activities to do with: personal interviewing and assessment; policy formulation; business assessment; marketing activities; output; the merits and demerits of particular initiatives; the success or failure of recruitment campaigns, advertising initiatives; image formulation; the success or failure of particular technologies, production methods; the ability of organisations and their specialist departments to plan, forecast, formulate policy and devise and implement strategies.

Other elements which impinge on the accuracy of data gathered and available are to do with: time lapses between the gathering, promulgation and interpretation of data; sampling errors; analytical errors; inexplicable inconsistencies; and the compounding of these, where inaccurate extrapolations are inevitable, if the gathering or analysis was inaccurate or flawed in the first place.

Managers must therefore develop a positive and healthy scepticism, questioning technique and enquiry into any data presented to them. This is not to promote managerial inertia – quite the opposite. Managers should ensure, however, that they do question and consider all aspects, and the full implications, of statistics, as the basis for accurate decision-making and initiative formulation. The ability to do this in the light of accurate and wide ranging data thus gathered is an aid to effective management and decision-making.

■ Index numbers

Index numbers show at a glance the overall direction of changes in a variable over a period of time. These variables can be virtually any regularly produced statistic. Those most frequently referred to are: the retail price index (RPI); wholesale price index; unemployment rate; national output; The *Financial Times* Stock Exchange Indices of the top 30 and top 100 shares; (FTSE 30 and 100); and exchange ratios. Industrial and commercial sectors also produce their own indices.

Bases are established, against which the subsequent movements are measured, in order to give accurate statistical variations. These bases are normally time – a base year or date; and percentage relatives – the most common of which are price, quantity or value; and weighting – where more than one item or variable is used on one index. In the expression of indices, the base year, base percentage relative, and any base weighting, are combined together and given a numerical value, a base number, against which future variations are to be expressed (see Figure 9.2).

The index thus published represents in a single figure the characteristics of a group of items.

Managers will tend to use the indices produced by their own sectors more than those produced nationally. These will be of greatest value to them in preliminary enquiry and assessment of their own sphere, and its component parts – wage rates, and the going percentage and composition of pay rises; market and marketing aspects, concerning such matters as price and price variations, trade volumes, the relationships between supply and demand; variations in related or substitute sectors (e.g. if the organisation is a seller of Spanish holidays, and sales are falling, it is necessary to know whether sales of holidays to other destinations are also falling, or whether their company is losing out at the expense of a substitute); and wholesale, warehouse, energy and transport indices and indicators. They are a useful source of information in the raising of causes of possible concerns, and 'early warning' systems; they may also indicate possible opportunities (such as the emergence of a highly competitive energy source, for example, which may indicate the opportunity to invest in a real fixed-cost advantage, and provide the seed for a business investigation in full into the matter).

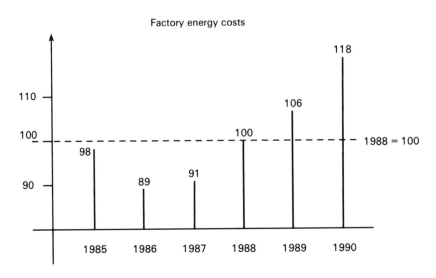

Figure 11.2   An index number

Managers use the various national indices as general sources of data and information. In particular, the annual rise in the RPI may give an indication of the level of wage rise to be demanded by the staff; while indices of wholesale price may be used as a starting point for a full investigation into the likely costs to be incurred over the coming period in the purchase of raw materials; or of inflationary pressures (usually) or sectors with which the organisation has trading and other commercial relationships. More generally still, the indices may indicate or imply such things as national or market confidence, recessionary pressures, or even 'green shoots' of recovery. Widely used in the media, they are of very limited true value to the manager in this way.

■ Probability

This concept provides a basis for assessing whether or not something will happen, or is likely to happen. It requires the assessment of one or more variables against a constant, or the assessment of two or more variables against each other. By doing this, possible, probable and likely outcomes of particular initiatives can be assessed and pre-evaluated. In such exercises the true and exact outcome will not be predicted; it is not a certain exercise. It is a valuable way of identifying the components of risk and uncertainty that may be endemic and unavoidable in a particular situation or initiative; and more generally, part of the 'early warning' systems that all managers should have in regard to their operations.

■ Accuracy and approximation

All data must be considered in the context of its collection, and any other pressures or constraints (e.g. time, resources) that are placed on this. The accuracy of the final data depends upon the soundness of the criteria on which the original collection was based; whether it was from primary or secondary sources. Other factors to be considered are time lag and rounding.

□ Time lag

This is the difference between the time when the information was collected, and when it is to be used; some statistics are soon out of date; and often business and public initiatives are planned to resolve future issues based on today's statistics.

□ Rounding

Whereby figures are rounded to the nearest manageable or usable element. An organisation's net profit for a particular year may be £56,203,459.52; for presentation and convenience this may be rounded to:

- £56,203,450
- £56,203,500
- £56,204,000
- £56,200,000
- £56.2 million
- £56 million
- £50 million

all depending on who is to use the figure and for what purpose.

■ Sampling

In relation to most business activities it is impossible to gain perfect information; sound methods of sampling must be used if data of meaning and value is to be gathered. Effective sampling may be used to gain valid and accurate impressions of markets, products, volume and quality of work, the nature of the work being carried out, the complexities of it, the intensities of work activities, staff turnover and absenteeism, and the regularity and severity of accidents.

The purpose of sampling is to learn information about the **whole** from the study of a **part**, providing results that would mirror those if a full survey were to be carried out.

☐ Sampling methods

Any sample must be representative of the population, activity or product under consideration. This may be ensured by a variety of sampling methods:

- **Regular**: whereby each *n*th product is chosen for testing; each *n*th person chosen for survey of their opinions.
- **Random**: whereby each person or product has an equal chance of being selected or tested; if a sample is chosen at random from a larger group or collection, it will exhibit the same characteristics as the whole provided that both are sufficiently large collections in the first place; random numbers may be used either as the starting point for this, or to select samples at each stage.
- **Stratified**: the grouping of populations and products into state or sub-groups, according to the needs of the data being gathered. This may be by age, location, occupation, street, town, country, urban, rural, for persons; or by date, time, shift, and line, in the measurement of products.
- **Multi-stage**: the purpose of this is to provide a measure of checking on one sample; and to identify where bias and inconsistency may arise. In the normal course of events, the stages are:

  - ⋆ piloting, to establish the fundamental soundness or otherwise of the methods to be used
  - ⋆ the main survey, in which the main data will be gathered
  - ⋆ and a follow-up survey among those initially surveyed, to establish any inconsistencies, perceptual failings, anomalies and bias that may be present.

- **Non-random and the use of quotas**: this is most prevalent in street surveys, whereby an interviewer may be required to get the responses of 50 persons on a particular day to a particular set of questions It is subject to a substantial degree of error, being additionally limited by the perceptions of the interviewer, external pressures on interviewees, and other variables (e.g. was it a Sunday, was it a town, city or village, where did the people interviewed come from?).

■ Validity, reliability and bias

At the outset of any proposed quantifiable or qualitative research, these elements must be considered. Research will be generally limited by additional constraints placed – accuracy, size of sample and populations, time and resource pressures. Within these constraints however, data gathered must be:

- **Valid**, that is, a measure or version of the truth; accurate (or a version of accuracy); and usable in the format in which it is presented

- **Reliable**, that is, the data gathered would be the same, or equivalent, if either a different sample were used, or if the sample had been surveyed at a different time in the same way.

Bias arises from a variety of sources, and while it is virtually impossible to eliminate (except through a full census), its origins and limitations can be recognised and accommodated. It comes from: the perceptions of the surveyors; the imperfections of the questionnaire and sampling methods; and any pre-conceptions or secondary agenda that has been included. Consideration must also be given to the sampling frame – the list, population or product range from which the sample is to be taken; partial response or non-response, misperception of the questions; and personal perceptions of the ranges indicated on such things as rating scales.

■ Census

A census is effectively a 100% sample. A full survey of the population is carried out in the UK every ten years (1971, 1981, 1991 – the next is in 2001). A census may also be carried out on particular sub-groups, e.g. all those exposed to radiation or poison may be surveyed for lasting effects. For business purposes census will normally be limited to attitude surveys at the workplace; or interviewing all leavers to find out why and where they are going; or getting all potential employees to fill in standard application forms. In terms of market research and product quality and reliability, census is not possible, and samples have to be taken.

■ Questionnaire

This is an instrument for gaining information from an informant for a particular purpose. Any such instrument must therefore be designed with specific and understood purposes, aims and objectives; and if possible, it should be piloted or tested to check that it does fulfil these purposes, or is likely to do so.

Having this right, however, provides a most valuable format for the gaining of equivalent information from a variety of sources, all for usage in a variety of managerial situations. Questionnaires are used, further, either as the means for structuring an interview, or as a more precise instrument in which specific questions are asked in the same way to each person (either orally or by presentation of the questionnaire to the subject for completion in their own way).

The questions used may be *open* (see Summary Box 9.3): where the subject is invited to expand their own response in their own words or style on given matters. Such questions are led by words such as 'who', 'what', 'where', 'why', 'how' and 'when'. The responses to these may be limited by the use of rating scales which may be either numerical:

SUMMARY BOX 11.3   Open and Closed Questions: Examples

Open
What do you like about Sweden?

Closed
(a) What I like about Sweden is: (tick box)

  • the scenery   ❏
  • the public transport   ❏
  • the food   ❏
  • other   ❏

(please specify) ....

(b) Do you like Swedish scenery   Yes   No

This illustrates the range and limitation that can be placed on responses. The ways in which information is asked for can thus be varied according to overall need, and in order either to give the respondent maximum opportunity for self-expression, or to limit this into preset and predetermined areas.

How important is it?   1   2   3   4   5
(please circle)

or verbal:

How important is it?   Very   Quite   Reasonably   Not   Not at all
(please circle)

It is normal also to ascertain some background information on the respondents for the purposes of classification, and to indicate any bias or external factors that may be affecting responses. Otherwise, the questions will be *closed*, eliciting precise and definite answers from the respondents (see Summary Box 9.3).

■ Operational research

Operational research is the use of quantitative methods in problem-solving. It is usually conducted by 'think tanks' and quantitative analysis units within organisations. Problems are considered and conceptual/mathematical/statistical/economic models are constructed to represent the system to be studied. The approach is to produce a model or simulation or 'mathematical game' version of what could/should happen in a particular set of circumstances. A rational model of the likely consequences of particular courses of action may then become apparent.

Operational research was originally used to solve military problems. Mathematical, statistical, economic and information sciences were applied to military situations; and one of the most famous (and most notorious) developments was the modelling of optimum shipping convoy sizes in the Second World War. It was also used to assess the logistics of moving large amounts of men, equipment and supplies around the battlefields of Western Europe towards the end of the Second World War. After the war, it was applied to industrial and commercial problems.

In industrial and commercial situations, this form of approach may be used in all aspects of organisational performance.

- **Blockage analysis**: blockages occur because organisational systems operate at the speed of the slowest part. Operational research is used to assess the effects of likely changes to the total process of the removal or repair of the blockage.
- **Production**: operational research is used in ordering the sequences of work, tasks, jobs, machine pressures and loading, and order scheduling. It may also be used to model for profit maximisation; volume maximisation; income maximisation; market dominance.
- **Marketing**: the relationship between organisations and their markets; the consequences of introducing or reducing the volume and range of products available; the effects of steady-state activities – distribution; vehicle and mailshot scheduling; direct marketing activities. In more extreme cases, operational research may be used to model the effects of market saturation – or at the opposite extreme, red-lining.
- **Queuing**: modelling the effects of increased customer flows; increased operations to reduce queues; and the effects on financial and other resources, and on the operations of the rest of the organisation. It is used to produce 'perfect models' of the optimum size of a particular part of the workforce concerned with managing and serving the queue.
- **Purchasing**: used to assess economic purchasing quantities; used to assess the differences between stockpiling and frequent regular deliveries; also used to assess the continuing relationship between the organisation and its sources of supplies.
- **Research and development**: used for example to produce analysis of the frequency with which new inventions become commercial products; the effects of research and development on other activities; the priority of research and development activities.
- **Communication**: used to analyse the relationship between quality, volume and effectiveness of communications and other aspects – e.g. strikes and disputes; absence and turnover; accidents; misunderstandings. It may also be used to analyse the effectiveness of committee systems, meeting groups, and general quality of information dissemination.

The greatest problem with operational research methods and techniques is that it produces perfect models.

Managers must understand that in practice this is never going to happen. A perfect model is only an indication of what would happen if everything was orderly and rational. In practice, nothing ever is. Again, therefore, the information thus produced is to be used, analysed and evaluated; and not adopted as a certain prediction for future activities.

■ Forecasting, extrapolation and inference

Forecasting, extrapolation and inference are concerned with facing the future with as much certainty as possible in the circumstances. Each depends upon the availability of high-quality and usable information for their accuracy and reliability. Each brings a slightly different point of view to the same problem.

Forecasting is a prediction of the future based on: knowledge and analysis of the present; knowledge and analysis of the past; and relating the two to the set of circumstances immediately foreseen. Forecasting further into the future is less certain. In managerial terms, it requires acknowledgement that business and commercial circumstances change and that operations and activities are affected by factors outside the manager's and organisation's control – for example, changes in customer behaviour and confidence; government activities; entry of new players into the sector; exit of players (especially a key player) from the sector; changes in production technology; changes in technology.

Extrapolation is the linear projection of the future based on current and historic statistics. It is a key output of operational research. Its value is in identifying linear trends. These are produced by statisticians, economists and information scientists for use by managers in their decision-making processes. It is not a decision-making process in itself.

Inference is the assessment of the likely state of the future based on a lack of complete (sometimes a lack of adequate) information. Inference leans heavily on relating the experience of previous similar situations to the present, and using this as the basis to make judgements and choose directions for the future.

Situational analysis (the basis of forecasting), the projection of statistics (extrapolation) and inference, together form the quantitative basis for qualitative evaluation and analytical judgements to be made by managers when they consider future directions and activities. It follows from this that information must be as complete as possible and that managers must know how to use it. They must know what is proved by this information and what is indicated by this information, the difference between the two and the strength of that indication.

■ Network analysis

This is the term used to embrace a range of organisation, scheduling, planning and control methods used in the ordering of complex projects and operational activities. The purpose is to identify in advance the shortest possible time in

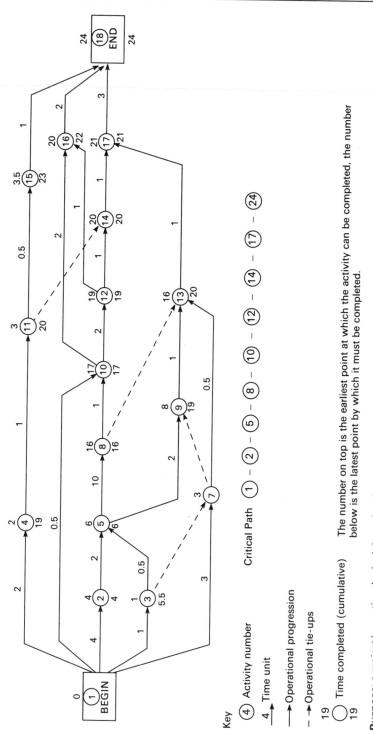

Key

④ Activity number

⟶ Time unit

⟶ Operational progression

--▸ Operational tie-ups

19
◯ Time completed (cumulative)
19

Critical Path ① – ② – ⑤ – ⑧ – ⑩ – ⑫ – ⑭ – ⑰ – ㉔

The number on top is the earliest point at which the activity can be completed, the number below is the latest point by which it must be completed.

Purpose: a project/operational schedule; a planning tool; a model against which to measure actual progress. Identification of critical incidents (those on the critical path). Identification of potential problems, blockages and hold-ups.

Figure 11.3 A network diagram

which such activities or series of activities or projects may be completed, or a new product brought on stream. From this, sub-schedules and activities can be worked out to establish the nature of resources, staff, equipment and other inputs that need to be present at given stages in order for this efficient and effective main schedule to be adhered to (see Figure 9.3).

The shortest and most effective route through such a schedule is called the 'critical path' – that is, the one that determines the speed of operations within it. Non-critical paths – that constitute flows of activity that have more flexibility in their inception and execution and timescale – will also be identified so that resources can be optimised at all stages of the work.

Critical incidents within the network will also be identified in advance. Each incident will be related to a set of criteria that contributes to the nature and extent of its critical configuration. Such criteria relate to matters concerning the difficulty, frequency, importance and value of the activity itself; scarcity and balance of resources; availability and conflicting demands on resources, expertise and equipment; and the consequences of delays on the critical incident to the rest of the schedule.

Such a network will then be used as a control mechanism, progress monitor, progress chaser (where desirable or necessary) and as a continuing means of monitoring and evaluating the whole series of activities and each component of the series.

■ Proof and indication

Effective managerial use of information must distinguish between proof and indication. At one level, statistics can prove anything (see Summary Box 9.2). This takes no account of the wider context nor of the interrelationship between one set of figures and others.

- **Cars**: a car dealership which sells 10% of its expensive models and 100% of its cheap models must take into account the likelihood (and the extent of the likelihood) that it has only sold all of its cheap models because the customers were first attracted by the expensive.
- **Hospitals**: an indication of hospital workload is likely to be the number of patients treated. If this rises by 20% it 'proves' increased workload. Again, this cannot be seen in isolation, and factors which would always have to be considered include: the number of patients returning for extended courses of treatment; for re-treatment following unsatisfactory treatment the first time round; and the number of patients attracted to the hospital following closure of other facilities elsewhere in the region.

From a managerial point of view, information and statistics are not therefore to be seen in isolation. They complete (or help to complete) a broader picture which consists at least in part of qualitative and behavioural aspects. Information, however complete, does not of itself make decisions or solve problems.

Problems, especially, are always bounded by a combination of information, deadlines and consequences – it is therefore certain that normally the solution to problems will be 'the best answer available on the day'. Information provides a basis (indeed part of the basis) for this approach. This is ultimately carried out based on the manager's judgement, analysis, evaluation and choice. It does follow that the greater the volume of relevant and useful information available, the greater the propensity, rationally, for effective and successful analysis – and therefore accurate decisions and effective solutions to problems.

■ Management information systems

The purpose of such systems is to 'oil the wheels' of the organisation, providing means for the effective transmission, reception and general communication of information. This must be in terms and formats that are efficient and effective, and that gives information in ways that are understandable, relevant, and above all usable. Such systems provide the basis for effective general business practices; and are specifically aimed at enabling sound decision-making.

■ Information systems and technology

Information systems are normally physical (at least in part) based on the retention of papers and documents recording the nature and volume of activities and providing material for internal and external consumption in all spheres – production, sales, marketing, staff management, finance and administration. Almost universally this is supported, and in many cases driven, by technology used to produce, store, retrieve, analyse and present information in a variety of different ways in order to meet divergent demands and according to the nature of the information and the purposes for which it is to be used.

■ Usage

Usage means addressing and analysing the organisation's needs for information, and the capabilities, capacity and durability of the systems that are being considered. It particularly concerns the volumes of information that are to be stored and processed and the nature and means of access required. It is especially necessary to pay attention to system design, workstation content and context, and location and hardware. In many cases, it is also necessary to consider integration with existing systems – both physical and electronic.

It is necessary to consider the nature and content of the relationship between the particular organisation and the system and software suppliers. This is likely to include after-sales and attention to teething troubles; training for all those who are to use the system; software upgrades; and replacing and servicing the hardware when necessary (see Summary Box 9.4).

■ System activities

Six specific business and management activities that impinge upon information systems may be identified:

1. Planning and organising of all work and support functions
2. Control mechanisms
3. The identification of blockages, either organisational or operational
4. The provision of linking elements and forums between departments and functions
5. Motivational aspects
6. Functional aspects: the ability to gain and gather accurate information from all functional and operational areas.

■ System data

Certain types of data required by the organisation may next be identified. Such data will take its format from the following elements:

- Long, medium or short term nature
- The extent of the accuracy required
- The volume to be stored, processed and retrieved, and the formats required for this

---

SUMMARY BOX 9.4   User-Friendliness

User-friendliness is the term used to describe the extent to which the needs of the system-users have been taken into account. Problems always occur when access and usage of the technology is complicated and when computer programmes have complex and convoluted access and instruction systems.

The best information (and production) technology is simple to understand and access, and straightforward to operate. It requires initial familiarisation and practice. This is normally provided by the supplying company. It also provides a variety of failsafe systems so that human error does not cause programmes to be wiped and large swathes of information and production capacity to be lost as the result.

User-friendliness is therefore a summary of the needs of the user. Lack of attention in each area normally results in a lack of willingness to use the system. This leads to a failure of thesystem to be operated to its full capacity; and, in turn, to incomplete information, inadequately stored, maintained and retrieved. The end result is to affect the quality the quality and decision-making of those using the system. It becomes discredited. Above all, it becomes extremely expensive and inefficient.

- What it is to be used for
- Who is to use it, and how they are to gain access
- How often it is to be used.

System design

Next must be considered matters to do with the design of the system or systems themselves:

- Whether to have one system or a set of related and interlocking sub-systems
- Modes and methods of access
- Frequency of access
- Questions of urgency of access, the value of access, and general matters of speed, accuracy, and methods of information processing
- The nature of the staff who are to use the system or systems, and their levels of quality, qualifications and trainability.

This is a fundamental consideration. If the system is too complex for the staff, and they are not capable of being trained to use it, either the system must be redesigned or staff hired who can use it in its current format.

System responsibilities

There are wider implications also to be considered. The most basic of these is to establish where overall responsibility for the system lies, and also where the devolved functional responsibilities are. There may be specific as well as legal constraints (apart from anything else) which it is critical to pin down; this is quite apart from questions of operational necessity.

System technology

Then there is the technology itself. Many organisations, functions and managers have been so carried away by the brilliance and capacities of both hardware and software that they have lost sight of their own specific requirements for it. This has to be balanced against the genuine lifespan of equipment in an age of constant technological revolution, update and obsolescence. As with other operational aspects, therefore, a strategic approach is required to the design, organisation and purpose of information systems; a system thus arrived at will invariably test more productivity for much longer than one that is technically more modern, but which has not had the same global regard to its purchase.

Alongside this is the possibility of purchasing 'off the shelf' information systems and software that can be installed and made operational very quickly, as opposed to the design and implementation of something that is tailor-made. The former will always be cheaper at the point of purchase; the true cost, however, has to be measured and evaluated over the full operational life of the system. There is also the wider question of the ability of complex organisations to accommodate effectively or satisfactorily the vagaries of something not specifically designed for them.

■ System security and control

Questions of control of information, and security of it, must be considered. Again this must be from the global or strategic point of view; a balance must be struck between use and value, questions of access, operational factors, and the power and influence of those who are responsible for the outputs. There are also more general elements of power and influence to be considered in regard to the information itself, its volume and quality and ultimate destinations and users.

■ System installation

There are behavioural aspects especially to be addressed. Lack of understanding of the technology, or a more nebulous disquiet or feeling of being threatened by it, will invariably mean either that the systems are not used at all, or else not used fully.

The installation of any system must therefore be accompanied by programmes of staff and management training, briefing, familiarisation, and overall appreciation designed to ensure that the system does indeed 'oil the wheels' of the organisation, rather than becoming an adjunct to it.

There are wider considerations for such matters as recruitment and selection processes, job design, and workplace layout, structure and design. The end result must be, overall, that the information system is fully integrated with all other organisation systems and activities; that those employed can use them, and are comfortable with them; and that the organisation as a whole has systems that contribute to its overall effectiveness, rather than detract from them.

■ System outputs

The data outputs from any system must be such that they are usable by those who receive them. Managers, in particular, do not normally require volumes of raw data; or if they do, they also require synopses and summaries and analyses indicating what the data itself indicates and giving pointers to the likely and suitable ranges of activities that the data implies. In this way management information systems are essential adjuncts to decision-making processes and the outlining, formulation and determination of strategic choices. They also give particular functional information in regard to the operational area in question.

Management information systems and the data that they generate must themselves be managed if they are to continue to remain effective and serve the organisation and its managers and fulfil the functions indicated above.

■ Conclusion

From a managerial point of view, therefore, statistics, information and the systems used are concerned with value and contribution. Statistics, mathematics and economics produce figures and information – it is the ability to analyse and evaluate that is the concern of the manager. For this to be successful and effective, specific concerns must be addressed.

■ Validity and reliability

The methods by which the data was gathered must be consistent. The data gathered should be from one of the methods indicated above. Where this has not been possible, or where the information gathering was incomplete or biased or skewed, the defect must be acknowledged. Ideally the data should be free from bias and subjective judgement. As in most cases, where this is not absolutely possible, defects must again be acknowledge. Where this is, as happens in many cases, virtually impossible, the data is to be treated with great degrees of scepticism (see for example, Summary Box 9.5).

As far as possible, the data gathered should be reliable – capable of validation in all equivalent situations and circumstances from which it was gathered. Again, if this is not possible, the fact should be acknowledged.

Managers therefore need to know and understand the basis or bases on which the information has been gathered if they are to use it successfully and effectively. It is necessary therefore, to have an understanding of the statistical and mathematical methods and the ability to use the figures in the pursuit of managerial effectiveness. For this to happen, managers need to know and understand:

- The basis on which the information was gathered and any specific constraints that were imposed such as time pressures, size of samples and access/lack of access to sources of information
- The context in which the information was gathered – the extent to which it was directed or prescribed; what information has not been taken into account (for whatever reason); who requested the information and why; what, if anything, it is intended to prove or indicate; what it actually proves or indicates
- Expert conclusions drawn by statisticians, mathematicians and information systems experts and their impact on managerial judgement, evaluation and analysis
- Uses to which the information may legitimately be put; uses to which it may not legitimately be put; the extent to which it is legitimate to use for other purposes information that was gathered for one purpose

---

SUMMARY BOX 9.5   The Generally Favourable Response

It is very easy to generate generally favourable responses (GFR). This is achieved as follows.

Example: marketing (upon the launch of a new product)

Interviewer:	Do you like this product?
Subject:	Yes
Interviewer:	how would you rate it on a scale of 1–10, where 10 is the most favourable response?
Subject:	About 7.
Interviewer:	Would you use it?
Subject:	Yes, I would.

Asking questions in this way is comfortable and reinforcing. But it is fraught with danger. Not enough follow-up information is demanded. It is certain to be clouded by: perceptions of what the rating scale means (different to every individual); the likeness (the subject will not wish to offend the interviewer); the question 'Would you use?' (very different from 'Will you use?' and 'And if so, how often?').

Example: staff references

Many organisations send out pro forma questionnaires to previous employers of potential employees. A common question on these is: 'Would you re-employ?', to which there is a range of GFRs, including: yes; yes if a suitable vacancy were to arise; probably; possibly; maybe; and so on.

The question is never asked as '*Will* you re-employ?'; or '*Will* you re-employ if a suitable vacancy comes up?'

The problem is bad enough in the latter case. In the former, the question is incapable of validation as it is based entirely on a set of personal perceptions (on the part of the responder) to a future hypothetical situation.

Example: questionnaire structuring

More insidiously still, GFRs are achieved through careful combinations of ostensibly direct, but actually leading, questions. It is for example, used by political parties in the pursuit of a vested interest as follows.

- **Question 1**: Do you believe that crimes against children should be stopped?
- **Question 2**: Do you believe that those who carry out crimes against children should be punished?
- **Question 3**: Do you believe that society should clean up those who carry out these crimes?
- **Question 4**: Will you support the death penalty?

The effect is at least three-fold. It leads people down a particular direction involving them in the desired train of thought. It produces (in fact) subjective answers to (overtly) rational questions. It makes overtly rational, but actually spurious, connections between questions 1–3 and question 4. And it is the answer to question 4 (not 1–3) that is then used by the vested interest.

- The wider context – the general extent to which the information may be used; its place in the overall scheme of things; the effects – both positive and negative – of taking one piece of information in isolation from others.

It is also important to recognise the difference between what can and cannot be controlled. Where organisations have to deal with factors outside their control, the best approach is to gather as much information as possible, to know as much as possible about those factors that are outside its control, and to cover the range of possible outcomes on the basis of the following spectrum (see Figure 9.4).

■ Currency

The other main issue to be addressed is the currency of the information. In general, circumstances change rapidly and information quickly becomes obsolete. To be effective, systems have to be kept up-to-date so that whatever is withdrawn and analysed is current also. This applies in all spheres. Production design, capability and quality may be superseded by others in the field and the organisation needs to know this in order to be able to respond. Human resource systems must be kept up-to-date concerning qualifications, length of service, employee history and staff capability. Marketing information must reflect

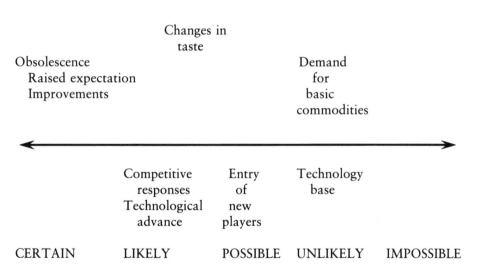

Note: There are very few elements that fall into the 'impossible' category.

Figure 9.4   Factors outside the organisation's control

current, not recent, states of the segments and niches in which activities are carried out. Sales information must reflect the current state of activities if there is to be any chance of effective forecasting, extrapolation and inference for the future.

Otherwise, the main conclusion to be drawn here relates to the managerial constructs that are to be placed on the quantitative data and information. This consists of ensuring that both the information and the methods used to collect, store and present it are suitable for the purposes of the organisation and the needs of the managers also. All quantitative data is only of value if it is available in ways that the organisation and those within it can understand and use. This must include the behavioural and perceptual aspects of it as well as the quantitative material itself. Above all, managers must have both faith and confidence in the budgeting information that they receive and the systems that produce it if these are to have in themselves any credence or organisational value.

CHAPTER 10

Financial aspects of management

■ Finance

Finance is the lifeblood of all organisations, in whatever sphere they operate. Companies in the private sector are required to make profits, that is, to generate a surplus of income over expenditure over a period of time, that supports the continuation of the business, and provides an adequate return to the backers. Public, social and health services, working to targets allocated by governments and other authorities, must use these resources to best advantage to satisfy the sectors that they serve, and reconcile with any constraints under which they may be placed.

Accounts are kept and produced for three main reasons:

- An essential check by the organisation on the state of its activities, income and expenditure in financial terms. This enables it to identify where resources are being consumed, in what volumes and the reasons behind this.
- The presentation of its financial state to stakeholders – staff, stockmarkets, stock and shareholders, banks, suppliers, customers, the community at large and the sectors in which it operates.
- Compliance with the law. Across the Western world, the law requires organisations to produce 'a true and fair' statement of their activities in financial terms, normally once a year, indicating the performance and state of the organisation in this way. This must be subject to external scrutiny and audit. Organisations have to pay tax and the extent of liability for this arises as the result of these accounting activities.

Accounts are produced by qualified and professional accountants, and other financial experts. They are produced in accordance with legal requirements as stated above. The accounting industry also has its own rules, codes of conduct and conventions which govern the ways in which they carry out their work and produce their results. Explanations and translations of these are often given in organisational, annual and other public reports, together with how these have been applied. Detailed explanations of these are available from the professional bodies of the accounting industry.

The managerial approach to accounts and financial aspects is concerned with the use, evaluation, interpretation, analysis and judgement of the financial data, what it means for the present and future of the organisation. It is one of the points of information used as the basis for effective decision-making. It enables a managerial assessment of current and recent performance in financial terms.

More specifically, effective and accurate accounts enable managers to pinpoint the following:

- **Costs**: these can be assessed from an informed view of the extent to which costs are justified; whether or not they represent effective usage of the organisation's resources; whether these constitute activities worth pursuing; whether improvements could/should/must/might be made in the given area
- **Income**: this can then be assessed on the basis of adequacy overall. It also enables a picture of income per product; per product range; per outlet; per region; and overall; to be built up
- **Returns**: attention to returns enables the organisation to assess the extent to which the income being generated represents an excellent, adequate, satisfactory or unsatisfactory return on investment, activities and cost. This is seen in turn, from a variety of points of view: the organisation's own desired levels of return; the time period over which the returns are to be made; and the performance of products, services and activities in their pursuit
- **Wider expectations** and **perceptions of satisfaction** based on sectoral norms and the interests of stakeholders
- **Comparisons** with the achievements of other organisations in the same or related sectors and activities
- Departmental, divisional, functional and sectional performance in the same terms.

■ Sources of finance

Companies and commercial organisations draw their financial resources from the following:

- Sale of shares, either to family, friends and colleagues (if the company is small and private), or else to the general public and other institutions, on the stockmarkets of the world if the company is 'public'
- Sale of loan notes and debentures which may be described as short term or fixed term capital and which must be repaid on the date specified
- Government grants and incentives issued either in the form of a company guarantee, or else in return for undertaking government contracts
- Retained income and profits from activities carried out
- Bank loans on which interest is repayable over the period of the loan. The loan itself is normally arranged under a form of contract and again, must be repaid at the stated time (or times).

Note: Gearing

Gearing is the relationship between bank loans and other sources of finance. The convention in the West is that gearing should be as low as possible, meaning that the balance of financial resources should depend as little as possible on bank loans. Conversely, Japanese companies tend to have very high gearing, though it should be noted that the majority of their loans come from nationalised banks underwritten and effectively guaranteed by the government; this is therefore seen as less of a problem in these circumstances.

Public sector corporations and organisations may also (as long as their Constitution allows) raise money in these ways. They are normally dependent upon government grants and budget allocations, given to them by departments and functions in place of share capital and which give them (or are supposed to give them) adequate resources to carry out their work.

In total, these sources of finance produce the capital base from which organisations operate. The capital base is there to underwrite and underpin activities, to acquire capital assets from which products and services are to be made and offered, and as a form of security for the organisation as a whole.

■ Investment, assets and liabilities

■ Assets

Assets are required by organisations to enable them to pursue their stated purposes.

□ Capital assets

Capital assets consist of premises, technology, equipment, and machinery to be used in the production of the organisation's offerings. They are sometimes referred to as fixed or tangible assets. Their acquisition is based on a combination of what the organisation can afford, the projected length of the asset's useful life and the uses to which they are best suited.

Capital expenditure is also made on acquisition of supplies (and suppliers); the means of distribution including vehicle fleets, containers, retail and other points of public contact outlets.

□ Intangible assets

Intangible assets consist of reputation, goodwill, confidence and expectation levels. They reflect the basis on which people come to do business with a particular organisation. High levels of goodwill and expectation are normally expected to translate into high levels of repeated business, increased reputation, and enlarging of customer demands and customer bases.

This may in particular be applied to brand names and images. Strong brand names (for example, Coca-Cola, Nescafe, Barbie) carry high and continuing levels of value. They each also have a commercial value in their own right, and the owning companies could (if they so wished) put them up for sale.

□ Short- and medium-term assets

These take the form of acquisitions made specifically for a purpose. Building companies acquire land banks on the basis that they will be able to build on these in the near future. Glassware and china companies acquire designs to be used on the next development of their products. Travel companies and agencies acquire banks of hotel rooms and airline seats to be sold on in the next season.

□ Long-term assets

These are acquired on the basis that the organisation is always going to need them. This especially applies to property and some forms of capital goods and production equipment.

□ Managerial assets

The concept of managerial assets represents the view that other elements of the organisation can, and should, be viewed as assets. This especially concerns:

- **The human resource**, especially where this has distinctive expertise; high reputation for quality, value and service; excellence in innovation, research and development activities; or rare and highly prized skills and knowledge
- **Markets**, especially those dominated by the particular organisation in terms, either of volume of business conducted or high levels of reputation
- **Command** of commodities, components or other valuable and highly sought-after scarce resources
- **Expertise** in pioneering and again, research and development; a list of successful and profitable inventions to product, to market
- **Excellence** and **expertise** of management and direction.

This view of assets takes elements from each of the previous aspects. It requires the application of a distinctive managerial perspective based on analysis, evaluation and judgement as well as taking the financial point of view.

■ Liabilities

Liabilities are the obligations and charges that are certain to be incurred or that are present as the result of the company's current activities. They are as follows:

- **Regular and continuing costs and obligations**. Of these the most regular and continuing is staff – all staff incur costs and have to be paid. Other regular liabilities include capital repayments; interest charges; supply, production and distribution costs; and other bills and charges incurred – especially fuel, electricity, rent, rates, heating and lighting
- **Activity related charges** which vary according to the nature of the organisation. The most universal are marketing activities, maintenance

charges, research and development and other pioneering and prospecting work
- **Short-term liabilities** incurred, for example, by hiring extra or specialised staff or equipment to get over a particular problem and for which a long term benefit is expected to accrue
- **Intangible liabilities** of which the most common is a bad reputation based on poor production, quality and volume; inability to meet deadlines; poor presentation; wrong and inappropriate images
- **Sudden liabilities** which occur based, for example, on the sudden obsolescence of products, sudden price drops, increases in the price of supplies or components, or production and other technology. When this occurs, the organisation has to decide very quickly whether it is going to try to rejuvenate that which it is already doing; or whether to remain in the sector or not. If it decides to do so, then it must meet the sudden liability as a consequence of this.

■ The relationship between assets and liabilities

From an accounting point of view, a relationship can be established between each designated asset and liability through comparisons and ratio analysis (see below). From a managerial point of view, a broader approach is necessary.

Something that is bought as an asset can quickly turn into a liability. Production and information technology, bought as a long-term investment, may be rendered obsolete at any time by new inventions. Building companies that bought land banks find that these become a liability if the demand for buildings dries up or if the price of land falls. Projects for which capital goods have been bought may be cancelled if other costs or unforeseen problems make the project no longer worthwhile.

■ Investment

The nature of investment is a key feature of the relationship between assets and liabilities. From a managerial point of view again, this relationship is to be seen from the perspective that anything bought as an asset may become a liability at any time when circumstances change, as illustrated above. There is therefore no certain return on anything. A piece of equipment that can produce 5,000 items a year for a designated useful life of ten years may have to be scrapped and written off altogether if a new and better machine becomes available, and the sectoral norm after two years.

■ Depreciation

Depreciation is an accounting convention which shows the period of time over which an item is gradually paid for, paid for in instalments, or written off altogether. It is important to remember that it is purely an accounting convention and not a managerial tool.

For example, the piece of equipment referred to in the previous paragraph may have cost £100,000. The organisation's accounting function may set out to depreciate it, quite legitimately from their point of view, at £20,000 per annum for five years. If it does become obsolete after two years, then the managerial stance must be to scrap it and replace it, whatever the accounting convention may say.

From this, arises a basic understanding of the managerial approach to investment. It involves recognising the financial nature of assets and liabilities, and the financial opportunities and constraints involved. It also means going well beyond this and recognising the strategic and operational opportunities and constraints involved, and the necessity to be able to bring this perspective to bear when required. It also has to be seen in the context of not being able to predict with any degree of certainty when these requirements may actually be. It further requires an understanding of the fact that the value of assets can both rise and fall; and can fall to the point where an asset becomes a liability.

From a managerial perspective also, investment is a continuous commitment, a condition and consequence of being in a particular sector. The specific nature of investment varies between sectors and between the organisations operating within them. Generally, however, this continuous commitment always covers:

- Staff expertise, training, improvement and development
- Organisational capability, capacity, improvement and development
- Systems improvement and development and refinement
- Brand and other marketing asset, reinforcement, development and enhancement
- Reputation, confidence and expectational enhancement
- Technology improvement, development and replacement.

All this is driven by the fact that in each of these areas, improvements and development are both possible and desired; and by the fact that everyone else is committed to them to a greater or lesser extent; and also the fact that those who are not certain to get left behind by those who are.

□ Investment appraisal

If this view of investment is adopted, it enables a much more informed and accurate approach to financial decisions to be taken by managers. These include:

- Whether to buy, rent or lease premises, staff, equipment and technology
- Whether to buy up stocks of supplies; whether to stockpile or to rely on frequent deliveries (just in time)

- Whether to buy up or lease transport and distribution fleets and other vehicles
- Whether to employ or sub-contract specialist staff and expertise
- The vagaries surrounding the useful life of each of these elements and necessary actions that may have to be taken concerning them at any time.

It enables a much more informed view to be taken of the opportunities and constraints of continued involvement in the sector. This part of investment appraisal takes account of:

- The levels of return that the sector is providing at present
- The levels of return that the sector may be expected to provide in the future
- The levels of return desired by the organisation
- Pay-back periods on particular activities
- Identification and evaluation of alternatives available to the organisation and the uses to which its resources could be put.

It is also necessary to look at costs specific to the particular sector. All sectors have their own particular cost and economics mixes. For example, the construction industry has extensive pre-project commitments including: gaining planning permission; permission to build; design times; public enquiries; arranging sub-contractors; arranging equipment; and all this must be funded as a condition of being in the sector. The level of investment and funding necessary must also take into account project completion; fitting out and refurbishment; and after-sales facilities. This is the time and cost frame against which those in the industry must work, and all sectors each have their own equivalent.

If short-term returns are required, the organisation in question will move out of areas where returns are only available over the long term. If long-term returns are required by companies working in retail and consumer goods sectors, the commitment is to ensure that a sufficient volume and quality of current products and a steady stream of innovations and improvements for the future are present.

More generally, any organisation requiring specific rates of return on investments, must work in or move to those sectors where these rates are possible. It is no use requiring a 35% annual return on investment, if the best return afforded by the sector is 10%. The organisation has then to decide whether it wishes to continue in the sector or not; to accept and try and maximise the returns based on the norms and possibilities; or to move elsewhere.

Financial data has therefore to be collected by the organisation to establish how this resource is being used, and to enable a managerial assessment and evaluation of this usage to be made. There is a control element in this, the ability to measure the costs of particular activities, as well as the whole. It enables the organisation to see where its money is tied up – for example, in stocks and storage, work in progress, raw materials, and goods in transit – and provide the basis of an assessment of this. It enables any slack, or stresses or strains to be identified. It is part of the wider necessity to provide a full range of management information.

■ Profit and Loss Account and Balance Sheet

Once the data is collected it has to be made available to both the internal and external environments. The external environment in the UK requires the annual presentation of a Balance Sheet, and Profit and Loss Account. These are governed by accounting conventions, and must be subject to scrutiny and audit. The Balance Sheet is a financial snapshot of the company on a stated day. It shows assets and liabilities in balance, and what the components of each are; this enables the wider business and financial world to make an informed judgement on the company's inherent strength and stability. The Profit and Loss Account is a representation of income and expenditure, showing a surplus or deficit on it (see Figure 10.1).

Company accounts must be countersigned as giving 'a true and fair reflection' of the financial state and performance of the organisation, by an externally appointed auditor.

Profit and Loss Accounts and Balance Sheets are normally presented as part of the annual report. As well as the figures, the annual report also includes statements by the Chairman and other top managers and directors concerning the well-being of the organisation; the nature, content and volume of activities and future plans.

■ Trends and comparisons

As stated in Figure 10.1, it is possible to compare one year's performance with another, both overall and line-by-line. This is useful up to a point.

To gain a more complete picture however, it is much more useful to take the same view over a longer period of time – often five years. This approach is the same – to take overall and line-by-line comparisons. Taking this longer view enables identification of more genuine trends and directions. It also enables 'blips', extraordinary items of sale and expenditure, share issues, special loans, to be set in context.

The Balance Sheet and Profit and Loss Account are primarily for external consumption, though much useful information can be gathered by anyone. Internal financial activities are organised around budgeting systems, accounts and finance functions. The relationship and appropriateness of these to the rest of the organisation must be established at the outset, and constantly maintained. These systems and functions exist to provide information and illumination for the organisation's main activities, and as the bases of maintaining and improving them.

■ Finance and strategy

The final element to be considered here is the strategic view of the organisation's finances, in relation to profits and surpluses, and budget allocation. In the case of profit, a balance must be struck between the short-term and long-term gain; and this may in turn require the reconciliation of shareholders' demands for

		1993 £ million	1992 £ million	
PROFIT AND LOSS ACCOUNT				
	INCOME	3188	3097	
	OPERATING COSTS	(2736)	(2771)	
	OPERATING PROFIT	452	326	
	INTEREST	(27)	33	
	PROFIT BEFORE TAX	425	359	
	TAX	(140)	(117)	(Brackets
	PROFIT AFTER TAX	285	242	indicate
	DIVIDEND	(82)	(72)	Subtraction)
	RETAINED PROFIT	203	170	

Figures are then normally given for earnings per share and dividend per share

		31 December 1993 £ million	31 December 1992 £ million	
BALANCE SHEET				
	FIXED ASSETS	2106	1996	
	Current Assets	1109	1043	
	Short term Creditors	(771)	(890)	
	NET CURRENT ASSETS	338	153	
	Total Assets	2444	2149	(Brackets
	Long term Creditors	(475)	(325)	indicate
	Liabilities and Charges	(299)	(359)	Subtraction)
	NET ASSETS	1670	1465	
	CAPITAL AND RESERVES			
	Share Capital	1470	1000	
	Capital Reserve	150	265	
	Other Reserves	50	200	
	TOTAL EQUITY	1670	1465	

Notes: It is used to give current and previous years figures for purposes of comparison. Thus, the overall performance can be compared, and also the line-by-line movements and charges.

Figure 10.1 Profit and Loss Account and Balance Sheet example

instant returns, with the need to ensure stability and continuity over a long period, possibly at the expense of a dividend pay-out. On the other hand, inert or bureaucratic budgeting systems often put pressure on managers to spend resources regardless of effectiveness because the money will otherwise be lost to the department or unit. Or the budget may be rigidly constrained, with the result that once the allocation is used up, the department is closed down or mothballed – as has happened regularly in UK public and health services in the early 1990s. Any strategic approach must therefore consider this, and any operational factors must be reconciled, if maximum effectiveness is to be achieved.

■ Financial resources and control

This is the background to the manager's position in relation to the financial resources available, and how they are to be used. The overall purpose is to illustrate the inherent responsibilities. It is also necessary to draw the relationship that exists between the actual cost incurred in doing something, the management of that cost, and the impression that it makes on the operation, the department, and the individuals concerned.

At the broadest end of the scale, the organisation has to generate enough income to survive and remain profitable and viable. There is thus a general pressure on managers to contribute to this in ensuring a steady flow of quality outputs that their customers and clients (whoever they are) will wish to continue to take up. There is derived pressure from this that is to do with ensuring that those resources input into the departments of individual managers, are suitable for their intended purposes of the requisite volume and quality and strike a balance between effectiveness, optimisation and flexibility.

The organisation also has to be able to determine the relationship between the extent of the investment in itself and the returns on that investment, both desired and actual. It has to determine and establish the price that it is to charge for its outputs in terms that are both acceptable to its markets and which provide this rate of return commensurate with the nature and level of business conducted. Such pricing policies will therefore normally seek to cover at least the variable costs (that is those actually incurred in the production of the output) and to make a 'contribution' to the return on investment, profit or surplus generated by the organisation. In sophisticated organisations with a multitude of offerings, this will relate to the range of output as a single entity and not to each item.

■ Costs

It follows from this that it is necessary to be able to identify a range of costs and to identify also their nature and behaviour.

Three costs are usually distinguished.

☐ Fixed costs (FC)

These are the costs incurred by the organisation, whether or not any profitable business of any sort is conducted. They consist of capital charges, premises costs, staff costs and administrative, managerial and support function overheads.

☐ Variable costs (VC)

These are the costs incurred as the result of engaging in direct business activity. They consist of raw materials, packaging and distribution costs. A price established for the item will, as stated above, normally seek to cover these at least; additionally it may make a contribution to the fixed cost.

☐ Marginal cost (MC)

This is the cost incurred by the production of one extra item of output, and reflects the extent to which the production capacity of the organisation may be extended without incurring additional fixed costs in the forms of investment in new plant, staff, equipment or machinery. There comes a point at which the production of an extra item does require these matters.

☐ Opportunity cost (OC)

Opportunity costs represent the opportunities foregone as the result of being involved in another area.

☐ Total cost (TC)

Total cost is the summary of all costs incurred by organisations as the result of engaging in particular activities and is the summary of fixed costs, variable costs, marginal costs and opportunity costs.

■ Cost apportionment

☐ Fixed and variable cost apportionment

These are the processes devised by the organisation for the purposes of identifying where these costs should be charged and apportioned. This is often known as the process of 'cost centring', and the activity thus identified is called the cost centre.

□ Profit apportionment

This is the converse of cost apportionment and is the organisation's method of ensuring the nature and sources of income generated by its various activities. This constitutes the identity of profit centres in the same way as cost centres above.

■ Break even

This is the point at which the balance between costs and income is established (see Figure 10.2 on page 314).

■ Asset valuation

The purpose of identifying, assessing and valuing the activities and resource as an asset is as part of the means of measuring their total contribution and worth to the organisation. Summary Box 10.1 shows the method adopted in such evaluation in response to the human resource. Equivalent approaches can be taken to 'hard resources' – production technology, capability, expertise, production volumes; and to 'soft' assets – reputation, goodwill and quality.

■ Ratio analysis

Ratios are used in financial management to identify, establish and measure particular performance aspects. The results and outcomes of the analysis of the ratios, and the level and quality of performance that they indicate, contribute to management knowledge and information, and become part of the process of assessment and evaluation.

These ratios include:

- **Profit ratio** $\dfrac{\text{Net profit}}{\text{Total sales}} \times 100$ Indicates percentage net return.

- **Selling costs:** $\dfrac{\text{Selling costs}}{\text{Total sales}} \times 100$ Indicates percentage consumed on Sales costs.

The same approach can be taken for energy, production, marketing, staff and distribution, as a percentage of sales.

- **Assets and liabilities**: $\dfrac{\text{Assets}}{\text{Liabilities}}$ a general ready-reckoner.

It is used to break the assets down into:

- (a) $\dfrac{\text{Long-term assets}}{\text{Long-term liabilities}}$

- (b) $\dfrac{\text{Current assets}}{\text{Current liabilities}}$

- (c)   'The Quick Ratio' or 'The Acid Test': $\dfrac{\text{Quickly realisable assets}}{\text{Current liabilities}}$

- **Debtors and Creditors**: $\dfrac{\text{Debtors}}{\text{Creditors}}$ indicates whether an organisation is paying out its bills more quickly than it is receiving payments.

- **Return on capital employed** (ROCE): $\dfrac{\text{Profit before tax}}{\text{Capital employed}}$ Gives rate of return on the investment.

The ratios thus provide distinctive measures of the particular activities. The information gained has to be seen in context however. For example, while a 'quick ratio' may show that a company could not easily cover its current liabilities, if these are not to be called in this does not matter. Similarly, different commercial and public sectors will have their own norms and expectations that have also to be taken into account – a 2% return on capital employed may sound low, but it may be twice the usual rate in the industry concerned. There is also the wider environment to be considered, and any opportunities, or difficulties; boom, or recession.

Different organisations have their own philosophies, means and methods of establishing what their fixed and variable costs actually are, how they are to be apportioned and what the desired rates and levels of returns are. The common purpose is to have methods, and to ensure that they are efficient and suitable to the organisation in question. It follows from this that methods of cost apportionment are neither exact nor linear but the subject of managerial and organisation debate and decision.

The main purpose of identifying the nature of these costs and their extent in given situations is as the basis of managerial assessment and decision-making. Costs should never become straitjackets outside which a department or function may not budget. It should always be remembered that the driving force of any organisation is its products and services and relations with its markets; costs and the management of them should never take the place of market imperatives. Only if this is achieved can a true assessment of the nature and extent of the

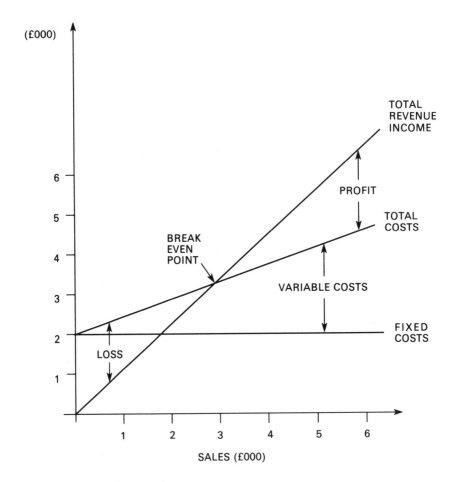

Figure 10.2 A break even diagram

effectiveness (in financial terms) of the organisation's activities be made (see Summary Box 10.2).

■ Internal markets

Internal markets are present in holding company structures, multinational organisations and health and public services. They are a combination of the following elements:

SUMMARY BOX 10.1   A Model of Human Asset Valuation and Accounting

1. The 'base' to be adopted is employment costs, which are measured (a) in total, (b) by staff category, (c) by operational division, (d) in terms of the added value (see Summary Box 11.3) that each contributes, and (e) by sectoral factors.

2. Return on these bases may be measured and assessed in the same way as for any other asset; and above all thus provides information for managerial discussion. Additional factors have to be taken into account in this particular regard however; these are: the opportunity costs of the current human resource (in regard to a new one or one that is a revamped or retrained or redeployed); measures of good will; the balance and mix of talents and capacities with operational requirements; human asset projections of cost, value, and benefit (related to the 'base' given above); and the **current** and **projected** asset values in each of these regards.

3. The concept of the 'human liability' must also be addressed. This is in regard to assessing any actual or projected occupational obsolescence, and consequent 'depreciation' of the asset; the full occupational liability; turnover and terminal losses; replacement costs; and refurbishment (that is, training and development) costs.

4. The assessment of the human asset can thus be conducted as a figurative balance of assets and liabilities, and provides a managerial ready-reckoner – a fresh means of the study of employment and the nature of the organisational investment in it.

5. As well as returns on (human) capital employed, there is information given in the planning, direction and disposition of resources; and the impact of this on the valuation, assets and liabilities of the organisation. This is also a means for the examination of the nature and effect of expenditure on the human resource; industrial relations; and organisation and employee development.

We can model this as follows:

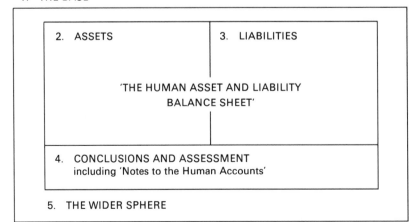

A Note on Return on Capital Employed (ROCE)

ROCE represents the nature and extent of the returns required by the shareholders in the organisation and other vested interests in it; it is useful as a comparator between desired and actual performance. It may also identify particular inefficiencies of resource utilisation. Finally, general returns on investment have their own distinctive comparators – for example the RP or rate of interest available on deposit accounts – which may serve as a bench mark for acceptable capital returns. On the other hand, returns should always be seen in terms of the nature of actual returns in the particular industrial or commercial sector in question.

1. The distinction between, and definition of, **purchasers** and **providers**, for the purposes of establishing a contracted arrangement; the position is further complicated by the fact that certain functionaries may be both purchasers and providers in different circumstances
2. The establishment of a **contracted agreement** between purchasers and providers, as the basis on which the relationship between the two is to be carried out in the future; essentially this will be agreed in advance of the business relationship, but will invariably require a 'continuity' or 'fine-tuning' clause, enabling matters that subsequently arise to be dealt with
3. The establishment of a **price-service return** and the ways in which the services are to be paid for; in multinationals this will generally be on a system of transfer pricing, using the most advantageous currency available to it; in other situations, a system of internal invoicing may be devised
4. The agreeing of quantity/volume, quality and timescale/deadlines **criteria** for each relationship established; what is included, what is not, and the scope and scale for varying each on the part of either party
5. **Transfer pricing**: for multinational and international companies, transfer pricing involves the selection and use of the particular currencies in which the organisation is to deal and on which it is to base its accounting, budgeting and other methods of control. It also includes setting prices through which internal transfers are to be made. These are subject to external audit and verification. For public organisations that create internal markets, this consists of putting a notional value on each of the people and activities concerned.

The emphasis of each element will vary; the overall constitution of any organisational internal market, however, must be to ensure an effectiveness of operation; and an efficiency of resource identification, allocation and evaluation on the part of the control, administrative and support functions of the organisation.

■ Budgets

As well as the actual components of a budget, there are wider purposes to be considered when budgets are being set.

Budgets and resource allocation

The budget is a plan (with sub-plans), that constitutes part of the process of managing the organisation, department, project or initiative. It aims to provide an accurate picture of where resources are being used, the speed and frequency of this, and the basis for making future judgements on the levels of finance required to meet particular targets (in terms of volume, quality and time).

SUMMARY BOX 10.2   Financial Measures of Performance from a Managerial Point of View

The following are useful managerial financial measures of performance. Their application and emphasis varies between organisations.

- **Income/profit**:
    - ★ per product; per product group or cluster; per product range; per activity; in total
    - ★ per employee – front line staff; support staff; in total
    - ★ per square metre; per outlet; per location; per region; per country
    - ★ per customer
    - ★ per hour/day/week/month/season/year
- **Fixed variable and total cost**: for each of these costs, calculations may be made
    - ★ per employee; per function; per activity; per department/division/section; per outlet; per location; per region; per country
    - ★ per square metre
- **Marginal cost**: marginal cost is usually best calculated
    - ★ per product; per outlet; per employee (if overtime or time off is given).

Notes:
1. Fixed and variable costs per customer can be calculated, but this is not normally very useful unless all customers are receiving the same regularity and level of service
2. Cost per function can be developed into a full cost–benefit analysis (see below). This is especially valuable when assessing the contribution of support functions and the effectiveness of primary (i.e. production and direct service) activities
3. Cost per customer is especially futile in assessing public services, health care and transport because the cost of providing given levels of service is more or less fixed. A hospital must be able to cope with maximum volumes of patients at all times and be able to provide the maximum range of services stipulated. Trains, buses and aeroplanes must stick to their schedules – one view is that, especially for trains and planes, there are no variable costs, they must follow their schedules, and that even to move empty on one route or between two destinations, is necessary, given that increased volumes of business are present further down the line.

The budget enables specific analysis and evaluation of the accuracy of the resource allocation process, and variances from it, and explanation of such variables. It provides an indefinable and quantifiable basis for corrective action – whether this is to do with profligacy in the use of the organisation's resources; or, at the other extreme, where a part of the organisation is being starved of resources essential for its effective operation.

At its core is the purpose for which the budget has been allocated. At the outset, this is usually based on an informed judgement of the likely level of resources required to do the job properly. Some measure of flexibility is also usual, and this should include the ability to restrict, as well as to expand or extend.

■ Budget components

A budget may identify the fixed costs associated with a department, division, function or activity in question. It is certain to identify the variable costs, relating these to given volumes of activities and providing sufficient resources to ensure that the desired volume and quality of activities can be carried out. It is likely also to identify the marginal costs incurred by getting involved in one-off special and additional activities. It is likely also to identify a relationship between resource utilisation and results.

There is likely to be some form of time constraint imposed. The work of accountancy often requires an annual statement of budget/resource utilisation even if the budget is not being operated to the same deadlines.

There is also certain to be some form of budget reporting required from a managerial and directional point of view to enable judgement on the effectiveness of this form of resource allocation and utilisation to be made (see Summary Box 10.3).

Two forms of budgeting should be noted.

- **Historic budgeting**: where the previous year's (or activities or projects) budget is taken as the starting point for the current allocation of resources. To be fully effective, it assumes that everything was correct and adequate in the previous period
- **Zero-based budgeting**: the opposite of historical budgeting and assumes that a fresh approach and consideration is required for current and future activities and periods. It requires a proper examination of the current and future activities, proposals and time periods, rather than reliance on historic figures as the starting point.

■ The budgeting process

The budgeting process should also include periods and elements of regular review, that allow more general and global evaluation of resource utilisation to take place.

SUMMARY BOX 10.3   Budgets: The Public Sector Example

This is an illustration of the shortcomings of the budgeting process and of what happens when budgets, rather than activities, become the driving force.

In the UK public services in the 1990s, at all levels, resources are allocated on an annual basis to support various activities. At the end of each 12-month period, the last budget is cancelled and a new one put in place. Any resources not used up over the period are lost and returned to whoever and wherever is responsible for providing them. There is therefore no incentive to conserve resources for a time when they might become useful in the future. There is every incentive to spend the resources, whether or not the activities are useful. There are two further effects.

1. **The budget cycle.** This works as follows. For the first 3 months of the cycle, activities are constrained while assessment of the resources in relation to activities is carried out. A steady-state is generated during the next 3 months based on this. Further restraints are applied during the third period of 3 months. The final quarter consists of a frantic attempt to use up everything not so far consumed because otherwise it will be lost.
2. **Closures and shutdowns.** Under this system these occur when the budget is used up due to pressures outside the organisation's control before the end of the cycle. Under this system it becomes 'more cost-effective' to have premises closed and staff and equipment idle, than to have them at work.

The very best that can be said for the system is that it can be seen where stated amounts of money have been spent. Apart from this, in virtually all circumstances, it is the wrong way to budget. It fails on all other counts, especially on that of devising budgets in support of real and desired levels of activities.

There are prescriptive, consultative and participative elements involved in the establishment of an effective budgeting process, and in its implementation. There should be not only a means of effective resource allocation, and wage monitoring, but also the means of ensuring that all those involved in its implementation understand fully the resource obligations and constraints under which they have to work. Even in areas of severe constraint – UK public and health services in the 1990s, for example – a better operational response will be generated if everyone concerned understands the nature and range of resource limitations.

Different methods of presentation of the budget and its elements will be used, depending upon the nature of those affected, their qualities and capabilities, and their responsibilities and obligations in the situation. Different figures will have different purposes and value to managers, accountants, operatives and professional staff, and due notice must be taken of this.

It is clear from this that part of the budgeting process must also constitute the means for the identification of conflicting areas – conflicting and divergent resource demands and pressures, for example – and their resolution and reconciliation. There is thus input from the budget to the task of both manager and accountant in understanding and explaining priorities, and to the professional and operative in the devising of, and prioritising of, their tasks and activities.

There is a requirement, finally, for an ability to reconcile control with flexibility, which in turn requires a measure of leeway for an otherwise productive initiative that needs a small extra resource in order for it to be fully successful, without at the same time destroying the credibility of the process. It follows from this that all budgets and budgeting systems must be specifically designed for the organisations, initiatives, operations, projects, staff and facilities in question; that while general principles and standpoints hold good, these must be applied as required to particular situations; and that therefore a universal set of precise rules is not appropriate.

■ Cost–benefit analysis

At its simplest, cost–benefit analysis is a quick and easy ready-reckoner method of establishing a basis on which a given initiative might be feasible or profitable (in whatever terms that may be measured), and of identifying those elements that require further, more detailed consideration before it is implemented. In this state, it simply requires correlating all the costs and charges that could possibly be incurred in such a venture, and setting them against all the values – benefits – that the completed item, project or product might bring.

Cost–benefit analysis also involves consideration of nine other areas:

- **Action choices** – the meaning of the costs and benefits of alternative courses of action in relation to each other.
- **Short, medium and long-termism** – the time periods over which costs are to be incurred; and over which results and benefits (and profits, in whatever terms they are to be measured) are to accrue; and the period over which they are required (either by the organisation, or its backers).
- **Values** – these are to be seen from both the economic and income generation point of view; and also in wider terms the impact on these to a greater or lesser extent Integral to cost–benefit analyses in terms of public policy are notions of the value of the quality and style of life; the value of recreational and optional facilities; the value of social and educational services; the value of general services to the population and its sectors.
- **Priorities** – related to values are the priorities ascribed by all business and public sectors to particular commercial and social undertakings; what is to be tackled first, and what the opportunity costs are in relation to those things lower on the list of priorities.
- **Initiatives** – and their wider impact; what they imply and the other activities that they lead to. An example of this in commercial terms is the concept of loss-leadership, whereby a commodity is offered at a price low enough to attract people to purchase it, in the expectation that they will buy other items from the outlet, thus generating increased activity and overall profit. It is also part of the process by which government regional aid is devised and delivered;

this activity is known as 'pump-priming' and is conducted on the basis that, by putting a certain resource block into an area, a measure of both commercial activity and public confidence will be generated.

- **Risk and uncertainty** – this is dealt with extensively elsewhere (see Chapter 5); it must be considered as part of the evaluation of costs and benefits overall.
- **Strategic aspects and overview** – by the consideration of products, projects, services and initiatives in this way, there are general benefits that accrue that in turn may offer a much wider approach to the actual matters in hand than was at first envisaged.
- **The relative valuation** – of different costs and benefits at the times, frequency and intervals at which they occur; and how to reconcile then when they occur at different points in time, or at least to understand the short-comings and imperfections of trying to do so.
- **The income-expenditure variable** – related in particular to values that accrue to those on different incomes; the relative importance to them of given or actual products and services; and the relative importance to them of different public services.

In this context, and using any specific numerative or quantitative methods necessary, a model for a detailed background, analysis and evaluation of both products and services, both public and private, can be drawn up. This also ensures that the widest possible constructs are placed on the given initiative, and that more nebulous concepts of social and intangible costs and benefits are assessed.

■ Conclusion

The main conclusion to be drawn is in recognising the difference between the work of professional accountants in producing figures, and that of managers in using, interpreting, analysing and evaluating them. In many ways, therefore, the work of the manager starts where that of the accountant finishes. Having said that, the manager must have the knowledge and understanding of how figures are produced, what they mean, what they state about the condition of the organisation as a whole and its particular activities.

It is necessary to recognise that, because of legal constraints, professional accountants tend to work in annual cycles. Managers should not be hide bound by this. Some managerial cycles are much shorter; others are much longer. In particular, the establishment of annual budgets needs extremely close attention – this is not to say that annual budgets are necessarily wrong, but they must be seen in an operational as well as financial context – and the operational drive must be paramount. And the archetype public sector approach indicated above is wrong and should be avoided.

It is also necessary to recognise the nature and content of investment. Investment is a long-term and continuing commitment on which is based the long-term continuity of the organisation. Profitability, profit maximisation, profit optimisation, are to be seen from this point of view. Long-term viability should never be sacrificed for immediate gain except where there is a crisis (and even then, if it is sacrificed, it is as likely to perpetuate the crisis as not). Long-term profitability means investing in all of those things that are to ensure that this does indeed happen – top quality staff, top quality products and services in the volumes and locations demanded by customers reinforced by high levels of quality, customer, confidence and reputation and, in turn, leading to repeat business. That is the context in which financial management is ultimately to be seen.

CHAPTER 11

Managerial performance

The purpose of this chapter is to bridge the gap between the acquisition of the skills, knowledge and aptitudes required of the manager and an understanding of the complexities and application problems in functional terms, so as to combine them together to generate effective and successful managerial performance in particular occupational configurations.

■ Evaluating managerial performance

Overall, the performance of managers will be judged on the success of the organisation in which they are practising, on the performance of their department, division or unit, and on the precise requirements of the managerial task within them. This, in turn, underlines the necessity of setting aims and objectives that serve as a benchmark for this measurement.

More specifically, for this purpose it is necessary to distinguish between those elements over which managers have control and those over which they have not. This enables the separation of actual performance from context and thus a much more valid evaluation can be conducted.

We have already established that the fundamentals of managerial success are the ability to communicate effectively, and to take effective decisions.

Within this broad setting managers bring their managerial qualities, and any other expertise – professional and technical skills – that they have together with their personal characteristics and attributes. The way in which they combine these is the key to the effectiveness and endurance of their performance. The elements contained in this section underline this. They also represent the ways in which they set their own standards, attitudes and values against which they expect members of their division, department, unit or function to measure up. They must also seek to engender a sense of pride on the part of all in belonging to the department concerned; a work ethic and team spirit that is productive, positive and harmonious as well as effective; and to generate a set of values for the department based on both moral and operational considerations to which all are able to aspire and which all are required to adopt. Finally, in operational terms, they must be able to identify, address and resolve problems and issues in ways that contribute to the effectiveness of their sphere of influence and direction, and that promote both behavioural harmony and business success.

Summary Box 11.1 shows how managers may model their problem-solving activities.

SUMMARY BOX 11.1   **A Problem-Solving Model**

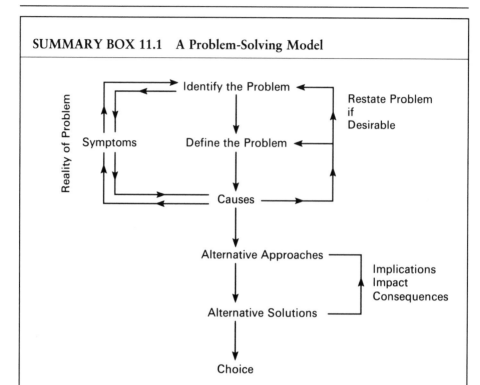

Purpose: to ensure that a rigorous and disciplined approach is recognised and understood as being necessary in all situations; or that it is adopted.
Points for consideration throughout the process must also include: the context and nature of it; when it is occuring; where it is occurring; why; its impact on the rest of the organisation, department or division; the extent to which it can be avoided; the extent to which it can be controlled; the consequences and opportunities of not tackling it (which is always a choice).

■ The department manager's role

This is a highly complex role. It requires both an understanding of the principle and practice outlined thus far and the qualities necessary to put them into effect in ways suitable to the function, operation and nature of the situation in which the manager has to work.

First of all the manager is the department's figurehead, the symbol or representation of it. As such, an image and identity is generated for the department in the whole organisation and with anyone else with whom they come into contact. Departmental managers represent it at meetings; they carry the hopes and aspirations of the staff at all times in all dealings with the rest of the organisation. It is the departmental manager's role and duty to fight the department's corner and to ensure that the interests of both department and staff are put forward and represented. In this function and according to the nature of the department in which they are working it will involve belonging to a wide range of professional associations, cluster groups and functional lobbies and to be an effective operator in all of these.

As well as representing the department, in such situations the manager is its spokesperson. This requires giving information both in the department and outside it.

Finally, the manager must have a decision-making capability that is suitable to the purposes of the department. Again, this involves drawing on capacities and capabilities and using them in ways suitable and effective in his or her own particular situation. In particular, part of this decision-making faculty must include an effective problem-solving method (see Summary Box 11.1). Again, the precise configuration of this will vary from situation to situation but essentially must address the basic process of identifying and defining the problem; assessing its causes; considering the variety of approaches that are possible and feasible in the situation; and deciding on appropriate courses of action.

Effectiveness in any managerial position requires both understanding and capability in these areas. If these are present there are additional benefits in terms of the creation of identity and pride among departmental staff. Finally, decision-making constitutes a critical part of the backcloth that is in any case necessary to managing effectively in any work situation.

■ Attitudes and values

Forming and nurturing the 'right' attitudes is an essential part of the managerial task, and any manager or supervisor must have a full grasp of this and be able to do it. If enthusiasm is infectious, so is negativity; it is very easy to have a demoralised workforce very quickly if certain matters are not picked up. In both multinational and public and health services this is manifest in the 'canteen culture', and has been partly responsible for engendering and perpetuating negative and undesirable attitudes. The overall purpose must be that everyone is happy, harmonious and productive on the organisation's terms and those of the manager and department in question. A clear and positive lead must therefore be given, and clear and positive attitudes engendered and formed.

Negativity, therefore, is to be avoided. Prevention of such attitudes is achieved through adequate and well-designed induction and orientation programmes so that every employee is given a positive set of both corporate and departmental values, a clear identity with the organisation and its purposes and confidence in the rest of the staff. Ultimately, people wish to feel good about the organisation and department for which they work.

Cure of bad attitudes is harder. In isolated or extreme cases, people who do not wish to work for the particular organisation will be dismissed. In large or complex organisations they may be moved somewhere with the view of reforming their attitudes and getting a positive response from them. Marks of envy must also be dealt with; office executives who wish for the sales persons' cars should be informed that, without the efforts of the sales force, there would be no office job. Similarly, as we have seen, professional and technical experts may feel a much stronger loyalty and commitment to their expertise than to the organisation which actually employs them to use it. In general departmental managers will address such matters either at the point at which they first assume their post, or when new members of staff come into the department. They thus set standards of attitude and conformity to which all are to aspire in the pursuit of the goals of the department. One manager's view of such 'ground rules' is given in Summary Box 11.2.

■ Setting goals

It is essential that all departments have clear aims and objectives and that all of those who work in them understand what they are and why it is the purpose of the particular part of the organisation to achieve them. It is invariably a feature of departments that malfunction, and staff who are demoralised or demotivated, that they are not clear about this purpose or of the requirements and directions of the part of the organisation for which they work.

The basis of setting objectives is: to give a clear statement of direction of the department and where it is going; to indicate proper courses of action; to indicate effective means of achieving these purposes; to provide a basis for eliminating that which makes no contribution to the stated objectives; to provide the basis on which plans and operational standards may be drawn up and to provide the establishment of meaningful standards of activity and control. They also provide the basis of accountability, that is the means of being able to check back when something has gone wrong and assess where mistakes were made.

Such aims and objectives should be written down to give high levels of credibility and to serve as visual reminders to all concerned. They should also be positive, and reflect both aspirations and achievement. They should be 'personal' and be drawn up in ways with which everyone in the department can identify. They must be challenging and motivating and reflect the theme of constant improvements and achievements wherever possible. They must be prioritised; they will not all be instantly achievable but will set a progression and configuration of the value of the work of the department. They must also be realistic without introducing measures of complacency or inefficiency.

Objectives must be measurable. This involves reducing any qualitative objectives wherever possible to a series of quantifiable measures. Where this

---

SUMMARY BOX 11.2   The Hard Line

'I believe in as hard a line as possible being taken by the management on the staff, a harder line being taken by the owners on the management and the hardest line being taken by the owners on themselves. Creating this environment is very difficult and so a strong approach must be taken in every area. The working atmosphere must be tightly controlled and be all-pervasive or it will not work. 'This seems contradictory to the 'kind' approach of Maslow or Rogers. I think it is necessary however if their dreams of what people are capable of are to be achieved.'

'The vital ground rules must be ascertained (no more, no less) and then they must be stuck to absolutely rigidly. The Japanese conformity approach should be made to look weak, when it comes to the ground rules. On the other hand, once these rules are adhered to, as much flexibility as possible should be allowed. In this way individuality is achieved through conformity. As long as the important things are taken care of, people can do what they want and express themselves freely through their jobs. I don't care how they do something as long as the end product is good. Mavericks who can work within the guidelines are welcome and a great source of creativity and inspiration.'

'It may be possible to summarise the ground rules into simply one thing. You must keep to your agreements. This encourages the development of the person's integrity, their ability to make choices and their sense of responsibility. It then gives us the opportunity to ask them to agree to what we really want, i.e., be at work at 8.00 a.m. If they agree to this, we will hold them to it, precisely. 2 minutes past 8.00 is not 8.00, and providing we can maintain enough front (and maintain this level of integrity ourselves) then we will pull them up on it.'

'Reasons are not relevant (e.g., the bus was late). It then becomes a matter of Personal Power, which we want to foster in the staff. It is possible to act as if you are responsible for everything that happens in your life whether it is true or not. Doing this eventually means it will end up as being true, in your reality. It is possible to look ahead and manipulate the environment. If you expect traffic then you can leave earlier. If they were paid £100,000 just for turning up on time, they would be there. This principle can be applied to everything we want, and although it may seem strange, in the long term it will benefit the individual as much as us.'

Source: David Scott, *Artisan Group Ltd Business Plan* (1993).

---

cannot be expressed it is often nevertheless possible to break an objective down into useful, specific and more controllable sub-objectives. For example, where phrases such as 'a matter of urgency' or 'as soon as possible' are used, these should be replaced with particular timescales or deadlines; the phrases quoted bind nobody to anything in reality and will be read as such by those involved.

Above all, goals, aims and objectives that are established must be clearly understood and valued by everybody. They must seek to combine the capacities and talents of everyone concerned in productive and effective effort and to reconcile the divergent and often disparate reasons that individuals within a department have for being there. Summary Boxes 11.3 and 11.4 give model goal and objective formulations.

SUMMARY BOX 11.3   Goals: Guidelines

In the interest of effective departmental performance, everybody should know the aims and targets to which they are working. If this is to be achieved a few simple rules must be followed.

1. Goals should be written down to give them greater credibility and to serve as a visual reminder
2. Goals should be positive and not negative, they should have precise aims and targets
3. Goals should be personal and related directly to the members of the department; they should reconcile the conflicting and divergent purposes that everyone has in being there
4. Goals should be specific, quantifiable and measurable
5. Goals should be challenging and motivate the department to work harder, more effectively and more productively than in the past – thus mirroring the concept of constant improvement
6. Goals should be realistic in these terms
7. Goals should be prioritised – they will not be instantly achievable
8. Goals should finally be understood and valued by everybody.

Source: Drucker (1954).

SUMMARY BOX 11.4   Objectives: an Example

A social service or welfare objective may be (and often is) written as follows:

- To promote the social well-being of groups with physical, mental and environmental handicaps, to enable them to function, as far as possible, as a community and within the community of their choice.

This is wrong. It is imprecise and unintelligible, and draws people away from it rather than to it. It is written in 'politician and bureaucrat-speak', and is thus full of opportunities for interpretation and again, will be read as such.

The approach is also wrong, therefore, unless what is actually desired is a clouding, rather than clarification of the issues raised. Assuming that clarity is what is wanted, the matter should be treated thus.

- In regard to each group of clients, the establishment of the following facilities and services . . . . by . . . . (a stated deadline).

Everyone is clear where they stand. Those working in the service have targets; the client group has expectations. There are included: performance achievement targets; measures of success or failure; and the basis of an operational review in relation to 'service' objectives.

■ Managing by walking about

Managing by walking about (MBWA) is an easy translation of one of the most important of managerial attributes: that of visibility. Furthermore, it also creates opportunities for productive harmony, early problem and issue resolution, and improvements in communications.

In behavioural and perceptual terms, the manager who is 'visible' is seen as approachable and acceptable. This will be reinforced by the manager who, while walking about, takes active steps to approach the staff members, get to know them, understand their jobs, their problems and their concerns. More specifically, MBWA underlines the essential qualities of trust, openness, honesty and integrity, as well as visibility. It fosters a communication forum and informal meeting point between manager and staff that demonstrates the manager's care and concern and enables small issues to be brought up and dealt with on the spot before they become big issues. Such behaviour is an essential cog in the process of continually appraising the performance of staff. It enables any misunderstandings on the part of anyone concerned to be raised and rectified quickly.

Such behaviour also fosters the quality of empathy in the manager or supervisor, and gives a full general knowledge and background to the hopes, fears and aspirations of those who work in the department. This is an essential prerequisite to the process of motivating the staff successfully.

Such behaviour reduces both the physical and behavioural barriers between the manager and staff. The closed door, large desk and executive trappings are not only physically imposing; they also present a perceptual barrier that the subordinate has first to overcome because they reinforce the differences in rank and status between the two: MBWA dilutes these.

Related to MBWA is the concept of leading by example; that is, the presence not absence of the manager when there is a crisis, and his or her energy and commitment in getting it resolved. Managers gain and improve their respect among their staff through their willingness to lead by example. Mark McCormack of IMG will go out with sales executives and consultants to demonstrate his own ability and preferred style in closing deals. Richard Branson of the Virgin Group regularly serves drinks and meals on his scheduled airline flights. Not only are they demonstrating their own willingness and capacity, they are also setting an example to and for their staff and keeping an active eye on the day-to-day operations of their organisation. It is also excellent general marketing among both staff and customers.

Mark McCormack of International Management Group (IMG) has developed his own variation of this – managing by ringing around (MBRA) or 'letting his fingers do the walking'. He employs this where it is impossible or otherwise overwhelmingly time-consuming for him to actually get to see the department or office in question; or where he judges a telephone call to be a more productive and sensible approach in the circumstances. The main principle remains, however – he always does one or the other.

MBWA is an essential tool for the manager and one that must be in constant use. If it is not, the staff will develop their own patterns and ways of working, their own means of problem and issue resolution, and control will pass out of the hands and office of the manager. In more sophisticated or complex organisations where there is a global, off-site, or other 'arm's length' supervision or direction mode, there should be an individual designated to act in the manager's stead, maintaining the visible face of the organisation and its management, taking the day-to-day decisions and resolving minor and operational issues before they become major crises.

■ Delegation

An easy to understand definition of delegation is 'getting work done through others'. This is the concept of handing over to a subordinate some part of the job that the manager is expected to carry out. Many managers are incapable of passing on work for others to perform. Common reasons for this are undue concern for supposed loss of prestige, fear of being superseded, personal interest in doing the job and lack of confidence in subordinates.

Managers may also seek to hang on to the tasks that they personally prefer to carry out in spite of the fact that they could and should be placed elsewhere in the department. These are excuses why not to delegate. Yet the only way by which managers can hope to concentrate effectively on their own priorities is by unloading as much of the remaining work as possible on to members of their staff. It is also an essential part of the processes of developing both the capabilities and capacities of the department and of the staff who work in it. Summary Box 11.5 gives Urwick's model for the manager's administrative/ delegatory function.

To build a full picture of the nature and extent of the process of delegation it is necessary to look briefly at some of the principles of delegation, their place in organisational structure and their impact on a manager's span of control (see Summary Box 11.5).

■ Attributes of the job and of subordinates

Effective delegation requires that managers know their strengths, weaknesses and capacities; and that they have a full understanding of the nature of the job; and what must be achieved – that is, its key results.

The manager must know also the level of knowledge and skill and the attributes and capacities of subordinates to be able to calculate what can be effectively and successfully delegated and what needs to be retained. The manager must thus know and understand the jobs of all subordinates; if not a thorough knowledge, then at the very least the key features of the job should be

SUMMARY BOX 11.5   The Elements of Administration

1. The principle of the objective – the overall purpose or objective for which the organisation has been constituted
2. The principle of group and functional specialisation
3. The principle of coordination and organisation
4. The principle of authority vested in one individual in the group; and reporting in a linear fashion within the organisation as a whole
5. The principle of responsibility by which all those in authority accept accountability for those working for them
6. The principle of definition of jobs, relationships, authorities and responsibilities
7. The principle of correspondence by which authority, responsibility and accountability are balanced
8. Span of control – ideally limited to no more than six persons per manager – see also Summary Box 11.7
9. The principle of balance is that of the structures, functions, systems and operations of the organisation
10. The principle of continuity – that is, the concept of the organisation's permanence.

Source: Urwick (1952).

known. The manager must also be able to understand key features of any new tasks quickly.

The method of delegation to adopt depends upon the workload. If this is heavy, it is necessary to use accepted channels to get to the core quickly. If the work situation permits, new channels can be developed. It is necessary next to consider the static and dynamic elements of this. The static elements are: forecasting, planning and organising. The dynamic elements are: motivation, coordination and control.

If managers are to fulfil these functions and discharge their main responsibilities they cannot also do the work; this constitutes the fundamental reason why work must be delegated. An established guideline is to delegate work down through the organisation, the staff concerned doing the utmost of which they are capable, usually resulting in an increase in morale through enhanced job satisfaction quite apart from any operational benefits. Delegation also allows the manager time to plan, coordinate and control by making more effective use of subordinates. They, in turn, will develop skills and potential and so assist in the improvement of their own prospects by greater involvement in the work of the organisation; via the process implicit in this of job enrichment, enlargement, progress and creativity, the level of job satisfaction of all subordinates would normally be expected to improve.

The key to delegation is the reconciliation of trust and control – that is, the trust that the subordinate feels the manager has in him; and the control that the manager has over the work of the subordinate. If the manager increases control, the amount of trust perceived by the subordinate decreases. If the manager increases trust in the subordinate and gives more responsibility then a degree of the manager's control must also be released.

Finally, whatever task is delegated, responsibility remains with the manager at all times. Responsibility is not delegated. To attempt to do so simply constitutes abdication of responsibility and will be reflected in the perceptions of employees, and also the reality when things do go wrong that the managers will look for scapegoats to blame rather than accepting what should remain their part in the affair.

■ Wait a minute

All managers should have a mechanism in some shape or form that constitutes a 'wait a minute' facility. This will be present in the formulation of policy or direction; the taking of decisions; and in the implementation of strategy. At departmental and other junior levels the purpose is to ensure that no inconvenient operational precedent is being set by taking a particular line to resolve what may seem a simple and one-off problem. 'Wait a minute' is not an abdication of decision-making ability or of decision-making itself. It need not take a 'minute'. It is simply to ensure that what is to be done has been questioned from every conceivable angle. It is more generally part of the monitoring, review, early and late warning systems that should be integral to all aspects of the manager's task. The presence of a 'wait a minute' facility does not of itself ensure that the right decision is taken, but it does at least afford a moment's further consideration. If this is all that is necessary to confirm that what is being done is truly for the good of the organisation and the fair and equitable treatment of the staff concerned, it is a moment well spent. Summary Box 11.6 considers three situations where 'Wait a minute' could usefully be used.

■ Control

All managers must have control mechanisms suitable to the department or unit concerned; and relating to the staff, resources and operations that are carried out within in it. This must apply even where the work in hand is of a professional, administrative, technical or qualitative nature. The overall function of control involves setting desired standards and measuring actual performance against them; from this, analyses of differences between the two will be made and remedial action will be taken where necessary (see Summary Box 11.7). It follows from this that objectives must be fully understood by all concerned, so that involvement in the control of the work necessary and any remedial action that becomes apparent is adopted and understood by all concerned.

SUMMARY BOX 11.6   Wait a Minute

- Nike, the sportswear corporation, tried to devise a global travel policy for their staff. In particular the focus was on who should travel first class, business class or economy class on the world's airlines. Should this be based on – the distance travelled; the part of the world to which the executive was travelling; the length of the journey; or the volume or value of business to be conducted?
- The Ceramics Industry Training Board summoned a meeting of junior field executives to its head office in Harrow, North West London. The junior executives were from all over the UK and overnight hotel accommodation was arranged for them.

  The meeting was unproductive and wasteful because two executives based in London were unable to attend. Because they lived in London no accommodation was found for them. On the day in question they were unable to travel because of a terrorist bomb. They also felt discriminated against, and slighted, by accident of their location in London.
- John Stevens, an official with an international bank at their London office, asked to be able to take two years' annual leave back-to-back (a total of two months) to visit friends and relatives in Australia. His request was granted.

  Mary Phelps, an official in an equivalent position and with longer service at the same bank put in the same request for the back-to-back leave to visit friends and relatives at Ullapool in Scotland. She underlined the request by stating that it would take longer for her to get to her destination than for Stevens to get to his.

SUMMARY BOX 11.7   Spans of Control

The span of control denotes the number of people who report directly to a particular manager or supervisor. The numbers vary greatly, influenced by: the nature and complexity of the work; the type of employees in question; the capacities of the manager or supervisor in question; the technology used in the particular section; the environment in which the work is being carried out (especially if this is dangerous or hazardous); and wider considerations of organisation structure and culture – in particular, where the archetype 'lean-form flat structure' is present spans will be large; while rigid hierarchies have small spans at each level. The balance that is to be struck is that which reconciles the need to manage, supervise, direct and control the operations or work in question with the other matters raised above. Each organisation (and very often this applies to individual departments) will establish their own rationale; each manager will translate this into that which is appropriate to their own situation. They may additionally appoint deputies, charge hands or other supervisors in situations where the work is complex or the total group large; or where there is a need or desire to generate a closer pattern of supervision. Finally, such posts may also be created as part of an organisation development programme or project.

The methods and mechanisms to be used will therefore be department or task specific; and linked to and in harmony with the overall methods adopted by the organisation. They must reconcile the necessity to produce clear results with the need to be flexible and objective in operation and economical and simple. Presentation of control information in ways that everyone can understand and have regard to is essential. It is necessary not only to indicate differences and deviations from required performance but also to provide the means of establishing the causes of these – where the failures are occurring, why this is so and what to do about them. Within this context managers will draw up and use their own control methods. These will include:

- **Forecasts**, based on the resources – staff, financial and technological – available; and in relation to the outputs that the organisation requires
- **Budgets**, for all the activities within the manager's sphere, covering such matters as staff, production, outputs, operational costs, administration, other overheads, cash and daily expenditure and possibly also an overall department reconciliation of these matters
- **Management information systems**, including the gathering and promulgation of information within the department and the reconciliation of this with desired levels of performance; these also provide a vehicle for the manager's contribution to the information systems and requirements of the organisation
- **Reporting systems**, designed to highlight any deviations and problems immediately, and to identify means by which such situations may be remedied; in any case, they should be able to provide information that can be used on an organisational basis for future planning and direction setting
- **Feedback**: part of the control process is the communication process which constitutes keeping the departments informed of its progress on a continuous basis; there is a control function inherent in the nature and content of feedback that is given; part of this may also be achieved through any performance appraisal scheme that is in place
- **Conflict**: part of the purpose of having control methods and procedures in place must be to ensure that conflicts or disputes between members of staff are resolved as quickly and effectively as possible
- **Control methods and means**: these should be integrated into the general review monitoring and process assessment that should be in place in all departments; to be fully effective they require full understanding on the part of all concerned – the manager, the staff and those other departments and units with whom they interact; they should also mirror the aims and objectives of the departments if they are to be fully effective.

Summary Box 11.8 lists the number of problems a manager may have to field even when events are outside his or her control.

■ Time

In simple terms, time at the workplace may be divided into productive time; non-productive or stoppage or downtime; maintenance time; and wasted time. It is necessary to recognise the prevalence of each element in any working

---

SUMMARY BOX 11.8   An Airline Manager Working in the Middle East

This manager regularly fields questions from powerful and influential people in his region. Problems handled have included:

- Why the daughter of a diplomat had to wait 20 minutes for an orange juice on her flight back to London.
- Why packages and parcels carried by a worldwide courier organisation had to go through security screening and not straight on to the airplane.
- Why it took two hours for a particular cargo to be cleared from the airport by customs.
- Why Europeans have to go through the full immigration procedure upon arrival in countries of the Middle East.

The point that each of these items has in common is that they are all outside the manager's control. They are nevertheless raised by customers and clients of his/her firm and he/she must therefore either deal with them or else find someone else to provide a suitable and adequate answer.

---

situation; what the composition of each element is; and from that to structure the work in order to maximise its usage of the time available (see Box 11.9). This may be developed a stage further into the operational and managerial structure that we have already noted – steady-state or day-to-day activities; crisis and emergency management; forward planning and forecasting; and innovation, research and development activities; and the balance of time to be spent on each. This is useful both as a vehicle for proposing an operational outline and as a method of measuring how the time resource is actually to be used and the effectiveness of it. From this, priority, crisis, wastage, overload and underload can be identified; and a time–resource–energy dimension put on each. The purpose is to ensure that what happens in reality accords with what managers think happens. Other dimensions and variables will also be included. These include the complexity and difficulty of the task in hand, the importance of it, the urgency of it, and the frequency of it. The value of what is done, whether derived or implicit, will also have a time configuration to it. What is therefore required is an attitude of continued questioning of time usage based on the premise that anything and everything can always be improved and made more efficient and effective.

From a managerial standpoint, therefore, time is a critical resource and impinges on all aspects of the managerial task; and above all, it is limited. It therefore requires both ordering and direction, the same as any other resource. Other general factors that have to be considered in this wider configuration are: the nature of the work; the personality of the job holder; the support systems available in order to ensure efficiency and effectiveness; the style of management adopted; the demands made by the staff on the manager's time; the management

---

SUMMARY BOX 11.9   Waste of Managerial Time

A report published jointly by the UK Industrial Society and BBC on 1 March 1993 drew as its main conclusions the following:

Managers spend up to 20% of their time or the equivalent of one whole day per five day working week in meetings. Furthermore, they spend up to a third of their working time on paperwork, routine and administration. The main time wasters identified were interruptions from colleagues, handling telephone calls that a junior or subordinate should have fielded, and dealing with untargeted bureaucracy and memoranda. The main operational cause of hold-ups was found to be computer problems and system failures.

The stark conclusion to be drawn from this is that managers represent an overpaid niche of the workforce, in relation to the quality of their output.

Operations, contributions and key results require better targeting, and better definition; and an understanding on the part of the organisations and their top executives of what the outputs required of their subordinates are and how these are to be achieved.

---

style of the superior and the way in which that impinges on the manager's time; the influences of the manager's colleagues and ways in which they impinge on the manager's time; the capabilities and capacities of those working in the department; and the capabilities and capacities of those in key relationships with the manager, especially any secretarial or personal assistant function that is present.

In order to maximise or optimise time usage, certain steps can be taken. The first is for the manager to be aware of the time issue. Part of the process that arises from this is to set priorities for the department; to set a pattern of delegation of tasks and activities; to produce suitable and effective work schedules; and to continuously assess the work in hand against time constraints as well as against constraints placed by other resource implications. Next the manager should identify those things that waste time. These may consist of long, unnecessary or habitual meetings or those which are procedural rather than executive in content; interruptions and the nature of these in his or her work; idle conversations; unnecessary bureaucracy, reporting systems and record keeping; the balance of travelling time against effective business conducted; and task allocations – especially the allocation of the easy tasks which should be conducted on a basis that leaves those of high capacity and quality to carry out key, critical or other activities that match their capabilities, not filling up their work schedules with items that are well within them.

The manager should also be aware of creative approaches to time management in terms of machine, equipment and plant usage; working patterns and shift arrangements; personal planning; the setting and maintenance of deadlines;

and giving clarity of purpose to meetings. There are opportunity costs of time usage and especially time wastage that can never be made up. All managers and their departments should have a system of time measurement that is suitable to its purpose; and that encourages efficiency and effectiveness of performance in regard to this resource.

■ Interpersonal skills and assertiveness

Everyone has interpersonal skills. For managers, these additionally constitute a tool that is essential to them in the pursuit of their daily occupation. They are instrumental in creating and reinforcing the management style adopted. They are part of the process of MBWA and the visibility that goes with this. They reinforce messages of honesty, openness and trust. They have implications for general levels and states of communication within the department; and for particular issues concerned with the handling of meetings and briefings within it (see Summary Box 11.10), the wider handling of public presentations, and the ways in which these in turn reflect on the department. The first and most important thing that a manager's use and application of his interpersonal skills will represent is the degree of trust and confidence in the staff and the basis on which they are to be treated. Overall it sets the tone and tenor for the whole department and its way of working. Managers will therefore apply their interpersonal skills in the following ways. They will never criticise members of staff either in public or on a personal basis when the problem is related to work. If there is a personal issue that requires managerial activity and concern this will be conducted in private and remain a matter between the manager and the individual. If it is necessary to criticise somebody's work performance, then it must be done in a clear and straightforward way with the emphasis upon remedy rather than apportioning blame. Effective criticism is always constructive; the end result must be to reinforce the importance of the individual as a member of the department. If it is possible such criticism should be reinforced by finding areas of work to be praised at the same time. In this way also, the work remains at the centre of the concern.

It follows from this that praise should be extended where it is due. It is a powerful form of recognition and a universal motivator. Every manager should avoid only dealing with staff when there are negative concerns. Praise makes the individual concerned feel identity, respected and important. It should be handed out whenever and wherever due, and it should be conducted in public.

The other manifestation of the manager's interpersonal skills is that of the particular pride and enthusiasm for the job, the work and the department. It is impossible that people working in the department will have any of these qualities if the manager does not have them. The best managers inspire and generate pride and enthusiasm by the ways in which they behave in relation to the department's work and the people carrying it out. It is the manager's job to

---

SUMMARY BOX 11.10   The Chair: Leading Meetings, Discussions and Briefings

---

- **Before the meeting**: the chair: establishes that a meeting is the best and most effective format for covering the matters in hand, and a suitable and effective agenda; sets the room, facilities and environment out in a way suitable for this matter; pre-briefs all those attending so that they know: what the nature of the meeting is; what their function in it is; what they are supposed to get from it; and the extent of their potential effect on the outcome of any resulting discussions. Finally, the chair will establish an effective order of business to be conducted and an application of general communication processes in ways suitable to the matter in hand.

- **During the meeting**: the chair has to strike a balance between allowing people's contributions and progressing the agenda in a suitable and effective way. If there are time constraints these should be made clear at the outset. Under such constraints contributions should also be limited so that all concerned get the opportunity to speak and to put their point of view forward. The correct atmosphere must be generated and maintained.

    The chair must also balance making sure that the matter in hand is kept to with allowing genuine opportunities for discussion and also the exploration of possibilities not previously thought of.

    The chair must know when to allow the discussion to continue and when to curtail it. Overall this aim must be to keep to the purpose and to move matters forward.

    A decision-making process should be published beforehand so that if there are decisions to be taken persons in attendance know what these are and how this is to be achieved (for example, through vote, through consensus, through the chair). Finally, nobody should be in any doubt as to the outcome of the meeting.

- **After the meeting**: it is invariably necessary for some form of follow-up to be effected. This normally takes the form of circulating a note, minutes or summary of what went on together with the main conclusions arrived at and decisions taken; and an indication of what is to happen next.

---

instil this feeling, and to promote this attitude among the staff and the interpersonal relationship with the staff is instrumental in this.

Above all, work should be a matter of enthusiasm; and a matter of enjoyment as well as fulfilment. Again, the interpersonal skills of the manager are instrumental in creating this background.

Other qualities of leadership that become apparent through the use of interpersonal skills are:- the courage of the manager concerned; job knowledge; self-control and self-discipline; sense of fairness and equity; standards of personal conduct and behaviour that reflect the standards required in the department; and a sense of humour. It is also a reflection of the interpersonal qualities of the manager that ensures that the correct and appropriate standards of dress, language and manners are established. This is particularly important in departments and units where dealings with the public are an everyday feature.

The purpose overall must be to establish an adult and assertive means of interaction within the department (see Summary Box 11.11). The prime purpose of the manager's interpersonal skills and approach in the situation is the promotion of effective work. These factors are an essential and integral part of this promotion; and without it actual standards will always fall short of the ideal.

SUMMARY BOX 11.11   Assertiveness

The following is an itemised configuration and summary of the manifestations of assertive behaviour and language.

- **Language**   Assertive language is clear and simple. It is easy to understand on the part of the hearer or receiver. The words used are unambiguous and straightforward. Requests and demands are made in a clear and precise manner, and with sound reasons.

  Weasel words, political phraseology, ambiguity, and 'get-outs' are never used.

- **Delivery**   Assertive delivery is in a clear and steady tone of voice. The emphasis of the delivery is on important and crucial words and phrases. The voice projection that is used is always even, and neither too loud nor too soft.

  Assertive delivery does not involve shouting, threatening, or abuse, at any time or under any circumstances; nor does it resort to simpering or whining.

- **Face and Eyes** The head is held up. There is plenty of eye contact, and a steadiness of gaze. The delivery is reinforced with positive movements that relate to what is being said (e.g. smiles, laughter, nodding; or a straight face where something has gone wrong).

- **Other Non Verbal Aspects** The body is upright (whether standing or sitting). Arms and hands are 'open' (in order to encourage a positive response or transaction).

  There is no fidgeting or shuffling, nor are there threatening gestures or table thumping; or other outward displays of temper.

- **Situational Factors** Assertive delivery is based on an inherent confidence, belief and knowledge of the situation, and the work that is done. Openness, clarity, credibility, and personal and professional confidence, all spring from this.

  Any clarity of purpose or delivery will inevitably be spoilt through having to operate from a weak position, or one which is not fully known or understood. In such cases, important issues are either clouded or avoided altogether. In extreme cases the people involved often interact aggressively or angrily in order to try to compensate for this basic lack of soundness, clarity or understanding.

This extends to giving negative messages; just because the message is negative, there is no reason for this to have any lasting effect upon the motivation and morale either of the staff member who is to receive the negative message or of the department at large. If it is necessary to deny someone a request, this should always be done quickly; the reason for the negative response should be made clear and should be the truth. The manager should never hide behind phrases like 'it's not company policy'. The reason given for the negative response should always be operational; and it should be clearly and unequivocally communicated.

The end result of all this is that the staff and manager each know where they stand in relation to each other; and that the interpersonal skills applied and relationship generated support this. It provides the basis for effective work transactions and ensures that disputes and misunderstandings are kept to a minimum. It also ensures that when these do occur they can be quickly and effectively remedied without lasting effect and, above all, negative consequences for the department as a whole.

■ Discipline and grievance

All managers handle matters concerning discipline and grievance at some stage or other. All discipline and grievance matters are covered also by employment law (see Appendix); and all organisations are required and expected to have procedures in place covering each that at least match the minimum standards recommended or set down by the law and codes of practice.

■ Discipline

Discipline is concerned with setting standards of performance, attitude and behaviour at the workplace in the interests of ensuring that everyone knows what is expected of them and that they conform to them. If the approach taken is both positive and understood by all concerned it follows that such problems are kept to a minimum. Any organisation is allowed and expected to set its own standards, and these will be reflected both in the nature of the work itself and also in regard to the expectation of customers (see Summary Box 11.12).

When problems do occur there are two facilities which managers should adopt in the approach to them. First is the manager's own intercession in the problem; the purpose of this must be to get the individual concerned back performing or behaving adequately and effectively. Normally, this will be achieved by having a quiet word with the individual, pointing out to him where his behaviour or activity is falling short of the required standard, ensuring that he knows what the required standard is and concluding the discussion with an agreement that this is now the way in which matters will be conducted.

SUMMARY BOX 11.12   Office Staff Practices, 1852

1. *Godliness, Cleanliness* and *Punctuality* are the necessities of a good business.
2. This firm has reduced the hours of work, and the Clerical Staff will now only have to be present between the hours of 7 a.m. and 6 p.m. on weekdays.
3. Daily prayers will be held each morning in the Main Office. The Clerical Staff will be present.
4. Clothing must be of a sober nature. The Clerical Staff will not disport themselves in raiment of bright colours, not will they wear hose, unless in good repair.
5. Overshoes and top-coats may not be worn in the office, but neck scarves and headwear may be worn in inclement weather.
6. A stove is provided for the benefit of the Clerical Staff.
7. No member of the Clerical Staff may leave the room without permission from Mr Rogers. The calls of nature are permitted and Clerical Staff may use the garden below the second gate. The area must be kept in good order.
8. No talking is allowed during business hours.
9. The craving of tobacco, wines or spirits is a human weakness and, as such, is forbidden to all members of the Clerical Staff.
10. Now that the hours of business have been drastically reduced, the partaking of food is allowed between 11.30 a.m. and noon, but work will not, on any account, cease.
11. Members of the Clerical Staff will provide their own pens. A new sharpener is available, on application to Mr Rogers.
12. Mr Rogers will nominate a Senior Clerk to be responsible for the cleanliness of the Main Office and the Private Office, and all Boys and Juniors will report to him 40 minutes before Prayers, and will remain after closing hours for similar work. Brushes, Brooms, Scrubbers and Soap are provided by the owners.
13. The New Increased Weekly Wages are hereunder detailed:

Junior Boys (to 11 years)	1/4d
Boys (to 14 years)	2/1d
Juniors	4/8d
Junior Clerks	8/7d
Clerks	10/9d
Senior Clerks (after 15 years with owners)	21/-d

The owners recognize the generosity of the new Labour Laws but will expect a great rise in output of work to compensate for these near Utopian conditions.

There will be occasions when this fails to work, and the procedures referred to above will therefore be invoked. The purpose of these procedures should always be to remove the cause of the problem. Stages in the procedure underline the standards required of the staff; and any and every warning issued by the manager or the organisation in the pursuit of a resolution of the problems will detail, in clear tones, the nature of it, steps taken to try and resolve it and the levels of performance now expected of the individual. These warnings will either be orally issued, or in writing; in either case a record will be kept by the manager concerned – as well as a procedural necessity it is also a legal requirement.

There are rules to be followed. Failure to follow these rules is a breach of the law and may be cited at industrial tribunal if the matter is serious and gets that far (see Appendix). The individual is allowed representation at a disciplinary hearing and also the right of appeal. The individual concerned must also be allowed to put his case and have it heard. Any finding against the individual must be communicated to him. This finding must reflect the nature of the offence and not be personally punitive.

All organisations designate a series of offences which, for whatever reason, constitute matters of serious or gross misconduct and for which suspension from work or dismissal or summary dismissal may be applied. It is normally accepted that such offences constitute breaches of the law – vandalism, violence, theft and fraud. However, in certain cases this may be extended to standards of behaviour on the part of the particular organisation – for example, failure to wear safety clothing on a building site may constitute a sufficient reason for dismissal, whereas this would not apply in other situations. Conversely, swearing at the place of work may constitute sufficient reason for dismissal for an individual working in a high-fashion boutique, whereas on a building site this would almost certainly not be the case.

When managers are called into action on this front, they need to ensure that they have their own strategy and purpose worked out for dealing with it effectively and speedily. The standpoint will always consist in the first place of establishing that the individual knows that there is a problem, and what the nature of that problem is; and then for asking the individual for his view and explanation of it. What the manager has then to achieve will have regard to the general needs of the department, the particular need to maintain standards, the particular need to sort out any misunderstanding if this is simply the case, and any wider needs of the situation. Only when the full facts of the case have been established will the manager make a judgement on it.

Above all, such a judgement will be reformative wherever possible, and punitive only as the last resort. Dismissal will be conducted only where this is the most suitable punishment for the offence (as in the case of breach of the law as detailed above), or where it is necessary for the wider maintaining of departmental standards, or where all other means have been tried and failed and where not to do would set a bad precedent. It is finally incumbent upon the manager to maintain records of all disciplinary measures conducted against staff members. Apart from the legal requirements it enables the manager to follow up cases and to ensure that any agreed new standards of behaviour and performance are being adhered to and maintained.

■ Grievances

As with discipline, the emphasis must be on resolving issues rather than institutionalising them and doing this quickly and effectively. In particular, if the individual concerned feels that insufficient attention is being paid to his case, he will feel slighted – he, after all, felt that the case was important enough to bring up and make an issue of in the first place.

Managers need to know again the scale of their own flexibility to act. They must also have regard to the wider situation – what implications are to be derived from resolving an issue in a particular way (or failing to resolve it).

The purpose again will be, within these constraints, the resolution of the matter in ways satisfactory to all concerned. Having said that, the overriding concern must be for the organisation or department; if it is necessary to disappoint a member of staff in this interest, this should be clearly communicated, together with the reasons for it.

Again, there are procedures to be followed and standards required by law; and, again, the overwhelming concern must be for justice to be seen to be done. If the individual does not like or does not agree with the manager's finding he should always be afforded the opportunity to appeal or to refer it to a higher level of authority in the organisation.

With both discipline and grievance the manager's standpoint must be to promote and set standards that keep all such activities to a minimum and to limit them as far as possible to cases concerning a genuine misunderstanding. Cases should be dealt with quickly and fairly, and should not be allowed to fester and rankle. Managers must, finally, be aware of the extent of their authority and freedom to act; and to understand when and where to seek expert assistance, for example in relation to those matters where there is a direct legal implication.

■ Negotiating

It follows from the consideration of interpersonal skills, discipline and grievance that managers will, from time to time, be faced with situations that require them to negotiate. Whether negotiations are simple and direct or long, complex and protracted, such activities must always be effective. Whenever managers enter into any form of negotiation, therefore, they must have their own aims and objectives and understand, above all, what their preferred outcomes are. In all such situations the best possible outcome is that which leaves everyone happy 'the win–win situation'. If the manager is to be effective in this area there are some basic ground rules.

First, managers should always pre-prepare their own case, establishing what they are seeking, when, where, how and why; must have regard to any constraints within which they have to act; and also to any opportunities afforded by a wider consideration of the matter in hand. Next, they must have an understanding (if not sympathy) with the position of the other person and of what they want, when, where, how and why, and of the merits and demerits of their particular case. Managers must again understand the extent of their authority in the particular situation. If they promise something they must be able to deliver it. If there is a ritualised position; or if there is a potentially explosive or extreme situation the manager must be able to deal with this, defusing any anger or bad feeling at least at the point of decision and implementation if not before. The creation of an effective environment for such negotiations is extremely important and must be conducive to getting the job done as required. This, therefore includes consideration of the behavioural, physical, psychological and role aspects of the situation; it will also have regard to any precedent set in the past and to the implications of setting such precedents in the implementation of whatever is to be agreed in the present. Finally, it is necessary to be aware of the continuing need to work effectively and harmoniously; even where the matter in hand is a serious dispute, this should not hide or obscure the basic requirement for the eventual promotion of an harmonious working environment.

There are particular skills and knowledge required in the negotiator (or negotiating team). These are to do with a strategic, tactical and situational awareness; empathy; judgement; situational understanding; and the ability to apply social and interpersonal skills in the right mix and in the right ways according to the nature of the situation.

Managers can and should be trained in the art, skills and processes of negotiating; as stated at the outset of this section it is an essential, integral and universal part of the job. All managers should therefore be competent at it and be able to handle such matters and issues in a satisfactory way.

■ Performance assessment

It is implicit in much of the above that the manager must be able to assess and judge the levels and quality of performance in his department and to measure it against the required standards, taking remedial action where necessary. This will be at the following levels. If there is a shortfall at departmental level he may need to conduct a range of activities to find out why this is so and to make his judgements from this. Such activities may consist of, for example, a walk-through of the processes and procedures of the organisation or department; an observation or sampling of departmental activities, harmony and cooperation; or the assessment and identification and remedying of blockages, again either in processes, procedures or the operations themselves.

At team level it may be necessary to institute a process of examination of the workings of the team in question to assess where performance is falling down, why this should be so and what is causing it. From this, a more accurate compartmentalisation and definition of this under one or more of the headings of attitude, conflict, processes, procedures, communication, decision-making and inter-relations should be possible. Furthermore, by undertaking such an approach the problem area may become apparent and remedy applied to it in the interests of reforming and recreating a positive and productive team.

At individual level a two-fold approach is necessary. One is to ensure that those in the department receive organisational feedback on the nature of their work, praise for good performance and quick and effective remedy for any shortfall. The organisation's formal appraisal methods may in any case require this and may use these methods as the means of allocating training, development, secondment, the next move and pay rises. In all these cases it will be important to the members of staff that such appraisal is carried out in accordance with expectations and generally effectively.

The other part of the approach to the individual here concerns the general monitoring of the work of the department by the manager concerned. Performance will actually be continuously assessed as part of the manager's 'leadership' role in the department. Effectively conducted, the manager will know the state of the department and the performance of it on a current and continuing basis. Issues will be remedied before they become problems, and problems before they become crises.

The final part of this activity is a continuous measure of performance against targets and objectives, the criteria against which the success or otherwise of his department will be assessed. Part of this requirement, therefore, is to see the department in this way and to be able to measure and judge its performance along these lines also.

■ Health and safety

We have already established the overall nature of responsibilities for health and safety (see Chapter 8). However, ultimately, the manager is responsible for all matters concerning health and safety within the department, and to ensure that everyone else in it understands their own place in this regard, and that they work and behave in ways that are safe and healthy. Managers have a variety of means and instruments at their disposal to ensure that this is achieved.

They are, in any case, responsible for all aspects of staff induction, training and attitude formation and health and safety must be an integral part of this. The required attitudes and standards are clearly indicated at this stage; in addition, the new member of staff is taught the emergency procedures and practices, and the importance of the use and wearing of any safety and protective clothing that may be necessary in the work. Emergency procedures and practices are to be learned and assimilated by all staff so that in the event of such an occurrence, effective and quick action can be taken both to remove people from the danger and in regard to the danger itself.

Safe behaviour patterns must also be devised. These support the required attitudes and also give effect to the procedures; above all, they ensure that any potential hazard in any part of the manager's domain is dealt with by whoever happens to be nearest to it.

Reporting of accidents is a legal requirement in the UK and also much of Western Europe and elsewhere. The purpose of doing this from the manager's point of view must be to provide information about work areas where accidents are occurring which can be assessed and analysed, and to take remedial steps from this, whether operational, organisational, developmental, or in regard to attitudes and behaviour.

In any department there must be an emphasis on prevention rather than cure that ensures that the actual levels of accidents is kept to a minimum. It is impossible to eliminate accidents altogether; however, by addressing work patterns and methods, attitudes and behaviour and by ensuring that adequate procedures exist and that everyone knows them, they can be kept to a minimum.

Managers will take general steps to ensure that the profile of health and safety in the department is suitable. This is done through the general promotion of safety, its importance in the total scheme of things and also matters relating to health and safety and emergency training and practices. It is also essential to ensure that standards once set do not fall and that accidents start to occur due to increased complacency or sloppiness in the day-to-day operation and departmental management. It should, moreover, be noted that there is a direct relationship between accident levels and staff morale: each feeds off the other and as accidents increase, so does morale decline.

■ Sickness

The manager will monitor the levels of sickness and absenteeism in the department and look to preventing this from arising. Much can be done in this regard by ensuring basic standards of comfort for staff, free from draught and dampness, and adequately heated and lit; and by ensuring that work stations and work methods are constructed in ways that do not give rise to repetitive strain injuries (RSI) of any sort. Training in specifics such as lifting will be given to ensure that back and arm strains do not occur. Those who operate VDUs will have their work structured with adequate breaks in order to prevent headaches and eye strain from occurring. Again, high levels of sickness absenteeism are generally indicative of low levels of morale and motivation among the members of departments.

Managers must be aware of all this and understand it. They must make interventions where necessary, conducting their own enquiries into accidents, sickness and absenteeism with the object of taking remedial action and the re-establishment of standards where necessary. Above, all if there is a bad accident or emergency in the department a full enquiry should be held and lessons learned so that it may be prevented from happening again.

■ *Realpolitik*

This is the art of survival in the organisation in which the manager is working (see Summary Box 11.13). It requires knowledge and understanding of the nature of the particular 'jungle' in question. From this managers will devise their own methods and means of becoming an effective and successful operator therein. They must be able to survive long enough to do this. It follows from this that they must understand and be able to work within the formal and informal systems of the organisation and to establish their place in them. Especially in the informal system they may require to find their own niches and from there go on and develop networks and support within the organisation. Large, complex and sophisticated organisations have series of 'cluster groups' determined by profession, location and status, and people in such situations must discover those that are suitable and make sure that they are involved in them to their advantage. They will develop a keen 'environmental' sense. This comprises, first, the ability to spot straws in the wind, indicating possible changes, developments, innovations or crises; second, the recognition of the departments and individuals where actual power and influence truly lie; third, sources of information within the complexities of the organisation; and fourth, 'managerial antennae' which are finely tuned to perceive any shifts in the other aspects or across the environment in general.

SUMMARY BOX 12.13   'After the Staff Meeting'

' . . . so I went to the leader, and I asked him to build me a wall for my back, so that when the knife came, I would be able to see it. And he agreed, and he built me my wall; but he left a hole in it, just in case . . . '

Source: Minisaga (Pettinger, 1988, unpublished).

Managers will assess their own position in the pecking order, the competition for power and influence and the qualities that they bring to the organisation's internal political situation. They will assess their own strengths and weaknesses in it, and the capabilities and capacities that are required in order to be effective and professional operators in the given situation.

They will identify where the inter-group frictions (and sometimes hostility) lie and assess the reasons for them. From this standpoint they will similarly assess the position of their department in the whole, and look to be able to lobby for support and influence where they are most likely to get it in the pursuit of these interests.

They must adapt their managerial style to the situation. For example, a highly open and task-orientated approach is not likely to work in a bureaucratic set-up.

By adopting it anyway, because of preference, the manager would simply throw away any advantages held and the political positioning necessary in order to operate in the environment. This would also impinge upon both the work and effectiveness of the department and its own regard in the organisation. Consider Summary Boxes 11.14–11.16.

Other factors that affect the political and operational environment in the organisation are as follows. There may be a question of role ambiguity, whether among departments or staff, where particular lines of activity, authority, job and task boundaries are not clearly delineated. There may also be more general problems in this area relating to lack of clarity of aims and objectives where departments are unsure of their remit and consequently operate in a void. Furthermore, departments may use this lack of clarity to push their own boundaries outward and build or extend their empires. Lack of clarity in the fields of performance and output standards also relates to this and leads to inter-departmental wrangles and conflicts based upon the consequent inevitable shortfall in performance and the necessity to draw attention away from that which relates to the department of the manager in question and towards other departments.

Throughout the operational environment there will also be various agenda that are to be followed. Departments and their managers have secondary and hidden agenda especially to do with the advancement of a particular course of action; but also, more generally, in the promotion of the department or its manager in the pecking order of the organisation. Unhealthy, negative competition may be engaged in by departments that has nothing to do with the pursuit of effective operations but rather negatively encourages success at the expense of other departmental failures and becomes a drive for power and influence in itself motivated by the need to gain the ear of the chief executive or in other spheres of influence.

The situation may be exacerbated by bad and inadequate communications and communication systems so that people find things out via the grapevine or other vested interests; in such situations especially, trade union officials prosper and flourish. There is a consequent increase in the numbers of disputes including those between departments; and an increase also in those disputes and grievances that get put on a formal basis and go either to arbitration or to the top of the organisation for resolution. Rules and regulations in such situations become the end and not the means to an end. Where such situations are allowed to persist over long periods of time, bureaucratic superstructures are devised and additional staff and procedures taken on and adopted, and such inter-departmental and organisational wranglings become institutionalised and part of the ways of working.

In such situations also information becomes a critical resource to be jealously guarded and to be fed out in the interests of the information holder rather than the organisation itself. Impurities are fed into information systems by vested interests and those seeking increased power and influence for themselves and their own unit or sector at the expense of others. In such situations, over-mighty

---

SUMMARY BOX 12.14   The Choice of Ministers

Machiavelli wrote that 'the first opinion formed of a ruler's intelligence is based on the quality of the men he chooses to be around him. When they are competent and loyal he can be considered wise, when they are not the prince is open to adverse criticism'.

The prince has 'an infallible guide for assessing his minister: if the minister thinks more of himself than of the prince, seeking his own profit rather than the greater good he will never be a sound minister nor will he be trustworthy'.

Source: Machiavelli, *The Prince.*

SUMMARY BOX 12.15   Over-mighty Subjects

In Sixteenth century England the Tudor Kings and Queens were burdened with what came to be known as their over-mighty subjects. These were the land-owning nobility whose support the monarch required to keep the peace in the outlying parts of the country and who, if support was not forthcoming, constituted a real threat to the monarch's position. This support was therefore generated by hiving off huge parcels of land, local ruling rights and general autonomy to the nobles in return for the continuing support for the Tudor dynasty. The Kings and Queens went on regular progressions throughout the realm to try to ensure that the bargains thus struck were adhered to; in practice, however, great areas of the country were effectively the personal fiefdoms of these nobles.

In organisations of today, 'over-mighty subjects' are found in areas equivalent to those described above. As well as location, however, organisations must beware of, and look for, these 'subjects' in key, critical and functional divisions and areas.

SUMMARY BOX 12.16   The Parable of the Spotlight

This is a recognition that, figuratively speaking one of the most powerful positions in any organisation comes about as the result of being able to 'shine spotlights' on other people; that is, to draw attention away from the workings of one's own department towards the workings (especially negative) of others. This constitutes the spotlight configuration. The purpose is to create a view of the department in the spotlight that is negative, at the same time creating an aura of greater darkness around one's own department in the position behind the spotlight, in which consequently it may not be seen so clearly.

---

subjects prosper, also at the expense of others (as do designated officials such as union representatives).

A manager must therefore recognise these components and vagaries of the work environment; and must be able to work his way around them, accommodate them, and where necessary, tap into them and feed into them in the pursuit of his own effective performance.

In the medium to long term the negative aspects outlined in this section have extreme demoralising and debilitating effects not only on the staff but also on the organisation itself and ultimately its customers and clients. The organisation must recognise such activities for what they are and take remedial steps wherever necessary and desirable. It is finally incumbent upon directors and general managers of organisations to take a global view of this situation and, where it occurs, undertake major activities and possibly organisation surgery necessary to remove it and to ensure that the organisation gets back on even track as soon as possible.

■ Conclusion

In the conduct of these variant and divergent activities, the manager is devising and implementing work methods, patterns and styles and a managerial approach that reflects these in the interests of getting productive, effective and profitable outputs from the department. This has to be seen from the widest of all angles. For example, taking time to induct a new member of staff may seem a profligate use of precious and expensive managerial time, but the payback on it will be seen, (a) when a problem has arisen due to the ignorance of the new member of staff or his lack of expertise or cultural awareness; and (b) in terms of the manager not having to waste time on resolving such an issue because of the time spent in induction. Similarly, resources spent on the department's ambience and environment may seem profligate in certain circumstances but the returns are measured in terms of low absenteeism, a general positive wish on the part of the staff to attend in the department, high levels of output, low levels of labour turnover and a productive and harmonious attitude in work activities.

The purpose of this chapter has been to outline the reality, diversity and complexity of the managerial task and its applications in both operational and project-type situations. The chapter is designed to demonstrate a range of the means and methods and approaches that are available for adoption in the pursuit of this; the quantitative methods discussed in Chapter 9 outlined a set of tools and sources of information that are also available in ensuring that these activities are pursued effectively.

The main additional point to make is that concerning the continuing obligation of professional practising managers to develop both their own expertise and the nature and functioning of their department. Again, we refer to the concept of 'continuous improvement' and the standpoint that, as perfection is not yet achieved, the process ever represents the art of the possible and not the fanciful. There is a very hard edge to this also – it derives from the universal drive for profitability and effectiveness: in the particular context of the business sphere of the 1990s, with its global and contracting markets, entryism and opportunism, technological advances and cross-market fertilisation, and the global nature of competitiveness and competition, any contribution that any managers can make in their own sphere that improves their own position and that of their organisation is of value. It follows from this that managers are obliged by virtue of their profession to keep abreast of all developments in the generic, managerial field as well those relating to the environment, function and operations of their particular organisation. Only by doing this are they able to maintain an effective, competitive and current position both for themselves and also for the department that they are leading and directing and of which they are the life and driving force.

CHAPTER 12

Managing in a changing environment

■ Introduction

The changes that have impinged on society over the period since 1945, and more particularly since the 1960s, in turn impinge on the management of organisations. These changes may be summarised as:

- **Technological**, affecting all social, economic and business activities; rendering many occupations obsolete and creating new ones; and opening up new spheres of activity, bringing travel, transport, distribution, telecommunication, industry, goods and services on to a global scale
- **Social**, the changing of people's lives, from the fundamentals of life expectancy and lifestyle choice, to the ability to buy and possess items; to travel; to be educated; to receive ever-increasing standards of health-care, personal insurance and information; to be fed; to enjoy increased standards of social security and stability, increased leisure time and choice of leisure pursuits; and all commensurate with increases in disposable income and purchasing power, and choices of purchase
- **Eco–political**, resulting in changes in all governmental forms; the state of flux of the EC, and the adoption of super-national laws and directives, and the single market; the collapse of the communist bloc and the USSR; the fragmentation of the former Yugoslavia into its component states; the emergence of Taiwan, South Africa, Korea and Vietnam as spheres of political and economic influence, taking their place in the business sphere
- **Expectational**, in which the changes may be expressed as from stability to a state of change itself, a state of flux; the change from the expectation of working for one company or organisation, to working for many, and the realisation that the former is increasingly unlikely; change in occupation, training and profession; change in political governance, and the instruments of state; organisations change their business (e.g. Virgin, from music into air travel) and expect their staff to change with them; hospitals in the UK reconstituted as 'business units' and offering medical services at a price or charge, and expecting staff and patients to go along with this; business is indeed 'thriving on chaos', and 'learning to love change', and this is increasingly expected by those who manage it.

However, the importance of understanding, controlling and managing this process is fundamental to its success. Rather than either passive acceptance, or allowing it to happen, managers must assume responsibility for, and direction of, the change process and the activities required to make it effective and

352

successful. There is a hard operational and commercial drive behind this, related to the business and operational *modus operandi* of the 1990s.

There is, finally, a managerial context. The great organisations of the past ten or so years are coming under pressure. Japanese organisations, and 'model' UK companies such as Body Shop, all experienced difficulties for the first time in the early and mid-1990s. This has involved fundamental operational and directional reappraisals by all. The true test of their total strength is the ways in which they handle these issues, and how they emerge from them.

■ The present and future of management

The purpose of this chapter is thus to highlight the concepts and issues that are of relevance and importance in the business and management sphere in the 1990s and beyond, and that constitute the background against which business is currently conducted and represent the current level of development of the field as an area of expertise in its own right.

Again, it must be stressed that essentially management is a qualitative subject and not an exact science; and that this extends into those spheres where quantitative methods are both present and operated (see Chapter 9). Everything is subject to interpretation and assimilation in particular circumstances.

Management takes place in a business sphere that is global and which draws its lessons and expertise from a global environment. There is therefore a reality of cross-fertilisation and exchange of ideas; and the potential for the development of this is virtually unlimited. There is a rich field of study to be drawn upon here before any manager, in any organisation, in any sector, in any country, can truly call themselves an expert. As we have already seen, while the main contributions have so far come from Western Europe, the UK, North America and Japan there is yet much to be drawn from Africa, the rest of Asia, South America and Australasia. There is thus no place for an attitude of insularity or complacency on the part of any manager from any organisation. Most of those organisations to which reference has been made, either in this book or elsewhere in managerial literature, have experienced difficulties as well as prosperity – and one of the tests of their true character, strength and expertise will be the way in which they handle these problems and overcome them.

It follows from this that the current nature and practice of management must be seen in the context of its environment. As often stated, this is both turbulent and changing. It is affected by recession and downturn. Also to be considered is the great rate of technological change. There is, further, the emergence of an Asian manufacturing bloc that has both technological and labour cost advantages. More generally, the bankruptcy, deprivation and social regeneration of the former communist bloc must be addressed. The population explosions, migrations, deprivations and famine of Africa must be considered. There is political and social turbulence in the Middle East, the Balkans and South

America. All these factors impinge on the business sphere. They generate business activities and operations that have to be managed. They generate pressures on resources and organisations. They generate economic, social and ethical factors that often make managerial solutions to problems, based purely on operational grounds, unacceptable or untenable (by whatever criteria the concepts and activities are measured). However, people working in the field are now able to recognise that there is great concern for deprived, war-torn and starving communities of the world; and that there are also direct ways of taking effective action in response to them; the adoption of the managerial (rather than the emotional or the political) perspective in these areas is what is required to generate a truly effective act.

This is the background against which the realities of management are currently drawn. There are general hopes (rather than expectations) of emergence from global recession, of economic expansion and of the resolution of the problems which face managers. There are more direct hopes in regard to the emergence, post-Cold War, of the countries of the former USSR; the emergence and development of the EC single market and its widening to accept new countries over the coming decades; and the development of realisation of the potential of the Asian manufacturing bloc to generate both economic expansion and greater resources over the coming period. In this context we now turn to particular managerial initiatives.

■ Management of change

The concept of the management of change is prominent because of the turbulence and ever-changing nature of the global economic system, as we have seen, and the relationships of organisations within it. This must be reconciled with the need of the managers of organisations to be able to have some influence, work within an environment that has these properties and to conduct effective and profitable business in spite and in consequence of it. Change impinges on everything. Markets, their size, scope, scale and nature are ever-changing. Technological advance is ever-more pervasive and ever-wider uses and adaptations are being found for technology. Work patterns, expectations and methods are constantly being altered and adapted while operations and activities are being globalised.

Change impinges on all aspects of organisational operations. This ranges from narrow productive and operational considerations to any ethical stance adopted by the organisation as part of its competitive positioning; to concepts of flexibility, responsiveness and quality; and all such matters pervade the whole culture and structure of the organisation. Since the end of the Second World War both business and public operations in the western world have tended to be established with order and stability in mind and many have been slow to adopt the ability to change as part of their way of working and existing.

A key phrase in all the excellence studies was articulated by Peters as 'learning to love change'. This flies in the face of the prevailing ethos in many western corporations, particularly those that are either complex or longstanding which have invested heavily over the period since the end of the Second World War in stability and order. What is required for effective change and the ability to promote it, live with it and harmonise with it successfully, is an understanding of this. The business world that people came into is not the same as that in which they are now being asked to operate; uncertainties and anxieties that arise out of this must first of all be stressed before they can be effectively and successfully managed.

■ Change catalyst and change agent

The concept of the change catalyst and change agent must be addressed. They may constitute one and the same thing; they may also be, as it were, different sides of the same coin – the catalyst for change may be the need to reform workplace industrial relations (for example) and the change agent the person given the responsibility of doing this.

The catalyst may be a person, event or factor, internal or external to the organisation. Whichever it is, it is that which brings the organisation to the realisation that we cannot go on as we are. It may be a very uncomfortable or even debilitating or destructive process in which the organisation and its managers are faced with unacceptable or unpalatable truths – the catalyst here is that which forces this out into the open. The catalyst thus provides the initial energy that sets the change of process in hand.

The agent is the person (or event, or phenomenon) that drives it. This may again be internal to the organisation (for example, an increase in the priority of marketing will become effective if the marketing director appointed to achieve it comes with a high reputation and track record in the field); or it may be external – a common use of management consultants by the organisation is to get them as external advisers to articulate to organisation stakeholders (especially staff shareholders) what may be unacceptable coming from within the organisation and from its top management team.

■ Attitudes, values and beliefs

Effective, lasting and operationally successful change is achieved only if attitudes, values and beliefs are addressed and the same universal importance placed on change as on operational and technological factors. They all impinge on each other: for example, the introduction of an automated production line leads to new job requirements, which leads to new job descriptions, which leads to new ways of working, which leads to revised staff handbooks and work agreements – and so on. Consequently the attempts to introduce an operational change in isolation (for whatever reason – and a common one in the UK used to be trade union pressure) simply results in the old stance being conducted less effectively on the new machine; while there may be a short-term gain in terms of expediency, in the avoidance of a labour dispute, in the longer term both operation and production will suffer.

■ Barriers to effective change

Barriers to effective change may be classified as either operational or behavioural.

■ Operational barriers

These are:

- **Location**: this is a barrier when, for whatever reason, it becomes impossible for the organisation to continue to operate in its current premises. Relocation has consequences for the re-settlement of famililies, re-training and organisation development. Even where the new premises are close by, it may affect access, work and attendance patterns. For greater distances, the consequences of widespread disruption have to be addressed. As well as personal consequences, this includes attention to organisation culture and structure.
- **Tradition**: this is a problem where there has been a long history of successful work in specific, well-understood and widely accepted ways. This may be underlined where a whole community has grown up around a particular industry or organisation and where this is a major provider of employment and prosperity (for example, coal mining, iron and steel, shipbuilding, engineering). If this has been steady for long periods, there are strong perceptions of stability and permanence.
- **Success (and perceived success)**: if the organisation is known or perceived to be successful in its current ways of doing things then there is a resistance based on 'Why change something that works?' Again, this is especially true if there is a long history of stability and prosperity. It is often very difficult in these circumstances to get workforces to accept that technology, ways of working and the products themselves are coming to the end of their useful life.
- **Failure**: this is a barrier to change where a given state of affairs has been allowed to persist for some time. The view is often taken – by both organisations and the staff concerned – that this is 'one of those things', a necessary part of being involved in a given set of activities. Resistance occurs when someone determines to do something about it – again, upsetting an overtly comfortable and orderly status quo.
- **Technology**: this is a barrier for many reasons. It is often the driving force behind jobs, tasks, occupations and activities. Their disruption causes trauma to those affected by the consequent need for job and occupation change, re-training, re-deployment – and often redundancy. Technological changes may also cause relocation to more suitable premises. Technological changes, in turn, cause changes to work patterns and methods. It has been one of the

driving forces behind the increase in home working where employees can be provided with all the equipment necessary to work without the need to come together at the employer's premises; and part-time working where the demands for maximisation on investment in technology and increases in customer bases have led to extended opening and operational hours. Technological change disrupts patterns of identity. It has led to flexible working, away from traditional job titles, restrictive practices and demarcation. Technological change has also disrupted traditions of representation and belonging to trade unions, and professional and occupational bodies. This has occurred as jobs and occupations have become obsolete, causing both the individuals and the bodies concerned to seek new roles.

- **Vested interests**: needs for organisational change are resisted by those who are, or who perceive themselves to be, at risk. Vested interests are found in all areas. They include senior managers, threatened with loss of functional authority; operational staff faced with occupational obsolescence; people in support functions no longer considered necessary; and those on promotional and career paths for whom the current order represents a clear and guaranteed passage to increased prosperity and influence.
- **Managerial**: the managerial barrier is a consequence of 'the divorce of organisation, ownership and control', where there is a divergence between the organisation's best interests and need for long-term survival, and the needs of individuals and groups of managers to preserve their own positions. Existing patterns of supervision may again provide both general order and certainty and specific career and promotion paths.
- **Bureaucracy**: the bureaucracy barrier occurs where patterns of order and control have grown up over long periods in the recording and supervision of activities and in the structuring of organisational functions. The problem is worst where the bureaucracy is large and complex, and a significant part of the total range of activities.
- **Redundancy and redeployment**: this is referred to above. It is a barrier in its own right because in the current context any proposed change carries redundancy and redeployment as possibilities and because it has so often been a consequence of other changes.

■ Behavioural barriers

The main barriers are as follows:

- **'It cannot be done'**: this is a barrier both to confidence and understanding and is based on a lack of true, full and accurate information concerning the matters which the organisation is proposing.
- **'There is no alternative'**: this comes in two forms. First, it is adopted by the workforce and interest groups in and around it (for example trade unions) that have a vested interest in the maintenance of the status quo either because it is familiar or because any change will result in loss of influence. This is especially true where business has been conducted in an effective and productive steady-state for a long period of time The other side of this is where directorates and managers adopt this as the one and only explanation for a change that is to take place. Conducted in isolation 'there is no alternative' simply becomes a challenge for others to think of alternatives. The matter requires explanation and communication in order to demonstrate to all those

affected that alternatives have indeed been considered and that what is now proposed represents the chosen strategic direction.

- **Lack of clarity**: if organisations have not sorted out the basis of the changes that are proposed, neither staff nor customers will go along with them with any degree of confidence or understanding; aims and objectives must be clearly understood as the prerequisite to successful and effective change, and communicated to those concerned in their own language.

- **Fear and anxiety**: these are human responses to concepts and situations that are unknown or uncertain. They are the initial response (or part of it) to any change that is proposed; and if allowed to get out of hand can become an exercise in the devising and promulgation of hypothetical scenarios that could in certain circumstances become problems on the changing landscape. Not only does this constitute a waste of organisational resources and a diversion from actual purposes, but such interaction among the staff feeds on itself, generating negativity and unnecessary internal turbulence.

- **Perfection**: at the point at which change is proposed suddenly everything concerning the status quo becomes 'perfect'. Anything that is proposed as an alternative has therefore to address this barrier. It is another manifestation of familiarity and comfort, and faced with the loss of this, such elements become highly worthwhile to retain.

For all barriers, the main issue is to avoid leaving a vacuum. Organisations have therefore to understand where the proposed changes are to lead and what their consequences are. Early communication is essential for the benefit of all concerned. The best employers give every opportunity to their workforce to be a part of their future before casting around outside for new staff and expertise.

In most cases most of these barriers, operational or behavioural, are present. The prevalence of each barrier will depend upon the particular situation, the nature and extent of the changes to be made and whether they are operational, locational, attitudinal, structural or cultural. To an extent, however, each must be addressed. The vehicle for this will always centre on communication. This must be effectively designed and the content delivered in the language of recipients. All media available will be used – briefing groups, plenary meetings, individual and group methods, oral and written modes, notice-boards, newsletters and other circulars. Overall they will address dates and deadlines for the given changes; the implications of them and their effects for staff; any range of alternatives that it may be necessary to offer; re-training, redeployment or redundancy; and some articulation of the future following the implementation of change.

■ Counselling and support

Following on from this, the behavioural barriers as they exist in an actual situation will be identified and an approach to them devised. It is first necessary to pin down those that need tackling before any successful or effective change can take place, those that require constant addressing throughout the whole period of change, those that will or may present themselves as hurdles later in the process and the likely timescales for these, the extent to which each will impinge upon the change effort if it is not effectively addressed, and any aspects of them that require further investigation.

It follows that this will require individual and group counselling and support methods and mechanisms to be put in place. These are for the purpose of reassurance, the continued addressing of lingering or persistent uncertainties, and they provide also the means of tackling individual cases. Moreover, they provide behavioural messages that in themselves reflect the organisation's concern for, and commitment to, its individuals and groups and have great implications for the overall presentation of stability, permanence and continuity.

A general stance of openness and assertiveness (see Chapter 11) in the management of behavioural aspects of change should always be adopted. If there is an issue of redundancy, for example, it is best to have it in the open and deal with it as soon as possible rather than allowing the grapevine to get to work. The language used to convey this (and all information) should always be that of recipients.

Addressing these matters in this way does not assume any dilution of the process. It rather emphasises the fact that the organisation will have sorted out both the required and proposed changes in advance and also the means by which these are to be effective. Only once this has been tackled in advance from a strategic point of view will effective implementation be possible. This also helps reflect the extent of the organisation's continuing relationship with its work-force and its customers, and reinforces these messages.

Finally, as change is not a linear process, opportunities for the organisation to reform and restructure other activities will generally present itself during its course. There may also arise historic, underlying or fundamental issues of culture, attitudes, beliefs, structures, values and ethics; the need to generate concepts of flexibility, dynamism and creativity among the workforce; and to reform more general or global perception of the organisation, its methods and relationships with customers and clients. The establishment of effective change processes and the successful stressing of the behavioural or human elements thereof should help constitute a springboard for future prosperity.

■ Changing culture

The concept implied here relates to the implication that what is currently in place is undesirable for a variety of reasons, that there is a vision or articulation of the desired state of affairs, and that a strategic approach can be (and once the decision is taken to proceed, must be) adopted to ensure that the required conclusion is arrived at. Consider Summary Box 12.1.

The process of changing culture is concerned with reforming the ways in which members of the organisation concerned think and believe, and also their prevailing attitudes. Therefore, while there are certain behavioural and opera-

---

SUMMARY BOX 12.1   Culture Change

This process was once defined as – unfreezing – transforming – refreezing. This has, however, lost credence to the extent that the idea of 'refreezing' is a misnomer in the current state of the business and managerial environment.

It is also possible to look at culture change in terms of force field analysis. This is where the forces that drive change and those that restrain it are separated out. Those that drive change are then energised and pushed on; those that restrain it are either removed or neutralised or else re-energised in ways productive to the desired outcome. This is a valuable concept but its weakness in application is the tendency to address operational matters rather than those that relate to attitudes, beliefs and culture. Changes in the latter therefore tend to be slow, diluted and hard to direct.

---

tional activities that can be usefully and positively addressed, the main thrust has to be at the core values, beliefs and ethos of the organisation itself and its staff, shareholders and other stakeholders; regard may also need to be given to both direct customers and also the views and values of the wider environment and society in which the organisation operates.

The process of change requires an acceptance and understanding that the prevailing culture is inappropriate, a willingness to do something about it, and a series of steps taken to reform it. The process additionally requires the understanding and adoption of the whole required culture and values that go with it by all staff in the organisation (this may be a consultative or directive process).

Manifestations of this will be reflected in changes at the operational phase, as we have seen. In addition, changes in managerial style and ways of working become necessary as do changes in job descriptions, job mix, organisational and structural aspects. It is impossible to contemplate cultural change without structural style or operational changes – they are all interrelated: it is simply that culture is the driving force (the reverse is also true, that it is impossible to effect operational change without having regard to cultural aspects, though operational change will not in itself change culture *per se*).

The process must be energised, resourced and driven if it is to stand any chance at all of lasting success; clarity of vision is required, and activities must be engaged in that address both the physical and human barriers to change. Effectiveness of communication and action will only be enjoyed if this is indeed so; in particular if the staff do not understand the need and value it, the resistance barriers will go up. In traditional organisations and others that have enjoyed long periods of permanence, order and stability the need for change is often very hard to put across (the Affluent Worker studies, for example, as we saw in Chapter 2, found that the staff expected steady-state work in return for an acceptable and increasing level of prosperity; where this is removed or destabilised the clamour is for the return to the old ways and not to seek some new order). Consider Summary Box 12.2.

SUMMARY BOX 12.2   External Force and Cultural Change

One study, conducted by Alan Williams and Paul Dobson of the City University Business School in the late 1980s, questioned whether culture change could be executed at all at least in the ways envisaged at the outset by organisations. Their study of 60 British organisations in the period 1985–88 across a wide range of industrial, commercial and public activities, concluded that culture change followed in the wake of organisation or operational change and that where it was effected this was because of external rather than internal driving forces.

■ Changing structure

The nature and complexity of organisation structures is self-evident and the reality of these structures forms a continuing thread throughout the whole of this (and many other) management books. What is at issue here is the nature of the structure, what it is supposed to achieve and its relationship with effective and profitable performance. Concerns in the field of organisation structure have been voiced by all authorities on the subject. The matter here is therefore both to articulate these concerns, and to draw conclusions from them.

There are historic problems with organisation structure. First, the history of organisation development indicates that structures are easier to put in place than they are to change, dismantle or rearrange. Second, the need for change, as we have seen, may neither be apparent nor recognised. Third, the structure has often provided a career progression path through the organisation that has been one of the attractions of working in it and staying in it; there is therefore a resistance to structural change on the part of the staff as well as the organisation itself. Full structures have often acquired a degree of permanence and stability throughout a period of business and organisational activity that has been conducted in an environment of permanence and stability also.

■ Organisation purpose

It is clear from this that there are matters to be addressed in regard to the structures of organisations. Like other structures they are devised to serve particular purposes and when that purpose is spent or concluded or moves on to another, the structure should move on also. For physical structures this will normally mean replacement or relocation; for organisation structures this process constitutes reform.

At the basis of this is the organisation's reason for being. From this, as we have seen arise the way in which it is operating and is to operate in the future, the size and scale of the organisation, its technology, its markets, and its staff. In turn, these are related to the nature of managerial style and direction and controls either required or implied. This is the reverse position of that which says 'we have a structure, therefore we must use it'; rather, it takes the opposite view that 'we need a suitable and effective structure and this is what it should be and should serve'.

■ Specialisation

The next point to be considered relates to the nature and degree of specialisation that is present. Current thinking and practice have tended to move away from highly specialised, functional divisions and departments. The functional expertise may well itself be required but it tends not to be so in traditional role patterns of organisation. Rather, the approach taken is to buy in expertise when it is required. Furthermore, organisations may ask for managerial and other key staff with a much wider range of expertise than was previously required; or they may train them in this much wider expertise in the period following the commencement of their employment.

■ Suitable structures

Related to this is the expense of carrying sophisticated structures and functional departments and the consequent addition of cost to the organisation. Sophisticated structures that tend towards functional specialisation and compartmentalised expertise are inherently unwielding and difficult to direct and harmonise with the core purpose of the organisation. While the higher bureaucratic concepts related to the permanence of organisations remain current together with the necessity to retain and develop its expertise, nevertheless traditional bureaucratic structures are increasingly being called into question as the most effective way of doing this.

Organisation structures that are to be devised increasingly therefore reflect the reappraisal of the ways in which functional expertise is required, rather than assuming that because it is required a department or division has to be set up for it. New structures therefore tend to reflect current principles of lean form and streamlining and flatness, especially when related to head office or corporate support functions. Other principles are placing responsibilities for quantity, quality, effectiveness and control on to managers as an integral part of their expertise; creating business units and profit centres that are themselves streamlined, empowered and which operate with a distinct clarity of purpose. Part of this purpose, furthermore, consists of fulfilling the organisation's functions but in ways which contribute to organisation performance and effectiveness rather than to serving the structured systems themselves. In some cases this has led to radical reappraisal of what the roles and functions of a head office (and the structures, systems and procedures that it devises) should actually be; and what constitutes an effective method of control; and how these can best be ordered and applied.

Above all, both the concepts and reality of structures of organisations increasingly reflect the other essentials of current business management practice – effective and suitable channels of communication; effective and suitable decision-making processes; the relationships between functionalisation and departmentalisation and value added to the organisation's outputs; closeness to the customer and the flexibility and dynamism that goes with it. Those responsible for the inception, design and structure of organisations are finding that what is required is an effective balance of the key aspects of control and permanence and direction, flexibility and dynamism; the ways in which organisations are to be constituted and reconstituted for the future will reflect this.

Traditionally, there has been evident a conscious decision taken by organisations to be centralised or decentralised, whether or not that was operationally desirable or appropriate; this extended to both structure and outlook. However, increasingly the question of centralisation or decentralisation is not a decision to be taken in this way but rather a matter that arises only in relation to the reality of effective performance. Having made this clear, there is a current tide of wisdom which indicates that the clearest path to this effectiveness lies in devolved autonomous business units. It is indicated in the 'shamrock' model (see Chapter 4) and other configurations of the peripheral workforce; and in the arm's length and privatised functions that are starting to appear in public, social and health services. It mirrors the hands-on, value-driven, lean-form approach recommended and promulgated by Peters. It mirrors the demands and drives for autonomy and executive authority on the part of business managers. Above all, what is indicated is a structure that is effective and suitable, reflecting the nature of the business and the ways in which work is to be conducted; and having regard to balancing the requirements of control and cost effectiveness.

■ Changing staff management

The reality of staff management is currently one of transformation: that is, of a fundamental shift in the perceptions of it, what it constitutes and what it should constitute; of the nature of managerial approaches to it; and of the expectations of it and what it should achieve on behalf of the organisation concerned. In the past the general approach has been coercive both in nature and operation; that is, the devising of structures and procedures to control the staff and contain the conflicts inherent in such a situation where based on confrontation.

This transformation is related to and driven by a combination of great advances in managerial expertise; advances in the understanding of human resource behaviour patterns and aspirations in work situations; technological advances; and changes in social expectations and aspirations. The general components and manifestations of this transformation have their basis in the assumption of professional expertise by managers. Particular configurations of this are as follows.

■ Patterns of employment

Developments in patterns of employment that reflect a combination of social obligation and economic requirements on the part of organisations have been and are taking place. Those organisations that have promised or implied lifetime employment to their staff have found that there is, inherent in this, a continuing obligation to train, re-train and redevelop staff. This has and does involve the development of alternative patterns of work and reformation of the workforce concept into that of 'the human resource' and all that this implies.

■ Performance and reward

An ever-more expert and precisely drawn relationship between pay, rewards, benefits and compensation packages offered to staff on the one hand and the nature of the performance and output requirements of them on the other is being developed. Above all, there is the realisation that steady-state salary scales and progressions are for steady-state organisations and environments; where neither is present this means of reward is inappropriate. Rewards and payment are therefore targeted; they are to be related to the achievement of objectives, and their effectiveness thus measured. It is furthermore necessary to develop both the concept of performance-related reward for administrative, professional and managerial activities, and to devise what constitute true and valid targets and aims in these areas of operation.

It follows from this that a greater understanding of the organisation's requirements of each staff member is necessary and a greater emphasis placed upon establishing what actually constitutes truly effective professional, technical, administrative and managerial output. It is true that performance indicators can be drawn in terms of standards of behaviour, quality of performance and exhibited and inferred general qualities of pride, commitment, enthusiasm and motivation; they have, however, to be established, assessed and measured by those in turn expert in the field and who understand the concepts themselves and how they are effectively to be applied in pursuit of the organisation's requirements.

A much more pragmatic view in business terms is thus taken of the human resource, bringing it into line with the approach to the other resources of the organisation. Staff are thus seen as the 'human asset' — that is, a reflection of investment, and on which returns are accordingly expected and to be assessed (see Chapter 9). There is a requirement for output and optimisation of efforts. There is also a value placed on genuine human assets that reflect the organisation's regard of them, the esteem in which they are held, the expectations held of them and aspirations for them. In the human asset, furthermore, there should be distinctive elements of pride, confidence and esteem held by the organisation for, and in, its people. This is also a contributory factor to the changes in work patterns and approaches to structural and cultural factors to which reference has been made above.

■ Staff as stakeholders

There is also the recognition of the position of the staff as a legitimate stakeholder in the organisation. A long held view in Japan and parts of Western Europe (especially West Germany) the concept is now becoming more widely accepted across the rest of the business sphere. Organisations are coming to realise that openness, honesty, participation, effective communication and the development at least of an operational consensus does not constitute dilution or loss of control but rather a means of focus for the development of the organisation, and generation of harmony and understanding are of benefit to everybody who works within it. Above all is the importance of the under-standing of the concepts, standpoints and reasoning behind it; the actual instruments used (works councils, briefing groups, and so on) will have value only where such understanding is found.

■ IR and staff relations

It is necessary now to address the particular field of IR and staff relations in this context. New and current approaches are concerned to ensure that these are conducted from a standpoint that is both cost-effective and suitable to the needs of the organisation. If direct relationships are drawn between the wider and more general aspects of staff identity and motivation and organisational performance profitability, it follows that the removal of the barriers of aliena-tion and demotivation where they exist is an essential feature.

Such approaches to IR therefore stem from an organisation-wide belief that there is a contribution to be made to profitability by the adoption of them. Standards are clearly established; and all staff are briefed in these. Managers are trained both to value their importance and to uphold them, and to conduct departmental industrial relations with a view of effectiveness in the same way as any other operational activity. Emphases are therefore concerned with problem-solving, decision-making and developing a conformist and harmonious wider environment and approach.

This means reappraisal of the concept, nature, role and function of IR on all sides. The nature of conflict inherent in the situation is still recognised; but it is addressed through the means of giving common cause and purpose to the situation rather than regulating and ordering the conflict itself. This requires a fundamental re-think on the IR role on the part of organisations, managers and units and employees' representatives in establishing their own role and preferred direction. It requires the adoption of a set of beliefs and values based on future aspirations rather than past traditions and places the emphasis firmly on organisations to deliver an aura and ethos that enables this to take place. It requires the basic arguments related to the 'price of labour' to be conducted from a strategic, enlightened and long-term perspective and for organisations to recognise the true implication of this. It requires, finally, the creation and adoption of IR policies that are effective and comprehensive in coverage, that reflect the need to address issue rather than process and that provide, above all, for a speedy and successful resolution of problems when they arise. The onus in all of this is on the organisation.

It follows from all of this that while the validity of the staff as a legitimate interest group is undiluted and genuine involvement is to be promoted, the means by which this is actually achieved will derive directly from the preferred IR standpoint of the organisation. In general terms, whatever is established will have its own constitution, remit, terms of reference and agenda that reflect the concerns of the staff on the one hand, and a forum for organisational and formalised involvement on the other. Its true effectiveness will always lie, however, in the extent to which the organisation views its staff as a legitimate interest group.

The approach to the human resource overall therefore reflects a combination of generally increased expertise and global fund of knowledge on which to draw. This is underpinned by an ever-developing understanding of the nature of HRM; and a hard business acumen that requires a return on people as on any investment. The human resource represents in general at least 50% of the organisation's total investment; and in service sectors this is very much higher, up to 90% in many cases. The required and developing approach to the human resource must be seen in these terms; this is part of the wider concept of the 'hands-on', value driven approach. Staff themselves must be regarded in this way as well as the outputs that they generate. The view adopted is therefore a combination of a measure of enlightenment and a true understanding of the concept of resource maximisation – one that recognises all the diverse and divergent demands inherent, identifies the nature of the prevailing organisation situation and reconciles each in productive, harmonious and above all profitable and effective activities.

■ Working with change

There are some more general considerations that affect organisations that now bear consideration. We have already established the reality of the concept of 'constant improvement'; and that this is itself part of the 'state of permanent change'. Moreover, technological advance and changes in market taste, in awareness and perceptions and wider environmental considerations reinforce this. The widening of horizons, choice and the resulting globalisation of business means that no market is safe or secure; that competition may come from any organisation of any nationality (or trans-nationality) from anywhere within the business sphere. The organisation that forgets this does so at its own peril. Flexible contracts, the changing nature of public services, general changes in lifestyle and aspirations also all impinge. It is therefore incumbent upon the manager to learn to love change and be comfortable with it and to regard the current turbulence of both the global business-sphere and the particular sectors of it as the natural environment in which to be successful and effective.

To complete this part of the picture it is therefore necessary to address and summarise the global concept of quality. The final part of this section is a brief summary of the main and distinctive features of Japanese management; as we have already stated, this is important in any consideration of management practice which has been shown to be both profitable and successful in the late 1990s.

■ Quality

'Quality' as a managerial concept is much in vogue in management direction and practices in the UK, EC and North America. It is endemic throughout the Japanese business and industrial spheres.

It is first necessary to recognise the conception of quality as part of a corporate state of mind, a core element of prevailing attitudes and values rather than as an adjunct to existing practices. It follows from this that the organisation's true commitments to quality will be reflected in the capabilities of staff employed; the tenor of sales and marketing efforts; levels of investments in plant, machinery and equipment; types of plant, machinery and equipment; induction, attitude formation, training and development programmes; and the style of IR and staff relations, supervision methods and managerial approaches that are adopted.

The organisational standpoint thus adopted is related to themes of 'obsession with excellence and quality' and the concern for quality as a moral standpoint. It is part of the background to the undertaking and part of the fixed investment in future success.

There is an obsession, first, with customer satisfaction, in terms both of the products or services offered, and the ways in which they are delivered by the organisation. This must cover the whole process from the acceptance of orders through delivery and dispatch to after-sales service. In many cases this is instrumental in the generation of repeat business. There is thus a strong element of long-term investment inherent in any true, genuine approach and attitude that has quality at its core.

There is an obsession, second, with staff excellence, in terms of their expertise, skills and knowledge. This must be underpinned, however, by a commitment to them that ensures that they are instilled with the attitudes necessary to deliver this expertise in the ways in which the organisation and its customers require. They must be paid and rewarded adequately. They must have their expectations and aspirations accommodated in the intention and pursuit of excellence. Again, this is regarded as a long-term, mutual investment and commitment between staff and organisation. It is not regarded as a purely instrumental or functional approach, or concept of employment.

There is an obsession, third, with the 'theme of constant improvement', the recognition that each and every aspect of the organisation, its products and services, its practices, procedures and operations, can be made to work better, more effectively in the pursuit of quality and excellence. Levels of investment in production methods and capacities, standards and lifespan of production plants and equipment will also be the subject of this commitment. Only the best equipment will do: that is, something which has all the attributes required to meet the output levels required in terms of speed, reliability, perfection, regularity and universality. The plant and equipment used is to be set at these levels before any item is produced and what is produced is to meet the standard each and every time. This is the production manifestation of 'right first time'.

The maintenance of operations at a continuing high-quality level is underpinned by both procedures and processes. The procedures include inspection, random sampling, testing and monitoring of products as they come off the line, and of the lines themselves during planned maintenance periods.

The processes reflect the concept of continued improvement and must include work improvements and quality improvement groups addressing both product and production methods.

Part of this must include the adoption of this obsession with quality by all concerned as a shared and core value and an active involvement in the improvement. Everyone's contribution is therefore to be valued. It also involves the adoption of the customer focus by all concerned, whether or not they deal directly with customers.

Quality assurance in service sectors, both public and commercial, is less easy to define, because each transaction is based upon a human request rather than a finished item. In practice, it is achieved in the commercial service sectors by breaking down each component of the service into something which is either measurable absolutely or into categories for which minima can be more easily defined.

Thus, for example, an insurance policy is the representation of a contract between one individual and the insurance corporation. It will state what the coverage given is in relation to the individual's own circumstances and dispositions, however, so that there is no doubt about the nature of the offering and expectation. As all insurance companies do this, the potential customer is able to make an informed choice and to question the organisation's representatives in any matter of which he is not sure. Similarly, the hotel starring system is a representation of the combination of ambience, facilities, room standard, restaurants and location, that is published in literature or brochures; again both travel agents and hotel staff themselves may be contacted to clarify any point.

In public services this now tends to be formalised by service level agreements and arrangements in which memoranda are drawn up specifying obligations and expectations on the part of the service users, consumers or purchasers and the providers of them. This is the direction that is increasingly being taken in the UK in the provision of local government activities (education, social service, repairs and maintenance, community housing and environmental health), and in the NHS, which now has its own internal market. In such arrangements, the precise offering will be agreed and a price fixed; there may be exclusions from it, or conversely a level of service above which the purchaser has to provide an additional payment.

■ Quality circles

The concept of quality circles was American and post-war in origin. It was exported to Japan which, in turn, made it an integral part of the continuous quality improvement process in organisations. A quality circle is a group of staff which meets on a regular basis to review the whole area of quality at the workplace. This involves identifying and clarifying problems, selecting issues from among these for resolution, organising and prioritising them, setting deadlines, timetables and target dates, and setting aims and objectives by which the improvements in the quality of the organisation's operations can be measured. To be effective, they require accommodation, resourcing and support from the organisation and a commitment to back the judgements of the quality circle. Organisations have to recognise that there is a pay-back, not only in improvement in quality or, at least, in problem identification, but that this is also instrumental in promoting the desired attributes of greater commitment, achievement, identity and participation by all concerned. Quality circles are voluntary, generating and selecting their own leadership, frequency and timing of meetings, and precise agenda format. Where they have worked, especially in Japanese companies, it has been because there is a greater cultural pressure to participate, together with an environment created that is both conducive to, and expectant of, a full measure of involvement (whether something is actually designated as being voluntary or not).

■ Japanese management

The concept, practices and approaches adopted by managers in Japanese companies are of interest for a variety of reasons. First, and most important, is clearly that concerned with commercial success; the Japanese 'economic miracle' of the period since the end of the Second World War is of critical global importance. However, there are other matters, both cultural and practical, which, merit careful study, impacting as they do upon the activities of all companies and sectors.

■ *Gambara*

There is a work ethic traditionally imbued by society that is manifest in a number of ways. A basic concept is *gambara* which means 'don't give up, do your best, be persistent, put in a great effort'. This lies at the core of the Japanese work ethic. There is also a high concept of service which is much more widely regarded than elsewhere in the world – service is regarded as being not only at the customer interface, but also over the lifetime of the products provided, and also for new products and models and their lifetime to the customer. The Japanese work for the good of their group and their company above all; the view adopted is that the whole only functions effectively when all its component parts are in turn functioning to full effect and capacity.

The relationship between work and society is vital. Bad business is regarded as a waste of the resources of the society. Service to the society is performed through the high industrial, commercial and managerial virtues of fairness, harmony, cooperation, continuous betterment of quality, courtesy, humility, adjustment, assimilation and gratitude. Responsibility in all these spheres is fostered through managerial arrangements at the workplace; and the inherent requirement for obedience, conformity and respect are combined with an enlightened and egalitarian view of society that is the equivalent of 'from each according to his means, to each according to his needs'.

The concept of interdependence also runs through Japanese companies. This also is viewed in the widest context. As well as relationships between organisation and customer, regard is given to those relationships between the individual at his work group, interrelationships between groups, the concept of self-restraint, cohesion and harmony, senior/junior and mentor/protégé relationships. The individual is valued for his contribution on all fronts: team, group, divisional and corporate.

Japanese management practices are designed actively to prevent problems from happening. This is distinct from elsewhere in the world where great store is often set by the ability of the manager to resolve problems. The Japanese manager is expected to resolve these as and when they do occur; this, however, should be kept to a minimum; organisation and managerial style reflect this.

The decision-making process is a combination of *nemawashi*, which means 'binding the roots' and has come to mean 'thorough preparation'; and *ringi*, which is the outcome of this. In practice, the process involves full consultation and the engagement of the cooperation of all those who are to be affected by a decision before it is taken. Preparation and pre-preparation time and effort is everything; and to those who do not come from within the culture, it is said that the process appears inert for a very long period. However, once *ringi* is reached, once everyone's support is engaged, it is understood that the matter in hand will go ahead at full speed from that point onwards, because there is nothing further to consider. The provision of information and the means for full participation, involvement and consultation on the part of all is critical to the success of operations if this style of management is to be adopted successfully and effectively. Japanese companies adopt a philosophy of 'management of the whole organisation', not a series of components. It is the effective functioning of the whole that is critical to operational success, not some of the parts only. To this extent adequate and effective communication and consultation systems are essential.

■ *Kaizen*

Kaizen refers to the constant progress of humanity, and the continuous striving for perfection. In management terms this has become 'constant continuous improvement'. It refers to all aspects of all organisations

- continuous staff training and development
- continuous product improvement
- continuous production and output improvement
- continuous attention to procedures and administration, to make this as simple and clear as possible
- continuous attention to the 'whole' – the Japanese organisation is seen overwhelmingly as one entity, rather than a collection of parts and divisions.

At its best, the result is continued output of high volumes of high quality products, often at premium (i.e. high) prices. This is supported by adaptation and innovation rather than creativity – the Japanese have no particular reputation for invention and creation; they are experts at taking existing products and improving each and every aspect. This is in time supported by an absolute commitment to high levels of investment in all aspects of staff, business and technology (see Box 13.4). It is reinforced by the high levels of expectations placed on staff, the high degree of conformity required, and the high levels of pay offered. Japanese companies set out to offer lifetime employment to their staff, and lifetime service to their customers. This can only be achieved if the company exists for a lifetime, and ensuring this is the required result of *Kaizen*.

■ *Mu*

Related to *Kaizen* is *Mu*, or complete openness. This constitutes a refusal to be hidebound by policies, constraints, directions and structures. It means being receptive to ideas, innovations, opportunity and potential; and engendering the qualities of vitality, flexibility, and adaptability, to organisations and their staff. The guiding principle of the company is to 'live for a long time', rather than to be 'the best airline' or 'the best car company'. It was this approach that enabled Mitsubishi to transform relatively easily from shipbuilder to car makers. Purposes and goals are set according to the demands and opportunities of the business-sphere, rather than preordained internal strategies – indeed, corporate strategy consist of having the staff, capital, technology and capability to respond to these demands and opportunities.

The next thread that runs through the practice of Japanese management may be summed up thus: the customer is king. Customers are the most important interest group to any company; without them there can be no business success. Customer satisfaction must be generated not only by the extent and quality of products and services currently offered, but also by the generation of new products to ensure that this goes on into the future. Implicit here also are two further features of Japanese management – continuity, the measuring of success over long periods of time rather than as something instant or short term; and the more general concept of continuous improvement.

In the pursuit of this the Japanese company sets great store by creative, innovative and extensive research and development activities. Only by investing and prioritising heavily in these areas is a continuing run of fresh offerings for the markets ensured. In addition, different applications for existing technologies may be found in this way, as are capacities for introducing a hitherto exclusive product to mass markets.

In the pursuit of this also, the Japanese company takes a very different view of failure from that elsewhere. Failure is when a commercially offered product fails to satisfy the customer. It is not a judgement generally made at the research or inception stage. Any product or idea that is generated, but which does not progress to the output stage, is nevertheless retained as the subject for the research or prudent activity, or else is kept in storage until market perceptions change and it can be commercially developed at a later date. Finally, while it may come to nothing in itself, the creative spark that engendered it may come up next with a market leader.

The stakeholders in an organisation and their relative positions of importance may easily be inferred from this. Staff come first – success is only possible through top quality, secure employees. The major Japanese corporations adopted philosophies of lifetime employment and have managed to practise this up to the present day (though there are signs of current difficulty in some organisations) customers are next. Third comes the shareholder, very often one of the large banks, and often, also, underwritten by the Japanese exchequer. In addition, shareholders are often customers of the companies that they underwrite. The emphasis on continuity, performance, satisfaction and the customer is therefore underlined again, rather than, as elsewhere, concentrating on dividends and shareholder benefits.

The other side of the coin is that Japanese consumers want the best. They expect this to extend across the entire range of consumer goods and services based on principles of continuity, service and quality outlined and inherent in the matters discussed above. Finally, authorities on Japanese management, style and practices are of the view that, while a certain amount of what is done can be ascribed to Japanese culture itself, nevertheless good management practices are good practices anywhere and everywhere. It is not the national characteristics of the Japanese that are to blame for managerial, industrial and commercial shortcomings of business elsewhere, but rather failings in those businesses and operations.

■ Japanese approaches to success

The rise of Japanese industry, and the domination of the global heavy manufacturing, technology, car and electronics sectors by Japanese companies, has also provided a rich source of material for management students. Over the period since 1960, Japanese industry has transformed its outputs and its reputation from low quality and customer confidence, to high quality and customer confidence; and Japanese companies are now the major supplier of electrical goods to the USA, Australia, New Zealand, and Western Europe, as well as being major players in the car, computer and banking sectors.

The components of success of Japanese companies over the period since 1960 may be summarised as follows:

1. **Conformity**: and the harnessing of this characteristic of Japanese society to the requirements of profitable business; in order for this to be successful, it requires vision and direction from the top of companies that is both profitable and worthy of respect from the staff and customers.
2. **Adaptation and adaptability**: very few of the products made by Japanese companies were invented in Japan; Japanese technologists, researchers and business developers have rather seen the potential of inventions from other parts of the world, adapted existing products for other purposes; been able to standardise production both to a high level of quality, and to a price that makes the products available to mass consumer markets; and been willing to promote and develop a full range of related products, and after-sales and back-up services to ensure a high level of repeat business.
3. The emphasis placed on the **long term**, rather than the immediate, return. There is an advantage in the financial system of Japan, which basically consists of the underwriting of Japanese business and industry by the government (at least over the short to medium term); this in turn allows both flexibility and confidence on the part of the industry to experiment, to pioneer, to develop new products and initiatives in the expectation of long-term success and profitability, without having short-term financial products or targets as priorities.
4. **Investment in staff training at all levels of the organisation**: for example, Nissan spent millions of pounds and dollars training production operatives at Washington, Tyne and Wear, UK, and Smyrna, Tennessee, USA, *before* a single car was produced; as well as the high quality of the finished product, the returns are measurable in terms of employee commitment, positive attitudes, identity (rather than alienation), and minute levels of absenteeism.
5. Concentration on, and commitment to, the **development of managers and supervisors**: especially in the areas of staff management and problem-solving

there is great pressure on the manager in a Japanese company to resolve issues successfully himself, rather than refer them through 'channels' (as in a more traditional Western bureaucracy); there is also a great cultural pressure not to get into institutionalised disputes, and above all, not to lose them.

6. **Single workplace status**: there is a strong social hierarchy in Japan; it is reflected to an extent at the workplace, in that the senior is worthy of respect; however, the workplace requires that this is translated into business needs only, and in this situation everyone is important in their role, whatever that may be; it is usual for everyone to wear the same uniform; to go through the same basic induction and orientation programme; to use the same facilities (e.g. canteen, restaurant and recreation); and to be on the same basic terms and conditions of employment.

7. A strong **identity** on the part of all staff with the company is both required and insisted upon: in managerial and professional occupations within the organisation this may involve, for example, working very long hours, taking an active part in corporate hospitality and business-related activities in the evening. Similarly, activities designated 'voluntary', are not voluntary to such staff in Japanese companies.

Consider Summary Box 12.3.

■ Foundations for the future

All of the factors and issues raised in this section concentrate on the drive for business and organisational quality, effectiveness and excellence. They reflect the fact that these constitute the major concerns of the business sphere in the last decade of the twentieth century. They are further underlined by the relationship that is drawn between the existence of these qualities in organisations and the success, effectiveness, growth and profitability of them that are considered to arise from the fact, either that they operate in these ways or that they exhibit these qualities.

The greatest mistake that anyone could make, however, is to believe that they constitute an end in themselves; that, once achieved, an organisation is guaranteed permanence and eternal profitability. This is not so. At their highest level (and if one is offering or preaching perfection) these concepts represent threads and strands that ought to run through the core of any organisation or undertaking; they constitute a standard of ethic, aura, belief and pride in the organisation that are increasingly recognised as the sound foundations on which business success must be built. They also represent the obsession with top quality of product and service and the central position of the customer in the activities of any undertaking and the critical importance of this. Such foundations require constant attention and maintenance as do the organisations, their structures, cultures and practices which are built on them. This is also the basis from which the next developments of the business and management sphere, and of managerial expertise are to come. It has taken the composition of the expertise and reality of management that is currently recognised thousands of years to develop this far; and this includes the globalisation of experience and practice.

a)

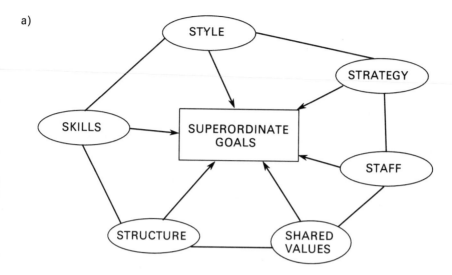

This is based on the management summary by R.T. Pascale and A. Athos 'The Art of Japanese Management', and is a variation on the 7S Model of Excellent Organisations. It illustrates the centrality of long-term commitment.

b)

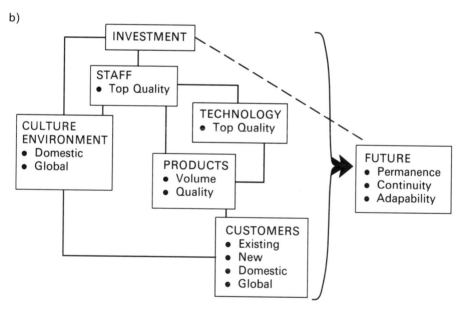

A systems approach to Japanese Management. The key input is INVESTMENT: the key output is a secure FUTURE.

Figure 12.1 Japanese management

SUMMARY BOX 12.3   Konosuke Matsushita (1892–1989)

Matsushita founded what is now the largest consumer electrical and electronic goods company in the world, and was also a much respected Japanese management guru.

He embodies all the principles outlined here. The three qualities that he required of his production processes were, high volume, high quality and low prices. Staff were taken on for life time employment and the company accepted any obligation inherent in that for re-training and development as new technologies came on stream and had to be used.

Matsushita was an advocate of different management styles, in different parts of the organisation. This should also apply in organisations of different size, technology, sophistication and complexity. Finally, management style must also change as the organisation itself changes, grows and diversifies; it is not possible to find a single successful formula by which it would work. He summarised this as: when to lead from the front; when to lead from the middle; and when to lead from behind.

He adopted the painstaking and deliberate expansion, development and diversification policies of the concept of *nemawashi* and *ringi*, so that risk was eliminated as far as possible from such initiatives and business success was, for a long period of time, assured.

He was a proponent of the business relationship between society and industry, advocating that it should be mutually profitable. Business operations that were not profitable should be closed down.

His leadership style was that of benevolent, enlightened and commercially orientated paternalism. He kept in constant touch with his senior managers, and also regularly visited all of his plant and production areas. He commissioned a company song which all employees had to sing at the start of each working day. He preached the virtues of self-sacrifice and self-discipline in the pursuit of company permanence and excellence. By doing this, all would benefit – company, customers, staff, and Japan.

■ Current managerial issues

In 1996 and 1997, and for the foreseeable future, the major issues facing organisations and their managers are as follows.

- **Technological advance**: and the opportunities that this brings in terms of increased opportunities for production, quality and durability; speed and flexibility of response to customer demands; and the capability to organise and develop workforces in ways that were simply not possible beforehand.
- **Investment**: the best organisations are increasingly taking the view that much greater attention is required. Investment in technology is viewed as a continued commitment, together with the need to change technology overnight almost, if and when radically new approaches are invented. Investment in the production and maintenance of high-quality staff is a prerequisite to long-term

and continued customer service and satisfaction, and therefore to long-term organisational well-being.

- **Culture, attitudes and values**: the best organisations are increasingly adopting and requiring their staff to adopt distinctive ways of doing things that:

  (a) support the organisation's own distinctive and considered view of how it should conduct its affairs

  (b) are capable of accommodating the differing, and often conflicting, interests of the employees

  (c) transcend local cultural pressures, meaning that both products and the ways in which they are produced and offered must be of a fundamental integrity, so that they are acceptable wherever business is conducted

  (d) create a basis of long-term mutual commitment serving the interests of the organisation, its customers, the wider community and its staff.

- **Business across cultures**: this especially applies to organisations operating in global markets. It applies also to a lesser extent to smaller organisations operating in a variety of localities. It constitutes the capability to 'play away from home' – understanding what is important to people in those areas and developing the capability to operate in those conditions and also other legal, social, political and economic constraints.

- **Strategy**: the capability to develop long-term clarity of purpose in all areas of activity, and taking the organisational steps to pursue it effectively. This means:

  (a) reconciling a range of conflicting pressures

  (b) learning global and general lessons from successes and failures

  (c) investment and commitment to the long term in terms of technology, markets, customers and employees

  (d) flexibility and responsiveness in the immediate term in the face of changing customer demands

  (e) generating staff loyalty and commitment through a determination to invest in their long-term future. This above all, means attention to training and development. It constitutes a mutual and continuous obligation. The view is also increasingly taken that long-term customer satisfaction can only be achieved through a commitment to staff excellence

- **Flexible patterns and methods of work**: this is based on a combination of the demand to maximise and optimise investment in production and other technology, together with changing patterns of customer requirements. This has led, for example, to longer factory, shop, office, public and private facility opening hours based in turn on the recognition that customers will use organisation services when it suits them. As organisations have extended their activity times, so they have found that extra customers have come to them and also that there is a great demand for short hours and other forms of part-time working and job opportunities on the part of employees and potential employees.

- **Ethics**: there is a realisation that there is a much greater propensity for consumers to use organisations in which they have confidence and that they can trust. This is based on the expectation of a long-term and continuously satisfactory relationship; and on the knowledge that, if this is not forthcoming with one organisation, it can be found with many others. There is also a much greater demand for work and staff relationships based on honesty and integrity rather than bureaucracy, barriers, procedures – and in many cases duplicity. If an organisation promises lifetime job security, then its first duty is to remain in being for that lifetime – and to do this, it must take a view of itself based on integrity rather than expediency.

■ The future of management

The purpose of this penultimate section of the book is to complete the picture; that is, to draw together the main threads, strands and implications so far discussed and to relate them to the environment both as it is now and also as it is envisioned for the future. Constant references have been made to the concepts and phenomena of the business sphere; the global nature of business and managerial activities; the close interrelationship between business and management; the universal nature of some activities and the highly specialised confines of others; and the ever-changing relationships and interactions between them.

First, the general level of debate concerning what management is and what it should be is being raised. This comes in a great variety of forms. There are ever-more management magazines, publications and broadsheets. There are ever-more successful business and management leaders publishing their memoirs, offering their own experience to the world, providing anecdotal or empirical lessons on which to draw. Functional managers have their own expertise mixes and offer lessons in those particular spheres. Particular business technology, operations and expertise recommend particular approaches to the management of the particular area, very often in the form of manuals and support literature, professional bodies, standards of education and skills and awareness provision. All these aspects create their own fora for debate and discussion; and this is being formalised and developed by professional bodies, managerial occupational categories, trade federations and associations and trade unions, all of whom are insisting increasingly on this as part of the continuing right of the individual to practise and to belong to the body concerned; or conversely as part of their continuing and developing obligations to their members and subscribers.

There is a great proliferation of business schools, business education establishments and private operators in the field of business and management education. The role and function of business schools in particular is ever-developing. The approach taken is multi-faceted. Primarily, this is the provision of business and management education at undergraduate and postgraduate levels; that is, the devising, organising and imparting of the body and knowledge of skills that, by common consent, constitutes the spate of expertise in the field at present. In particular, the globalisation of the MBA and other Masters degrees in management as a statement of general worth and value in the field is becoming ever-more important. There is also a proliferation of pre-vocational, vocational, certificate and diploma courses and qualifications in business administration, general management and functional or specialist management (often in conjunction with a professional body or occupational sector). Beyond this, courses for experienced and professional people wishing to acquire this new body of expertise both for advancement and enlightenment in the fostering and development of expert practice is also gaining in recognition and value. Finally, many business schools offer short courses related to particular management skills and knowledge also catering for the full range of capabilities and capacities.

Much of this work is driven by the necessity for recognition and qualifications on the part of both organisations and their managers. Any formalised contracting arrangement normally requires the provision of a body of suitably recognised and qualified staff, a formal statement and note of their expertise which (apart from anything else) provides the basis for contract assessment, compliance and insurance. This is particularly affected by privatisations, project work, approaches and other formalised contract compliance regulations that are coming into being in both Western Europe and the emergent Eastern Bloc. This is likely to become especially important in the placement of public works and services; the development of regeneration activities based on infrastructure health and social service projects; and the particular requirements of purchaser–provider arrangements and arm's length activities that may arise from this. In summary, there is a balance to be struck between formal education, personal qualities, capacities and capabilities, organisational and environmental pressures and the increased complexity of the management. This is certain to develop further in the coming period.

It follows from this that the nature and concept of management is not one which leads itself *per se* to a relationship with promotion (at least not without inherent capacities and capabilities on the part of the potential promotee being assessed and evaluated in advance). Management is from all of the above standpoints a designated expertise, increasingly professionalised, and likely to progress to a highly expert and organised status. It follows also that one will choose management as an occupation at the outset of one's career rather than another functional activity from which one may be 'promoted' to a managerial position. The individual is therefore likely to commence as a management trainee and to progress to junior, middle and senior or 'competent' and expert, and 'diverse' manager; in the same way as in another field one starts off as a junior doctor and then progresses to houseman, registrar and consultant; or from junior plumber to experienced and expert consulting status. The envisaged managerial progression is in parallel to this rather than a bureaucratic move or an adjunct at the top of it.

The levels of expertise, excellence and capability in the field impinge in the same way in the business and management sphere as do other professional expertises in other areas. Just as in the field of medicine an ever-greater range of viruses, illnesses, injuries and incapacities can be identified and treated, so there is an equivalent application in the field of management. An ever-greater range of knowledge is available and coming on stream in relation to all aspects of the business and management sphere – expertise available to the professional manager in pursuit both of their profession and the particular job also in which they finds themselves a practitioner at the present. The converse is also increasingly recognised; that is, that an absence of this expertise impacts directly on the performance of the manager. This in turn has a derived negative effect on the business performance of the organisation in that it removes part of the competitive edge that would be present if the manager had the qualities, capacities and expertise referred to; at present any such organisation would have to compete without benefit of these elements. It is self-evident, therefore, that there is an ever-greater expectation placed on managers. Expert, qualified, educated and trained, their contribution is not only valued but valuable. The costs of employing expert managers are coming increasingly to be regarded as part of the investment necessary for effective and continuing business performance and one on which returns can be measured in both quantitative and qualitative ways.

The expectations of organisations, it follows again, are changing. There is a move away from sophisticated functional and bureaucratic structures towards the lean forms referred to above. Career paths are not therefore to be based on a progression through such a labyrinth based on a combination of loyalty, expertise, accommodation and service; but rather on expertise alone and the ability of the manager to develop this and apply it in an ever-widening range of situations rather than his ability to survive the bureaucratic jungle. The path followed is at present increasingly envisaged as being task, project and customer-related and mirrored in the way in which he combines his personal, professional and operational qualities, education and capacities.

■ The business sphere

Constant reference has been made to this concept throughout the book; by way of completion it is necessary to address certain key features of it that are of both importance and prominence in the last part of the twentieth century and beyond.

■ Investment

A greater understanding of the requirement of investment and the true nature of business and organisational returns on investment is clearly indicated. Much has been made of the Japanese approach to both. These levels of investment have ensured sound foundations on which the organisation itself is built. They have also ensured the purpose of, and continued updating of, high quality capital equipment and plant that ensures a constant flow of new products and a high level of quality of the output (see Summary Box 12.4). This is all driven by the consuming business need to gain and keep customers and to meet the twin aims of giving satisfaction and maintaining loyalty. This level of investment has also extended to the generation of high quality staff. Part of the level of investment related to this has been the necessity to generate and maintain high levels of motivation and corporate identity. This is manifest also in the generally high levels of pay and terms and conditions of employment that such organisations always deliver as part of the commitment required in adopting this particular style of management. These levels of investment and resource commitment have

---

SUMMARY BOX 12.4   Investment

The apocryphal tale is told of two groups of managers, one British and one Japanese, who each ran a production line employing 20 people.

A machine was invented that could do the work of this line but which only needed one person to operate it.

The British managers went home with heavy hearts because they knew they would have to make 19 people redundant.

The Japanese managers went home with glad hearts because they were going to get 20 new machines; they were going to expand output by a factor of 20; all the staff were going to get re-training and a fresh place of work; and they would not be adding to the wage bill.

---

enabled high volumes of high quality output to enter into the consumer goods market over the period since 1945 and more especially over the period since 1970, representing the period when Japanese industry expanded, internationalised and ultimately globalised, inwardly investing into Europe, North America, the Middle East and New Zealand, bringing with it untold commercial and consumer benefits.

This is therefore a fundamentally different approach to the nature and philosophy of business from that which prevails in more traditional sectors of the west. Japanese investment objectives are based in the long term and require a long-term commitment and growth. Stakeholder satisfaction is seen in the returns afforded over these long periods by the permanence of business and its enduring commercial viability rather than instant returns looked for in other areas of the business sphere. From this standpoint comes the confidence that is a prerequisite in the commitment of resources to research, development, experiment, piloting and bringing on stream the range and diversity of products for consumption. It is clear that there are lessons to be drawn from this approach. These are a total confidence in the quality and entity of the organisation itself, its staff, its products and its services. Consideration must also be given to the strategic nature and attitude to investment and returns on it. Longer-term views of organisation direction and the reflection of this in attitudes and approaches on the part of both shareholders and other stakeholders and interest groups are clearly required. The same must apply to public and health services – short-term, cost-restrained, budget-driven services and projects simply ensure that a poor quality of service is delivered at high charge to the stakeholder.

Related to this is a reappraisal of the nature of organisation resources, and above all the generation of capacities and capabilities and their maximisation. We have dwelt at this in some length in relation to organisational aspects. Operationally this is likely to lead to a reappraisal of all business and organisation activities in all sectors with a view to establishing the optimum possible returns.

The same is required of profit assessment and appraisal. Profitability is increasingly to be seen as an organisational state over a long period rather than a configuration of a six-monthly or annual profit and loss account. The adoption of both the conception and the reality of the long-term view is critical to the enabling process required of the development of long term business and public strategies. Confidence in both must also be seen. Again, a major reorientation and re-education process has to be undertaken in regard to those who are responsible for the devising, generation and support of these activities.

There is implicit in all of this the proposal that both the development of new sectors and the regeneration of existing industries and commercial and public services require this long term view to be taken. Levels of investment are to be generated for the purpose of securing these in the long term. This flies in the face of certain current attitudes in certain sectors of short-term shareholder and stakeholder satisfaction, the payment of instant dividends and (in public services) political expediency.

There is a paradox to be addressed here also in relation to the strategy of organisations. On the one hand, plainly, they are competing for business in their sector however this is defined (and this includes reference to national, continental, trans-continental and global markets). However, the nature of activity, especially at global level, is much more sophisticated than the traditional economic model; organisations are adopting strategies of pooling resources, expertise and capital in pursuit of this so that 'super sectors' are being developed – the Channel Tunnel for example, is dependent on Japanese banks for financial support and thus on the strength of Japanese manufacturing industry where these banks gain the income and resources from that enable them to do this.

■ Concern for the environment

This is a matter of universal, political, economic and social priority at present; and is likely to become more extreme in the future. It has direct implications for business and managers. It is also plainly related to the investment concept detailed above. It affects ultimately all aspects of the business sphere. Globally, there is a balance that must be struck between developing, economic and business activities in order to support a world population that is expending at a great rate (the population of the city of Cairo goes up by 1 million every seven months, for example) and one which has short-term needs; and preserving the world so that it may support life and a quality of life further into the future.

At organisation level there is a necessity to consider the effect of operations on the environment, in relation to all business aspects. Marketing policies and activities, for example, may demand levels of packaging to preserve the product, to demonstrate it to its best possible advantage and to meet public and sectoral expectations. On the other hand, both the packaging itself and the technology used to produce it may be consumptive of resources themselves and also create high levels of pollution or waste. Production and operations and the technology related to this also create drains on the world's resources. They create waste and effluent which also have to be managed and disposed of. Human resource policies in certain parts of the business sphere (for example the UK) provide high-quality, prestige cars to go with particular occupations; these cars are very often resource-intensive in production and highly consumptive of fuel.

The net result is that strategies and policies for managing the environment have to be devised globally, sectorally and organisationally. This requires organisations and their managers to place the environment at or near the top of their list of priorities. It requires them to take a much wider view of the true cost of operations. Related activities may therefore include reorientation of marketing and product presentation and a parallel re-education along these lines as part of the total strategy aimed at changing customer expectations in this way (and reconciling this with the positive, persuasive wider marketing activities). It also requires organisations to take a longer-term view of production processes. The approach required is that which relates both to responsibility for, and the adoption of, procedures and practices which truly address the problems of the disposal of waste and effluent and for which organisation provision must be made in strategic, operational and investment terms.

■ The changing nature of public services

The restructuring of municipal, public and health services requires a mention here, as do the related concepts and realities of service level agreements and arrangements (we have made reference above to the privatisation which often accompanies these). The strategic conception relates to the stated need to revitalise and regenerate these services, to restructure them, to improve the quality and effectiveness of their management and to make them more efficient. This is all based on the premise that it can be achieved only if the organisations responsible are freed from bureaucratic, state or other authority control. Managers will in turn be free to conduct and provide and order these services in the ways in which their expertise directs. This is of a special importance when the nature of these services is considered – they are the primary, critical, health, social and education activities that are ever-more in demand, ever-expanding and the object of ever-higher social and public expectations. The same thinking has been applied to public utilities and strategic state industries. In the UK, gas, electricity, water, telecommunications and some research have all been privatised or transferred from government to shareholder ownership. Others, especially the railways and postal services, are set to follow in this path.

There are configurations of public policy to be considered; and also overt political concerns. From a managerial standpoint the reorientation of industries, utilities and services, the related culture and structure changes, and the regeneration of them, together with the continual drive for improvement and increased effectiveness, are the major concerns. The reality of what has been achieved so far and what is envisaged for the future is creating and enlarging the total sphere of management and opening a vast range of new opportunities for expert managers. These changes impinge on all aspects of management, all functional areas and the fields of operations and project activities also. The related conception of autonomy of service units also generates managerial opportunities. In summary, what is envisaged is nothing less than a complete reorganisation of the utilities and services concerned; if this is to be truly and effectively achieved very high levels of managerial expertise covering all the elements that we have discussed are to be required.

The paradox of all this concerns the necessity to reconcile the volatile and turbulent environment and business sphere and great advances in both technology and expertise with the conception of stability and permanence (and the levels of investment necessary) to ensure that this can be achieved. The strength of organisations, their directions and strategies chosen and those responsible for their implementation must be such as to be able to accommodate all of this. In the past the best organisations have been able both to devise and meet market opportunities, and to generate activities in these terms, balancing the supply and demand side of opportunities afforded. In the future added complexity will be given by the size and nature of those markets and the scale and scope of the investment, technology, production methods and activities necessary to fill them effectively and profitably. At the capital investment end, this clearly indicates the generation of global and trans-national joint ventures. At the technological end there are implications for universal application, utility and compatibility. This is from both an organisational and operational standpoint. It is also necessary in the particular pursuit of global business and activities. Additionally, the concepts of product and service quality related to the raising of expectations and meeting them are now firmly in place. Again there is a relationship between levels of investment and technological excellence. This mixture must then be capable of performance in this volatile global economy and business sphere. Organisations have to be able to reconcile these configurations of strength and permanence, therefore, not only with technological and expertise advances, but also with the business and operational qualities of flexibility and responsiveness and the speed of that response.

The nature of management therefore requires transformation in both concept and approach. The basis of knowledge and expertise requires adaptation in the same way and from the same standpoint as the lawyer or the doctor – it is the beginning, not the end of the activities of the true professional; in the same way it is the foundation for development and progress and not a body of knowledge of passing interest only. When this transformation is effected, business activities and the organisations that conduct them will take great leaps forward in all activities related to all aspects of the business sphere. The truly expert manager must also have the same qualities of passion, conviction and commitment that other experts demonstrate in the pursuit of their chosen paths.

The processes, qualities and expertise of business and management outlined here and their interaction and interrelationship both among themselves and with the wider business sphere and environment are having great and lasting effects on business practices. The transformation effected is to generate the creative and energetic aspect in the business sphere and to develop the nature and level of expertise in as many ways as possible. Management is thus no longer a straitjacketed or bureaucratic process; above all, it is not the equivalent of administration. Both business and management are ever-developing concepts, phenomena and realities. Their progress and transformation are limited only by the capacities and capabilities of those who work in them in whatever sector or aspect.

Finally, as we have said, these constitute global and universal activities and it follows from this that 'good practice is good practice wherever it is found'. It is ever-more evident that this is so and that any true expertise, whenever it is found and from wherever it is drawn, provides an increase in both understanding and in the fund of knowledge, skills and capabilities of the expert manager. The professional and expert manager has therefore to bring above all to his chosen profession a willingness, openness and capacity to learn, develop and preparedness to draw lessons from wherever they may become apparent and to assimilate these lessons in regard to his own expertise. This covers the whole spectrum of business and managerial activity with opportunities afforded in all sectors across the whole world. This is the scale and scope of the range and potential offered to the truly expert manager. The whole field therefore opens up opportunities that are truly exciting, challenging and adventurous for anybody who wishes to take advantage of them and who has the qualities, capacities and personal attributes to do so.

Appendix: Employment Law in the UK

■ The legal framework

The sources of employment law are the same as all other legal areas.

- **Statute law**: defined by acts of parliament.
- **Criminal law**: consisting of offences against the nation or the Crown.
- **Civil law**: allowing for the resolution of disputes between individuals.
- **Precedent**: in which a judgement on one case is held to apply to others of a similar nature.
- **Custom and practice**: in which legal status is accorded to something that has gone on for a period of time.
- **European law**: the ultimate point of reference for any UK citizen on any legal matter including employment.

Recourse to the law for alleged breaches is the same as all other legal areas – the Courts, Court of Appeal, House of Lords, and the European Court of Justice. Employment matters may also be taken to Industrial Tribunal.

■ Fairness and reasonableness

All organisations are unique and because they vary so greatly the test of what is fair and reasonable in particular sets of circumstances is always applied. Fairness and reasonableness is based on a combination of:

- The size of the organisation, the resources at its command and disposal
- The nature of business and activities, the technology and equipment used, commercial and operational pressures
- The nature of people employed, their skills, knowledge, qualities and expertise
- Ways of working, including interpersonal relationships
- Respect, value and esteem for staff and customers, honesty and integrity, and ordinary common decency
- Specific legal standards (for example, health and safety, product quality and description, trading standards).

Fairness and reasonableness applies to conduct, behaviour and performance; and to both employers and employees.

■ Natural justice

Quite apart from any legal obligation, natural justice demands that people are treated equally and fairly and with respect and honesty in all walks of life; and work (or indeed lack of it) plays a significant part in everyone's life.

■ Best practice

Standards of staff and human resource management set by ACAS, the Department for Employment and expert bodies such as the Institute of Management and the Institute of Personnel and Development establish what is known as best practice. Best practice is a combination of fairness and reasonableness, honesty and integrity, natural justice, together with the operational ways of organising and directing people in order to optimise organisational performance.

■ Precedent

Workplace and Industrial Tribunal cases are treated as distinctive and individual and therefore on their own merits. Tribunal judgements do not set precedent. Precedent is only set in employment law cases where these are referred on or pursued beyond Employment Appeal Tribunal and into the mainstream judicial system.

■ Areas covered by employment law

■ Contract of employment

This is the basis of the relationship between employer and employee. Not later than two months after starting work, any employee who works more than eight hours per week must receive a written statement giving:

- The name of the employer and the employee
- The date when the employment began, taking account of any period of employment with a previous employer which counts as continuous with the present
- Pay or the method of calculating it, and payment interval
- Terms and conditions relating to hours of work, holiday entitlement, other time off including public holidays and holiday pay
- Job title or brief description of job
- Place of work or places, along with the employer's address
- Any other specific or stated terms of employment.

This is the principal statement and must be contained in one document. In addition, the following information must also be given or be reasonably accessible to the employee:

- Health and safety matters reflecting the employer's duty of care
- Terms and conditions relating to sickness, injury and sick pay
- Any pension arrangements
- The length of notice the employee must give and receive
- The period of employment, if it is temporary or fixed term
- Particulars of any collective agreements by which the employee is to be bound
- Any specific conditions that apply when the employee is to work outside the UK for more than one month
- Any disciplinary rules applicable to the employee and the person to whom employees can apply if dissatisfied with a disciplinary decision or if they have a grievance about their employment and the procedure to be followed
- Any implied terms of employment, and employee obligations

Information given in job advertisements, job descriptions or other company information may also constitute part of the contract of employment.

Any change to the written particulars must be consulted on and agreed, and notified in writing to employees individually within one month of the change. If there is any dispute about the written statement, either the employer or the employee may refer the matter to an industrial tribunal.

■ Collective agreements

This refers mainly to any trade unions that the employer recognises and the right of the employee to join or not. It normally constitutes a statement of the specific terms and conditions by which both employer and employees are bound, and the specific procedures that are to be followed.

■ Discrimination and equality of opportunity

All organisations are required by law to be equal opportunity employers. It is illegal to discriminate between people when offering employment, promotion, pay, training and development or any other opportunity on all of the following grounds:

- Racial or ethnic origin and religion
- Gender, including pregnancy, marital status and retirement age
- Disability (except where the employer's premises do not provide suitable access)
- Membership of a trade union, refusal to join a trade union, insistence on joining or not joining a trade union
- Spent convictions for previous offences and misdemeanours (although there are many occupations exempted from this including teachers, doctors, lawyers, social workers, banking and finance).

Discrimination may be either direct or indirect.

Direct discrimination is overt – the straightforward refusal of work or opportunities on any of the grounds indicated above. Indirect discrimination occurs where a condition or restraint is placed, the effect of which is to bar, restrict or jeopardise the opportunities of people from each of the groups indicated above.

■ Health and safety

An employer may not order or request an employee to carry out work that is hazardous or unsafe without first providing the correct protective equipment, clothing and training where necessary. An employer may not request, order or coerce an employee into carrying out any unsafe or hazardous activity.

It is the duty of employers to provide as far as reasonably practicable a healthy and safe working environment. It is the responsibility and duty of all to ensure that this is maintained and that accidents, hazards and emergencies are notified and rectified immediately.

■ Maternity

All female employees are entitled to 14 weeks' maternity leave regardless of length of service or hours worked. For those who have more than two years' continuous service the period is 29 weeks.

Pregnant employees are allowed time off with pay for ante-natal care.

On returning from maternity leave, the employee has the right to return to her previous job or (if this has ceased) to suitable alternative work.

■ Time off

Employers must allow reasonable time off from work for employees to carry out the following:

- Public duties, including Justice of the Peace, members of local authorities, tribunals, health authorities, governorships of schools and colleges, boards of prison visitors; jury service if the employee is called
- Duties connected with the activities of recognized trade unions, including representation of members and training
- Looking for work and attending job interviews, retraining, career and occupational counselling after employees have been declared redundant and before they have left
- Maternity (as above).

■ Redundancy

Employers may dismiss – make redundant – employees whose work no longer exists or where fewer employees are required to carry out existing levels of work. Where redundancies are declared the employer must disclose the following:

- The reasons for the redundancies
- The numbers and descriptions of employees affected
- The criteria for selection
- The means and dates on which the dismissals are to be carried out.

Employers must consult with any recognised trade unions as soon as it becomes known that redundancies are to occur. This must happen even if only one employee is to be made redundant.

Alternatives – short-time working, short term lay-offs, transfers, redeployments, early retirements and calling for volunteers – must all be considered and rejected as impractical before compulsory redundancies take place.

The minimum consultation periods are as follows:

- 90 days in the case of 100 or more dismissals in a 90-day period
- 30 days in the case of ten or more dismissals in a 30 day period

otherwise consultation must begin as early as possible.

Employees who are dismissed because of redundancy are normally entitled to a lump sum payment. The amount depends on age, pay and length of service as follows:

For each year of continuous employment

- from age 41 to 64, 1.5 weeks' pay
- from age 22 to 40, 1 weeks' pay
- from age 18 to 21, 0.5 weeks' pay.

In 1997, £220 is the maximum weekly pay that is taken into account and 20 years the maximum service. The maximum redundancy payment is therefore £6,600 (i.e. 20 years' service between 41 and 64 = 30 x 220).

The amount is reduced by one-twelfth for each month of service completed over the age of 64, so that at 65 (the statutory retirement age) no payment is due.

The employer must give the employee a written explanation of a redundancy payment.

■ Transfers of undertakings

The Transfer of Undertakings (Protection of Employment) regulations (TUPE) safeguard employees' rights when there is a change of employer following a change of ownership, takeover, merger or privatisation. It also applies where there is a change of status – for example, from public to private sector, from building society to plc.

The effects of the TUPE regulations are:

- The existing contract and terms and conditions of employment are transferred in their entirety to the new employer, including continuity of service. The transfer may not take place with the purpose of reducing pay levels and other terms and conditions of employment.
- Recognition rights of trade unions are transferred if the new body maintains a distinctive identity.
- Dismissals related directly to the transfer of the business are automatically unfair.
- Both the old and the new employer must consult and provide advance information to any recognised trade unions and to all employees who are to be affected. This must include: the timing of the transfer; the reasons for the transfer; legal, economic and social implications for those affected.

■ Industrial action

Industrial action may be conducted in the pursuit of a legitimate trade dispute. A trade dispute occurs between employer and employees on one or more of the following grounds:

- Terms and conditions of employment
- The physical conditions in which people are required to work
- Dismissal, termination or suspension of employment of one or more employees
- Allocation of work or duties
- Matters of discipline
- Membership or non-membership of a trade union
- Facilities for officials of trade unions
- Machinery for negotiation or consultation and other procedures relating to any of the above matters, including the recognition by employers or employers' associations of the right of a trade union to represent employees.

Industrial action must be preceded by a postal ballot independently scrutinised (for example, by the electoral reform society). Those responsible for conducting a ballot (normally a trade union or staff representative) must give seven days' notice of their intent to hold a ballot. They must notify the employer of the outcome and give seven days' notice of any industrial action intended.

■ Payment

Payment must be made at the intervals stated in the contract and this must consist of the amounts stipulated.

Itemised pay statements must be issued at each interval. These must show the gross pay; the net pay; and the amount of each and every deduction made.

■ Individual rights

Individual rights at places of work have been clarified and strengthened over recent years. This has been partly due to UK government legislation and partly due to the European Union (EU). The main individual rights are:

- The right to fair and equal treatment regardless of length of service, hours worked or whether designated a full or part time employee
- The right to employment protection (protection from unfair dismissal) after two years' continuous service regardless of hours worked or whether designated a full or part time employee
- The right to join a recognised trade union or to refuse to join it; the right not to be penalised, victimised or harassed for joining or refusing to join
- The right to adequate and continuous vocational and job training
- The right to a healthy and safe working environment
- The right to information, consultation and participation on key workplace issues and other matters of relevance and importance
- The right of access to personnel files and other information held (whether on paper or database)
- The right to be represented or accompanied in all dealings with the organisation, especially matters of grievance or discipline.

□ Notes

The great majority of applications made to industrial tribunal are by individual employees. The orientation of the tribunal is therefore towards the individual. Where there is any doubt over the merits and strengths of the case of applicants and respondents, the tribunal normally orders the case to proceed.

Where there is any question that any of the rights indicated above have either been breached or not upheld, the tribunal will normally order the case to proceed.

It is the employer's duty to uphold the rights of individuals. The onus is therefore placed on the employer to be able to prove or demonstrate to the satisfaction of the tribunal that individual rights were upheld. It is the employer's duty to ensure that all employees are informed of their rights.

Employees may not be induced or coerced to sign away all or part of their statutory rights, nor is any such signature legally binding.

■ Case examples

Recent cases that have acquired legal status and set precedent are as follows.

■ Polkey v. A.E. Dayton Ltd

'Organisations must follow procedures when dismissing an employee' (Lords).
The ruling was as follows:

- In a case of incapacity an employee must be given fair warning and a chance to improve
- In a case of misconduct, investigating fully and fairly and hearing what the employee has to say in explanation or mitigation of their conduct
- In a case of redundancy, warning and consultation with affected employees and adopting a fair basis for selection and taking reasonable steps to redeploy those affected.

The tribunal which considered Polkey's case held that the employer had breached the correct procedure but that the result would have been the same if the procedure had been followed. This was rejected by the House of Lords. The Lord Chancellor stated: 'It is what the employer did that is to be judged, not what he might have done.'

■ Heywood v. Cammell Laird

'Equal pay means pay and not equivalent benefits' (Lords).
Jean Heywood worked as a cook at Cammell Laird. For this work she was required to have a recognised qualification. She argued that her qualification was of the same level as those of men working elsewhere in the company, and that therefore her work was equivalent to that of those men. She was paid less than those men.

The company acknowledged that they paid Mrs Heywood less, but because she received a free meal every day, this made her total reward package up to a level equivalent to that of the men with whom she was making the comparison.

The House of Lords rejected this and ordered the company to make up her pay to the same level as that of the men.

■ Brown v. Stockton-on-Tees Borough Council

'Pregnancy may not be used as a criterion for redundancy' (Lords).
Maria Brown worked for Stockton-on-Tees Borough Council. She worked in a group of four female staff. The Council made two members of staff redundant and singled Mrs Brown out as one of them because she was pregnant. If **last in first out** had been used to determined redundancies, Mrs Brown would not have been made redundant; no other criteria for redundancy was published.

The Lords upheld the view that pregnancy was not a valid ground for redundancy; and that to make someone redundant because of their pregnancy amounted to discrimination. The Lords went on to state that criteria for redundancy must be published in advance of redundancies; failure to do so means that last in first out (lifo) will apply.

■ Price v. The Civil Service Commission

'Age constraints must not be indirectly discriminatory on grounds of gender' (Court of Appeal).

Belinda Price worked as a civil servant and, at the age of 36, put in for a promotion to the next grade. The Civil Service Commission turned her down on the grounds that she was too old and that everyone who made the particular grade had to do so by the age of 29.

Ms Price countered this by saying that she could not have achieved this because she was out of the workforce for ten years bringing up children. She was otherwise a good and effective worker; the only thing militating against her promotion was her age; and that because of circumstances, this discriminated indirectly on grounds of gender.

The Court of Appeal upheld this view, stating that the particular age barrier was less favourable to women (and therefore discriminatory) than to men.

■ Burchell v. British Home Stores

'Allegations of misconduct must be fully investigated before any action is taken against an employee and before an employer comes to a decision as to what is to happen' (Court of Appeal).

Burchell was dismissed for misconduct by British Home Stores without being given the opportunity to state his case. The Court of Appeal laid down three guiding principles to ensure that natural justice would be upheld:

- The employer should show that there was a genuine belief that the employee was guilty of the misconduct under consideration
- The employer must carry out a reasonable and thorough investigation into the case
- As the result of the investigation, the employer must have reasonable grounds for maintaining the belief

Each point is now always considered and questioned by tribunals where cases arising from misconduct occur.

■ European Court of Justice

The following judgments were issued by The European Court of Justice after they had exhausted the tribunal and UK legal systems.

■ Swift v. British Rail

'Retirement age and the opportunity to retire must be the same for all employees regardless of gender.'

■ British Rail v. National Union of Railwaymen

'Union membership agreements – the closed shop – are illegal and may not be enforced; no-one should be forced to join a trade union or any other organisation against their will (nor should they be prevented from joining a trade union or any other organisation if they so wish.'

■ Procedures

Procedures exist to set standards of performance, conduct and behaviour at places of work and to ensure that everyone knows what is expected of them and that they conform to this. They ensure fairness and equality of treatment for everyone.

All organisations must have procedures for handling and managing discipline, grievance, disputes and dismissal. These have to meet standards prescribed by ACAS and the Department for Employment. They must:

- be in writing
- state to whom they apply
- be applied evenly to everyone concerned regardless of rank or occupation
- be accessible, available for inspection and available for use at any time
- be capable of being understood and followed
- be fair and reasonable
- indicate the disciplinary actions which may be taken in given sets of circumstances
- indicate the levels of management which may take particular actions
- provide for matters to be dealt with quickly.

■ Discipline

Disciplinary procedures must always include the following.

■ General rights

- The right of the individual to know the case against them and to confront their accuser
- The right to respond to the case and present their own point of view

- The right to representation at each stage, either by the representative of a recognised trade union or other person of their choice
- The right to receive in writing a definitive statement of the conclusion and outcome of the case at each stage
- The right of appeal against the conclusion and outcome at each stage.

■ Offences

Offences normally fall into the following categories:

- Minor offences and misdemeanours
- Repetition of minor offences and misdemeanours
- Serious misconduct
- Gross misconduct.

The nature of each varies between organisations. Organisations must normally indicate the kind of offences that fall into each category.

■ Warnings

Minimum standards require for a series of at least two warnings (and many organisations have three or four). These may either be written or oral; when oral they are in any case normally confirmed in writing.

The general aim is to ensure that the employee is aware that an aspect of their conduct, behaviour or performance is unacceptable and giving cause for concern. The warning must confirm this and state the remedial action that is necessary.

For poor performance this normally includes retraining or a restatement of the standards of activity that are necessary and acceptable.

For shortfalls in behaviour and conduct, this normally includes a restatement of what the required standards are and why they are necessary.

For both performance and conduct, warnings will normally include a date in the future on which a review of progress is to be carried out.

■ Recording

Warnings are recorded on the individual's personnel file (or equivalent) for set periods of time. Time periods are stated in the procedure and notified to the individual in each case.

It is normal for warnings for minor offences to be kept on file for periods of between three months and two years. Records of more serious offences may be retained for longer periods. The most serious offences are kept on file for life.

There are no rules governing this. The only requirement is to be fair and reasonable. The organisation must balance its need to set and maintain standards with the requirement of individuals not to have their career or their prospects irreparably harmed by relatively minor incidents.

At the end of the stated period, the warning is removed from the file. It may never be used or referred to again.

■ Serious misconduct

For matters of serious misconduct is it acceptable and legitimate to place individuals on a final warning. This is confirmed to the individual in writing as the result of the hearing and assessment of the case.

Organisations must indicate the kind of offences that constitute serious misconduct (though the list need not be exhaustive). These normally include persistent bad time-keeping, persistent poor performance, rudeness and insubordination.

■ Gross misconduct

For gross misconduct it is acceptable and legitimate to move straight to dismissal. This is normally called summary dismissal. This is also confirmed to the individual in writing as the result of the hearing and assessment of the case.

Organisations must again indicate the kind of offences that constitute gross misconduct (though the list again need not be exhaustive). These normally include vandalism, violence, arson, sabotage, theft, dishonesty, sexual misconduct, sale and publication of confidential information, other breaches of the criminal law, and harassment, persecution and victimisation of members of staff.

For both serious misconduct and gross misconduct procedures must be followed. However serious the alleged offence, the individual is still entitled to hear the case against them, to face their accuser, to respond, to be represented and to appeal against the findings.

Where dismissal does occur the reasons stated for dismissal must be the real reason for dismissal. This must be notified in writing to the individual and to anyone else who requests the information (for example, the Department for Social Security).

■ Suspension

For serious offences it is acceptable and legitimate to suspend employees from work while a full investigation into the matter is held. Suspension is normally on full pay. The reasons for suspension and the date and time from which it becomes effective must be confirmed in writing at the point at which the decision to suspend is made.

■ Disciplinary hearings

For all disciplinary hearings the employee must be informed of the following:

- They must be notified, either orally or in writing, that they are required to attend a disciplinary hearing. The words 'disciplinary hearing' must be used. They must be informed of all the rights indicated above, including the rights to be accompanied and represented.
- They must be informed of the case against them, who has brought it and why. They must be given the opportunity to face their accuser. They must be informed of the nature of the case, whether it potentially constitutes a minor offence, repeat offence, serious misconduct or gross misconduct.
- They must be asked to give their explanation of the events and situation.
- They must be allowed (but not excessive) time to prepare their case. They must be allowed to call witnesses and gain access to documents and papers that affect their case.

■ Grievance

All employees have the right to raise issues, concerns and problems with their employer. This normally consists of:

- Raising the matter with the immediate supervisor, either informally or formally
- If there is no satisfaction, raising the matter with the next level of management
- If there is still no satisfaction, raising the matter with upper levels of management including ultimate reference to the chair, managing director, chief executive officer or equivalent
- The right to have present a witness or observer and to be represented
- The right to appeal against the proposed resolution if this is felt not to be satisfactory
- The right to receive the outcome or resolution in writing.

Most issues are resolved to the satisfaction of everyone at the initial stage. The rest exists to ensure that serious matters – especially victimisation or discrimination – can be fully and adequately dealt with.

There is an exception to this. Where the employer has fewer than 20 employees, formal grievance procedures are not required. However, employees must be told the name of the person who should be approached if they have a grievance or concern.

■ Personnel records

Complete up-to-date records constantly maintained are essential. They must include copies of the contract of employment and other terms and conditions. They must also include copies of all formal communications between employer and employee, and especially notes of warnings, conduct, behaviour and performance. Other documentation is also useful – especially general notes, file notes, diary entries, records and minutes of meetings, performance appraisal statements and other general features.

The purpose is to provide an accurate and truthful record of the period of employment. This material is also invariably both useful and required if the employee does at some stage make a complaint at a tribunal.

■ Sources of information

■ Expert bodies

□ Advisory, Conciliation and Arbitration Service (ACAS)

ACAS is an independent statutory body funded by government grant. It is the recognised national source of expertise, advice, information and guidance on workplace industrial relations and staff management. ACAS publishes guidelines and codes of practice on discipline, grievance, dismissal, employment practices and the content and use of procedures. These are available from offices of ACAS, either free or for a small charge.

The general role of ACAS is to promote workplace harmony, understanding and well-being.

- **Advice**: ACAS may be contacted at any time, either by post or phone on any aspect of workplace, industrial relations or staff management for general advice and information. ACAS officials also arrange and carry out briefings and training sessions by agreement.
- **Conciliation and mediation**: ACAS may be contacted at any time to arrange conciliation and mediation in disputes that are likely to become serious if they are not resolved quickly. ACAS searches for common grounds and areas where agreement might be reached and makes proposals for tackling other issues. ACAS also conducts conciliation and mediation in all applications to tribunal as stated above.
- **Arbitration**: ACAS may be contacted at any time to arrange arbitration in disputes where there is no apparent possibility of resolution. Both parties normally agree to be bound by the arbitrator's findings (though this is not required by law). The arbitrator hears both cases and then makes recommendations based on their assessment of the merits. The result may be wholly in favour of one party or a compromise between the two, or some alternative solution.

In all cases that come to hearing, the tribunal normally requires satisfaction that the advice, proposals, recommendations and guidance of ACAS have been followed. Where this has not occurred, good reasons must be shown. Where both parties agree to be bound by the findings of an arbitrator, good reason must be shown if one party then decides not to accept these findings.

□ Health and Safety Executive (HSE)

HSE is also an independent body funded by government grant. It is the recognised source of expertise, advice, information and guidance on all matters concerning health and safety at work.

The HSE publishes advice and guidelines on general health and safety matters. It has a statutory right of access to all work premises. It carries out inspections, advises on safety matters, and in extreme cases, may close down premises or parts of premises where these are considered to be unsafe or unhealthy.

Where a case arises from health and safety matters the tribunal always requires satisfaction that the advice, proposals, recommendations and guidance of the HSE have been followed. If this has not occurred good reason must be shown.

□ Department for Employment (DE)

The DE publishes booklets and leaflets giving advice and information on changes to the law and the implementation of regulations. It is the duty of employers to ensure that they keep themselves up-to-date with current employment legislation.

A tribunal never accepts ignorance of the law as a defence – whether on the part of applicant or respondent.

□ Commission for Racial Equality, Equal Opportunities Commission, Disablement Resettlement Officer

These bodies provide independent advice and guidance, and act as a source of information on employment law and related matters. Their advice and guidance is normally considered to be the highest form of expertise available.

In tribunal cases where the advice and guidance of these bodies has been sought, the tribunal will normally place great emphasis on their recommendations.

☐ Trade Unions, Employers' Associations, Professional Associations, Independent Associations

These bodies provide advice and guidance and act as a source of information on employment law and related matters to their members. Their advice and guidance carries no particular presumption of expertise. It is, however, generally of high quality and represents the state of knowledge and information available.

Tribunals may choose to place emphasis on the recommendations, advice and guidance given by these bodies.

■ Laws and regulations

The main laws, and their coverage, are as follows:

☐ Equal Pay Act 1970

- **Equal pay**: the right to receive the same pay and other terms of employment as an employee of the opposite sex working for the same or an associated employer if engaged on like work, work rated as equivalent or work of equal value.

☐ Employment Protection (Consolidation) Act 1978

- **Pay**: the right to receive an itemised pay statement.
- **Maternity rights**: the right not to be unfairly dismissed for reasons connected with pregnancy; the right to paid time off work for ante-natal care; the right to return to work following absence because of pregnancy or confinement.
- **Medical suspension**: the right not to be unfairly dismissed on medical grounds; the right to receive pay for suspension on medical grounds.
- **Redundancy**: the right to be consulted by the employer about proposed redundancies; the right of recognised independent trade unions to be consulted by the employer about proposed redundancies; the right to receive payment when made redundant; the right to receive an itemised statement of redundancy payment; the right to pay and time off in the event of redundancy to look for other work or to make arrangements for training.
- **Time off for public duties**: the right to time off for public duties.
- **Trade union membership/non-membership rights**: the right to pay and time off for trade union duties; the right to time off for trade union activities; the right not to suffer dismissal or action short of dismissal for trade union membership or activities or non-membership; the right not to suffer action short of dismissal to compel union membership; the right not to be unfairly dismissed for trade union membership or activities; the right not to be unfairly dismissed for non-membership of the union; the right not to be chosen for redundancy because of trade union membership or activities, or non-membership of a trade union.

- **Unfair dismissal**: the right not to be unfairly dismissed for any reason; the right to receive a written statement of reasons for dismissal
- **The right to receive a written statement of terms of employment and any alterations to them.**

□ Race Relations Act 1976

- **Race relations**: the right not to be discriminated against in employment, training and related fields on grounds of colour, race, nationality, ethnic or national origin.

□ Sex Discrimination Act 1975

- **Sex discrimination**: the right not to be discriminated against in employment, training and related fields on the grounds of sex, marriage or pregnancy.

□ Transfer of Undertakings (Protection of Employment) Regulations 1981

- **Transfers**: the right of unions to be informed and consulted about the transfer of an undertaking to a new employer; the right not to be dismissed on the transfer of an undertaking to a new employer.

□ Employment Act 1980

- **Trade union rights**: the right not to be unreasonably excluded or expelled from a trade union.

□ Employment Act 1988

- **Trade union rights**: the right not to be unjustifiably disciplined by a trade union; the right of recourse to a tribunal if discriminated or disciplined by an employer concerning trade union rights; the right of trade unions to hold secret ballots on employer's premises.

□ Wages Act 1986

- **Payment of wages**: the right of all staff not to have deductions made from their wages unless allowed by statute by the contract of employment or with the individual's prior written agreement; the right of everyone to an itemised pay statement.

☐ Disabled Persons (Employment) Acts 1944 and 1958

- **Disability**: the general right not to be discriminated against in employment because of a registered disability; the duty of employers with 20 or more employees to employ a minimum of 3% of registered disabled people; the right to complain to tribunal if discriminated against or disadvantaged by virtue of disability.

☐ Rehabilitation of Offenders Act 1974

- **Spent convictions**: job applicants and employees are not under any legal obligation to disclose information about previous convictions; the right to deny a previous offence when the conviction for it is **spent** – a person has served their punishment and been rehabilitated (there are a large number of occupations which are exempted from this rule – especially working with money, people and property; and working within the legal, law enforcement and emergency services).

☐ Trade Union Reform and Employment Rights Act 1993

- **Employee rights**: the right not to be dismissed for exercising statutory employment rights regardless of length of service or hours of work; the right of women to 14 weeks' maternity leave regardless of length of service or hours of work; the right to healthy and safe working premises and activities regardless of length of service or hours of work.
- **Transfers of undertakings**: the regulations governing business transfers are extended to cover non-commercial undertakings.
- **Trade unions**: individuals are given the right to join the union of their choice; the deduction of union dues from pay must be authorised in writing by the employees every three years; the duty of an employer to inform and consult union representatives about collective redundancies is re-stated.
- **Industrial action**: strike ballots must be postal and independently scrutinised; unions must give employers seven days' notice of their intention to hold a strike ballot; unions must give employers seven days' notice of the industrial action intended; injunctions may be sought by anybody affected by unlawful or unofficial industrial action to prevent this from taking place.

☐ European Union Law

European Union Law is broadly superior to UK Law; any case that reaches the European Court of Justice will be judged by this as the final conclusion to the matter in hand.

The particular concern of European Union Law is the strengthening and upholding of individual rights in all aspects of life – and this includes employment. The main areas of concern are:

- **Freedom of movement** for workers and self-employed persons across the European Union
- **Protection of employment** and **remuneration**; adequate vocational training
- **Freedom of association**, especially the right to join trade unions and associations, or not to join trade unions and associations
- **Information consultation** and **participation** of employees on major workplace issues
- **Health** and **safety** at work
- specific **protection for stated groups of employees**, especially children, adolescents, elderly persons, disabled persons; equal treatment for men and women.

The general principle is that current UK legislation reflects the demands of EU law and standards. It is especially important to note that any case that does reach the European Court of Justice will be judged by persons who take a European perspective.

Bibliography

■ General bibliography

M.K. Ash (1985) *On people Management*, MacDonald.
E.F.L. Brech (ed.) (1984) *Organisations*, Longman.
E. de Bono (1984) *Lateral Thinking for Managers*, Pelican.
T. Burns and G.M. Stalker (1968) *The Management of Innovation*, Tavistock.
R. Cartwright *et al.* (1994) *Management*, Blackwell.
A. Chattell (1995) *Managing for the Future*, Macmillan.
P.F. Drucker (1955) *Management by Objectives*, Prentice-Hall International.
———— (1993a) *The Post Capitalist Society*, HarperCollins.
———— (1993b) *The Ecological Vision*, Transaction.
P.F. Drucker (1986a) *Drucker on Management*, Prentice-Hall International.
———— (ed.) (1986b) *The Practice of Management*, Prentice-Hall International.
———— (ed.) (1988) *The Effective Executive*, Fontana.
———— (ed.) (1990) *Frontiers of Management*, Heinemann.
W. Goldsmith and D. Clutterbuck (1990) *The Winning Streak*, Penguin.
J.H. Goldthorpe *et al.* (1968) *The Affluent Worker, Vols. I, II and III*, Cambridge University Press.
J. Harvey-Jones (1990) *Making it Happen*, Fontana.
R.M. Kanter (1985) *When Giants Learn to Dance*, Free Press.
F. Kast and J. Rosenzweig (eds) (1985) *Organisation and Management*, McGraw-Hill.
D.R. Koontz *et al.* (1984) *Organisations*, Longman.
P.A. Lawrence (1984) *Management in Action*, Routledge & Kegan Paul.
P.A. Lawrence and K. Elliott (eds) (1988) *Introducing Management*, Penguin.
P.A. Lawrence and R. Lee (1984) *Insight into Management*, OUP.
R.S. Lessem (1985) *The Roots of Excellence*, Fontana.
———— (1987a) *Intrapreneurship*, Wildwood.
———— (1987b) *The Global Business*, Prentice-Hall International.
———— (1990) *Transforming Management*, Prentice-Hall International.
T. Lupton (1984) *Management and the Social Sciences*, Penguin.
N. Machiavelli (1986) *The Prince*, Penguin Classics.
M.H. McCormack (1983) *What They Don't Teach You at Harvard Business School*, Fontana.
———— (1989) *Success Secrets*, Fontana.
A. Morita (1987) *The Sony Story*, Fontana.
R. Pascale (1989) *Managing on the Edge*, Simon & Schuster.
R. Pascale and A. Athos (1983) *The Art of Japanese Management*, Fontana.
L.J. Peter (1970) *The Peter Principle*, Penguin.
T. Peters (1989) *Thriving on Chaos*, Macmillan.
———— (1992) *Liberation Management*, Macmillan.
T. Peters and N. Austin (1985) *A Passion for Excellence*, Collins.
T. Peters and R. Waterman (1982) *In Search of Excellence*, Harper & Row.
J. Rice (1995) *Doing Business in Japan*, Penguin.
A. Roddick (1992) *Body and Soul: The Body Shop Story*, Ebury.

R. Semler (1992) *Maverick*, Free Press.
R. Stewart (1991) *Managing Today and Tomorrow*, Macmillan.
L.F. Urwick (1947) *Elements of Administration*, Pitman.
J. Woodward (1970) *Industrial Organisation: Behaviour and Control*, OUP.

■ Strategy

H.I. Ansoff (ed.) (1985) *Business Strategy*, Penguin.
R. Buchholz (1982) *Business Environment and Public Policy*, Prentice-Hall International.
C.R. Christensen *et al.* (1987) *Business Policy: Text and Cases*, Irwin.
E.F. Johnson and K. Scholes (1993) *Exploring Corporate Strategy*, Prentice-Hall International.
R. Pettinger (1996) *Introduction to Corporate Strategy*, Macmillan.
M.E. Porter (ed.) (1990a) *Competitive Strategy*, Macmillan.
M.E. Porter (ed.) (1990b) *Competitive Advantage*, Macmillan.
J.L. Thompson (1990) *Strategic Management*, Chapman & Hall.

■ Behaviour of organisations

J.H. Adair (1975) *Leadership*, Cambridge University Press.
R.M. Belbin (1986) *Superteams*, Prentice-Hall International.
E.H. Berne (1984) *Games People Play*, Penguin.
D. Biddle and R. Evenden (1989) *Human Aspects of Management*, IPM.
D. Buchanan and A. Huczynski (1985) *Organisational Behaviour*, Prentice-Hall International.
D. Cartwright (ed.) (1959) *Studies in Social Power*, University of Michigan.
D. Drennan (1992) *Transforming Company Culture*, McGraw-Hill.
A. Etzioni (1964) *Power in Organisations*, Free Press.
J. French and B. Raven (1959) 'The Bases of Social Power', in D. Cartwright (ed.), *Studies in Social Power*, University of Michigan.
J. Groucutt and P. Griseri (1996) *In Search of Ethics*, Technical Communications.
C.B. Handy (ed.) (1990) *Understanding Organisations*, Penguin.
C.B. Handy (1984) *The Future of Work*, Penguin.
P. Harris and R. Moran (1991) *Managing Cultural Differences*, Gulf.
J. Henry (ed.) (1992) *Creative Management*, Open University.
P. Hersey and K. Blanchard (1982) *Management of Organisational Behaviour*, Prentice-Hall International.
G. Hofstede, (1980) *Cultures Consequences*, Sage.
J. Kenney and R. Reid (ed.) (1992) *Training Interventions*, IPM.
R.S. Lessem (1989) *Managing Corporate Culture*, Gower.
R. Likert (1967) *The Human Organisation*, McGraw-Hill.
F. Luthans (1989) *Organisational Behaviour*, McGraw-Hill.
A. Maslow (1960) *Motivation and Personality*, Harper & Row.
A. Mumford (1989) *Management Development*, IPM.
H. Owen (1985) *Myth Transformation and Change*, Collins.
M. Pedler, J. Burgoyne and T. Boydell (1991) *The Learning Company*, McGraw-Hill.
R. Pettinger (1996) *Introduction to Organisational Behaviour*, Macmillan.
M. Reddy (1991) *The Managers' Guide to Counselling*, Methuen.
E. Sternberg (1995) *Just Business*, Warner.
B. Taylor and G. Lippett (1984) *Management Development and Training Handbook*, McGraw-Hill.

V. Vroom (1964) *Work and Motivation*, John Wiley.
V. Vroom and E. L. Deci (1992) *Management and Motivation*, Penguin.
P. Warr (ed.) (1987) *Psychology at Work*, Penguin.
A. Williams and P. Dobson (1991) *Changing Culture*, IPM.

■ Management of organisations

K. Back and K. Back (1982) *Assertiveness at Work*, McGraw-Hill.
R. Blake and J. Mouton (1986) *The New Managerial Grid*, Gulf.
C.B. Handy (ed.) (1990) *The Gods of Management*, Penguin.
C.B. Handy *et al.* (1981) *Making Managers*, Penguin.
D. Katz and R.L. Kahn (1978) *The Social Psychology of Organisations*, Wiley.
R. Pettinger (1996) *Managing the Flexible Workforce*, Technical Communications.
W.D. Rees (1990) *The Skills of Management*, Routledge.
W. Reddin (1970) *Managerial Effectiveness*, McGraw-Hill.
E.F. Schumacher (1986) *Small is Beautiful*, OUP.
G. Sereny (1996) *Albert Speer: a Biography*, Macmillan.
R. Tannenbaum and W. Schmidt (1958) *How to Choose a Leadership Pattern*, Harvard Business Review.
M. Trevor (1992) *Toshiba's New British Company*, Policy Studies Institute.

■ Marketing management

M. Baker (1992a) *The Marketing Book*, Institute of Marketing.
————— (1992b) *Marketing*, Macmillan.
V. Buell (1990) *Marketing Management*, McGraw-Hill.
E. Clark (1988) *The Want Makers*, Hodder & Stoughton.
W. Cohen (1986) *The Practice of Marketing Management*, Macmillan.
J. French (1992) *Principles and Practices of Marketing*, Pitman.
W. Keegan (1990) *Global Marketing Management*, Prentice-Hall International.
V. Packard (1960) *The Hidden Persuaders*, Penguin.
V. Packard (1957) *The Waste Makers*, Pelican.
G. Randall (1992) *Marketing*, Routledge.

■ Human resource and industrial relations management

R. Cartwright *et al.* (1994) *Personnel Management in Practice*, Blackwell.
K. Cheatle (1996) *Code of Employment Practice*, NCVCCO.
A. Ferner and R. Hyman (eds) (1992) *Industrial Relations in the New Europe*, Blackwell.
S. Kessler and F. Bayliss (1992) *Contemporary British Industrial Relations*, Macmillan.
B. Livy (1989) *Corporate Personnel Management*, Pitman.
A. Rodger (1958) *The Seven Point Plan*, National Institute of Industrial Psychology.
M. Salamon (1992) *Industrial Relations*, Prentice-Hall International.
G. Salomon (1992) *Human Resource Strategies*, Open University.
K. Sisson (1991) (ed.) *Personnel Management in Britain*, Blackwell.
D. Torrington and L. Hall (1992) *Personnel Management: A New Approach*, Prentice-Hall International.
D. Walton and A. McKersie (1965) *A Behavioural Theory of Labour Negotiations*, McGraw-Hill.

■ Operations management

E. Adam and R. Ebert (1990) *Production and Operations Management*, Prentice-Hall International.

M. Bresnen (1990) *Organising Construction*, Routledge.

K.B. Clark and T. Fujimoto (1991) *Product Development and Performance*, Harvard.

D. Cleland and W. King (1988) *Project Management*, Van Nostrand Reinhold.

M. Cuming (1984) *Managers' Guide to Quantitative Methods*, ELM.

G. Davis and M. Olsen (1985) *Management Information Systems*, McGraw-Hill.

E. Gummesson (1991) *Qualitative Methods in Management Research*, Sage.

J. Heizer and B. Render (1991) *Production and Operations Management*, Allyn.

R. Layard (ed.) (1980) *Cost-Benefit Analysis*, Penguin.

K. Lockyer (1992) *Quantitative Production Management*, Pitman.

L. Long (1990) *Management Information Systems*, Prentice-Hall International.

J.J. O'Neil (1989) *Management of Industrial and Construction Projects*, Heinemann.

R. Pettinger and R. Frith (1996) *Measuring Business and Managerial Performance*, STC.

J. Van Horne (1990) *Financial Management and Policy*, Prentice-Hall International.

G. Welsh *et al.* (1984) *Budgeting: Profit Planning and Control*, Prentice-Hall International.

M.E. Wright (1980) *Financial Management*, McGraw-Hill.

Index